The social psychology of everyday life

All too often social psychology concerns itself with situations far divorced from the realities of everyday life. In *The Social Psychology of Everyday Life*, Michael Argyle concentrates on real-life settings and emphasises the practical applications of what psychology is able to tell us.

Taking social psychology out of the laboratory into everyday life, Argyle provides an up-to-date review of what is known about some of the most interesting and important areas of social psychology, embracing biological, historical and social factors as well as psychological ones. He looks at central areas that make up our everyday lives and covers many of the most pressing concerns of the day: conflict and aggression, racial prejudice, leisure, work and unemployment, religious beliefs, social class, relationships, health and happiness.

Written by one of the leading social psychologists of our day, this comprehensive account of the psychology of everyday life will be an important text for students of psychology, sociology and education, and for all those whose courses include a psychology component.

Michael Argyle is Reader in Social Psychology at the University of Oxford and a Fellow of Wolfson College. He is the author of many articles and over twenty books, including *The Psychology of Happiness* and *Cooperation* (both also published by Routledge).

The social psychology of everyday life

Michael Argyle

London and New York

First published 1992
by Routledge
11 New Fetter Lane, London EC4P 4EE

Simultaneously published in the USA and Canada
by Routledge
a division of Routledge, Chapman and Hall, Inc.
29 West 35th Street, New York, NY 10001

Reprinted 1992

Typeset in Times by Selectmove Ltd
Printed and bound in Great Britain
by Mackays of Chatham PLC, Chatham, Kent

British Library Cataloguing in Publication Data
Argyle, Michael *1925–*
 The social psychology of everyday life.
 1. Social psychology
 I. Title
 302

Library of Congress Cataloging in Publication Data
Argyle, Michael.
 The social psychology of everyday life/Michael Argyle.
 p. cm.
 Includes bibliographical references and indexes.
 1. Social psychology. 2. Social interaction. 3. Social groups. 4. Attitude
 (Psychology) I. Title.
 HM251.A782 1991
 302–dc20   91–17444
                                                CIP

ISBN 0–415–01071–3
    0–415–01072–1 (pbk)

Contents

Figures and tables

FIGURES

TABLES

Preface

Social psychology is becoming boring, abstract, remote from real life. This book is an attempt to bring it back, to deal with some of the most interesting and important topics. These include two which are fairly new to social psychology – health and happiness – and two which have not hitherto been generally recognised – leisure and social class.

In all of these fields there is a substantial body of good research, and research which has been done in field settings or with realistic experiments. I have done research and written books on most of these topics; the highlights are presented here in a briefer and much updated form.

I am grateful to many people for their ideas and comments, for collaboration in research, and for reading chapters, especially to Nicholas Argyle, Rupert Brown, Peter Collett, Geoff Evans, Adrian Furnham, Monika Henderson, Steve Hobfoll, Mansur Lalljee, Sonia Livingstone, Luo Lu, Kathy Parkes, Ben Slugoski and Yair Hamburger.

Ann McKendry put it on the word processor with amazing skill and accuracy. My wife, Sonia, greatly improved style and clarity. The Leverhulme Trust financed some of the recent research reported, and earlier work was supported by the ESRC.

Michael Argyle
Oxford
January 1991

Chapter 1

Introduction

RESTORING THE TRUE CONTENTS OF SOCIAL PSYCHOLOGY

Social psychology is about social behaviour and the effect of social relationships and situations. This should open the door to a tremendously rich and fascinating range of phenomena. And social psychologists have developed a brilliant methodology for studying them: laboratory experiments of great sophistication, very ingenious manipulations and control groups were thought up, so that it could be demonstrated that the experimental variable was the true cause of the effects on dependent variables.

It was part of this tradition to study what were believed to be the fundamental, underlying processes of social behaviour. The result had been, however, that once social psychologists got their hands on a problem it had a way of being replaced by very abstract reformulations so that it all but disappeared, and all the familiar detailed contents were lost. The 'experimental' method led to other-worldly situations in which subjects sat in little rooms in total isolation and pressed buttons, or sat in little rooms and answered strange questions.

Take the study of small social groups, one of the 'classical' fields of study. The groups studied consisted usually of 2–4 students, all strangers, who were asked to solve little problems, for 15–20 minutes, or guess lengths of lines, pull on ropes, cheer or clap. This offered a kind of bogus generality, in the hope that universal truths would be discovered, which would apply to any kind of real group. Nothing was said about the special peculiarities of committees, families, groups of friends, juries, therapy groups, religious groups and so on. It was apparently not necessary to know anything about any of these actual groups to study 'groups' in general.

One of the favourite topics of small group research was the formation of group norms, apparently a universal group phenomenon. There was almost no interest in whether the norm was about not killing, loving your neighbour, working hard, not working hard, telling the truth or deciding which clothes to wear.

Take the study of beliefs and attitudes, another classical field of social psychology. Attitudes could be about religion, politics, race, soap or coffee, it didn't really matter, because it was thought they all functioned in the same way and could be studied by the same little laboratory studies. Did it make any difference whether beliefs were in the after-life, the inferiority of other racial groups, the effects of smoking or the height of Mount Everest? Again it was not necessary to know anything about religion or politics, race, soap or coffee.

Experiments in social psychology have sometimes lost all touch with reality, in the pursuit of ingenious manipulation of variables, and have become a kind of theatre of the absurd. In well-known experiments, subjects have been made to dress up in hooded Ku-Klux-Klan outfits while delivering electric shocks to other people, or have been ordered to give apparently fatal shocks to other subjects, or been paid considerable sums of money to tell lies, or to eat fried grasshoppers. They have been wired up to real or imaginary physiological equipment, had one hand in freezing water while the other hand filled in questionnaires, been led to believe that other subjects were having epileptic fits or that the laboratory was on fire, or been insulted by experimental confederates. What on earth these subjects thought they were doing we shall never know. This is worse than can be found in other fields of psychology, though rivalled by experiments in which worms were taught to turn left, ground up and fed to other worms to see if they learned anything, or experiments in which rats were asked to choose between Mozart and Bartok.

Meanwhile, in the pursuit of abstract fundamental principles of social behaviour, social psychologists have managed to eliminate the actual contents of groups, beliefs and the rest, by passing social phenomena through a kind of filter or sieve, through which most of the interesting material dropped, leaving just the highly abstract components which were believed to be more important.

This book is about some of the missing contents of social psychology. I have chosen some key examples. It starts with interaction and relationships, but in a way that deals with their rich contents. For groups I have described, in different chapters, groups of friends, working groups and religious groups. For attitudes, I discuss religious, political and racial attitudes. Some of the topics are recent arrivals on the social psychology scene, not yet in the textbooks – happiness and health. Others are not yet recognised as part of the subject at all – leisure and social class. Some topics I have tackled in a different way – inter-group conflict.

Conversation (Chapter 2): The book starts with one of the most central topics in social psychology – social interaction, but focusing on one of its main features, talk. This had been neglected by linguists, for whom language consisted of marks on paper, not utterances in social situations. Social psychology did little better, treating it as an abstract S-R process, and found little more than that questions sometimes led to answers. However, an in-between field has developed, the 'social psychology of language', which has analysed a number of distinctive phenomena – accommodation, politeness, inter-subjectivity, conversational rules and skills, as well as the different kinds of conversation over the telephone, in political speeches, between friends and by men and women, different social classes and different personalities. This is a field in which good experiments have been done, as well as good field studies, and they have needed a lot of skill and ingenuity. As for the other topics discussed in this book there are important practical implications, in this case for helping those who are bad conversationalists.

Social relationships (Chapter 3) were discovered by social psychologists quite recently. However, they assumed that all relationships are much the same as one another, are all like friendship and love, can be explained by abstract principles such as exchange theory, and can be studied by little games. I believe that this is a mistake, and in this chapter give a detailed account of five different relationships – friendship, love and marriage, work, parent–child and kinship. We shall see that there are great differences between these relationships, in their biological basis, the kind of bonding, the rules and the activities pursued together. As well as following rules, the right skills must be acquired in order to establish and maintain relationships.

Work (Chapter 4) is nearly always done in groups, under supervisors, in a hierarchy. The nature of the work, and the relations between workers, take very different forms at different historical periods, and with different kinds of technology. Work cannot be studied in the laboratory without taking account of the complexities of work settings. The first social psychological approach was the Human Relations movement, which emphasised the importance of working groups, supervisory skills and job satisfaction, but overlooked technology, organisation and wage incentives. However, social factors are most important, not only as sources of job satisfaction, but also of absenteeism, labour turnover, mental health and productivity. Field studies of various kinds, including field experiments, have been very successful here, and have provided important clues to how to solve some of the serious problems connected with work – low job satisfaction, poor health and social conflict.

Leisure (Chapter 5) has scarcely been studied at all by social psychologists, although we spend several hours a day at it. Sociologists have carried out mainly descriptive studies of how much leisure we have and what we do. The interest of psychologists is different: what do people do when they have a more or less free choice, what is the motivation for leisure, why do people watch so much TV, which kinds of leisure make people happiest? Some kinds of leisure create social problems; some people don't know what to do with their leisure, such as the unemployed; some don't seem to be making the best use of it. There are other important questions here: could leisure replace work, or work be made more like leisure, and what exactly is the difference between them?

Religious beliefs, behaviour and experience (Chapter 6) may be true, but they are also social phenomena, and affected by social variables. They can be looked at as examples of beliefs and attitudes, but there are distinctive contents of the beliefs to be explained. Religion can be looked on as an example of a social group, but religious groups have distinctive practices, and they convert people. Much valuable information comes from social surveys, and from field studies of special groups, such as converts, the terminally ill and members of sects and cults. There has been some successful use of experimental methods too, in a realistic way, on the effects of drugs, sensory deprivation and fear of death, for example. There are a number of intellectually intriguing theories, about the possible social origins of religion, most of which remain to be tested.

Aggression and conflict between groups (Chapter 7): The psychological basis of aggression has been extensively investigated, sometimes by rather bizarre experiments, but does not help us much to understand or prevent real conflicts between groups. Research by social psychologists on inter-group conflict has mostly been confined to laboratory studies of artificial groups who are found slightly favouring their own members, and again tells us nothing about what can be done about real conflicts. In an attempt to get to grips with the real thing, in this chapter a number of cases of true conflict between groups are discussed, using whatever empirical evidence research workers have been able to obtain – about tribal wars, racial prejudice, football hooligans and modern war. Only in the case of racial prejudice has it been possible to carry out much rigorous research so far.

Social class (Chapter 8) has been left mainly to sociologists in the past, indeed it is one of their favourite topics. Social psychologists too are very interested in how social behaviour, beliefs and relationships vary with class. This is the case of cross-cultural psychology closest to home, showing alternative ways of conducting social affairs, and with the promise of explaining these differences. We are even more interested in social interaction and relationships *between* classes, in their attitudes towards each other and in social mobility between them. There is not much scope for experimentation here, apart from studies of small group hierarchies, which may provide models of the class system. Most of the research has been done by surveys, and field studies of selected groups.

Health (Chapter 9): Illness is not only produced by germs and viruses; it is also caused by stress, while the effects of stress are offset by supportive relationships and affect some 'hardy' personalities less than others. New variables are important here, such as health behaviour (drinking, diet and so on), and compliance (with doctor's orders), and new kinds of explanation, such as the impact of relationships on the immune system. Research on these factors enables us to explain the differences in health between men and women, and different classes. It also opens the way to preventive measures directed at health beliefs and behaviour, to modify exercise, diet, smoking and drinking, and even to alter certain aspects of personality.

Mental health (Chapter 10): Here we draw partly on research in social psychiatry, but also on social psychological work on the social behaviour of patients, and field studies of the effects of stress, social support, and personality. There is much detailed knowledge in each of these spheres. New social variables appear, such as coping style; new personality variables, like hardiness. Again this provides an explanation of the variation of mental ill health with gender and social class. Social factors can be used in the prevention of mental disorder, such as stress management and exercise, and in treatment, such as social skills training.

Happiness (Chapter 11), or subjective well-being, is a new topic in social psychology, and one which has been taken up with enthusiasm. Previously there had been surveys by sociologists, which had mainly found demographic variations in happiness. Social scientists have now found more important sources, through field studies of relationships, work and leisure, through laboratory experiments on mood induction, and longitudinal studies of links with personality. We are now getting down to explaining some of the findings; for example, why extraverts score so high on measures of happiness. A lot is known about the effects of happiness, on health and sociability, and on how happiness can be enhanced.

THE NEED FOR GOOD RESEARCH METHODS

Most of the topics discussed in this book have been studied partly by experimental methods, some good, some bad. By bad experiments I mean experiments in which there is little similarity to real life, or where there is no social interaction. In the Prisoners' Dilemma Game, for example, pairs of subjects cannot communicate and must make decisions in ignorance of what the other will do. In 'minimal group' experiments subjects are led to believe that they belong to a group which never meets, and where the members have little or nothing in common. By good experiments I mean those where real emotions or relationships are generated, even though on a reduced scale, and real social behaviour takes place. It must be admitted that the line between good and bad experiments is a very fine one, difficult to draw, and drawn in different places by different people. In practice, it depends on the judgements of the 'refereeing classes', those who are asked to referee journal articles, book manuscripts or proposed conference papers.

There are many areas where it is not possible to design laboratory experiments with any pretence of realism, so field studies must be resorted to. Field experiments have had some success in certain areas such as helping behaviour, but these are usually confined to short-term contacts between strangers. Social surveys and similar field studies can be very informative but usually do not tell us what is causing what. Does attributional style cause depression, or is it the other way round? Does watching violent TV films make people violent or vice versa? A straightforward survey cannot tell us. One solution is the longitudinal study in which subject samples are approached twice, at intervals of 6, 12 or more months. Statistical analysis can then reveal the directional path. Another method is the 'quasi-experimental' design, in which carefully selected and contrasted samples are studied, perhaps at two points in time. For example, the mental health of school-leavers was assessed before they left school; later the effects of employment and unemployment could be found (p. 93). Within this framework a great variety of important topics can be studied; for example, the effect of personality, of different cultures, the causes of health, mental health and of happiness.

Realising the difficulties with experiments, some have been tempted to resort to case studies, with the promise of rich descriptive material and no problems of artificiality. These can indeed be a valuable source of hypotheses, especially in a new field, but it is a great mistake to stop here, without testing these hypotheses by more rigorous methods – after all, most hypotheses are wrong; one can usually think up six explanations for anything, so at least five of these will be wrong.

However, research isn't just a matter of collecting data, there's plenty of that already. It is done to understand the social world – that is, to generate ideas and theories which lead to testable hypotheses – and also help us to understand events and to control them. In the bad old world of artificial experimentation the theories were arid and abstract, drawn from cognitive psychology (such as balance theory), or economics (like exchange theory and so forth). I believe that these abstract theories have led to a total lack of practical application. What can be done to solve any actual problems by knowing about balance, exchange, equity, dissonance, or inter-group theory? All they really suggest is that human nature needs to be changed.

However, when we start to look at the actual phenomena, a much richer set of ideas becomes available. From the study of social interaction (Chapters 2 and 3) come ideas about communication and relationships, with roots in linguistics, and in ethology and evolutionary theory. Other topics discussed in this book take us to sociology and anthropology, medicine and psychiatry. This richer theoretical base also leads to richer practical application.

Chapter 2

Conversation

Most social psychology books nowadays have no chapter on talk, yet this is central to nearly all social behaviour. And it is no good just leaving this topic to linguists to deal with, because their interests are different – mainly finding the rules which govern the composition of sentences. Speech makes possible cooperation over work and leisure, and the conduct of relationships; work, leisure and relationships consist to greater and lesser degrees of talk. Conversation is the realm of shared vocabulary and ideas, of shared rules and understandings.

Linguists sometimes present language as printed words on paper. This is a mistake: the real unit is the utterance by one individual to one or more others, in a situation, in a conversational sequence, where he or she is trying to influence the other. Utterances are units of social behaviour, but they are very special units, since they use words and grammar, and convey meanings. Conversations similarly are special sequences of behaviour with a complex structure, and they require special skills to perform properly.

Social psychologists study conversation by experimental or other objective methods using quantification. The results are published in psychological journals like the *Journal of Language and Social Psychology*. Where linguists study conversation, such as in 'conversation analysis', they study a few examples and infer the existence of rules, rather like the rules of grammar (Roger and Bull, 1988). In the present chapter I shall draw primarily on research of the first – namely, experimental and quantitative – variety.

Why do people talk so much; in other words, what are the functions of talk? There are quite a number of them, and they can be classified in different ways.

The central use of language is probably in

1 conveying information, asking questions about, and discussing, other people, objects or events;
2 influencing the behaviour of others, by requests, orders, persuasion or instructions;

3 speech acts, such as 'I declare this garden party open' – which are not true or false;
4 sheer gossip, chat and jokes, directed more towards strengthening and enjoying social relationships than to communicating any serious information;
5 regulating encounters with 'hello', 'thank you' and similar utterances;
6 expressing emotions and attitudes to others, by groans and cries, but also by the contents of speech.

(Robinson, 1972)

The kinds of conversation which are found in different situations take quite different forms. We describe some of these later – conversations on the telephone, political interviews on TV, making friends, seeing the doctor, for example. Those who can't talk effectively in these situations are at a great disadvantage, and those who can't converse in common social situations become isolated and distressed. They can, however, be given special training.

THE ANALYSIS OF CONVERSATION

Speech acts and shared vocabulary

The basic unit of language, it is now believed, is not the printed word but the spoken utterance. An utterance is a piece of behaviour. Austin (1962) drew attention to utterances such as promising, ordering, apologising, judging guilty, declaring garden parties open, and making bets, which he called 'performative utterances'; they are neither true nor false, but they affect what is going to happen. He went on to argue that all utterances do things in this way, can be looked at as items of social behaviour which are intended to influence the hearer in some way. They are all 'speech acts'. However, utterances are special kinds of social behaviour, because of the way in which words and grammar create meanings.

Utterances have to be carefully planned, so that they will be understood by the listener, be received in the intended manner – for example, as a joke or an order – and lead to the intended results – for instance, he laughs or he obeys. This means imagining his or her point of view, 'taking the role of the other', 'inter-subjectivity'. Experiments have shown that most speakers do this most of the time. For example, people say things quite differently depending on whether they are speaking to a expert or an ignoramus, a child or a dog, and depending on what they think the other person knows already and is able to understand (Krauss, 1987). Lawyers use far fewer technical legal expressions when examining witnesses than when arguing with other lawyers in courtrooms; defendants use far less criminal jargon and swear less when in court than when being interviewed by their lawyers.

If garage mechanics are asked a question about adjusting a car engine, they move rapidly down the hierarchy of technicality, if it becomes clear that the questioner doesn't understand.

Many mental patients are deficient in seeing other people's point of view; Blakar (1985) found that schizophrenics couldn't cope with a problem-solving task about finding a route on a map, but this was when the two subjects had been given slightly different maps.

Two people cannot communicate unless they have some shared language. First they need some shared vocabulary; that is, a number of words with same or similar meanings. A lot of the interaction between a mother and a child aged 18–24 months, consists of the child learning the labels for objects. By the age of 6 most children know over 14,000 words; that is, they have picked up about 9 a day.

Interactors also need some shared information or common ground that can be taken for granted, and that each assumes the other possesses. Many utterances add new information to old; for example, 'the coffee machine has conked out again'. This shared ground is cumulative, it builds up during the course of a conversation, such as in a tutorial or a school lesson. Between people who know one another well or who belong to the same group or community, or who work together, there is extensive common ground (Clark, 1985). The better two people know each other the easier it is for them to identify individual people, objects or places, either by names, or by shorthand description.

Shared context is important in helping people to convey clear messages. Many utterances are ambiguous without a context, since many words have more than one meaning; for instance, 'Where is the bank?' We all possess a great deal of background knowledge, which we share with other people when we enter social situations. One way of looking at shared background knowledge is in terms of 'scripts', which describe standard sequences of events – for example, when going to a restaurant – and which could be used to instruct a computer in what to say and how to understand the answers when ordering and paying for a meal at a restaurant.

Two speakers need to share a 'definition of the situation', as sociologists call it. By this is meant the basic nature and purpose of a situation, and the roles of each person in it. This can be indicated by the nature of furnishings and decoration, which can hint that a relaxed social event is about to take place, or serious work, or a police interrogation (Argyle, 1991).

Non-verbal accompaniments of speech

Non-verbal communication (NVC) plays several essential roles in conversation: it adds to and completes the meaning of utterances, it provides feedback from listeners, and it helps with synchrony and coordination.

NVC from the speaker

A speaker emits a variety of NV signals, which are closely coordinated with his speech.

(1) Tone of voice

The pitch pattern of an utterance 'frames' it; for example, as a question (rising pitch at end), suspicious and hostile, funny, sarcastic, serious and so on. Stress can be placed on particular words to emphasise them, or to indicate which of several possible meanings are intended; for instance, 'they are *hunting* dogs'. Voice quality also indicates emotional state; for example, depressed people speak in a low, slow, voice, with falling pitch. It can indicate attitude towards the other – friendly or hostile, dominant or submissive. And accent shows social class and regional origins. All of this information can be obtained from a single short utterance.

(2) Pauses

Speakers spend 30–40 per cent of the time in silence. There are longer pauses if the topic is difficult, and these are for 'thinking time'. Pauses often come at the beginning of clauses, and are probably used to plan the clause. Some are just hesitation pauses with or without 'ers', while the speaker works out what to say next. It has been found that conversations between friends have many fewer pauses than those between strangers (Markel, 1990).

(3) Gestures

While people speak, they gesture with their hands. These gestures illustrate what is being said; for example, by copying shapes, objects, movements, relationships, by pointing, or as 'batons' to mark new points. Gestures are simultaneous with the words they illustrate, or come slightly before them. They send useful information, as experiments have shown in which people describe shapes or movements with or without using their hands. Gestures develop in children at about the same age as speech – for example, becoming more abstract – and are controlled by the same areas of the brain; gestures and speech are a joint production. 'Emblems' are quite different: these are symbolic gestures which replace words, such as the hitch-hike sign and various rude gestures; they are not used much during conversation.

(4) Gaze

Speakers look at listeners quite a lot of the time – about 40 per cent for strangers 2 metres apart, more than this if they like each other or are further apart. They look in glances of about 3 seconds, which include mutual glances of about 1 second. Gaze is closely coordinated with speech: speakers look just before the ends of utterances, and at major grammatical breaks, in order to collect feedback on listener reactions. They look away when they start to speak and at hesitant periods, to avoid cognitive overload; if people are asked to gaze continually, they can do so, but speech errors increase.

NVC by the listener

While people are in the listener's role they send a lot of NV signals, though they may not be aware of it.

(1) Vocalisations

These include uh-huhs and similar grunts, as listening signals. There are also feedback signals such as 'good', 'really?', and sometimes listeners help out by finishing the sentence for the speaker.

(2) Gestures

The main one is head nods, small ones to show continued attention, larger and repeated ones to indicate agreement. Head shakes are quite rare.

(3) Facial expressions

Those of listeners are an important source of feedback information. Mouth and eyebrows can show that a listener is puzzled, or understands, agrees or disagrees, is pleased or annoyed, disbelieving or angry.

(4) Posture

This indicates degree of alertness or sleepiness, and some more specific reactions as well. If listeners are bored they prop their heads up, if interested they lean forwards, if they disagree they tend to fold their arms.

(5) Gaze

Listeners look a lot more than speakers, often 70–75 per cent of the time. They are looking to pick up the NV accompaniments of speech, together with some lip-reading if they are deaf. The reason that it is less than 100 per cent is presumably, as in the case of speakers, in order to reduce either cognitive overload or arousal.

The gestural dance

We have seen that there is some synchrony of bodily movements between people in conversation: as they start to speak they look away and start gesturing; as they stop speaking they do the opposite. However, a much finer degree of coordination of bodily movements at fractions of a second has been reported by some investigators. McDowall (1978) found no evidence for this in statistical analysis of 6 persons' bodily movements, filmed at 8 frames per second. On the other hand most of them were strangers and any gestural synchrony would be weaker than for two people. Two people in conversation do adopt congruent postures, usually mirror images, and when they do so there is a stronger feeling of rapport: if an experimental confederate copies the other's bodily movements he or she is liked more. It looks as if there is a 'gestural dance', though not at the split-second timing originally proposed (Argyle, 1988).

Conversational sequences

Conversations consist of sequences of utterances. Socially unskilled people, who will be discussed later, often have difficulty in managing these sequences: they don't know what to say, or they say something that is regarded as inappropriate by others. We need to know what to teach them, and how to train them. This can be looked at as a fundamental theoretical question: rules of grammar specify how to put words in order to make sentences; what are the rules for putting utterances in the right order to make conversations?

A set of conversational rules was suggested by Grice (1975), which can be summarised as follows:

1 provide no more or less information than is needed,
2 be relevant,
3 tell the truth,
4 be clear.

No empirical evidence was offered in support, though it is quite likely that most people would agree with the rules if asked, even though they often break them. However support for (1) has been provided by experiments in which it is found that speakers on the whole provide listeners with information that is needed, rather than telling them what they know already. Support for (2) is given by everyday experiences, as when A says 'I'm out of petrol', and B replies 'there's a garage round the corner', A will assume that this is a relevant response, and that the garage probably sells petrol and is open. Support for (3) is provided by experiments on 'irony', if A says 'What a delightful day' (when it isn't), the assumption that A means to tell the truth leads to taking this as a case of irony.

On the other hand there are certainly occasions when speakers are often not entirely open, helpful or frank. First, teenagers, when asked by their parents where they have been and what they have been doing, provide a familiar example. Secondly, politicians, subjected to hostile questions on TV, are often very evasive, or answer a quite different question. Thirdly, in committee work, diplomacy, cases of industrial and military secrets, and many other work settings, people often do not feel free to make relevant and helpful conversational contributions. Furthermore the rules are often broken in the interests of politeness, especially the first. And it must be admitted that if conversationalists did keep to Grice's rules all the time it would make for very boring, formal kinds of conversation – no jokes, metaphors, amusing exaggerations or irrelevancies. But above all these conversations would be regarded as very impolite.

Perhaps we can taken conversations apart by looking at pairs of utterances; such pairs are possibly the building blocks from which longer sequences are constructed. The most familiar pair is question–answer: the second utterance is closely related to the first, and its meaning is incomplete without knowing about the previous utterance. For example, 'about 90 miles' conveys no information at all unless we know that it is a reply to some question. The first utterance of the pair has some compelling power to 'project' a relevant response. Question–answer is the most common type, but there are a number of others such as request–comply (or refuse), summon–answer, offer–accept (or refuse), thanks–acknowledge, greetings, and partings (Clark, 1985).

We said that the question–answer sequence is a common building block of conversation. Often a question leads to a straightforward and relevant answer, but this is not the only possibility. The reply may be another question, which often results in an insertion routine, as in

> A: Are you coming tonight?
> [B: Can I bring a guest?
> [A: Sure.
> B: I'll be there.

A question may be open or closed; an open-ended question usually results in a fairly long answer, especially if non-verbal encouragement is also given.

The importance of adjacency pairs is shown by the fact that an utterance is to some extent predictable from the one that went before. In a study of conversations between pairs of students who did not know each other, Thomas (1985) found that:

1 disclosing information about self was reciprocated in 23 per cent of cases;
2 expressing beliefs was reciprocated in 19 per cent of cases.

Here, and in other studies, the question–answer sequence was the most common. However Clarke (1983) found that 3 previous utterances are taken into account. Artificial dialogues were constructed, where subjects had access to 0, 1, 2, and so on previous utterances; when they knew 3 the resultant dialogue was judged as good as or better than real conversation.

One suggestion is that groups of 3 utterances are a basic building block, where the third acknowledges, thanks, terminates, or in some other way responds to the second part of an adjacency pair (Tsui, 1989). My own preference is for 4-part units, which can be seen most clearly where one speaker is in charge, and has a plan, is trying to obtain certain responses from the other. As with driving a car, or other motor skills, an interviewer or teacher knows how to take corrective action to produce the results he wants. If the other does not talk enough, the solution is to ask more open-ended questions, and to show more interest in or approval of what is said.

Here is another example of corrective action on the part of an interviewer (I) with a respondent (R):

I_1:   asks question
R_1:   gives inadequate answer, or does not understand question
I_2:   clarifies and repeats question
R_2:   gives adequate answer

or

I_1:   asks question
R_1:   refuses to answer
I_2:   explains purpose and importance of survey; repeats question
R_2:   gives adequate answer.

(Brenner, 1980)

In practice the other person is not just a passive stooge, but may also be pursuing goals of their own, in the form of reactions desired from the interviewer. Here is a case of this happening in an interview between a college admissions tutor and an applicant.

I_1:   How well did you do at physics at school?
R_1:   Not very well, I was better at chemistry.
I_2:   What were your A-level results?
R_2:   I got a C in physics, but an A in chemistry.
I_3:   That's very good.

Another kind of sequence is where a repeated cycle of utterances is followed. Flanders (1970) found that there are repeated cycles of this kind in the school classroom, as shown in Figure 2.1. He maintains that the skills of teaching consist partly of the ability to control these cycles, and to shift from one to another. Thus the teacher might start with a short cycle: Lecture (by teacher) – Question (by teacher) – Answer (by pupil). The teacher could then shift to a longer cycle which included more pupil participation and initiative by stimulating and reinforcing such moves on the part of pupils.

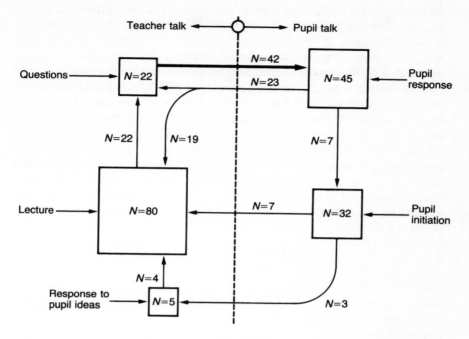

Figure 2.1 Cycles of interaction in the classroom
Source: Flanders, 1970

Synchronising utterances

When two or more people are talking, they take turns, and the turn-taking is surprisingly efficient. Many gaps between utterances are less than ⅕ second, the normal reaction time; people do not usually interrupt – about 10 per cent in tutorials, though more than this in political interviews on TV. How is this synchrony achieved?

One solution offered was in terms of the verbal contents. Sachs, Schegloff and Jefferson (1974) argued that a speaker produces a unit of conversation, of various kinds, and that listeners can recognise the type of unit and anticipate its end-point. The speaker may select the next speaker (if several others are present), by addressing a question, complaint, request, tag-question, and so on to a particular person. Or the speaker can leave it open, and the next speaker selects himself. However, as Ellis and Beattie (1986) point out, if there are long utterances, as in TV political interviews, there are a number of possible end-points: which one does the other person take as the ending, and start speaking? The answer is that non-verbal signals are also important here.

One NV ending signal had already been found, by Kendon (1967). He found that if a speaker did not make a terminal gaze just before ending an utterance there was a longer interval before the other replied, so evidently the terminal gaze acted as an end-of-turn signal. However, later work found that this signal is only effective when the general level of gaze is low, as between strangers. It was then found that listeners make use of a number of signals given off by speakers, in combination; the more there are, the clearer it is that the speaker is coming to the end of his utterance.

Pitch contour is one cue: ending a sentence with a falling pitch, or with a rising pitch in the case of a question. *Ending gestures*: speakers return their hands to rest at the ends of utterances; keeping one or both hands in the air is a powerful way of keeping the floor. *Grammatical ending*: Sachs and colleagues were partly right about the contents of utterances – the ends of utterances can be judged, and also anticipated, from the structure of the sentence, and in a later experiment this was found to be more powerful than falling pitch (Sachs *et al.*, 1974).

Speakers pause and look up in the middle of long utterances. How can listeners tell whether the speaker has come to the end of the utterance or not? If the speaker intends to say more, the pause and gaze will be shorter, there is no falling pitch, and the hands are still active.

How can a listener take the floor, if someone else keeps talking all the time? Would-be speakers show signs of arousal, make vigorous head nods, anticipatory hand movements and yes-yes noises; they wait until the speaker pauses and then interrupt; if he or she still goes on talking the last move is to speak louder.

Interviews on radio and TV now play an important part in the news and the political process; these interviews have a special pattern of turn-taking. The convention has been established that the interviewer is in charge, he opens and closes the conversation, and asks the questions. He may introduce other material but this is assumed to be preliminary to a question and is not responded to. While he appears neutral, he asks questions which are designed to probe and challenge, sometimes attributing them to third parties. The interviewer is supposed just to answer the questions, but often takes the opportunity to argue for his position and to defend himself and his party. Sometimes the interviewee rebels, and asks questions back, refuses to answer, or leaves the studio, but this constitutes a news event in itself (Greatbatch, 1988). More often he evades the issue.

Beattie (1983) noticed that Mrs Thatcher appeared to be interrupted a lot in these interviews, and this was confirmed in a comparison with an interview with Mr Callaghan. He analysed one of her interviews and showed it to groups of judges in various forms. He found that judges could not distinguish between ends of utterances and points at which she was interrupted, from the typescripts alone. However, they could do so from silent video, audio, or video with sound. Further analysis showed that she was using falling pitch in mid-utterance as well as at ends of utterances. Since utterance endings could be detected from video without sound, there must have been a visual cue too, perhaps terminal gaze.

Several years later Bull and Mayer (1988) analysed 4 Thatcher and 4 Kinnock interviews. They did not find that Mrs Thatcher was interrupted more than Mr Kinnock, but she did complain more, with words like 'No, please let me go on', and 'May I just finish', though Kinnock also complained. There are in fact a lot of interruptions in these interviews – every 53 seconds on average. And the reason is clear: Mrs Thatcher evaded the issue in 56 per cent of her answers, Kinnock in 59 per cent, and 39 per cent of interruptions were for evasive answers. Mrs Thatcher also evaded questions by making personal attacks on interviewers, which deterred them from that line of questioning.

Politeness

Everyone agrees that 'politeness' is desirable, but what exactly does it consist of? The dictionary is not much help – 'having good manners, being refined, cultivated, courteous' and so on, which does not tell us what to do. How about 'forms of speech which are as far as possible agreeable and rewarding to others'? I say 'as far as possible' because being polite need not require constant flattery and agreement.

Politeness could be seen as a number of social skills, and several have commonly been proposed (Lakoff, 1973; Leech, 1983).

(1) Being friendly

Making an encounter enjoyable, warm acceptance of the other person, is perhaps the key to politeness, from which the rest follows. This is partly done by words, but even more by the non-verbal style in which utterances are delivered.

(2) Care of other's self-esteem

Interactors should work hard to avoid damaging the 'face' or self-esteem of the other. Praise or reference to success of other should be maximised, those of self modestly minimised.

(3) Avoid constraining the other

For example by direct orders or requests. Children learn to replace 'I want a sweet' with more indirect versions. Indirectness is more polite because it leaves the other free to choose. 'Would you mind answering the phone?' is more polite than 'Answer the phone'. It is possible to place utterances on a scale of indirectness from 'mitigation' to 'aggravation'. Mitigation is where orders or requests are given as questions, hints or suggestions, with reasons; aggravation is the opposite – 'Answer the bloody phone'. Linde (1988) found that in air crews with good safety records there was a higher level of mitigation – it keeps up social relationships and does not challenge the captain's authority. There was more mitigation when addressing superiors. But in accidents and emergencies, real and simulated, there was less mitigation, and it could lead to disaster, because such messages were much less likely to be acted on.

(4) How to say 'no' or disagree

In Japan it is very impolite to say 'no', and questions are avoided for which this might be the answer. For us too it is more polite to emphasise points of agreement and minimise disagreement, as in 'Yes, but . . .'. Disagreements should be wrapped up in utterances which contain agreements or other positive components, including positive non-verbal elements (Leech, 1983).

(5) Making repairs

When someone has broken the rules, or has frustrated or offended the other in some way, he usually tries to make things right by a 'repair'. Holtgraves (1989) asked a sample of subjects what they could say if someone was disastrously late for an appointment. The most common move was to express regrets, and in 55 per cent of cases a combination of moves was used. They fell into three clusters: concessions (regrets, apology, often including an account of what happened), excuses and justifications. These three types fitted the mitigating–aggravating dimension, where concessions are most mitigating, and justifications most aggravating.

(6) Avoid rule-breaking

There are many kinds of behaviour which are commonly regarded as impolite, through breaking normal rules of behaviour. Examples are interrupting, breaking into queues, talking too much, or telling unsuitable jokes.

Rules of politeness vary between situations. In a study which pre-dates the publication of most of these rules we asked subjects to rate the importance of 20 rules for each of 8 situations. The results are shown in Figure 2.2.

The rules in the top cluster were thought to apply to all the situations mentioned, and can be regarded as rules of general politeness. The last cluster consists of additional rules for parties, where evidently a further degree of politeness is needed; the party rules did not apply to the other clusters of situations, which were work or informal social situations.

In university seminars, in Britain at least, it is quite normal for people to disagree sharply, and this is perfectly acceptable if done in a friendly way, but without any 'wrapping up'. In 'banter' between males, there is a lot of what

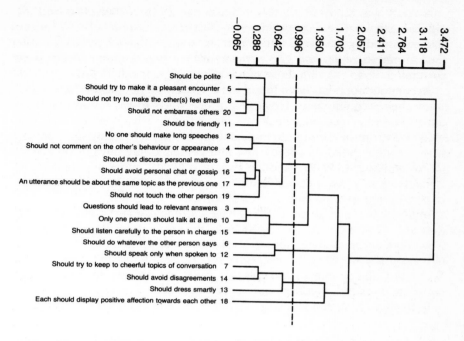

Figure 2.2 Clusters of rules in common social situations
Source: Argyle *et al*, 1979

looks like face-damaging rudeness, but this is usually acceptable as friendly teasing without hostile intent. In another study of rules for relationships we found that it was widely agreed that one should joke or tease friends. While this held for British subjects it was not found in Japan or Hong Kong – where there is much more concern with face (Argyle, 1987).

Accommodation

Two speakers often 'accommodate' to each other; that is, they change their speech styles to be more similar. This can be in respect of the language spoken (such as in French- and English-Canadian encounters), of accent (as between people of different social classes), loudness or length of utterance. They do so partly in order to be accepted by or integrated with the other, and partly to be understood better. An interesting example comes from the study of conversations between Americans and Japanese. The Japanese give many more back-channel responses, grunts and head nods, probably because they speak in shorter sentences, so that there are more pauses, where back-channel responses would be appropriate. When Americans and Japanese speak to each other, there is accommodation on both sides – the Americans use more, the Japanese fewer back-channels (Figure 2.3).

A study was made of a girl in a travel agency in conversation with 51 different clients. She accommodated to class-related aspects of their speech such as sounding the initial 'h', so that she sounded h's 3.7 per cent of the time at one extreme, and 29.3 per cent at the other, and her speech style correlated .76 to .90 with those of her clients (Coupland, 1984).

Accommodation has been found to be successful: people are liked more when they accommodate. However, in one study it was found that if an interactor converged on speech rate, accent *and* verbal contents, this was seen as patronising or ingratiating, and there was more liking for a person who accommodated on speech rate and contents only but not on accent (Giles and Smith, 1979). Another person is liked if more apparent effort is involved, as when speaking another language, and if the motive appears to be a design to break down cultural barriers.

Individuals converge more if they have a strong need for approval, and if they are of lower power, so, for example, the lower-status Puerto Ricans in New York accommodate more to blacks than vice versa. And convergence depends on possessing the necessary repertoire – you can't converge on Welsh or Chinese unless you know the accent or language, though you can converge on speed, loudness and, as we have seen, class-related accents.

Individuals of higher levels in organisations, and of higher social classes,

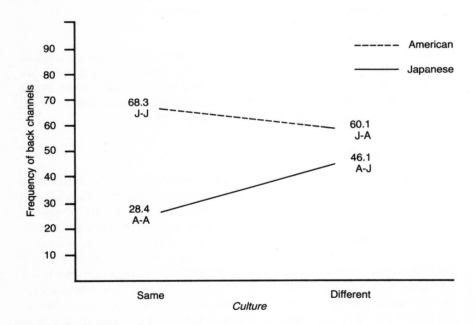

Figure 2.3 Accommodation in American–Japanese conversations
Source: White, 1989

speak faster with a more standard accent. These differences are preserved, so that there is some 'divergence' between different levels. However, if two individuals from different levels come together, in a cooperative task, where they have equal standing, both converge towards a similar accent and speed. This was found in an experiment using nurses of different levels of seniority (Thakerar *et al.*, 1982). In some other settings, as we have seen, the lower-status individuals converge more.

There can also be divergence if people do not wish to be accepted by the other, and on the contrary want to emphasise their status or their separate group identity, as in some ethnic settings like the Flemish and French in Belgium. This prevents too much accommodation between males and females since they want to keep to male or female norms of speech. When males and females meet they accommodate to one another in certain ways – such as length of pauses, and they over-accommodate on utterance length, but actually diverge in some other ways; for example, women laugh a lot more (Bilous and Krauss, 1988).

Making and keeping friends

In our early experiments on non-verbal communication we found that if a stranger behaved in a friendly non-verbal style (in face, tone of voice and so on) this created a much more friendly impression than friendly words. This was supported by other studies; for example, showing that people who had difficulty making friends were deficient in their use of such positive non-verbal cues (Trower, 1980).

However Ellis and Beattie (1986) pointed out that it is possible to express positive attitudes towards other people by using more subtle verbal forms than 'I like you', such as agreeing and paying compliments. Similar findings have emerged from the study of the behaviour of extraverts with strangers – they are very good at getting to know strangers quickly (Thorne, 1987).

I maintain that a positive non-verbal manner is very important, and the following non-verbal signals have been found to be effective in communicating a friendly attitude:

proximity:	closer; lean forward if seated
orientation:	more direct, but side by side for some situations
gaze:	more gaze and mutual gaze
facial expression:	more smiling
gestures:	head nods, lively movements
posture:	open with arms stretched towards other rather than arms on hips or folded
touch:	more touch in an appropriate manner
tone of voice:	higher pitch, upward pitch contour, pure tone
verbal contents:	more self-disclosure

We turn now to the verbal side of making friends, and the kinds of utterance suggested by Beattie and others. The first group of utterance types are all cases of 'rewardingness', which is an important source of friendship.

1 *Paying compliments* This is one of the main forms of verbal rewardingness, and often includes, in English, the word 'nice'. This overlaps with the politeness rule about maximising praise of the other.
2 *Pleasure talk* Talking about pleasant events, keeping to cheerful topics of conversation. This kind of conversation has been found to enhance feelings of joy and reduce depression.
3 *Agreeing* The purpose of these conversations is not to solve problems but to further the relationship, so if possible one should agree with what has been said.
4 *Use of names* The other is addressed by name, preferably first name. The word 'we' is used to signal shared activities, feelings, group membership, cooperation.
5 *Being helpful* It is very rewarding to provide or offer help, in the form of information, sympathy or practical help.
6 *Humour* This makes social encounters more enjoyable, and signals a positive attitude to others. Humour breaks down social barriers, reduces tensions, increases joy, and produces shared feelings and attitudes; for example, to the object of humour.

The next group of verbal moves is concerned with developing the relationship, rather than being rewarding.

7 *Reaching for similarity* Speakers try to find things which they have in common – people and places, opinions and beliefs, interests and knowledge. This is most important, since friendship depends on shared interests, which can be talked about or engaged in together.
8 *Questions*, especially questions taking a serious personal interest in the other, and suggesting some self-disclosure. They must not be too intimate, or the politeness rule of respecting privacy will be broken. The level of intimacy depends on the stage which the relationship has reached.
9 *Self-disclosure* The reply should be at a sufficient level of self-disclosure, matching and perhaps going a little beyond what has been disclosed by the other. The development of friendship depends on self-disclosure; it has been found that part of the trouble with lonely people is that they keep to impersonal topics of conversation, like sport and politics.

Friends spend a great deal of their time together talking. What do they talk about? There are 5 main areas of conversation:

(a) sheer sociability – jokes, casual chat about recent activities, and simply enjoying each other's company;
(b) gossip – news about friends and acquaintances;
(c) discussing common interests – for example, in leisure activities and self-disclosure of feelings and thoughts;
(d) providing information and solving problems; the social network is often the best source of information or advice;
(e) social support, for those who are distressed. However, it is better to involve people in cheerful activities, or to try to solve their problems, than to dwell too much on distressing events.

We have found that conversations between friends are governed by powerful informal rules, which if broken often result in loss of a friendship. Table 3.4 shows the things that should *not* be said to friends (p. 53).

CONVERSATION OVER THE TELEPHONE AND VIDEOPHONE

Conversation over the telephone is different, because all visual information is lost; the videophone keeps visual information, but there is still physical separation. The study of conversation in these modes is theoretically interesting, and also practically important; it would be useful to know how far either of them could replace business meetings, for example.

The main difference which has been found between telephone and face-to-face conversations is that telephone conversations are more task-oriented – for example, there is less praise of the other, more information given; they are also shorter, though utterances are longer (Rutter, 1987). While this has been found in a number of experiments in the lab and with people at work, I doubt whether it applies to telephone conversations between teenagers and their friends, or between sisters, or mothers and daughters; in my experience these conversations are certainly not short, and I very much doubt whether they are task-oriented either.

However, there are more questions over the telephone, and over video, compared with face-to-face (Table 2.1). This may be because there is less certainty over how the other is reacting. Here video and face-to-face are better than telephone. In view of the role of non-verbal signals in synchronising, it was expected by research workers that synchrony could be worse over the telephone. However, several studies have found the very opposite: over the telephone there are *fewer* interruptions or long pauses (see Table 2.1). The explanation is probably that in face-to-face it is possible to send positive non-verbal signals which prevent the annoyance or breakdown of interaction which interruptions could produce.

Table 2.1   Conversation over the telephone and videophone

	Face-to-face	Telephone	Videophone
Number of interruptions (in 15 minutes)	14.7	9.0	
Duration of interruptions (secs)	18.7	9.4	
Length of mutual silence (secs)	18.9	14.4	
Length of utterances	25.7	34.3	
Percentage questions	14.4	22.9	21.5
Acknowledged signals	7.2	3.6	4.7

Source: Rutter, 1987

It is also interesting that there are more back-channel acknowledgement signals in face-to-face conversations. This is interpreted by Rutter as another sign of the spontaneous and relaxed nature of normal conversation, contrasted with the task-oriented formality of the other media. There are, however, more vocal back-channels over the telephone – partly replacing head nods and the rest.

What is the difference between these three media in terms of the effects of conversation? For simple transfer or exchange of information, all three are equally good. For problem-solving, again there is no difference, though people enjoy it more in face-to-face conversations. With bargaining and negotiation a very interesting difference has consistently emerged: over the telephone the person with the stronger case – for example, in simulated management–union negotiation – always wins, while in face-to-face and video this is often not so; when there is vision, interpersonal considerations, such as wanting to keep on good terms with the other, influence the outcome of negotiations.

How about purely social aspects of conversation? A stranger is rated most friendly after a face-to-face conversation, compared with video, telephone and writing, in that order, though video is close behind face-to-face. It is evidently difficult to establish a close or intimate relationship without seeing the other person. This has been described as the 'coffee and biscuits problem' – the need for a relaxed sharing of food and drink, and sociable chat, in order to establish a warm relationship (Short et al., 1976).

There are further problems about the use of these media. Most of us have learned how to use the telephone, how to manage without vision, and also how and when to make a call, how to begin and end it. We have as yet no such skills or routines for using videophones, and this may explain why they have not caught on. There are major new problems here, how much attention need be paid to clothes and hair, or the tidiness of the room, for example.

POLITICAL SPEECHES

In previous historical periods influence was exerted by leaders, politicians and prophets by word of mouth at public meetings. Roosevelt made much use of the radio, and later political leaders have used TV. The Kennedy–Nixon debates influenced many of those who saw them to vote for Kennedy, partly because of his evident persuasiveness and charm, partly because of the less favourable impression created by Nixon's face. The percentage of voters who said they would vote for Kennedy increased from 44 per cent to 50 per cent – though there was little change of attitude on political issues.

Atkinson (1984) recorded a number of British political speeches and observed that 'spontaneous' applause was often produced by certain rhetorical devices such as lists of three and 'contrastive pairs', in both cases with appropriate emphasis and pauses. This was followed up by Heritage and Greatbatch (1986), who analysed 476 speeches at party conferences. They found that whether or not rhetorical points led to applause depended on the use of non-verbal emphasis, especially terminal gaze at the audience, increase in loudness, increased pitch or loudness variation, and a change of rhythm or gestures. When 2 or more of these were used there was more than a 50 per-cent likelihood of applause, with one 25 per cent and with none 5 per cent. The content of what was said also affected the enthusiasm of the reception – which was greatest when other parties were being attacked, and when the pro-majority position was being put forward.

Arthur Scargill is a very effective political speaker, certainly in terms of generating an enthusiastic response. Bull (1987) analysed a speech by Arthur Scargill in which there were 25 rhetorical points, of which 22 received prolonged applause. The most successful rhetorical devices were contrasts, 3-part lists, and 'headline punching' (the speaker proposes to make a declaration or promise, and then makes it). In the sections which produced most applause he used strong hand movements; for example, '*they* say . . .' (left-hand gesture), but '*we* say . . .' (right-hand gesture).

There has been a lot of research on the American Presidential debates. Leathers (1986) describes how he trained Carter for his debates with Ford. Despite his reputation for not being able to walk and chew gum at the same time, Ford emitted a much more credible image at the first debate:

a high level of gaze;
powerful gestures, such as a karate chop;
arms and feet spread wide in an assertive posture; and
loud volume of speech.

Carter, on the other hand, displayed a great deal of downward and apparently shifty gaze, a high blink-rate, weak and self-touching gestures, a narrower and rather passive posture, and he spoke very quickly, dropping his voice at the end of sentences, with a lot of disfluencies. Leathers claimed to have altered Carter's behaviour, and he was judged to have won the second debate by most people, and his media advisers thought that this was partly due to his changed pattern of NVC (Leathers, 1986). (Another reason may have been that Ford apparently didn't know where Poland was, in the second debate.)

Some political and religious leaders seem to have a 'charismatic' quality, which commands attention, and attracts people to them. It is not known exactly what makes people charismatic. Atkinson suggests that it may be due to the use of intense gaze, extensive use of gesture, and the rhetorical devices already mentioned. The contents are surely important too. Religious leaders have often generated a lot of emotional enthusiasm in their hearers by talking of the terrors of hell or the imminence of death.

Social class

It is familiar in Britain that accent varies with class, and the same is true in other countries. Linguistic analysis shows that lower-class speech varies in the sounding of certain phonemes, is more ethnic or regional, and sounds less confident or eager. In the USA lower-class people sound *th* as *t*, and *r* is less voiced (in, for instance, 'bared'). However, people of all classes have a range of speech styles, and in casual, informal speech move towards the working-class style. In careful speech, such as reading aloud, lower-working-class Americans showed 'hypercorrection'; that is, they went beyond upper-middle-class speech in sounding their *r*s (Labov, 1966). This shows how accent may be used as self-presentation, to improve apparent social class.

In Britain, and elsewhere, accent is used as a cue for social class, and is probably the main cue. It is found that an individual's class can be judged quite accurately from short samples of speech. A correlation of .80 between perceived and actual social class has been reported; it drops only to .65 if speakers are all asked to assume an upper-class accent (Ellis, 1967). When Giles and Powesland (1975) used a technique whereby a single speaker made recordings with a variety of accents, it was found that accents were placed by judges along a dimension of generalised prestige, as shown in Figure 2.4.

'Received pronunciation' (r.p.) is the name for standard, educated South of England speech. When the (supposedly different) speakers were rated on a number of scales, those with superior (r.p.) accents were rated as having greater self-confidence, intelligence, ambition, leadership, prestige and wealth, good looks and height, occupational status and cleanliness. However, subjects who were themselves Welsh, Scottish or Yorkshire, while agreeing that the r.p. speaker was more intelligent than the rest, thought that the speaker with their own regional accent was more friendly, generous, good-natured, and had a greater sense of humour. The r.p. speaker was usually found to be more persuasive in experiments, subjects cooperated with him more, and said they would be more likely to employ him.

The verbal components of speech also vary with class. In many societies there are 'high', or official, and 'low', or informal, varieties of speech.

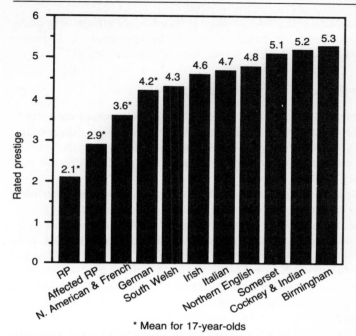

* Mean for 17-year-olds

Figure 2.4 Prestige of different British accents
Source: Giles and Powesland, 1975

Bernstein (1959) described the 'restricted' code which he believed was normally used by working-class people in Britain, and the 'elaborated' middle-class code. Research has confirmed these ideas, and clear differences in verbal style found in a number of cultures. It is found that middle-class speech has:

> longer, more complete, sentences,
> better grammar,
> more subordinate clauses,
> is more impersonal, has few pronouns.

It follows that middle-class speech should permit more accurate and efficient communication, and this has been confirmed in experiments. But, as with accent, individuals vary their speech style, and are more likely to use the elaborated code in more formal situations; however, middle-class people have a greater range here, and vary the code more in different situations, though they are unlikely to use the characteristic restricted code tags 'didn't I?' and 'wasn't he?'. Working-class people depart much less from their preferred code.

Bernstein suggested that the functions of the two forms are different. Middle-class speech is for the clear transmission of information, working-class speech is for sustaining social relationships in face-to-face groups. The codes used in different classes are passed on partly by education, but also by the way mothers reply to children's questions (Robinson, 1978).

GENDER DIFFERENCES IN CONVERSATION

Men and women tend to talk about different things. Groups of men like to talk about money, work, sports, competition, and like teasing one another, while women talk about family, friendships, feelings, clothes, health and food. Women engage in more self-disclosure, talk about more intimate topics, especially to other women.

In mixed-sex pairs and groups, men talk more on average. They also interrupt a lot more; on the other hand women often challenge these interruptions, so it is by no means a matter of women being submissive. But when women interrupt, they ask questions leading to more male talk. Men tend to be dominant in these conversations in a number of ways; as well as talking and interrupting more, they talk more loudly and control the conversation more, while women make more polite listening signals like 'that's right', which are not intended to interrupt. When men have real power or expertise, they control even more; women do not change their style (Leet-Pellegrini, 1980).

Lakoff (1975) proposed that women's speech has a number of characteristic features – more questions, tag questions (such as 'didn't I?'), hesitations, intensifiers, hedges (like 'sort of'), and rising intonation. Much of this can probably be best interpreted as politeness, keeping up the smooth flow of conversation. It could be interpreted as insecurity and hesitancy; however, questions are effective in controlling the topic, and 'you know' demands attention, and checks that the other is listening. These are ways of turning an insecure conversation into a successful one (Fishman, 1980). Women also express doubtfulness ('may', 'might'), and use many more 'intensifiers' ('it was so beautiful'). There are typically masculine expressions ('oh shit', 'what the blazes is going on?'), and feminine ones ('oh dear', 'that's adorable'). Women laugh more, especially when feeling uncomfortable, and make many more back-channel responses.

The main gender difference in voice quality is that women's voices are of higher pitch, partly for anatomical reasons, but partly because women tend to smile while they speak, which produces a higher-pitched sound. The resonance pattern is also different, male voices having more energy at the lower pitches. Women use more intonation, twice the pitch range of men in one study; women 'italicise', where men are 'deliberate'; women use sharp upward gradients, as in surprise, the bright and cheerful style, exaggerated when speaking to children (and taken off by Joyce Grenfell). Men keep to the same steady pitch, or use a falling pitch.

Women have often been found to be more fluent that men; they have fewer pauses or other speech errors. Their grammar is more correct, and their sentences more complete and more complex, from an early age. Women use more standard r.p. speech, in these respects and in terms of accent. When women are heard speaking in this way, they are rated both as more masculine (adventurous, independent), and also as more feminine (attractive); that is, as more 'androgynous' than women speaking in regional accents. This may be partly because r.p. accents are rated higher on masculinity for both sexes (Smith, 1985; Ellis and Beattie, 1986).

Overall the speech style of women is directed towards keeping a pleasant conversation going, and pursuing the goals of cooperation, friendship and social support. Men are more concerned with the task, often at the expense of the relationship, and with competition and dominance rather than cooperation (Argyle, 1991).

CONVERSATIONS IN DIFFERENT SITUATIONS

Conversations differ greatly in different situations – for example, at interviews, parties, church services, over the telephone, at committees. Here are some of the ways in which they differ.

Vocabulary

The vocabularies used may be quite different, between, for example, a physics seminar, a church service, and mother–infant conversations. Take dressmaking:

> Stitch armhole facing back to armhole facing front at shoulders and sides.
> Pin facing to armhole edge, RIGHT SIDES TOGETHER, matching notches and seams. Stitch.
> GRADE seam allowances. Clip curves.
> Turn facing to INSIDE. Press.
> Top stitch $3/_8''$ (1 cm) from armhole edge (Gregory and Carroll, 1978).

Criminals use special slang, partly with the purpose of preventing outsiders from understanding. Such special vocabularies have been found for professional gamblers, pickpockets, smugglers, drug addicts, prisoners and others. These argots have been described as 'antilanguages', since they use an alternative vocabulary to that used by 'straight' society, and this has the additional function of creating and maintaining an alternative social reality.

High and low forms

In formal situations people use more careful speech, corresponding to the 'high' version of the language, the 'elaborated code' in Britain. For

informal situations they use the 'low' or 'restricted' code. The high version
is more grammatically correct, has more subordinate clauses and a larger
vocabulary. The low version is more casual and also more personal, with
more questions and more pronouns. The high version is for the efficient
exchange of information, the low one for sustaining interpersonal relations
(Brown and Fraser, 1980).

Figure 2.5 shows how class I people shift towards the low style, for
informal settings, with fewer relative clauses and shorter sentences.

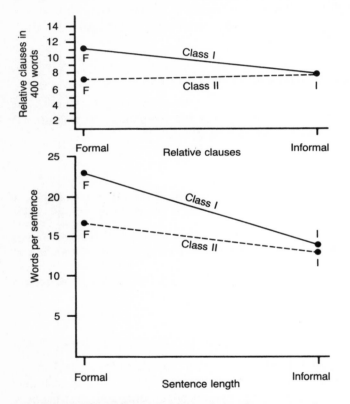

Figure 2.5 Effect of social class and situation on speech
Source: Lindenfeld, 1969

Categories of utterances

There are a number of basic utterance types:

    statement: conveys information
    question: seeks information
    order, instruction: influences another's behaviour

gossip, chat, jokes: sustains social relationships
promises, bets, names, etc.: creates a changed state of affairs.

The Bales (1950) scheme for categorising utterances into 12 types was widely used (asks for suggestion, gives suggestion, agrees and so on), and it shows clear differences between situations – for example, in the number of jokes made, or questions asked. However, it became clear that some situations required special categories of behaviour, in order to record psychotherapy, management–union bargaining, and mother–child interaction, for example. In order to record what is happening in psychotherapy, categories are needed which distinguish between a Freudian 'interpretation', and a Rogerian non-directive reflection, for example.

It is also necessary to analyse the contents of conversation, the non-verbal signals, and the bodily actions, used by a doctor with a patient, for example. Elements of behaviour are grouped differently: we found that asking about work and about private life would be regarded as similar on a date, but quite different at work (Argyle, Furnham and Graham, 1980).

Sequences of utterances

Some situations are more or less scripted, so that everyone knows what to do. This is literally true in a play, largely true of a church service, and partly true in a restaurant or a shop. In some other situations, one person has a plan, and tries to make the other follow it too – as in an interview or teaching.

A visit to the doctor consists more of a sequence of *episodes*. Byrne and Long (1976) reported the following phases:

1 relating to the patient,
2 discussing the reason for the patient's attendance,
3 conducting a verbal or physical examination or both,
4 consideration of patient's condition,
5 detailing treatment or further investigation,
6 terminating.

They found that all six phases occurred in 63 per cent of interviews, and that sometimes part of the sequence was repeated.

Sometimes both are trying to achieve a goal, and use strategies to influence the other, as in negotiations and decision-taking. Or neither has any particular plan or goal and just responds to the other's last speech, as in purely social situations, though there is probably a goal of seeking the other's affection or approval.

Rules

Every situation is governed by rules, mainly informal rules. The rules develop because they are 'functional'; that is, they help the participants to attain the goals of that kind of situation. We found the rules governing a variety of common situations for Oxford students, and these are given in Figure 2.2. The functional importance of rules can be seen from a number of situation-specific rules; for instance, 'make sure your body is clean' and 'answer truthfully' (seeing doctor), and 'don't pretend to understand when you don't', and you 'should say what problems you are having' (tutorial).

Personality differences

There are great individual differences in speech and conversational style; some of these are linked to familiar personality dimensions.

Extraversion has been most widely studied. Extraverts, and people who are socially competent, speak in voices that are louder, faster, higher pitched, and with fewer pauses. Their voice quality is not breathy (as introverts' voices are), but more resonant, harsh and metallic. They talk more than introverts, and with less delay before replying (Scherer, 1979). They make rapid social contact, and do so by speaking in a warmer, more enthusiastic way, and by asking questions, agreeing, paying compliments (Thorne, 1987), and in a different verbal style, using more verbs.

Neurotics, and anxious people, also talk fast, but with pauses and other speech errors, a breathy voice, and shorter utterances. Socially anxious people are often socially unskilled and bad conversationalists. They may fail to initiate conversational topics, just giving brief replies when spoken to. They are often very egocentric, and talk about 'me' a lot. In depressed people there is a special voice quality – slow, low-pitched, with falling pitch, and of weak intensity. There is little talk and little initiation of topics.

Dominance and assertiveness: People who talk fast and loudly are thought to be dominant and assertive. These people are more directive, interrupt more and make less use of polite mitigation.

Schizophrenics have a distinctive speech style, which is monotonous, of low pitch and loudness, and breathy; there is some evidence for a 'hollow', non-resonant voice quality. Some schizophrenics do not talk at all; those who do have difficulty in turn-taking and keeping to relevant topics.

Common types of conversational failure

There are a number of ways in which individuals can be 'bad conversationalists' – either they cannot keep a conversation going at all, or they fail to reach the goals of the conversation (personal or professional), or they annoy other people and are found unrewarding and are avoided. These are serious failures of social competence, and result in social isolation and loneliness, and ineffectiveness at work and in everyday situations. The variations below correspond to the basic processes already discussed; all are familiar both in clinical practice with neurotic patients and in everyday life.

(a) Turn-taking

One of the commonest failures is talking too little. This is partly due to failure to initiate conversational topics, so that others have to do all the work and keep the conversation going. Other people often do this by asking the silent person questions, for which they get short answers, so that the conversation can easily turn into a kind of interview. Giving *short* answers is part of the trouble.

    Q. Where do you come from?
    A. Didcot
        (*long silence*)

A more skilled move here would be to make a double or 'pro-active' response, for example,

    Q. Where do you come from?
    A. Didcot: there's a very interesting railway museum there; have you seen it?

In addition to keeping the conversation going this seeks shared experience and interests.

A much rarer problem is talking too much, and this is much more difficult to deal with. Both problems reflect insensitivity to the reactions of other people and to the normal rules of conduct of social encounters.

(b) Ego-centricity

This is not taking account of the point of view of others. We have seen the importance of designing speech acts so that they are understood and have the desired influence on others. Neurotic patients are very egocentric, in talking about 'me' a lot, and showing very little interest in others. This can lead to communication failures, as when an American lady at a party, when I asked her where exactly her home town was, looked at me as if I was a total idiot and said, 'Why, it's just over the state line', which left me none the wiser.

(c) Failures of politeness

These can take a number of forms. People can damage another's self-esteem, be boastful rather than modest, constrain the other by direct demands, interrupt, disagree or say 'no' without softening it. They can fail to use indirect, 'mitigated' forms, though we saw earlier that these may fail to produce the necessary actions in crisis situations.

(d) Self-disclosure

A common failure on the part of individuals who feel lonely or can't make friends is insufficient disclosure about themselves, especially about their feelings. A rarer problem, described by Berne (1966), is too much self-disclosure, found in some neurotics. Asking questions which are too personal is the other side of this. Normally there is gradually increased disclosure as two people get to know each other, up to a limit, and it is closely reciprocated. In professional situations of course it is *not* normally reciprocated.

(e) Attitude to others

A common failure is simply not being friendly enough, and we have seen that this is partly done verbally, partly non-verbally. The verbal signals for friendliness were described earlier (such as compliment, agree, use name). Failure to send these signals is common on the part of people who can't make friends, surly adolescents, and sometimes people at work. On the other hand it can also be a mistake to be too warm – for example, in professional and work relationships – and the precise level of intimacy needs to be very carefully controlled. Many people have jobs where they have to be friendly towards their clients – nurses and teachers, for example. Air hostesses have a special problem here and need to make particular efforts to manage their verbal and non-verbal communications.

(f) Failures of cooperation

In all social situations it is necessary to take account of the other's goals and point of view, and to integrate these with one's own. In a social conversation, for example, this means not simply being interested in the other, but discovering and developing joint interests. In negotiation the skill is to find a solution which gives maximum joint profits. In leadership and persuasion it is essential to discover and appeal to the other's needs and show how they can be met.

(g) Coping with different situations

It is important to use the appropriate speech style, which is different for home and work, for parties and committees, along the formal–informal dimension, for example. It is also necessary to display the appropriate emotional state, in words as well as non-verbally. We found that the rules for parties include 'should keep to cheerful topics of conversation'. It is possible to *display* the appropriate emotion, by control of the contents of speech and of non-verbal signals such as tone of voice and facial expression. It would be very ineffective if a doctor, psychiatrist, nurse or teacher showed that they were depressed or angry when dealing with clients.

Some situations need special conversational skills, which have to be learnt; for example, in psychotherapy, committees, school teaching. We have seen that they may involve special kinds of utterance, special sequences, as well as the special rules which govern these situations.

CONCLUSION

Language is not marks on paper, nor is conversation an S-R sequence. Conversation is an intricate, cooperative skill, for two or more, and this skill is needed for all social behaviour. A range of important phenomena has been uncovered unique to this field, such as inter-subjectivity, accommodation and politeness. Conversational sequences are complex, and only partly understood. Non-verbal signals play essential roles, in synchronising and in the back-channel. Special verbal skills are needed to make friends, over the telephone, and in other situations, and there are major differences of speech style with gender and social class. Failure to master conversational skills, either in general or for particular situations, leads to problems, but people can be trained in using the knowledge now available.

REFERENCES

Argyle, M. (1987) *The Psychology of Happiness*. London: Methuen.
—— (1988) *Bodily Communication*. 2nd edition. London: Methuen.
—— (1989) *The Social Psychology of Work*. 2nd edition. Harmondsworth: Penguin.
—— (1991) *Cooperation: the Basis of Sociability*. London: Routledge.
Argyle, M., Furnham, A., and Graham, J.A. (1981) *Social Situations*. Cambridge: Cambridge University Press.
Argyle, M., Graham, J.A., Campbell, A. and White, P. (1979) The rules of different situations. *New Zealand Psychologist*, *8*, 13–22.
Atkinson, M. (1984) *Our Master's Voices*. London: Routledge.
Austin, J. (1962) *How to Do Things with Words*. Oxford: Oxford University Press.
Bales, R.F. (1950) *Interaction Process Analysis*. Cambridge, Mass.: Addison-Wesley.
Beattie, G.W. (1983) *Talk: An Analysis of Speech and Non-verbal Behaviour in Conversation*. Milton Keynes: Open University Press.
Berne, E. (1966) *Games People Play*. London: Deutsch.
Bernstein, B. (1959) A public language: some sociological implications of a linguistic form. *British Journal of Sociology*, *10*, 311–26.

Bilous, F.R. and Krauss, R.M. (1988) Dominance and accommodation in the conversational behaviours of same-and mixed-gender dyads. *Language and Communication*, 8, 183–94.

Blakar, R.M. (1985) Towards a theory of communication in terms of preconditions: a conceptual framework and some empirical explorations. *In* H. Giles and R.N. St Clair (eds) *Recent Advances in Language, Communication and Social Psychology*. London: Erlbaum.

Brenner, M. (1980) *The Social Structure of the Research Interview*. New York and London: Academic Press.

Brown, P. and Fraser, C. (1980) Speech as a marker of situation. *In* K. Scherer and H. Giles (eds) *Social Markers in Speech*. Cambridge: Cambridge University Press.

Bull, P.E. (1987) *Posture and Gesture*. Oxford: Pergamon.

Bull, P. and Mayer, K. (1988) Interruptions in political interviews: a study of Margaret Thatcher and Neil Kinnock. *Journal of Language and Social Psychology*, 7, 35–45.

Byrne, P.S. and Long, B.E.L. (1976) *Doctors Talking to Patients*. London: HMSO.

Clark, H.H. (1985) Language use and language users. *In* G. Lindzey and E. Aronson (eds) *Handbook of Social Psychology*. New York: Random House.

Clarke, D.D. (1983) *Language and Action*. Oxford: Pergamon.

Coupland, N. (1984) Accommodation at work: some phonological data and their implications. *International Journal of the Sociology of Language*, 46, 5–32.

Ellis, A. and Beattie, G. (1986) *The Psychology of Language and Communication*. London: Weidenfeld and Nicolson.

Ellis, D.S. (1967) Speech and social status in America. *Social Forces*, 45, 431–7.

Fishman, P.M. (1980) Conversational insecurity. *In* H. Giles, W.P. Robinson and P.M. Smith (eds) *Language: Social Psychological Perspective*. Oxford: Pergamon.

Flanders, N.A. (1970) *Analyzing Teaching Behavior*. Reading, Mass.: Addison-Wesley.

Giles, H. and Powesland, P.F. (1975) *Speech Style and Social Evaluation*. London: Academic Press.

Giles, H. and Smith, P.M. (1979) Accommodation theory: optimal levels of convergence. *In* H. Giles and R. St Clair (eds) *Language and Social Psychology*. Oxford: Blackwell.

Greatbatch, D. (1988) A turn-taking system for British news interviewers. *Language in Society*, 17, 401–30.

Gregory, M. and Carroll, S. (1978) *Language and Situation*. London: Routledge and Kegan Paul.

Grice, H.P. (1975) Logic and conversation. *In* P. Cole and J.L. Morgan (eds) *Syntax and Semantics*. vol. 3. *Speech Acts*. New York: Academic Press.

Heritage, J.C. and Greatbatch, D.L. (1986) Generating applause: a study of rhetoric and response at party political conferences. *American Journal of Sociology*, 92, 110–57.

Holmes, J. (1990) Hedges and boosters in women's and men's speech. *Language and Communication*, 10, 185–205.

Holtgraves, T. (1989) The form and function of remedial moves: reported use of psychological reality and perceived effectiveness. *Journal of Language and Social Psychology*, 8, 1–16.

Kendon, A. (1967) Some functions of gaze direction in social interaction. *Acta Psychologica*, 26, 22–63.

Krauss, R.M. (1987) The role of the listener: addressee influences on message formulation. *Journal of Language and Social Psychology*, *6*, 81–98.

Labov, W. (1966) *The Social Stratification of New York City*. Washington, DC: Center for Applied Linguistics.

Lakoff, R. (1973) The logic of politeness; or minding your p's and q's. *In Papers from the Ninth Regional Meeting of the Chicago Linguistic Society*. Chicago: Chicago Linguistic Society, pp. 292–305.

—— (1975) *Language and Women's Place*. New York: Harper and Row.

Leathers, D.G. (1986) *Successful Nonverbal Communication*. London: Collier Macmillan.

Leech, G.N. (1983) *Principles of Pragmatics*. London: Longman.

Leet-Pellegrini, H.M. (1980) Conversational dominance as a function of gender and expertise. *In* H. Giles, W.P. Robinson and P.M. Smith (eds) *Language: Social Psychological Perspective*. Oxford: Pergamon.

Linde, C. (1988) The quantitative study of communicative success: politeness and accidents in aviation discourse. *Language in Society*, *17*, 375–99.

Lindenfeld, J. (1969) Social conditions of syntactic variation in French. *American Anthropologist*, *71*, 81–8.

McDowall, J.J. (1978) Interactional synchrony. *Journal of Personality and Social Psychology*, *36*, 963–75.

Markel, N. (1990) Speaking style as an expression of solidarity: words per pause. *Language in Society*, *19*, 81–8.

Robinson, W.P. (1972) *Language and Social Behaviour*. Harmondsworth: Penguin.

—— (1978) *Language Management in Education*. Sydney: Allen and Unwin.

Roger, D. and Bull, P. (1988) *Conversation*. Clevedon: Multilingual Matters.

Rutter, D.R. (1987) *Communicating by Telephone*. Oxford: Pergamon.

Sachs, H., Schegloff, E. and Jefferson, G. (1974) A simplest systematics for the organization of turn-taking in conversation. *Language*, *50*, 696–735.

Scherer, K.R. (1979) Nonlinguistic indicators of emotion and psychopathology. In C.E. Izard (ed.) *Emotions in Personality and Psychopathology*. New York: Plenum.

Short, J., Williams, E. and Christie, B. (1976) *The Social Psychology of Telecommunications*. London: Wiley.

Smith, P.M. (1985) *Language, the Sexes and Society*. Oxford: Blackwell.

Thakerar, J.N., Giles, H. and Cheshire, J. (1982) Psychological and linguistic parameters of speech accommodation theory. *In* C. Fraser and K.R. Scherer (eds) *Advances in the Social Psychology of Language*. Cambridge: Cambridge University Press.

Thomas, A.P. (1985) Conversational routines: a Markov chain analysis. *Language and Communication*, *5*, 287–96.

Thorne, A. (1987) The press of personality: a study of conversation between introverts and extraverts. *Journal of Personality and Social Psychology*, *53*, 718–26.

Trower, P. (1980) Situational analysis of the components and processes of socially skilled and unskilled patients. *Journal of Consulting and Clinical Psychology*, *48*, 329–39.

Tsui, A.B.M. (1989) Beyond the adjacency pair. *Language in Society*, *18*, 545–64.

White, S. (1989) Backchannels across cultures: a study of Americans and Japanese. *Language in Society*, *18*, 59–76.

Chapter 3

Social relationships

In some ways this is the central chapter of the book. Relationships are the basis of social support – one of the main sources of happiness, and of mental and physical health. Relationships are central to the main activities of everyday life, of work and leisure, to be described later. In addition to being major sources of happiness, relationships can also be sources of conflict and unhappiness. The divorce rate has been rising steadily in most parts of the world. In Britain it is now about 40 per cent – the highest in Europe. This causes great distress, including ill health and mental illness, as we shall see later, and can be very damaging to the children. Many people have difficulty in making friends, or can't keep their friends, and become isolated and lonely. In Britain 24 per cent of the population say they sometimes feel lonely, 8 per cent of them once a week or more; this too is a source of distress, including depression and suicide. Some have difficulty in coping successfully at work, because they can't get on with superiors, subordinates or co-workers. Can we do something to help all these people?

Relationships are central to our conceptual schema for the analysis of social behaviour. This draws on socio-biology, which explains the evolutionary origins of relationships, and it draws on theories of attachment, the functional analysis of rules, and other concepts.

In all human culture there is the same set of social relationships, though they can take varied forms (for example, some allow more than one wife). They are:

> friends
> marriage, and other kinds of cohabitation
> parent–child relations
> siblings and other kin
> work relations, especially between mates and with supervisors
> neighbours.

This list can be divided up further, and in one of our studies we distinguished 22 relationships, all of which could be found in Italy, Japan and Hong Kong as well as in Britain.

THE PSYCHOLOGICAL BASIS OF RELATIONSHIPS

Relationships are a new topic for psychology. Can we explain them?

Socio-biology provides an important part of the explanation. The theory of 'inclusive fitness' proposes that the welfare of genes is the primary biological goal. Therefore systems of behaviour evolve which do this, such as producing offspring, and looking after them and other close kin (Hamilton, 1964). There are many forms of help and cooperation in the animal kingdom, and most can be explained in this way. For example, the probability that one animal will help another is often directly proportional to the degree of genetic relatedness. Birds may delay reproduction to be 'helpers at the nest' of a sibling, and this results in greater survival of the young. There is also mutual help and cooperation between non-kin; chimpanzees help their 'friends' find a mate; and lions cooperate over hunting. This can be explained by a second evolutionary model – reciprocal altruism, which can develop under certain conditions. Cooperation may evolve in whole groups, if cooperation pays off; this can happen if there are a lot of isolated but homogeneous breeding groups, as was the situation for hominids in the period 300,000 to 100,000 BC.

Animal behaviour is mainly innate, but human behaviour is greatly affected by culture and learning. Do these innate, evolution-derived, processes explain human behaviour and relationships? There are powerful grounds for thinking that such innate biological processes apply to us too. The inclusive fitness model is supported by the fact that 86 per cent of people will give kidneys to their own children, fewer to other kin, and very few to anyone else (Fellner and Marshall, 1981). Child neglect and abuse is very rare for biological children, compared with adopted or step-children. Kinship is the main basis of relationships in most cultures. In modern society it is still important: most inheritance is to kin, and major help – during illness, for example – is from the family.

Humans have innate equipment for the necessary kinds of communication – for example, facial nerve and muscles – and innate motivational systems such as sex. Human infants seem to be programmed to communicate, interact and form relationships, though they do need socialisation experience to develop these skills. Similar social relationships are found in all cultures, and are similar to those found in animals, especially birds and non-human primates. Some of the differences between men and women are culturally universal, and can be explained biologically: women seek a reliable and supportive mate, men look for an attractive one, and are interested in fertilizing females as well as looking after them.

There are interesting cultural differences in all relationships. A man may have several wives or a concubine; there has been a historical shift towards one wife, greater equality of roles, and recently towards shorter duration of marriage. Choice of partner through romantic love is the norm in the

Western world; elsewhere arranged marriages are more common.

Third World families are much more extensive – that is, more relatives are recognised and live together – and kinship is the dominant type of relationship. The ecology may be a factor: the importance of kinship for working-class people in Europe is probably due to their low geographical mobility, so that they tend to live near their kin. In a number of Third World cultures there are varieties of formal friendship, such as that of blood brothers, whereby friends are made into a kind of pseudo kin.

Notice that sex, like eating and drinking, is immediately rewarding, as well as leading to important long-term goals. All patterns of behaviour which are biologically important give such rewards. The explanation is that members of a species who have developed the reward system are more likely to engage in the behaviour, so that they and their kin are more likely to survive. This explains why relationships are such powerful sources of satisfaction (Argyle, 1991).

Social systems. Social relationships such as marriage, friendship and the rest are very complex affairs; they are far more than two people liking each other. And while they may have some things in common, there are a lot of obvious differences between them. In marriage, for example, two individuals normally share all their worldly goods, and their bed, and produce children: none of these three things happens in friendship or other relationships.

In some ways relationships are like games. In order to understand or play a game, one needs to know the *goals* which are being pursued (sometimes literally), and the *rules* which must be followed to do so. Chess would be a poor game unless the players had to take turns. Furthermore, the rules form a system, so that if one rule is changed it is often found that others need to be changed too. Rules define *roles* which players, or people in relationships, should perform. Games have special moves which are allowed, relationships have *activities* – both can be regarded as steps towards the goals. *Skills* are needed for both.

Rules are *functional*; that is, they make the attainment of goals possible. The rule of the road makes it easier to get somewhere without collisions. And note that there are two alternative versions which have been adopted in different cultures. Examples of relationship rules with an obvious function are driving on a certain side of the road, and not talking during concerts. Other relationship rules are less obvious. For example, the strict rules of etiquette surrounding doctors, lawyers and other professional people have the function of maintaining a certain distance, so that doctors and others can obtain intimate information without becoming too familiar or involved. We shall discuss the rules of relationships below. One result is important – the rules are different for different relationships, reflecting the nature of each relationship, and the special problems which need rules to deal with them. And the rules vary between cultures, which have developed somewhat different versions of each relationship.

Reinforcement and exchange. Many theories of relationships and especially of friendship, have been based on the idea of reinforcement and exchange of rewards. Many studies have shown that individuals who are rewarding are liked more – when they are friendly to others, helpful and cheerful, for example. Positive non-verbal signals, smiling and the rest, are signs of liking and are particularly important. Experiments have shown that experimental confederates who agree, or smile, are liked more than those who disagree or frown. These findings have been incorporated successfully into social skills training; for example, increasing rewardingness in marital therapy, and teaching positive non-verbal signals to social isolates.

There has been disagreement over whether or not equity is important for relationships; that is, whether it matters that people are getting more or less than they put in to a relationship. Van Yperen and Buunk (1990) carried out a longitudinal study of 736 married couples and found that feelings of equity predicted marital satisfaction and not vice versa, especially for women; the effect for men was rather weak.

However, being rewarded by the other is not the only source of interpersonal attraction and bonding. In close friendships people are often concerned with the needs of the other. Hays (1985) found that the best predictor of the survival of student friendships was the *sum* of rewards plus costs; in other words, doing things for the other was a positive factor. Clark (1986) showed that in 'communal' as opposed to 'exchange' relationships people are more concerned with the needs of the other, do not keep track of rewards or costs to themselves, and enjoy doing things for the other. As we shall see later, friends particularly enjoy doing things together, especially leisure activities. The other is instrumental to the rewards, but it is the experience of embeddedness, of cooperative interaction, that is important.

Love, marriage and kin are affected by reinforcement, and training in rewardingness has been used as part of marital therapy. However, there is evidence that reinforcement is not essential for kinship relations to persist, and furthermore they usually last for ever. This could be the result of the biological process described – concern for those with shared genes – or it could be due to early bonding between parents and children and between siblings.

Socialisation and learning. Whatever biological basis relationships may have, they are also the result of learning experiences, though the capacity to make use of these is itself innate. The attachment of infants to their parents or other caretakers has such an unlearnt basis, but also depends on the extent of maternal warmth and responsiveness (Bowlby, 1969). Mothers form closer relationships with their daughters, and this may explain why women form more intimate relationships later.

In the family children learn by observation and modelling, by reinforcement and by instruction about how each kind of relationship should be conducted in the culture. Everyone builds up a picture, often rather vague, of (for example) the difference between friends and sisters, what is supposed to happen in marriage, and how to bring up children. We shall see later that it is important to have the right information on these topics. When things go wrong in a relationship – for example, after the breakdown of a marriage – people spend a lot of time thinking about it, to work out an explanation, partly to protect themselves from acknowledgement of failure (Harvey *et al.*, 1982). And it has been found that when couples are in conflict they tend to blame each other, and to attribute the other's behaviour to personal characteristics like selfishness (Orvis, Kelley and Butler, 1976).

The skills of relationships also have to be learnt. Knowing about them is not enough, any more than knowing about springboard diving enables you to do it. Practice and coaching are needed too. Friendship skills are probably the first to be acquired; love and work relationships are different and have to be learnt later. Most of the individuals with social skills difficulties need help with relationship skills, and training can be focused on these.

THE MAIN FEATURES OF RELATIONSHIPS

In this section I shall describe the main features of which relationships are composed. In order to describe a game, to explain to someone who wanted to play it, the same kind of features would be mentioned – goals, moves, rules and the rest.

Goals

What are people trying to do in a relationship? We carried out studies in which people rated the importance of lists of goals for different relationships. Three factors usually appeared. These were:

1 Own physical well-being,
2 Social acceptance and so on,
3 Task goals specific to the situation.

The three factors for a nurse dealing with a patient are shown on the left hand side of Figure 3.1.

We also asked subjects to rate on a 5-point scale the extent to which each goal was instrumental to, independent of, or interfered with other goals. This showed the amount of conflict versus instrumentality, and other scales elicited the direction of such relationships; links between goals both within and between persons were found. Figure 3.1 shows the perceived goal structure for nurse and patients; it can be seen that the nurse's goal of looking after the patient leads to patient's well-being, but that this is in conflict with the nurse's own well-being.

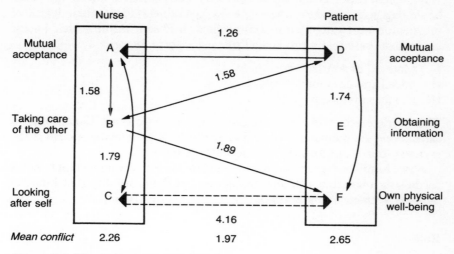

Figure 3.1 The goal structure in nursing
Source: Argyle et al., 1981

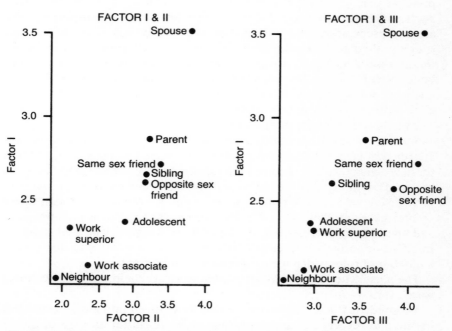

Figure 3.2 Relationships plotted on the satisfaction dimensions
Source: Argyle and Furnham, 1983

It might be expected that the satisfaction received from relationships would be similar. Argyle and Furnham (1983) asked subjects to rate their degree of satisfaction with a number of relationships on 15 satisfaction scales. Factor analysis of these scales produced three orthogonal factors:

I   Material and instrumental help
II   Social and emotional support
III   Common interests.

The average scores for each relationship on these three dimensions of satisfaction are shown in Figure 3.2. It can be seen that the spouse is the greatest source of satisfaction, especially for Factor I.

As we saw in earlier chapters, relationships confer very important benefits for health, mental health and happiness, but there are different kinds of benefits from each relationship.

Rules

The theory we propose is simply this: rules are created and changed in order that situational goals can be attained. It is a familiar psychological principle that an individual person or animal will discover routes to desired goals, either by trial and error or by other forms of problem-solving. We are now proposing an extension to this principle: *groups* of people will find routes to their goals, and these routes will be collective solutions, including the necessary coordination of some behaviours and the exclusion of other behaviours by means of rules. Unless such coordination is achieved, group goals will not be attained. Harris (1975) offered an explanation of the Indian rules protecting cows in terms of the value of cow-dung as fertiliser and fuel, of oxen for pulling farm implements, and so on.

Spouses, children, neighbours and people in professional relationships are ruled by laws; those in work relations are ruled by contracts. In addition there are many widely endorsed but informal rules – behaviour which it is believed ought or ought not to be performed in each relationship. Argyle, Henderson and Furnham (1985) carried out pilot interviews to obtain a pool of informal rules: there were 33 rules which might apply to any relationship, and up to 12 more for each of 22 relationships. Samples of 60 adult subjects rated the importance of each rule for each relationship. For each there were a number of rules which it was agreed were important.

The most general rules, which applied to most relationships in 4 cultures were as shown in Table 3.1.

We predicted that relationships would be grouped into intimate and less intimate in respect of the rules which apply. A cluster analysis of the 22 relationships using only the 33 common rules produced the clusters shown in Figure 3.3.

The first cluster consists of intimate relationships: here the rules are for

Table 3.1 General rules for relationships

Rule no.		Number of relationships in which mean showed high endorsement	Subjects' responses in the high endorsement category across relationships (%)
31.	Should respect the other's privacy	22	90.0
19.	Should not discuss that which is said in confidence with the other person	21	83.3
32.	Should look the other person in the eye during conversation	21	72.5
17.	Should not criticise other person publicly	16	65.4
20.	Should not indulge in sexual activity with the other person	15	54.9
22.	Should seek to repay debts, favours or compliments no matter how small	14	62.3
18.	Should stand up for the other person in their absence	12	62.6
30.	Should share news of success with the other person	12	58.3
1.	Should address the other person by their first name	11	56.7

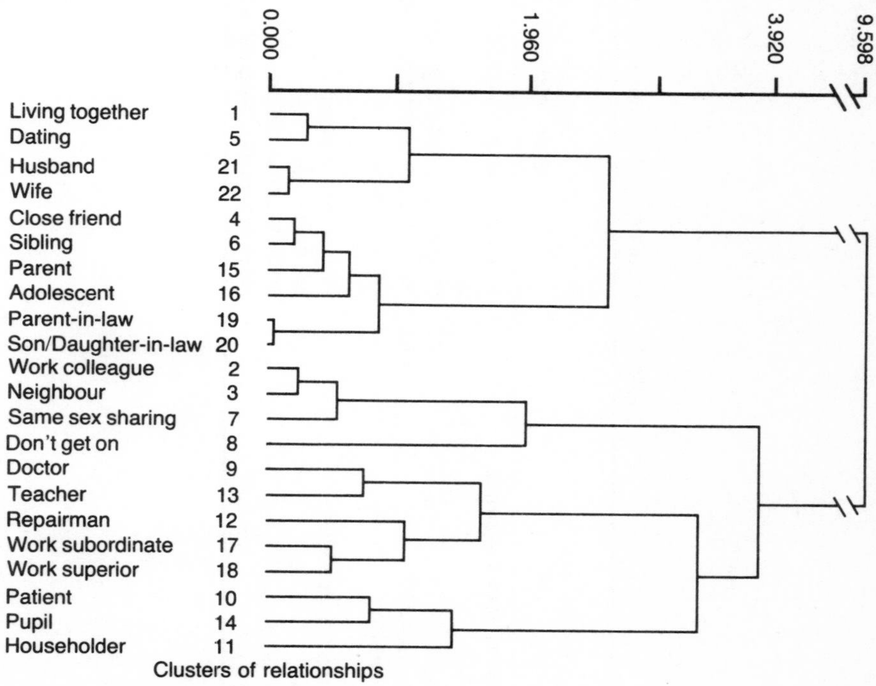

Figure 3.3 Clusters of relationships
Source: Argyle, Henderson and Furnham, 1985

Table 3.2 Situations and activities most chosen for certain relationships

Friend, similar age Mean ratio 1.26		Spouse Mean ratio 1.64		Work colleagues, liked, same status Mean ratio 1.11	
Situations above this ratio		*Situations above this ratio*		*Situations above this ratio*	
Dancing	2.00	Watch TV	2.61	Attend lecture	2.11
Tennis	1.67	Do domestic tasks together	2.48	Work together on joint task	1.56
Sherry party	1.63	Play chess or other indoor game	2.31	Together in a committee	1.55
Joint leisure	1.63	Go for a walk	2.28	Morning coffee, tea	1.50
Pub	1.60	Go shopping	2.15	Casual chat, telling jokes	1.35
Intimate conversation	1.52	Play tennis, squash	2.03	One helps the other	1.31
Walk	1.50	Informal meal	1.93		
		Intimate conversation	1.91		
		Have argument, disagreement	1.84		

expressing and maintaining intimacy. The other cluster was of less intimate, work relationships: here the rules were for avoiding intimacy and for the efficient performance of tasks.

Rule systems implicitly prescribe the roles between the participants. At cricket, in baseball, there are a number of distinct parts to be played – batsman, bowler, wicket-keeper, umpire and so on. Relationships too are role systems. An important part of roles is the power which occupants have over those in other roles.

For example, in marriage, for a long time and in most cultures, wives had an 'expressive' and nurturant role inside the home, while husbands had an 'instrumental' role in finding food, earning money, building houses and dealing with the world outside. Pressure from women is causing these roles to change in three ways: more women have jobs, and sometimes have better jobs than their husbands; they have more equal power; and they do less of the housework than before, though they still do most of it.

Activities

The things that people do together in a relationship are like moves in a game; they are the moves allowed to reach the goals. In a study by Argyle and Furnham (1982), 60 subjects, in 4 age and sex groups, were asked how often they had engaged in 26 activities with others in 7 different relationships during the previous month. One of the analyses extracted the most characteristic activities for each relationship by calculating the relative frequencies for each (Table 3.2).

This shows, for example, that the most characteristic activity with a spouse was watching TV. (Later research has shown that being in bed together is even more characteristic.) Factor analysis of the data produced a general intimacy factor, based on items such as intimate conversation, informal meals and watching TV. Spouse was by far the highest on this factor, friends intermediate, work-mates lowest.

We shall discuss below in more detail the characteristic activities for a number of relationships. As Table 3.2 shows, they are strikingly different.

Forms of attachment

We shall discuss the nature of attachment for several kinds of relationship later. The parent–child relation has a distinctive and powerful form of bonding, either due to 'selfish gene' processes or to the intensity and intimacy of early interaction. Lovers and spouses become attached in a similar way, as is shown by the great distress from divorce or bereavement. Kin, such as siblings, usually have a life-long attachment, little affected by reinforcement. The attachment between friends is different: it is clearly affected by rewards, especially the enjoyment of joint leisure, and signs of affection from the other. Close friendships made in early life may endure for ever, rather like kin, suggesting that some similar kind of bonding has taken place. Work relationships are often more superficial; the rewards arise from help with work, but also enjoying each other's company at work. There is usually little sense of loss when leaving a place of work.

Concepts and beliefs

A number of investigators have studied ideas and relationships; for example, they have asked people to rate the properties of friendship. There is convergence in finding the following properties; authenticity, affection, confiding, help, trust, companionship, self-respect and conflict (Davis and Todd, 1982). Love, on the other hand, is characterised by needing the other, caring for the other and possessiveness (Rubin, 1973). It is possible to find the dimensions, the conceptual space that people use to compare relationships. Wish *et al.* (1976) found 4 perceived dimensions by using *multidimensional scaling:* equal versus unequal; cooperative and friendly versus competitive and hostile; socio-emotional and informal versus task-orientated and formal; and superficial versus intense. However such dimensions are not really continuous variables, in that there are no relationships between marriage and siblings, or between work-mates and neighbours, any more than there are games between polo and chess.

The ideas that people have of relationships are partly due to the mass media, and many investigations have been made of how relationships are represented or misrepresented in TV soap operas and advertisements (Livingstone, 1990).

It is important to have more or less correct ideas about relationships. Socially inadequate and isolated adolescents have been found to have concepts of friendship like those of young children – focusing on benefits to self but lacking the ideas of commitment and loyalty (La Gaipa and Wood, 1981). Mentally disturbed people also have inadequate understanding of relationships, and men seem to have less understanding of them than women (Burnett, 1986). We shall see later that friendships depend on keeping social networks intact, which is not widely realised. Indeed the whole study of social relationships can be valuable in providing a better understanding of the nature of different relationships.

Skills

All games, like tennis and cricket, require special skills which need to be mastered. Simply understanding the game and knowing the rules is not enough. In the case of friendship there are the skills of making friends, and of maintaining friendships. For marriage there are some quite different skills, for avoiding and dealing with conflicts, negotiating solutions when there is disagreement. Just as people can be taught how to hit tennis balls, so too can they be taught how to make friends, and stay married. Methods of training in relationship skills will be described later.

There may be some skills which are needed for all relationships, such as rewardingness, capacity to cooperate by finding jointly satisfying solutions to problems, and engaging in verbal and non-verbal interaction sequences.

THE MAIN RELATIONSHIPS

Friendship

Friends are people who are liked, whose company is enjoyed, who share interests and activities, who are helpful and understanding, who can be trusted, with whom one feels comfortable, and who will be emotionally supportive. At least this is what people say if asked what they understand by 'friends'. We shall report research on what friends actually do together, and what they get out of it. There are different emphases: so for men, friends are people to do things with, like shared leisure; while for women friends are people to confide in, who will be emotionally supportive. To anticipate again, for young people friends are expected to be entertaining, for old people friends are expected to be useful and helpful. Another difference is between communal and exchange relationships, as described earlier.

The number of friends whom people have varies with the level of closeness specified, but is typically about 5 'close' friends, 15 'friends', 20 members of the social network (this may include kin), and a far greater number of acquaintances. It is possible to measure the level of liking between 2 people by asking them to fill in scales such as 'How much do you like or dislike X?' (10-point scale). Perhaps a better measure is the frequency of interaction, or time spent together, and another is the level of self-disclosure of intimate information.

For animals, and in developing cultures, friends are biologically important – they help and cooperate over defence, food-gathering and in other ways. In the modern world they are mainly for sociability and fun. Friends come from various sources, but mostly from work, from neighbours, and from leisure groups and clubs, while some endure from childhood (Parker, 1964). They are people with common interests, who find each other congenial, who are brought together in the environment. Sometimes friends come in groups; for example, groups of teenagers, who go around together. It is usually better to think of networks of friends, where A knows B and C, but not D, and so on. Friends usually form networks rather than clearly bounded groups, though networks do have some dense clusters.

We shall see shortly that friendship serves important biological, psychological and sociological goals. Does it also confer immediate rewards, as sexual behaviour does? Friendship is a major source of joy, as a 'bleeping' study by Larson (1990) shows (Figure 3.4). Subjects were bleeped on random occasions, when they filled in scales, reporting who they were with and their emotional state. They were clearly happier when with friends.

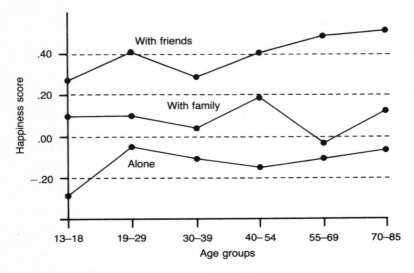

Figure 3.4 Positive affect with different companions
Source: Larson, 1990

How is this joy created? It is partly because of the enjoyable things that friends do together (see Table 3.2). In addition, friends send each other a lot of positive non-verbal signals – smile, gaze, touch, tone of voice and so on, which produce immediate positive reactions (Argyle, 1987).

Various attempts have been made to find the motivational basis for friendship activities. The most successful are the needs for affiliation and intimacy. The need for intimacy was defined as 'the motivation to seek a warm, close and communicative exchange with others', and was measured by a projection test. Subjects write stories based on vaguely drawn pictures; high scores are given when they write about union, harmony, surrender, positive affect and intimacy; high scorers are found to spend more time talking to friends, are good listeners, and engage in a lot of self-disclosure (McAdams, 1988).

Friendship formation goes through a number of stages – 'filters' that have to be passed. *Proximity* is the first. Frequency of contact in turn depends on proximity, so friendship develops more easily if people live near each other, work in the same office, or meet at the same church or club. This works very well for students, but less well for adults – because adult neighbours often have too little in common. *Similarity* is the second filter – two people must

Table 3.3 Five kinds of social support

Cluster	Variable	R with own cluster	R with next highest cluster
1	*Information*		
	Job opening info.	.78	.02
	Job contacts	.80	.01
	Housing search aids	.13	.02
2	*Services*		
	Minor household aid	.64	.07
	Minor services	.45	.06
	Major household aid	.42	.13
	Organisational aid	.20	.04
	Household items	.50	.14
3	*Companionship*		
	Doing things together	.45	.03
	Discussing things	.70	.01
	Sociability	.39	.02
	Formal group activities	.24	.01
4	*Emotional*		
	Major services	.25	.09
	Family advice	.65	.12
	Minor emotional support	.66	.06
	Major emotional support	.53	.12
5	*Financial*		
	Small $	.60	.16
	Big $	.58	.04
	Housing $	.39	.02

Source: Wellman, 1985

be sufficiently similar, especially in attitudes and beliefs, social background, social status, and above all share the same interests. Surprisingly similarity of personality is not necessary. As for *rewardingness*, Jennings (1950) found that the popular girls in a reformatory were the ones who helped and protected others, encouraged and cheered them up, made them feel accepted and wanted, and were concerned with the feelings and needs of others. It is when friendship becomes close or 'communal' that friends become much concerned with the needs of the other. In training someone in how to make friends, rewardingness is a good place to start.

A fourth filter is *development of regular meetings*. An essential early step is for one person to suggest a meeting – coffee, pub or tennis, perhaps. The frequency of interaction may increase, by dint of having lunch twice a week, playing squash, sharing accommodation, going on holidays together. They now become dependent on each other for the rewards of each other's company and from the activities like tennis, that take more than one person to play.

Self-disclosure is the fifth filter. As people get to know each other better, they are prepared to discuss more intimate topics. They trust each other to treat this information as confidential, and begin to treat each other as confidants with whom they can discuss their problems, and from whom they can rely on receiving social support. Self-disclosure is very important: one of the reasons that some individuals feel lonely, it is now known, is that they do not have sufficiently intimate conversations with their friends.

Friendships usually do not last for ever, and there is usually a period of *decline*. This is less dramatic than divorce and takes place gradually. One common reason is that one or the other moves further away. We shall see that another common cause is the breaking of rules, especially 'third-party' rules about handling the network. Or one party may find more interesting things to do or more interesting people to do them with.

What do friends do together? We asked about the frequency of various activities and the results were shown in Table 3.2. In another study we factor analysed 37 kinds of leisure activity, most of them done with friends, and found 5 factors (see p. 124).

From these and other studies it looks as if friends do three main kinds of things together – have conversation, provide help and spend joint leisure.

Conversation

Friends spend a great deal of time talking. This takes place over meals, over drinks in pubs, while drinking tea or coffee, while walking, in each other's homes, at cafés and restaurants, while on outings together, and while taking part in shared leisure activities. Indeed it is an almost constant activity during the time friends are together. Young people from 15 to 25 in particular spend a great deal of time together, often every day, up to 3 hours a day, and more time later on the telephone talking to the same people.

This conversation takes several forms. A lot of it is sheer sociability – jokes, gossip about friends and news about local events. There is discussion of common interests, from politics to religion to gardening and Scottish dancing. Friends are a most useful source of information and advice; networks are a most useful source of information and advice; the network can help you find accommodation, a job or a good doctor. Friends provide social support for people with problems, by sympathy, advice, or being a good listener, a confidant.

Help

Friends often provide help, though less than kin do. Wellman (1985) found several help factors – help with domestic affairs, financial help, and advice and information. It is in Third World countries like India that help from the social network is particularly important. In our own culture friends are primarily, but not only, for fun. For young people between adolescence and marriage, friendship is the most intense relationship, and they do reckon to provide help within their power to provide it. This would not usually include much material help, such as money or accommodation, since they cannot provide these.

However, help is not always well received, if it carries the implication that the recipient is incompetent, or reduces his or her freedom of action or if reciprocity is not possible.

Shared leisure

Shared leisure is a central part of friendship. Figure 3.2 showed that satisfaction from shared activities is very high for friends. A lot of leisure is spent in clubs, classes, teams, or other groups. This is an important source of friends, and we shall see later that it is an important predictor of happiness.

Why do people need friends? We saw that friends are biologically important to animals. The study in Figure 3.2 shows the three main kinds of satisfaction for humans. The first is *instrumental and material help*. Friends are not so important as family, but among the young and old, and in some cultures, friends are an important source of help. In addition the friendship network confers collective benefits by increasing social integration, and as a result cooperation in the community (see Table 3.3). The second kind of satisfaction is *emotional support*. We shall see that friendship networks contribute to mental health. People are lonely either if they lack a close relationship, or if they lack interaction in social groups. The third kind of satisfaction, *shared activities*, especially in joint leisure, is the explanation of why friends are a major source of joy, either because the activities are enjoyable, or because of the exchange of positive non-verbal signals (Argyle and Lu, 1990).

Table 3.4   Friendship rules and break-up of friendships

	Moderately or very important in breaking up friendship (%)	Slightly important in breaking up friendship (%)
Being jealous or critical of your other relationships	57	22
Discussing with others what was said in confidence with him/her	56	19
Not volunteering help in time of need	44	23
Not trusting or confiding in you	44	22
Criticising you in public	44	21
Not showing positive regard for you	42	34
Not standing up for you in your absence	39	28
Not being tolerant of your other friends	38	30
Not showing emotional support	37	25
Nagging you	30	25

Source: Argyle and Henderson, 1985

However, friends are particularly important, are often the main source of social support and other benefits, at two periods of life – for the young before marriage, and for the over-sixties, after retirement and after widowhood.

There are informal rules of friendship. We found that people in England strongly endorsed a number of rules, including rules about rewardingness, such as 'should strive to make him/her happy while in each other's company'.

In order to test whether these rules were of any importance in practice we studied a sample of broken friendships. It was found that the lapse of friendship was attributed in many cases to the breaking of certain rules, especially rules of rewardingness and rules about relations with third parties; for example, not being jealous and keeping confidences. (Table 3.4)

Friendship also requires certain skills, both for making friends and for keeping them. In order to make friends, we can make use of some of the processes leading to friendship. Take proximity and similarity: it follows that it is a good idea to join a club in your neighbourhood, or choose from the people at work. For rewardingness: improve positive non-verbal communication, rewarding verbal styles (take an interest, pay compliments, and so on), and other forms of reward. From the known stages: follow the usual sequence of inviting to a date, making meetings more frequent and regular, find common interests, increase self-disclosure. To keep friends there are two main points – keep the rules, especially third-party rules, and keep up the rewards.

Some people are socially isolated or lonely. Loneliness is greatest among those who are single, who live alone, rarely see their neighbours, or are unemployed. Those who are unable to find friends or form other social relationships are people who are lacking in certain social skills, such as low rewardingness, social anxiety and low self-esteem (De Jong-Gierveld, 1990). Some individuals feel lonely, even though they spend a lot of time with friends; their problem is insufficient self-disclosure, not talking about personal topics. These conditions can be corrected by social skills training, as described below (p. 66f). It may be possible to find more friends without training – join a club, class, or other group in the neighbourhood. This will contain others with similar interests who live near – ideal conditions for friendship formation.

As people become older they spend more time alone. It is found that elderly people feel *less* lonely than younger ones, especially men, although many are in fact living alone. This may be because they attribute their isolation to factors beyond their control, such as retirement and bereavement, and they are no worse off in comparison with others, so that there is no loss to self-esteem; loneliness is redefined (Shute and Howitt, 1990). Or it may be because they feel a need to be alone, and solitude has a positive side. For poets and others it is necessary for creativity; for adolescents it may be necessary for developing autonomy and identity formation; and for everyone it may be necessary just to get away from the pressures of other people. Those who are able to cope well with being alone are less depressed or ill and more satisfied with life. Older people become better at being alone (Larson, 1990).

Some people have a much stronger need for friends than others. Extraverts like a lot of social life, especially in teams or groups, and they like noisy parties and dances (Argyle and Lu, 1990). People with strong needs for affiliation or intimacy, on the other hand, seek close relationships, including heterosexual close relationships; they are good listeners and develop a strong concern for the other (McAdams, 1988).

Love and marriage

By romantic love is meant a strong feeling of sexual attraction towards another person, usually of the opposite sex, together with a need to be with them and to look after them. Compared with friendship, there is sexual desire, a stronger sense of caring, and exclusiveness. Scales for measuring it include all these components.

It particularly happens to young people; American students between 19 and 24 report 5–6 romantic episodes, and to have been in love 1.25 times (Kephart, 1967). If two people get married, the passionate state of romantic love slowly gives way to a different kind of love – 'companionate love', consisting of deep attachment and strong affection, but with less sexual excitement (Argyle and Henderson, 1985). Love often leads to cohabitation or marriage; about 92 per cent of people in Britain get married, at least once. There are different kinds of marriage, partly depending on whether one or both partners have jobs, and how much sharing and companionship there is as opposed to independence.

Courtship, like friendship, develops over time. Mate selection is an important biological process. The biological basis of love is to attract and retain mates, reproduce with them, and for the female to find a mate who will look after her and the infants (Clark and Reis, 1988). And while romantic, sexual love does the job for a limited time, it is later replaced by companionate love. Some empirical support is provided for this theory from a study by Buss in 37 cultures (1989). Subjects were asked what they looked for in a potential partner. Males valued youth (aged under 25) and physical attractiveness in women – perhaps reflecting their fertility. Females valued the financial capacity of potential mates, such as ambition and industriousness. They also preferred somewhat older mates – there is a correlation between age and income. This reflects the primitive need for a mate who is a good provider and can look after wife and children. In another study, using American students, Buss (1988) found that males and females used different techniques for attracting mates, which reflect the different mating interests of the two sexes. Females did it by wearing provocative and sexy clothes, by attention to cosmetics and hair, and by flirting; men, by displaying or boasting about their wealth and accomplishments and showing how strong and fit they are.

There is also a cultural component to love; the two-factor theory proposed that love is based on a combination of (any) physiological arousal, and cognitive factors, the presence of an appropriate member of the opposite sex, and belief in the love ideology. Laboratory experiments have found that physical exercise or other sources of arousal increases the romantic attraction of males to an attractive female (White *et al.*, 1981).

Courtship proceeds via parties and dances, to dates, and activities of increasing intimacy. As an affair develops the couple spend more time together and in more situations, positive feelings increase, and are expressed, there is more self-disclosure, increased concern for the other, a shared sense of unity and commitment, and more bodily intimacy. Huston *et al.* (1981) found several different kinds of 'trajectory' towards marriage: accelerated, accelerated but with reversals, and prolonged (over 3 years). There are several formal stages, such as announcing an engagement, moving in together and getting married (Argyle and Henderson, 1985).

People in love spend a lot of time together. What do they do? They do much the same things as friends – talking, eating, dancing, walking and son on – but they do it away from other people. There is a much higher level of self-disclosure and discussion of intimate topics. And a lot of time is spent most agreeably in 'affectional activities' – a combination of sexual activity and intimate conversation, and this intimacy may include intercourse. There is a lot to argue about. Braiker and Kelley (1979) found that as couples progressed from casual dating to marriage the frequency of arguments and problems increased, although feelings of love also increased. The cause of this conflict is that as two people get to know each other better, and do more things together, more differences emerge, which have to be discussed, worked through and compromised over.

Attachment between lovers is rather similar to that between infants and mothers, and indeed uses some of the same kinds of baby-talk and bodily contact. Perhaps one is derived from the other? Shaver and Hazan (1988) proposed and found evidence that the three kinds of infantile attachment distinguished by Ainsworth lead to similar styles of adult love attachment: secure, avoidant, and anxious/ambivalent.

Special social skills are required to engage successfully in courtship. Young men who were more successful in dating girls were found to be more fluent at saying the right thing quickly, and agreed more; they smiled and nodded more. Other non-verbal signals which are important here are gaze, pupil dilation (unfortunately not under conscious control), proximity, bodily contact and grooming. Above all, physical attractiveness is most important.

Is marriage going out of fashion? In their survey of values in Britain, Brown *et al.* (1985) found that only 14 per cent of people thought so – more among those who were divorced, had an unhappy home life, were unemployed or had left-wing political attitudes. Most felt that a child needs both parents. Married couples do a lot more things together, and Table 3.2 showed some of the characteristic activities. Marriage could be described as cooperation over the basic biological activities of sex, the procreation of children, child-rearing, providing food and eating together, looking after each other and the home. In addition married couples spend a great deal of time talking, to discuss and solve problems – to resolve disagreements, and to help each other with personal problems. There is also joint leisure, and shared social life with friends and kin.

Love and marriage are certainly very rewarding. Being in love is probably the greatest source of joy. And marriage is the relationship which provides the greatest satisfaction, as Figure 3.2 showed. On the other hand, love is not based on seeking rewards: caring for the other is a central activity for love (Clark and Reis, 1988). This suggests that love is not about seeking rewards, but about seeking intimacy and communion. In any case love is a very inefficient way of seeking rewards – 'Romantic relationships pose a particular problem for theories of people as cool-headed accountants seeking maximal rewards' (Kenrick and Trost, 1989) – since it is far too impulsive and emotional. The motivation is partly sexual, but partly the need for intimacy (McAdams, 1988).

Companionate love can also be seen as a kind of bonding. Marriage produces a high degree of bonding, in most cases. This is shown by the number of years that most couples spend together, and the distress experienced after bereavement or separation, assumed by research workers to be the greatest source of stress, and resulting in an elevated rate of mental disorder and death from heart attacks (Stroebe and Stroebe, 1987).

As we shall see in later chapters, marriage provides substantial psychological benefits. These include better health and increased length of life – caused by couples looking after each other, better health behaviour, and the activation of the immune system. There is greatly increased psychological health, due to the availability of an intimate confidant, and help with problems. Happiness is much greater, for similar reasons, and the availability of a partner to cooperate in both leisure and domestic work.

There is a lot of conflict in marriages, as Figure 3.2 showed; one of the characteristic marital activities is 'arguing'. This is simply because there are so many things, large and small, to be agreed about. Part of the solution is for the partners to be better negotiators, able to arrive at constructive, cooperative solutions. Marriages are happier when the partners can see the other's point of view; for example, 'Before I criticize my partner I try to

Table 3.5   Rules for both spouses in marriage

1   Show emotional support
2   Share news of success
3   Be faithful
4   Create a harmonious home atmosphere
5   Respect the other partner's privacy
6   Address the partner by first name
7   Keep confidences
8   Engage in sexual activity with the other partner
9   Give birthday cards and presents
10 Stand up for the other person in his/her absence
11 Talk to the partner about sex and death
12 Disclose personal feelings and problems to the partner
13 Inform the partner about one's personal schedule
14 Be tolerant of each other's friends
15 Don't criticise the partner publicly
16 Ask for personal advice
17 Talk to the partner about religion and politics
18 Look the partner in the eye during conversation
19 Discuss personal financial matters with the other partner
20 Touch the other person intentionally
21 Engage in joking or teasing with the partner
22 Show affection for one another in public
23 Ask the partner for material help
24 Show distress or anxiety in front of the partner
25 Repay depts and favours, and compliments

Additional rules for the husband

1   Look after the family when the wife is unwell.
2   Show an interest in the wife's daily activities.
3   Be responsible for household repair and maintenance.
4   Offer to pay for the partner when going out together.

Additional rules for the wife

1   Show anger in front of the partner.
2   Don't nag.

Source: Argyle and Henderson, 1985

imagine how I would feel in his/her place' (Long and Andrews, 1990). Part of the solution is to keep to the informal rules which it is generally believed should be followed in marriage (Table 3.5).

Rules also define roles, and marital roles are changing in the modern world. Already families have become smaller, and many marriages do not last for ever – about a third in Britain. There has been pressure from women for equal say in decisions, for them to have careers, and for husbands to share the housework. However, dual-career marriages are stressful and difficult to operate, especially when there are children. Perhaps some further new rules will develop.

We can get some ideas about the skills needed in marriage by looking at the kinds of behaviour found in happy marriages. The main ones are set out below:

1 Pleasing verbal acts (such as compliments) and few negative ones (such as criticisms and complaints);
2 Pleasing non-verbal acts (such as kisses, bodily contact, presents, helpful behaviour);
3 An enjoyable sex life;
4 A lot of time spent together – for example, in leisure activities;
5 Agreement over finances;
6 A problem-solving approach to matters to be decided;
7 Acting as a sympathetic confidant to the other.

Work relationships

Nearly all work is done in groups or larger organisations, because most jobs need more than one person, and more than one kind of skill, to do them. This is true of all human societies, including those primitive societies which are otherwise 'individualistic' or 'competitive' (Mead, 1937). Work relationships are the result of people being brought together by the work: for example as work-mates on assembly-lines, or in offices, members of teams such as aircrews, or where one is a supervisor, assistant, inspector, technical advisor, or client. These are all rather different work relationships; another way of dividing them up is by different degrees of closeness, as will be shown shortly.

People become work-mates because they have applied for jobs and have been selected, sometimes one by the other, more often by different people. These relationships have a strong formal component, defining the relationship, for example, between teachers and pupils, officers and men, salesmen and customers. In addition, some degree of informal variation on the formal relation develops over time, as two people get to know each other, and may become friends to some extent. There has been disagreement in the research literature over how important these relationships are, and in Chapter 4 we describe four degrees of closeness in work relationships (p. 80–1).

Work relationships are a major factor in job satisfaction, and therefore for happiness as a whole. They are instrumentally satisfying since they provide help and cooperation with the work itself, so that greater rewards can be obtained. In primitive societies this includes catching large animals and building houses. In modern society it might include financial gains, promotion, recognition for good work done, and the economic survival or other success of the group or enterprise. The social satisfactions from work-mates are similar to those of friendships, and include a lot of conversation and fun, but little in the form of leisure pursuits. We found that much greater satisfaction of both kinds is obtained from those in the closer relationships.

Relationships at work convey benefits for mental health and health. Research on this is discussed in Chapter 5.

There is quite a lot of conflict between people at work, but this is partly contained by the emergence of informal rules. The rules which we found are given in Table 4.3 (p. 81). Rules 3, 4, 6 and 9 are directly concerned with maintaining cooperation over work. Many of the other rules are concerned with maintaining positive relations between workers, and preventing common causes of friction.

Social skills are needed to cope successfully with these relationships. Work-mates need skills of cooperation, being sensitive to the needs and feelings of others, being able to compromise and arrive at ways of meeting the needs of self and others. Supervisory skills are more complex, and will be described in detail in Chapter 7.

Parent–child relations

Most children in Britain are brought up in families, with an average of 2.3 children, though an increasing number live with one parent or with one parent and a step-parent. This is a relationship which begins when the child is born, and usually endures to the death of the parent, taking quite different forms at each stage. Infants start by being part of a totally integrated biological system with their mothers, and in this period both sides seem to know how to communicate and interact, without need of instruction. For some years they are completely dependent for food, care and protection. Gradually children become more independent, and at adolescence partly break the bond by various kinds of rebellion and hostility. Soon the grown-up child resumes a close but now more equal relationship, and eventually it may be the parent who is dependent.

The characteristic activities of parents and children are well known – and quite different from those in other relationships. Parents feed their children, and meals are major family events. They supervise, discipline and train children in acceptable ways of behaving. There is a lot of conversation – which teaches children language, and later many other things. Parents and children show each other affection, with a lot of bodily contact in the early years. Parents help children in many ways, and later children are expected to help in the house.

A powerful attachment develops between children and parents or other caretaker, and this explains why the relationship is so enduring. It is probably partly due to shared genes – parents and children on average share 50 per cent, the process of 'inclusive fitness'. Attachment also depends on the nature of mother–child contact, and is strongest when the caretaker feeds the child, plays and engages in social stimulation, involving bodily contact, looking and smiling.

This relationship provides a great deal for children, since they are totally

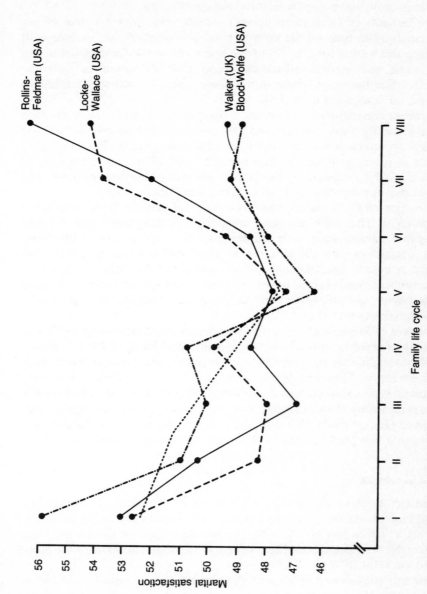

Figure 3.5 Marital satisfaction at different stages of the family life cycle
Source: Walker, 1977

dependent on their parents, not only for bringing them into existence, but for continually feeding, housing, clothing and protecting them, over a number of years. They also receive a lot of physical affection, are given pocket money, and played with for some hours a day.

The benefits of children to parents are obvious – a great deal of joy and satisfaction, help on the farm in rural communities, and people with children live a little longer. There are also costs in the form of stress and hard work, and marital satisfaction – and probably happiness – hit low periods when there are babies in the home, and even worse when babies become adolescents (Figure 3.5).

A recent American study found that when married couples have children in the home they worry more, and have lower marital happiness, but that there is no effect on health, anxiety or overall happiness. These negative effects of marriage increased between 1957 and 1976, and in the case of wives could be explained by the greater number of mothers at work, and the greater number divorced (McLanahan and Adams, 1989).

The style of child-rearing used by parents affects the later personality of the child. The most important component is acceptance and warmth. Accepting parents love their children, spend a lot of time with them, their interaction with the children is warm and rewarding, rather than critical or hostile, and they have a high opinion of the children. A second important component is the use of discipline which is neither too permissive nor too strict, and which uses explanation, pointing out the consequences of one's behaviour for others.

Styles of child-rearing vary along other dimensions, and in this way pass on the kinds of personality and behaviour that are valued in the culture. Children may be brought up to be aggressive, achievement-orientated, individualistic or cooperative. Handling adolescents is particularly difficult. The most successful style in our culture is a 'democratic' one, where the child participates in decisions, there is a moderate degree of control and full explanations are given (Elder, 1962). This is similar to leadership in other settings except that here it is in the context of a close and emotional relationship.

Kinship relations

In most cultures kinship is the main basis of relationships. In the modern world kin outside the home are much less important, and consist mainly of parents, children and siblings who live elsewhere, grandchildren and some cousins. Nevertheless about 50 per cent of the strongest ties outside the home are to kin (Hill, 1970).

The activities shared by kin are different from those with friends. Some live together (for example, unmarried siblings), and in working-class circles children usually live quite close. There is frequent contact between parents and adult children, and between sisters. Meetings usually take the form of visits, at home, for a meal or sometimes to stay. Nothing much is actually done, apart from eating and talking; the talk is about one another's welfare, and the family news. More major help is provided for kin than in any other relationship. A lot of this help is domestic, provided by women, for a wife who is ill, or having a baby, or looking after elderly parents. Table 3.6 shows the results of a study of three generations in Minneapolis.

Table 3.6   Help given and received by kin, USA, (percentages)

		Parents	Married children	Grandparents
Economic	Given	41	34	26
	Received	17	49	34
Household	Given	47	33	21
management	Received	23	25	52
Child care	Given	50	34	16
	Received	23	78	0
Illness	Given	21	47	32
	Received	21	18	61

Source: Hill, 1970

It can be seen that 50 per cent of parents help their children with child-care, 47 per cent with household work, 41 per cent with money, and that help flows in both directions, though more from older to younger. Finally there is inheritance of property, most of which is passed on to children or other close kin.

Kin show a high degree of bonding, as is shown by the long duration of these relationships, often in the absence of much reinforcement. The inclusive fitness model is probably part of the explanation, though intimacy in the early family between parents and children, and between siblings is another source of attachment. And different kinship systems have developed by 'social evolution' in different cultures. An example is the rule of descent from one parent, found in agricultural societies. The direct result is the formation of large, strong kinship groups who can band together for mutual protection and support. However, this is usually combined with the rule of exogamy – marrying into other family groups – which has the effect of creating bonds, mainly female ones, between the different clans.

What kind of benefits does kinship produce? We saw in Figure 3.2 that parents and siblings are major sources of satisfaction, especially in material and instrumental help, and we saw above some of the forms this takes. This is very important in Third World cultures where the kinship network replaces social security, and other public sources of help in developed cultures. We have seen the material help provided in our own country. More important perhaps is the social and emotional support, especially that received by women, who often depend for it on their mothers or sisters.

There are also conflicts between kin, and especially between siblings. During childhood there is a lot of rivalry, and in later life they compare their achievements; in one study 71 per cent of adults had rivalrous feelings towards their siblings. There can be discord over inheritance, and sharing the duty of looking after elderly parents. Nevertheless, the unbreakable bond persists, and is especially strong between sisters.

DEMOGRAPHIC VARIATIONS IN RELATIONSHIPS

Social class

In Britain different social classes have different kinds of friends. Middle-class people choose their friends cautiously, mainly from work, neighbours or clubs, they invite them home, introduce them to one another, and do various things together. Working-class people see a lot of the neighbours, and there is a lot of mutual help here – lending sugar or money, baby-sitting, and so on – and they see various mates from pub, club or church but only in that setting, in a group, and do not invite them home – only kin are invited home (Allan, 1979). These are very different kinds of networks.

Working-class people keep up closer kinships ties in most cultures, and in Britain *do* invite kin into the home. The main reason is that working-class kin live much nearer together; children do not seek education or jobs in distant places or move away as middle-class children do. Working-class people in Britain are most likely to seek help when in trouble from kin, middle-class people from friends (see p. 206).

Working-class people get married younger (4 years younger in Britain) and have babies sooner. They are on average less happily married, because the couples do less together and working-class husbands tend to be poor confidants. Mixed-class marriage is much worse.

Age

Friendship is quite different at different ages. For young people, during adolescence and up to marriage, friendship is the most important relationship, some spend 3 hours a day together and more on the phone. Marriage, children and work cut down time spent with friends, until in middle age they are seen much less often. In old age, after retirement, often widowed, friends become important once again.

Courtship and falling in love are mainly for the under thirties; the median age of marriage for men in Britain is 26, for women 23.3. Children are born during the following few years, and have left home when the parents are in their early fifties. About a third will have separated or divorced, and often married again. Those left settle down to a quieter kind of love, enjoying the 'empty nest', their shared leisure activities and their grandchildren.

Gender

Women form closer, more intimate friendships (with other women); they talk a lot, and provide one another with social support. Male friendships are less intimate, and instead of talking men do things together, like playing squash. They also form groups and clubs more readily.

It is women who hold kinship systems together, especially through the female–female links between mothers and daughters, and between sisters. They may see each other every day, and often provide domestic help as well as social support.

For men, relationships at work are important, and as we have seen some work-mates become friends, while others are regularly seen for lunch or coffee at work, though not outside. Relations with work colleagues may last for many years, and form a world-wide network in some professions, including psychology. Help and cooperation from these work-mates is often essential to successful completion of tasks and career success.

For some women at work the social contacts are more important than the work. Women in senior positions usually handle their subordinates in a more caring and a more democratic way than the corresponding men.

Culture

Friendship is found in all cultures, but it can be more formal than in ours. Australian 'mateship' developed in the early days among miners and stockmen, isolated in the bush, with very few women. They needed a friend who could be trusted to stand by them. Another form of friendship is the forming of 'blood brothers', either by cutting the skin and rubbing in each other's blood, or by drinking some of each other's blood. This occurred in the ancient world, and is still practised in parts of Africa. The purpose is to create an alliance between individuals or groups, so that the other can be trusted absolutely, or perhaps to turn an enemy into a friend.

Marriage varies a lot between cultures – Muslim marriages (up to 4 wives, very easy divorce), Indian (arranged by families), traditional Chinese (wife plus concubine), and 'swinging' or 'open' marriage with no rules of faithfulness. Recent historical changes have led to smaller families, working wives, more emphasis on love and fulfilment, and greater equality. Dual-career couples are increasingly common, and are finding life rather stressful.

Kinship networks are much more extensive and important in Africa,

India and the rest of the Third World. If you want a job, or want almost any kind of help, the kinship network is the best place to turn. In parts of Africa it is difficult to become rich or start a business because so many 'brothers' want a share. In China respect is paid to elderly parents, as is a substantial proportion of the income of unmarried children.

Work relationships are more hierarchical in Japan and most countries outside Western Europe and North America. In Japan managers are trained for obedient behaviour in hierarchies by management courses in which they are compelled to go on 25-mile route marches by night, on little food, ordered to shout or sing the company song, and to learn and recite meaningless texts. Work relations in Japan are different in other ways too: working groups are kept intact for many years, and there are strong conformity pressures. In less developed parts of Africa, and here before the Industrial Revolution, work was done in groups of relatives and neighbours, and was not separated from leisure.

In a cross-cultural study of rules, we found that in Japan and Hong Kong there were stronger rules for avoiding face – for example, not criticising in public, for keeping harmony in groups, obedience in hierarchies, and for concealing emotions (Argyle, 1987).

TRAINING FOR RELATIONSHIPS

There is a very high, and increasing, rate of divorce in all Western countries, causing a great deal of distress to those concerned, and making their children unhappy, often later mentally disturbed or delinquent, and such effects are worse than those from the death of a parent. Many people are isolated, live alone, have no friends. Can such individuals be helped? I shall describe three kinds of training which are in current use, and then suggest some general and possibly more powerful ways of training people for relationships.

Marital skills training

Several kinds of marital therapy are used in the USA, based on research into marriage. They usually emphasise rewardingness, sometimes with points being awarded or special 'love days'. Couples may be taught to resolve their problems by 'contracting'. For example she agrees to more sex, if he agrees to more conversation. Partners may be trained to be better senders and receivers – for example, of non-verbal cues for emotions, and intentions – sometimes using video techniques and modelling; listening skills are improved and empathy increased. A common problem in unhappy marriages is 'negative reciprocity'; that is, a negative communication by A leads to a negative one from B. Another is simple lack of skills of negotiation, which are described later (p. 188). It is possible to include training in such sequences of interaction. Clients may need some social skills training to learn how to put their case to their spouse tactfully, and constructively. Above all, they can be trained in how to negotiate solutions to problems, how to find the best solutions for both, and to be prepared to give way, and compromise. A success rate of about 65 per cent is claimed (Gurman and Kniskern, 1978). In Britain Marriage Guidance is extensively used. Marriage guidance counsellors are unpaid, and are not professional social workers or psychologists. They are, however, trained and experienced in dealing with marital problems, and act as lay therapists with couples. They listen, they try to help the couple solve their problems as a neutral third party, they usually offer guidance or advice, and they do their best to preserve the marriage.

Friendship training

Many people who receive social skills training (SST) (for example, at psychiatric out-patient clinics) complain principally about difficulties in making friends (Trower et al., 1978). We have found that such people are indeed deficient in social skills; they are often poor conversationalists, are unrewarding and unassertive, fail to send positive non-verbal signals, and are very egocentric. The usual method of training is by role-playing, with videotape playback. There are three stages: coaching and modelling (by showing a video of competent performance); role-playing; playback of video and comments by trainer. This general procedure is quite effective, though special methods may be needed to train in NVC, or to discourage egocentricity, and a good understanding by the trainer of conversational processes is needed to correct problems in that area.

Training for supervision and other professional skills

Supervisors of working groups, teachers, doctors and many others now receive training in how to manage these relationships. Sometimes it is done by role-playing exercises, at a training centre, where other trainees play the other roles. It is better to have some real clients or patients, and teachers are often trained by 'micro-teaching' – with a small class for a short period. Sometimes it is impossible to reproduce the real-life problems in a training centre; the alternative is training on the job. Police are sometimes trained on the beat by a 'tutor constable' in this way.

Courses are designed to provide the social skills needed for the job. For example, one training course for industrial supervisors included role-played exercises on the following topics:

Orienting a new employee
Giving recognition
Motivating a poor employee
Correcting poor work habits
Discussing potential disciplinary action
Reducing absenteeism
Handling a complaining employee
Reducing turnover
Overcoming resistance to change.

Use can be made of detailed research findings in planning such training.

The use of educational methods

There is a lot that can be learnt about relationships, and people are often ignorant of the facts of life in this area. They may not realise that friends come in complex networks, which have to be handled very skilfully, or that loneliness is the result of insufficient self-disclosure, that married couples often have rows, since there is so much to decide about, or that when adolescent children are rebellious and difficult, this is nearly always for a fairly short period. Better understanding about relationships is needed for some people.

Much of this information is contained in rules; for example, the third-party rules for friendship. These rules are the result of generations of experience, and if broken can lead to disruption of relationships, as we have seen. One of the most strongly endorsed marriage rules we found is 'be faithful'. Some people say they have an 'understanding' with their partners and so don't need to keep this rule. Again research shows that breaking the rules is likely to result in loss of the relationship. Part of education for relationships could be learning the rules.

Relationship-focused SST

Knowledge of a skill is not enough; as with pole-vaulting, practice of the skill is needed too. SST can be focused on the special skills needed for friendship, marriage or other relationships.

CONCLUSIONS

Relationships are central to social behaviour, though they are usually excluded from laboratory experiments. It makes a great difference whether you are dealing with your friend, enemy, spouse, work-mate or a sibling. Some relationships are biologically important and partly unlearnt (for example, parent–child and other kin), they are partly learnt from the culture, and the components, like rules, are functional (that is, they help with goal attainment). They are rewarding, but also cooperative, and the motivation often includes a concern for the other.

Relationships can be analysed in terms of the goals pursued, the typical activities, the rules, the form of attachment and the skills needed. They are a most important source of happiness, health and mental health. Friendship is a great source of joy and help, often arises out of shared leisure and needs special skills. Love and marriage provide the greatest satisfaction, have powerful bonding but also a lot of conflict, which can be avoided by keeping to the rules and having the right skills. Work relationships are important for job satisfaction and mutual help at work. Parent–child relations produce great satisfaction, long-term attachment and help, but a lot of stress at certain periods.

There are differences between the forms of relationships, in different social classes, ages, for men and women, and in different cultures. It is possible to use all this knowledge to train people for marriage, friendship and other relationships.

REFERENCES

Allan, G. (1979) *A Sociology of Friendship and Kinship*. London: Allen and Unwin.
Argyle, M. (1987) *The Psychology of Happiness*. London: Methuen.
—— (1991) *Cooperation: the Basis of Sociability*. London: Routledge.
Argyle, M. and Furnham, A. (1982) The ecology of relationships: choice of situation as a function of relationship. *British Journal of Social Psychology*, *21*, 259–62.
—— (1983) Sources of satisfaction and conflict in long-term relationships. *Journal of Marriage and the Family*, *45*, 481–93.
Argyle, M. and Henderson, M. (1985) *The Anatomy of Relationships*. London: Heinemann; Harmondsworth: Penguin.
Argyle, M., Furnham, A. and Graham, J.A. (1981) *Social Situations*. Cambridge: Cambridge University Press.
Argyle, M., Henderson, M. and Furnham, A. (1985) The rules of social relationships. *British Journal of Social Psychology*, *24*, 125–39.
Argyle, M. and Lu, L. (1990) The happiness of extraverts. *Personality and Individual Differences*, *11*, 1255–61.
Bowlby, J. (1969) *Attachment and Loss*. Vol. 1. *Attachment*. London: Hogarth.
Braiker, B. and Kelley, H.H. (1979) Conflict in the development of close relationships. *In* R.L. Burgess and T.L. Huston (eds) *Social Exchange in Developing Relationships*. New York: Academic Press.
Brown, J., Gerard, D. and Timms, N. (1985) Marriage and the family. *In* M. Abrams *et al.* (eds) *Values and Social Change in Britain*. Basingstoke: Macmillan.
Burnett, R. (1986) Conceptualisation of personal relationships. D. Phil. thesis. Oxford University.
Buss, D.M. (1988) The evolution of human intrasexual competition: tactics of mate attraction. *Journal of Personality and Social Psychology*, *54*, 616–28.
—— (1989 Sex differences in human mate preferences: evolutionary hypotheses tested in 37 cultures. *Behavioural and Brain Sciences*, *12*, 1–49.

Clark, M.S. (1986) Evidence for the effectiveness of manipulations of communal and exchange relationships. *Personality and Social Psychology Bulletin*, *12*, 414–25.

Clark, M.S. and Reis, H.T. (1988) Interpersonal processes in close relationships. *Annual Review of Psychology*, *39*, 609–72.

Davis, K.E. and Todd, M. (1982) Friendship and love relations. *Advances in Descriptive Psychology*, *2*, 79–122.

De Jong-Gierveld, J. (1990) Developing and testing a theory about loneliness. Paper to conference of International Society for the Study of Personal Relationships, Oxford.

Elder, G.H. (1962) Structural variations in the child rearing relationship. *Sociometry*, *25*, 244–62.

Fellner, C.H. and Marshall, J.R. (1981) Kidney donors revisited. *In* J.P. Rushton and R.M. Sorrentino (eds) *Altruism and Helping Behaviour*. Hillsdale, NJ: Erlbaum.

Gurman, A.S. and Kniskern, D.P. (1978) Research on marital and family therapy: progress, perspective and prospect. *In* S.L. Garfield and A.E. Bergin (eds) *Handbook of Psychotherapy and Behaviour Change*. New York: Wiley.

Hamilton, W.D. (1964) The evolution of social behavior. *Journal of Theoretical Biology*, *7*, 1–52.

Harris, M. (1975) *The Rise of Anthropological Theory*. London: Routledge and Kegan Paul.

Harvey, J.H., Weber, A.L., Yarkin, L. and Stewart, B.E. (1982) An attributional approach to relationship breakdown. *In* S. Duck (ed.) *Personal Relationships*. Vol. 4. *Dissolving Personal Relationships*. London: Academic Press.

Hays, R.B. (1985) A longitudinal study of friendship development. *Journal of Personality and Social Psychology*, *48*, 909–24.

Hill, R. (1970) *Family Development in Three Generations*. Cambridge, Mass: Schenkman.

Huston, T.L., Surra, C.A., Fitzgerald, N.M. and Gate, R.M. (1981) From courtship to marriage: mate selection as an interpersonal process. *In* S.W. Duck and R. Gilmour (eds) *Personal Relationships*. Vol. 2. *Developing Personal Relationships*. London: Academic Press.

Jennings, H.H. (1950) *Leadership and Isolation*. New York: Longman.

Kenrick, D.T. and Trost, M.R. (1989) A reproductive model of heterosexual relationships: putting proximate economics in ultimate perspective. *Review of Personality and Social Psychology*, *10*, 92–118.

Kephart, W.M. (1967) Some correlates of romantic love. *Journal of Marriage and the Family*, *29*, 470–4.

La Gaipa, J.J. and Wood, H.D. (1981) Friendship in disturbed adolescents. *In* S. Duck and R. Gilmour (eds) *Personal Relationships*. Vol. 3. London: Academic Press.

Larson, R.W. (1990) The solitary side of life: an examination of the time people spend alone from childhood to old age. *Developmental Review*, *10*, 155–83.

Livingstone, S. (1990) *Making Sense of Television*. Oxford: Pergamon.

Long, E.C.J. and Andrews, D.W. (1990) Perspective-taking as a predictor of marital adjustment. *Journal of Personality and Social Psychology*, *59*, 126–31.

McAdams, D.P. (1988) Personal needs and personal relationships. *In* S. Duck (ed.) *Handbook of Personal Relationships*. Chichester: Wiley.

McLanahan, S. and Adams, J. (1989) The effects of children on adults' psychological well-being. *Social Forces*, *68*, 124–46.

Mead, M. (ed.) (1937) *Cooperation and Competition among Primitive Peoples*. New York: McGraw-Hill.

Orvis, B.R., Kelley, H.H. and Butler, D. (1976) Attributional conflict in young couples. *In* J.H. Harvey, W.J. Ickes and R.F. Kidd (eds) *New Directions in Attributional Research*. Vol. 1. Hillsdale, NJ: Erlbaum.

Parker, S. (1983) *Leisure and Work*. London: Allen & Unwin.

Parker, S.R. (1964) Type of work, friendship patterns, and leisure. *Human Relations*, *17*, 215–19.

Rubin, Z. (1973) *Liking and Loving: an Invitation to Social Psychology*. New York: Holt, Rinehart & Winston.

Shaver, P.R. and Hazan, C. (1988) A biased overview of the study of love. *Journal of Social and Personal Relationships*, *5*, 473–501.

Shute, R. and Howitt, D. (1990) Unravelling paradoxes in loneliness: research and elements of a social theory of loneliness. *Social Behaviour*, *5*, 169–84.

Stroebe, W. and Stroebe, M.S. (1987) *Bereavement and Health*. New York: Cambridge University Press.

Triandis, H.C., Bontempo, R., Villareal, M.J., Asai, M. and Lucca, N. (1988) Individualism and collectivism: cross-cultural perspectives on self-ingroup relationships. *Journal of Personality and Social Psychology*, *54*, 323–8.

Trower, P., Bryant, B. and Argyle, M. (1978) *Social Skills and Mental Health*. London: Methuen.

Van Yperen, N.W. and Buunk, B.P. (1990) A longitudinal study of equity and satisfaction in intimate relationships. *European Journal of Social Psychology*, *20*, 287–310.

Walker, C. (1977) Some variations in marital satisfaction. *In* R. Chester and J. Peel (eds) *Equalities and Inequalities in Family Life*. London: Academic Press.

Wellman, B. (1985) From social support to social network. *In* I.G. Sarason and B.R. Sarason (eds) *Social Support: Theory, Research and Applications*. Dordrecht: Nijhoff.

White, G.L., Fishbein, S. and Rutsein, J. Passionate love and the misattribution of arousal. *Journal of Personality and Social Psychology*, *41*, 56–62.

Wish, M., Deutsch, M. and Kaplan, S.J. (1976) Perceived dimensions of interpersonal relations. *Journal of Personality and Social Psychology*, *33*, 409–20.

Chapter 4

Work

Work is a central, and essential, part of life. It is necessary for animals as well as humans, to provide food, shelter and protection from enemies without and disruption within. We humans have a lot of additional needs – for clothing, entertainment, travel, education and all the elaborate services to which we have become accustomed. To produce these, workers in 1870 worked 60 hours a week; the working week has now fallen to 38 hours for most people, though many do overtime, and professional workers and those with their own businesses often work very long hours.

Work consists of doing things to raw materials in order to change them into a more finished product. It is this finished product which is needed by others, and for which they will pay. The car industry changes sheet and other metals into cars, the textile industry changes yarn into clothes. All work can be seen in this way, including medicine, research, transport, entertainment and writing. Work cannot be understood apart from its technological setting. It takes quite different forms in different historical periods and in different cultures. Comparing work in Britain, Japan and Third World countries, not only is the technology totally different, but so is the incentive system and the social relationships. The same is true if we compare work today with work in the Industrial Revolution, the Middle Ages, and the Roman empire.

Work, as we now know it, generates a number of serious social problems. Perhaps psychology can suggest how they could be tackled.

1 Although many people enjoy their work a great deal and have high 'job satisfaction', there are others who do not. About 12 per cent of people in Britain say they dislike their jobs, and another 45 per cent only 'quite enjoy' them; 84 per cent of unskilled steel workers and 79 per cent of unskilled car workers would not choose the same job again (Table 4.4).
2 On the whole work is good for us, but there are some who are made ill or mentally ill by stresses at work. Stress is produced by the same occupations which cause low job satisfaction; for instance, when the work is repetitive, or has time pressure and low status.

3 Some people simply don't like work, as they have experienced it, and either avoid doing it or do as little as possible.

4 Others are depressed or ill because they are unemployed. The study of unemployment has led to the discovery that work produces a number of hidden benefits, only realised when people lose them. One reason that people feel unhappy in our culture when they are out of work is because they have been socialised into the Protestant work ethic.

5 There is a traditional conflict between employers, or managers, and the workers, leading to stoppages, strikes and lack of cooperation. A lot is now known about the ways in which strikes develop. New forms of consultation, 'industrial democracy', can do much to improve things.

6 There are other problems in large organisations due to the sheer size and number of levels in the hierarchy, resulting in alienation at lower levels. This has serious consequences, not only for job satisfaction but in high rates of absenteeism, labour turnover and accidents.

7 Technological change, especially the introduction of automation and computers, is changing the nature of work in several ways. These include deskilling, unemployment and breaking up working groups.

Working arrangements differ greatly in different cultures, and historical periods. They are changing fast at the present time. The reasons for change are mainly economic and technological, together with changing ideas about management. Psychologists have something to contribute – how to make work more enjoyable and less stressful, more intrinsically rewarding, how to reduce absenteeism, labour turnover, accidents and conflicts between groups. We have most of the knowledge already about how to do these things; this chapter explains how.

THE BIOLOGICAL AND HISTORICAL ORIGINS OF WORK

Ants are famous for their work, and especially for their cooperation over work. One ant-hill may weigh several tons and house a million ants, which all cooperate over the work. Most of it is done by 'worker ants', sexless females. There is division of labour and cooperation among the workers. Several specialised castes have evolved, such as soldiers – large ants with big jaws, living larders – which hang motionless and swell up to a large size when full, and agricultural ants – with further sub-divisions for cutting leaves and caring for fungus gardens. In a number of ant species, the workers do very little work, but instead make raids on the nests of other ants of a different species, led by their soldier ants, overcoming the others, and carrying off the worker pupae to their own nest. Once they have been born these slaves are put to work cleaning the nest, foraging for food and caring for young.

In addition to keeping slaves, some ants have an equivalent of farm animals, such as aphids like greenfly, which suck juice out of plants and excrete a sugary substance, which can be 'milked'. The aphids can suck sap out of plants, which the ants cannot. Going further down the animal scale, ants keep plants, by cultivating fungus gardens, sometimes on a large scale, excavating as much as 40 tons of soil (Wilson, 1971).

For animals work leads directly to their food or other rewards. Animals work partly through unlearnt, instinctive mechanisms and partly through simple learning. Monkeys and apes are most similar to humans. Curiously they work much less hard than we do. Food grows on trees and only needs to be picked, supplemented by insects, lizards and other small beasts. Chimpanzees use a simple tool to eat ants; they poke a stick into the nest until it is covered with ants and then lick them off. Most apes and monkeys construct simple nests to sleep in at night, high up in the trees away from predators. Nests are very simple, made by bending branches, and are constructed in a few minutes. A great deal of time is spent in pleasant social interaction, the adults grooming each other or copulating, while the infants play (DeVore, 1965).

The nature of work has seen a series of fundamental changes during the course of human history. In the earliest and most primitive societies, people were hunters and gatherers, and made simple dwellings from skins or branches. There was no money, and work was not a separate category of activity, since everyone worked, and did so most of the time. Children were taught the patterns of work behaviour in their families. This was partly by imitation, since they could constantly see adults working; instead of playing, children were given scaled-down weapons and tools to use. In early settlements there was farming and use of animals, there was barter, and some division of labour as different craft skills developed. Work was still an integral part of life, not separated from leisure or family life, but some now worked for money.

In the ancient civilisations of Greece and Rome, most of the work was done by slaves, and manual work and working for wages was despised. Large groups of workers were paid, or in the case of slaves, compelled to work in large workshops and building enterprises, under the harsh supervision of soldiers, monks or other slaves, until the whole system collapsed. The large and often useless building enterprises were the first historical signs of achievement motivation.

Under the medieval feudal system the serfs worked in exchange for protection by the lord of the manor, and use of a strip of land. The serfs accepted their obligation to work and fight for their superiors, for little reward; work was regarded as a moral and religious duty, and necessary for salvation; it was also enforced by law. Agricultural work and handicrafts were thought of as necessities of life, and were accompanied by many of the satisfactions of more primitive village life – it was closely linked with social life, church festivals and sport (Thomas, 1964). Feudalism in turn collapsed when the peasants left for better jobs in the towns, and landowners found that they could do better by paying wages and charging rent for land.

In the cities small workshops developed with a master craftsman and his apprentices. In the 'domestic system' families did work sent out by master craftsmen, paid by piecework. During the sixteenth and seventeenth centuries in England, early capitalism was beginning, with growth in mining, fishing and manufacturing. The Industrial Revolution proper came later, between 1769 and 1850 in England, with the discovery of steam power, and various inventions in the textile industry, the use of iron and steel, and the appearance of factories. Large numbers of men, women and children worked long hours, often under unpleasant conditions. They were unwilling workers, often idle or drunk, and there was now a clear contrast between work and leisure.

Working conditions improved, partly through the influence of trade unions, but the nature of work then deteriorated with the growth of Taylor's scientific management, and of time-and-motion study, which divided jobs into meaningless simple tasks, and Ford's development of the assembly-line, which introduced machine-pacing. The reaction to the boredom and alienation produced job-enlargement, and other ways of making work more varied and interesting, including making whole groups responsible for tasks. However, these changes are now being overtaken by the even greater changes in work generated by automation and computers, sometimes described as the 'Second Industrial Revolution', which will be discussed later.

The Industrial Revolution was traumatic for many workers and produced a great deal of conflict between workers and employers, because people were quite unused to the conditions of industrial work. Industrialisation in Africa has proceeded slowly because Africans are not accustomed to working regular hours, under supervision, at a regular speed with standard methods. Children need to be socialised to work, under the prevailing working conditions. It is at school that children first learn to work – at a set task, at a certain time, under supervision, cooperating with peers, and where there are rewards and sanctions for productivity.

By the age of 7 most children in Britain are expected to tidy up their toys, either alone or with a parent. Only 18 per cent of children do regular household chores, such as washing up, more girls than boys, and more in middle-class homes. A further 53 per cent earn money from their parents for doing jobs (Newson and Newson, 1976). Adolescents are not always very helpful around the house, and may be accused of 'treating it like a hotel', though some contribute to the family income. Work in the home, both self-care and family chores, is the earliest work to be done, and may be a kind of training for work later. Mothers direct it, partly because it needs to be done, but also to train children in self-discipline. A study in Australia found that

> In effect, the significance of work to mothers appeared to lie primarily
> in its being an index of socialisation into true concern for her for others
> in the family, and into a full understanding that 'making a contribution'
> was an integral part of being a member of the family.
>
> (Goodnow and Delaney, 1989)

Adolescents have to choose an occupation from a wide selection, though
the local choices are more limited. The choice depends on images of
professions from various sources, which may be quite inaccurate. Choice
depends on ability, and on personality. Jobs may be tried out during
vacation, or a series of jobs may be tried. Once a job is taken, there
is more socialisation, in the form of training courses, influence of peers,
instructions from superiors. New employees who are given formal induction
training in groups have higher job satisfaction (Zahrly and Tosi, 1989). If
a person settles in the job, and there is a stable work period, he or she
starts to see it as a career, has hopes for promotion, becomes committed
to the organisation or profession, its goals and values, and the job becomes
central to the personality.

However, there are some young people for whom work socialisation fails,
and who never learn to find work rewarding. Some find it difficult to work
regular hours under supervision, some never discover a kind of work that
they want to do, or they prefer some leisure activity. Others may decide
to delay the decision about what to do. University life and graduate work
may provide such a period of 'moratorium', and this may be followed by
one or more years spent in remote countries overseas, wandering about
looking for an identity.

People are motivated to work in a variety of ways. For animals and
for primitive men, there are immediate rewards in the form of food
and shelter. Later many worked for money, which can be exchanged
for biological rewards, and money has been the main incentive for work
for several centuries now. Money really is an effective motivator. For
example, changing over from payment by time to piecework (payment by
results) produces a large increase in output: increases of 40–60 per cent in
output are common. A recent American meta-analysis of 330 intervention
programmes found that a change of financial incentives had the greatest
impact, of 2.12 times the standard deviation in 13 studies (Guzzo et al.,
1985). However, all these figures are probably exaggerated since whenever
an incentive scheme is introduced other improvements are made as well; for
example, improvements in methods of working, or delivery of supplies.

Piecework also creates a lot of management problems, friction between
workers and restriction of output, and in any case can only be used for
certain repetitive, easily measurable jobs. A number of alternative schemes
are in use, such as 'measured day work', where there is a regular wage plus

a bonus if a certain rate or standard of work is maintained. Another scheme is to give bonuses based on merit ratings, and this can be used for any job, including those of managers and professors.

However, money is not the only motivation for work. The amount of money people want to earn depends on how much their friends and neighbours have, how large the family is, whether they are trying to buy a house or car, the availability of hire purchase and so forth. There are a number of people who have to choose between better and less well-paid jobs, and choose the latter – for example, clergymen, research workers, hospital orderlies, or those who just want to live the simple life.

It is obvious that many people enjoy their work, that many do voluntary (unpaid) work, and that many put a lot of effort into serious, work-like leisure activities. It follows that intrinsic motivation in some form affects work behaviour. What are the characteristics of jobs which make them intrinsically interesting and enjoyable? Hackman and Oldham (1980) proposed that 5 job characteristics motivate work performance. These are:

1 skill variety
2 task identity (completing a satisfying and recognisable whole)
3 task significance (impact on others)
4 autonomy
5 feedback (information on success).

Many studies have shown that job satisfaction is greatest for workers doing jobs with these characteristics. However, not everyone likes work that is interesting or challenging. Some actually prefer work that is dull and repetitive. But many, especially at senior levels, are motivated to achieve. For managers the desire for promotion is a major incentive, more so than for manual workers; for them the next step-up is more often to start their own small business, in which they can use their skills.

Organisations differ in how their members are motivated. Industrial workers may be motivated primarily by pay, but fear of punishment is present in all organisations, especially in prisons, and in most armies – where men can be shot for not fighting – and was the main incentive for Roman slaves. A third kind of incentive is important in research establishments, hospitals, and voluntary and professional organisations, where the members work because they believe in the importance of the organisation's goals, and are personally committed to them. This is a factor for many people at work, especially when they become committed to the organisation.

There are some people who simply like work for its own sake. This can partly be traced to the Protestant work ethic (PWE) of Calvin and Luther (see p.151). Most people are distressed at being unemployed (though not at being retired), and many say that they would carry on working, even though it was economically unnecessary.

Does the PWE produce harder work? There is not a great deal of research here, but what there is has found that PWE correlates with such work behaviour as the rate of performance at laboratory tasks, more constant attendance at work, and greater commitment to the organisation (Furnham, 1990). The PWE is still alive today, and it is strongest in Protestant countries. Table 4.1 shows the scores for large samples found in the European Values Survey for 1981.

Table 4.1   Intrinsic work ethic scores by country

| | | Factor 1 scores* | | | | |
		Low (0–3)(%)	Medium (4)(%)	High (5–8)(%)	Factor 1 means	
	Spain	70	12	18	2.92	(N = 2,303)
	Belgium	66	14	20	2.64	(N = 1,145)
Catholic	Ireland	54	18	28	3.45	(N = 1,217)
	Italy	46	19	35	3.77	(N = 1,348)
	France	45	16	39	3.79	(N = 1,200)
	Holland	60	16	24	2.99	(N = 1,221)
Mixed	Ulster	52	18	30	3.49	(N = 312)
	Germany	50	16	34	3.75	(N = 1,303)
Protestant	Denmark	41	19	40	3.65	(N = 1,182)
	Britain	41	19	40	4.02	(N = 1,168)

Source: Giorgi and Marsh, 1990

It can be seen that although the PWE was stronger in Protestant countries, there was a lot of variation, especially between Catholic countries – France, for example, coming out rather high and Spain the lowest (Giorgi and Marsh, 1990).

GROUPS AND RELATIONSHIPS AT WORK

People come together to work partly because most jobs take more than one to do, and so that there can be division of labour where different individuals specialise in different skills, in order to share the use of capital equipment, and simply because they enjoy one another's company. For most work, working in groups is inevitable. Even in the most individualistic and uncooperative societies, like that of the Eskimos, cooperation is necessary – to catch whales, for example, and in other parts of the world to build large houses. Indeed this is one of the roots of sociability (Argyle, 1991).

The benefits of group working are particularly marked for small work-teams, where the members have chosen to work together, or have come to like each other. Van Zelst (1952) put together cohesive teams of bricklayers on the basis of a sociometric survey and found that over an 11-month period the cohesive groups achieved 12 per cent more output, with a 16.5 per-cent reduction in costs for materials, and a reduced labour turnover.

It is possible to develop work-teams to advantage; for example, into autonomous and flexible groups. It is even possible to replace the ever unpopular assembly-lines with such groups. This was done in one of the Volvo factories in Sweden, where each work-group now has it own entrance, coffee area and small workshop. Car bodies are placed on carriers whose speed, although computer controlled, can be altered manually, making variation possible. Each group does its part of the assembly together, men working in pairs, and is responsible for quality control. The cycle of operation is about 20 minutes (Francis, 1986). There have been many similar experiments. In most cases there are substantial improvements in productivity and job satisfaction (Pasmore et al., 1984). Team-building consists of discussion of relationships, goal-setting, clarifying roles and problem-solving, and usually leads to improved group cohesion and altered norms. Sundstrom et al. (1990) analysed 13 examples and found increased performance in 4 out of 9 cases where it was measurable. And team-building is a major source of job satisfaction.

The nature of work-teams depends on the technology. An interesting example is provided by the Longwall method of coal-mining. Traditionally 42 men worked on 3 shifts under a single supervisor, doing 3 different jobs – cutting, filling and stonework. The three groups were dependent on each other, but never met, so there were accidents and low productivity. By reorganising the groups so that all 3 jobs were done on each shift cooperation increased, together with greater productivity, and reduced accidents and absenteeism (Trist et al., 1963). This and other studies by the Tavistock Institute show how the same technology can be combined with different social arrangements.

Work-teams can be created by the physical environment. Sundstrom (1986) described how a group of clerical workers was installed inside a steel-mesh cage; they worked hard but had time for a lot of fooling about, such as 'sniping' with elastic bands. The cage was altered so that the group came under improved surveillance from managers, who imposed better discipline, but with the result that the group no longer kept up with the work schedules. Homans (1951) had a theory about working groups. He argued that people come to work in order to get the work done and to be paid for it; they have to cooperate with other people, then discover that they like some of them, and start engaging in extra social activity with them. This 'secondary system' then affects the work. Those who play games together later help each other at work, and sub-groups and informal leadership hierarchies are formed, which influence cooperation at work.

A lot of decisions at work are taken nowadays by groups, such as committees. This takes up much time, but are the decisions better than those reached by individuals? Experiments in which groups of managers tackle management problems find that they are better than the *average* group member, and for younger managers at least a little better than the *best* member (perhaps the best individual members were better among the older managers) (Webber, 1974). The use of committees has the further advantage of enabling different interests to be represented and of increasing commitment to what is decided.

What is the nature of work relationships? How are they different from other relationships? Some studies have found that work relationships can be superficial and unimportant. We thought it likely that under some conditions, such as belonging to a stable work-team, close relationships might be quite common. We suggested that 4 degrees of closeness might usefully be distinguished:

1 *Friends outside work* include people who become friends in the usual sense (that is, are seen outside work); many friendships are formed at work. Managers and professional people make friends at work easily as a result of leisurely lunches and events which spouses can attend.
2 *Friends at work* include others who are seen regularly for lunch, or at coffee breaks, but who are not seen outside the work place. Goldthorpe *et al.* (1968) found that while 55 per cent of car workers had one or more close friends at work, only 27 per cent saw them outside, and only 16 per cent invited them home.
3 *Friendly working relationships* include others who are seen quite often at work, and with whom social contacts are on the whole rewarding, but

Tables 4.2   Percentage of workers engaged in work and social activities more than several times a day at work

	With			
	Social friend	Friend at work	Work colleague	Disliked colleague
Helping other with work	52	32	18	8
Discussing work	49	52	32	17
Chatting casually	72	63	26	15
Joking with the other	72	54	24	13
Teasing the other person	46	32	18	20
Discussing personal life	30	19	13	11
Discussing personal feelings	26	10	5	5
Asking for or giving personal advice	33	19	8	6

Source: Argyle and Henderson, 1985

Table 4.3 Rules for co-workers

1 Accept one's fair share of the work load
2 Respect other's privacy
3 Be cooperative with regard to the shared physical working conditions (e.g. light, temperature, noise)
4 Be willing to help when requested
5 Keep confidences
6 Work cooperatively despite feelings of dislike
7 Do not denigrate to superiors
8 Address the co-worker by first name
9 Ask for help and advice when necessary
10 Look the co-worker in the eye during conversations
11 Do not be over-inquisitive about each other's private lives
12 Repay debts, favours and compliments no matter how small
13 Do not engage in sexual activity with the co-worker
14 Stand up for the co-worker in his/her absence
15 Do not criticise the co-worker publicly

Source: Argyle and Henderson, 1985

who are not seen regularly for lunch or coffee.
4 *Work relationship only.* These are a minority whose company is not enjoyed, and who are only seen at all because of the work.

Table 4.2 shows the activities which were shared more often by those in the closer relationships. It can be seen that the friends engaged more in a range of both work and purely sociable activities.

There is often conflict and friction within working groups, over rivalry for promotion, easier or better-paid jobs, for example. There is more conflict in working groups than among friends outside work since it is not so easy to leave, and because there are special sources of friction in the work place. In a study of the informal rules applicable in a number of different relationships it was found that the rules listed in Table 4.3 were relevant for co-workers and provided a key to the sources of friction at work. The existence of these rules indicates that friction may occur when fairness, cooperation, help, mutual support and privacy are brought into question (Argyle and Henderson, 1985).

Primitive societies are famous for their elaborate ceremonies, and these are believed to be important in maintaining social cohesion and cooperation. Modern working groups have their rituals too. Such rituals are often associated with eating and drinking, holidays, and celebrating arrivals and departures. They probably contribute a lot to in-group feelings.

Groups may divide into smaller sub-groups, especially when the original group is large. A group may divide on the basis of age, race, pay, or doing different jobs. There is often competition, friction or rivalry between such groups. However, networks of links between members of different groups can be important in reducing the amount of conflict in organisations (Nelson, 1989).

WORKING ORGANISATIONS

From early times people have worked not only in small social groups but also in organised social groups. The behaviour of the present members is therefore to a considerable degree *programmed*. Each person occupies a position – such as slave, feudal lord of the manor, merchant capitalist, shop steward – and associated with each position is a standard pattern of behaviour, or *role*. These roles *interlock* – for example, there was a standard pattern of interaction between a feudal serf and his lord of the manor. We are now dealing not with the personalities or behaviour of individuals, but with the functioning of whole social systems, where anyone could be replaced, and is so replaced when they leave.

Working organisations take different forms at different periods, and in different cultures. This is partly due to ideas about organisation. Early in the present century Taylor's ideas of 'scientific management' were very influ- ential, based on the way the Army was run. There should be a small span of control, written responsibilities, economic incentives, bureaucracy and simple jobs. The Human Relations movement introduced very different ideas – the importance of working groups, democratic supervision and job satisfaction. Nothing was said about economic incentives, technology or organisational design. Contemporary ideas are more complex, and emphasise the import- ance of fitting organisations to technology and the outside environment, and of integrating individuals and groups inside the organisation.

It has been found that the shape of organisations varies with the technology. Woodward (1965) found that the number of levels in the supervisory hierarchy was typically 3 in unit or batch production, 4 in mass production and 6 in process work; the span of control also varies, being greatest for mass production. She reported that the most successful firms of each type were those that were near the typical structure for each type of work.

In traditional industry large firms have mechanistic structures; that is, strong hierarchy, centralised control, high division of labour, and a great deal of formality in the form of written rules and job specifications. On the whole these are sources of low job satisfaction. However in a faster-moving situation, like the electronics industry, more 'organic' structures develop, with weak hierarchies, flexible division of labour, decision-taking at all levels and a lot of lateral communication (Burns and Stalker, 1961). In a study of tape-recorded encounters between supervisors and subordinates it was found that in organic firms there were fewer orders but more questions from superiors, and more upward initiation of interactions (Courtright *et al.*, 1989).

As a result of research into the effects of different kinds of organisation, it is possible to give some advice abut which work best. Size may be necessary for use of expensive central equipment, but larger organisations are found to have lower output per man ($r = -.23$ in a meta analysis by Gooding and Wagner, 1985), lower job satisfaction, and higher absenteeism, labour turnover and accidents. Flat as opposed to tall organisations – namely, those with a larger span of control and fewer levels in the hierarchy – are generally preferred. Organic structures do better with a faster-changing environment, mechanistic if things are static. This is an example of a contingency theory – that firms which adopt structures which are appropriate for their environment survive, or that they learn by experience and change towards the shapes which work best. Lawrence and Lorsch (1967) found evidence for this theory at the departmental level: those departments facing more uncertain environments adopted less formal structures; that is, fewer written rules and job descriptions.

One of the main problems with working organisations is the conflict which often develops between owners, or managers, and labour. While there are certainly common, shared interests here, there are usually conflicting interests too; for example, workers are paid less, and are laid off when such action is economically advantageous to the firm. In Britain 58 per cent of full-time male and 50 per cent of female employees belong to trade unions, more among the older ones and those in lower classes (Reid, 1989). Twenty-four per cent have taken part in or would willingly take part in an unofficial strike; over 50 per cent feel exploited or taken advantage of at work. Fifty to sixty per cent would like more participation in their immediate affairs, while a few would like to take part in more distant decisions affecting the whole company (Wall and Lischeron, 1977).

Strikes and stoppages are usually triggered by particular incidents – a worker is laid off, or an agreement broken – but often take the form of demands over pay; however, they are made more likely when there is low job satisfaction, militant trade-union leaders, and unskilled management. Conflict seems to be endemic in hierarchical structures, where those at the lowest levels feel frustrated and alienated.

There are ways of improving relationships within working organisations. Having fewer levels in the hierarchy, smaller plants, and more democratic-consultative styles of supervision all help. The introduction of various kinds of industrial democracy helps even more; for example, joint consultative committees (UK), workers' councils (Yugoslavia), worker directors (Germany) and quality circles (Japan). Surveys show that there is widespread desire for this, especially on the part of skilled workers. And where it has been introduced, job satisfaction has usually increased, and so has productivity (Miller and Monge, 1986).

SOCIAL SKILLS AT WORK

We said above that people at work play organisational roles. However, they play these roles in varied ways, and in particular with different degrees of competence in dealing with other people.

Wherever the effects of social skills can be measured, substantial effects of social skills have been found. Take supervision of working groups: good supervisors may produce 2 times the output, $1/8$ the complaints, $1/5$ the absenteeism and labour turnover, of other supervisors. Take selection interviewing: while some interviewers can raise the validity of selection based on the dossiers alone from .40 to .70, others actually reduce it. Similar findings are reported for selling, psychotherapy and many other work skills (Argyle, 1989).

It is important to understand what social skills are like. In some ways they are like motor skills, such as driving a car, where rapid corrective action is taken when necessary. The moves made are now social signals; for example, an interviewer asks open-ended questions to get the other to talk more freely. But verbal utterances have to be delivered in the right non-verbal style: indicating warmth and encouragement in this case. It is essential to consider the other's point of view – social influence only works if the right kind of persuasive considerations are presented. Most social skills involve cooperation, and this requires intricate turn-taking, and keeping up a coordinated sequence of related moves. This is not entirely a matter of conscious planning, since the finer elements become automatic, like keeping balance on a bicycle.

There are other aspects of social competence which are more conscious, following rules; for example, an interviewer should be aware of the conventions of the interview – that personal questions may be asked if they are relevant to the selection, that the interviewer can take notes, and so on. Training courses on dealing with people from other cultures or social classes include information about the relevant customs and conventions; for example, when buying from and selling to Arabs.

Supervision of working groups is a central job in almost all kinds of work. It is a difficult relationship, and is unsuccessful unless the right skills are used. Two dimensions of supervisory style are particularly important. The first is *initiating structure*; that is, telling people what to do, scheduling the work, letting subordinates know what is expected, and motivating them. This certainly affects performance or output. And it has to be done skilfully, or job satisfaction falls.

The second is *consideration*; that is, looking after subordinates, being friendly and approachable. This dimension particularly influences job satisfaction, and consequently absenteeism and labour turnover. Productivity depends on a combination of initiating structure and consideration – as described by the 'path–goal' theory. House (1971) proposed that the main function of supervisors is to point out the path to successful performance and to see that this leads to rewards for subordinates. It was proposed that subordinates will work harder if the leader makes the satisfaction of needs contingent on effective performance. The relative importance of these two dimensions is contingent on the situation; for example, more supportive supervision is needed with frustrating tasks, more direction when tasks lack structure (especially for authoritarian subordinates).

There is a third dimension of supervisory style, *participation*: democratic and persuasive leaders allow their subordinates to participate in decisions, sometimes by means of group decision-making. With participation there is usually greater acceptance of decisions and commitments to carry them out; without participation there can be resistance and hostility. Job satisfaction is usually greater under participatory supervision, and absenteeism is less.

Does the intelligence of supervisors make a difference? Fiedler and Garcia (1987) have found that intelligent leaders of a variety of kinds are more effective in that their groups have a higher rate of performance. However, this occurs only when the leader is directive and not under stress (especially interpersonal stress from his or her own boss), and the group members are supportive of the leader.

House has developed the concept of *charismatic* leadership – leaders who can inspire and encourage, and cause subordinates to change their goals and aim for higher ones. The charismatic or transformational style is conceptualised as communicating a vision and a mission, maintaining a positive image in the minds of others, and providing inspiration and encouragement by his or her presence. Leaders can be rated by subordinates on such scales, and those with high scores have been found to be successful in a variety of settings – persuading workers to abandon low productivity norms, in combat, management, and even, it is claimed, for American presidents (Fiedler and House, 1988).

Subordinates can have some useful social skills too – for influencing their superiors, for example. Six social techniques are commonly used, in this order: reasoned arguments, ingratiation, exchange of benefits, assertiveness, appeal to higher authority, and forming a coalition (Schriesheim and Hinkin, 1990). These methods of influence are used more by subordinates under task-centred than under person-centred superiors, and especially after a second influence attempt by the latter (Derluga, 1988).

Managers need the same skills as supervisors, and some other skills too. They spend a great deal of their time with other people, about 66 per cent, and more than this in the case of senior managers. Managers need to be good with people, not just being nice to them but understanding what is going on, and how groups and organisations work. They must be able to design work-flow systems and administrative structures, and set up committees.

There are also a number of set-piece skills, some of which all managers will need to master: selection interviews, appraisal interviews, personnel interviews (that is, with unsatisfactory workers), committee chairmanship, negotiation (such as with unions or other firms), and the presentation of material to an audience (such as clients).

Every kind of work requires special skills: academics have to give lectures, classes and tutorials; doctors have to handle patients, sometimes to change their behaviour or to give bad news; clergy must take different kinds of church services, give sermons, talk to distressed parishioners; politicians have to make speeches, negotiate agreements, appear on TV. An account of most of these skills is given elsewhere (Argyle, 1983, 1989).

How can people best be trained in these skills? For many years they learned simply by doing the job, but this is a very ineffective way, and various forms of training are now widely used. Follow-up studies have found that they have a substantial effect on objective measures of performance, as well as on-the-job satisfaction of others (Burke and Day, 1986).

Role-playing is increasingly used, especially for specialised skills, like interviewing. A list of topics (skills to be taught) is drawn up; one is tackled at each session. Trainees are usually handled in groups of 6–7. A session starts by the trainer explaining the skill, and showing a videotape to be modelled; each trainee then role-plays for about 7 minutes with another trainee as stooge; a videotape is then played back and discussed, and constructive comments are made. The main problem is helping trainees to generalise what they have been taught to their real work situation, by giving them 'homework'; that is, asking them to try the new skills out. (See also p. 66ff.)

On the job training. For some jobs, like that of the police, and perhaps management, it is difficult to create a realistic replica of the real thing in the lab. An alternative is to train on the job, by means of a trainer who spends time with trainees, sees them in action and makes constructive comments. This method is commonly used for teachers, and is coming in for other skills. Having a mentor is good for promotion prospects. In addition to help and advice, it provides modelling for trainees, and also provides an entry into the social network (Dreher and Ash, 1990).

Educational methods. Lectures, discussion, reading and films are well-known ways of teaching in other areas. They can make a valuable contribution to SST too, especially where there is a lot of information to assimilate, as in intercultural training. However, skills cannot be acquired from knowledge alone and all skills need practice as well.

PERSONALITY AND WORK

There are several areas of personality which are relevant to behaviour and experience at work. To predict success at work, intelligence is found to be the most powerful, with correlations of about .50, especially for management and other higher-level jobs (Schmitt and Noe, 1986). For manual jobs, measures of motor coordination, mechanical ability, arm strength and so on are successful. For management and all jobs dealing with people social competence is essential. One of the best selection methods here is by Assessment Centres, where various leadership and situational exercises are used: these always give good predictions to later success. Little use is made of personality tests for selection; they don't work very well, partly because it is so easy to cheat. However, research has shown that some personality variables are relevant to work success, and these will be described below.

Type A personalities used to be famous for their heart attacks (p. 239), as well as for working hard, but research has shown that it is not a unitary trait. It is now well established that it is the irritability, or aggressive component, which is connected to heart attacks; the somewhat independent component of achievement striving leads to high performance for some occupations (Bluen *et al.*, 1990). Achievement motivation has been found to correlate with success for sales personnel, managers in small firms, scientists and other academics, and entrepreneurs. These are all people who can achieve success by their own efforts. Managers in larger organisations have to achieve success through the efforts of others. McClelland and Boyatzis (1982) found that, for non-technical managers in such firms, success depends on high-power motivation combined with low affiliative motivation; that is, a desire to influence people rather than make friends.

We saw earlier how important entrepreneurs were during the Industrial Revolution, and they are still very important today in starting new enterprises. They are found to have a special kind of personality. In addition to having a strong motivation to achieve, they often have somewhat deviant personalities, making it difficult for them to fit into large organisations. Case studies have found that some entrepreneurs at least are non-conformist, rebellious, distrust authority, are unwilling to work with others, and come from families where they were not appreciated, or from marginal minority groups, giving them a great drive to succeed and establish a new identity (Kets de Vries, 1977).

Most people prefer work that is varied, interesting, challenging and that uses their skills – the components of jobs which make them intrinsically rewarding for most people (Hackman and Oldham, 1980). Whereas some workers have this 'growth-need strength' and are motivated and satisfied by complex and demanding jobs, others are not. The former want to accomplish something, learn and develop themselves. There is some disagreement about the percentage of workers for whom this is important, but it probably includes most managers and technical staff. There are other workers, paid less, and doing more boring work, for whom it is not important, and who work mostly for the pay (Goldthorpe *et al.*, 1968), though perhaps too for the social life.

Attitudes and values affect how individuals get on at work. We saw the importance of the PWE at an earlier period. Does the PWE produce harder work? Not a great deal of research has been done here, but what there is has found that the PWE correlates with such work behaviour as the rate of performance following negative evaluation – especially if the subjects received unearned rewards, more constant attendance at work, and greater commitment to the organisation (Furnham, 1990).

'Workaholics' are probably extreme products of the PWE, although their intrinsic motivation is probably also very high. They work very long hours, spend little time with their families, have almost no leisure time, take no holidays and are clearly addicted to work. It is found that they enjoy their work very much, and are happy with their lives (Macholowitz, 1980). The tendency can be measured by their agreement with questionnaire items such as:

Most people who don't succeed in life are just plain lazy.
I feel uneasy when there is little work for me to do.

(Mirels and Garrett, 1971)

Job satisfaction is greater if people can find work that suits their particular interests, values and personality, and on the whole they gravitate towards such jobs. So, for example, in a survey of 1,500 managers it was found that they were somewhat more extraverted and less neurotic than the population norms; those in sales and personnel were the most extraverted, research and development people and consultants the least (Eysenck, 1967). And

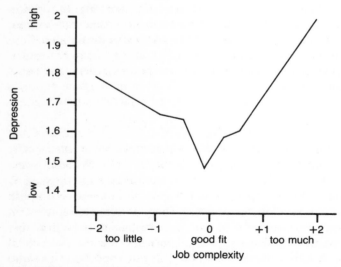

Figure 4.1 Job complexity and depression
Source: Caplan *et al.*, 1975

Rosenberg (1957) found that students high on his people-oriented scale chose social work, medicine, teaching and social science; students scoring high on his self-expression scale chose architecture, journalism and art; students scoring high on extrinsic-reward orientation chose sales, hotel management, estate agency and finance.

The difficulty of the job held is correlated with degrees of depression, as shown in Figure 4.1.

Men and women tackle work rather differently. To start with, they tend to do different kinds of jobs. Many women work in one or two main types of job. Some are teachers, nurses, social workers or personnel officers, all of whom look after other people. Some women are secretaries, clerical workers, or shop assistants, all of whom help other people and work in small groups. Women have different motivations and values related to work – they value the social side of work more than men do and have more friends at work. And women want to be helpful to others, and are concerned with creativity and self-expression, rather than just making money. In supervisory positions women have a somewhat more democratic and caring style, though the difference is not great (Eagly and Johnson, 1990). And as managers women have problems – of fitting into and being accepted by a largely male management world. There are few women in top management: in Britain 6 per cent are women, in the USA 2 per cent; men do not consider that women have the necessary management qualities, a view not shared by the women (Metcalfe, 1990). Most women at work have the problem of looking after the home as well, especially if they are working full-time and have children. The dual career family is rich but stressed. Nevertheless most women at work are happier and in better mental health than those not at work, and a little more satisfied than the men. For married women at work, more stress arises from the home and caring for children than from the work. However, not all jobs for women are equally satisfying, and clerical workers enjoy their work less than those who have more autonomy.

THE CAUSES AND EFFECTS OF JOB SATISFACTION

Most people work a lot of the time. They do it partly, in some cases mainly, because they are paid to do so, or need the fruits of work themselves. How far do they also enjoy doing it? The most widely used measure is a very simple one. Overall job satisfaction can be assessed by simple questions such as 'Choose one of the following statements which best tells how well you like your job? I hate it, I dislike it, I do not like it, I am indifferent to it, I like it, I am enthusiastic about it, I love it' (Hoppock, 1935). Another question is to ask if you would do the same job again, and this reveals large differences between occupations (Table 4.4). More sophisticated measures obtain scores for different components of job satisfaction – with pay, the work itself, the other people at work and so on.

How satisfied are people with their jobs? A number of surveys show that a little over half the working population say they are very satisfied, about 35 per cent fairly satisfied, and 10 per cent definitely dislike their work (Argyle, 1989). In order to find out what makes work satisfying we can look at the conditions under which satisfaction is highest. Some work is *intrinsically satisfying*, if it has the characteristics of skill variety, task significance, and so on, described earlier, though we have just seen that not everyone finds such jobs rewarding. However, many people feel very satisfied when deeply involved in challenging work, which uses their skills and leads to recognition of success. And for many individuals, if the work is too easy, they get depressed (Figure 4.1).

There are large differences in satisfaction between *occupations*, as shown by this survey of how many would choose the same job again (Table 4.4).

Table 4.4   Percentage of workers who would choose the same work again

	%
Mathematicians	91
Lawyers	83
Journalists	82
Skilled printers	52
Skilled car workers	41
Skilled steel workers	41
Textile workers	31
Unskilled car workers	21
Unskilled steel workers	16

Source: Blauner, 1960

Other surveys find that professional people are the most satisfied, followed by managers, clerical, skilled and unskilled labour.

Pay is certainly important, especially as a source of dissatisfaction. Across the population pay is a quite minor predictor of happiness, but within organisations relative pay is important, especially how far workers think that they are being paid equitably, in comparison with others (Berkowitz *et al.*, 1987).

Social factors are important – belonging to a friendly and supportive working group, having a superior who uses the right skills, and belonging to an organisation which is fairly small, has few levels in the hierarchy, and where there is participation in decision-taking.

Individual differences. Job satisfaction is partly innate, as twin studies show (Arvey *et al.*, 1989). Extraverts have more job satisfaction, those high in neuroticism less, as with happiness in general. Also important is the 'fit' between person and job, both in terms of ability, and also challenge, sociability and values.

Why do people find work so satisfying, indeed one of the most satisfying things in their lives? It is because certain activities are intrinsically rewarding – activities that use skills, complete tasks and have an impact on others; it is because of the social satisfaction of work, the opportunity to achieve success, and probably because pay makes it rewarding. Job satisfaction is an important goal, which should be maximised for its own sake. It also has a number of further consequences. Do happy workers work harder? They do, to some extent, especially in the case of supervisors and those in higher levels of skill (Petty *et al.*, 1984), though it is not known how far satisfaction causes higher performance. Happy workers are absent less; they stay longer in the job – their labour turnover is less, and here the causal chain has been confirmed.

Job satisfaction correlates quite strongly with overall life satisfaction. A number of studies have been carried out to discover which causes which, and both directions of causation have been found.

Absenteeism is a major problem at work – $13^{1}/_{2}$ days off per year per employee in England – and one consequence is a higher rate of accidents, through workers being unfamiliar with the work (Goodman and Garber, 1988). It is increased by job dissatisfaction, but is partly due to other demands, for example, from the families of women workers. About half of it is partly due to genuine sickness. And it is greater for less skilled workers, though it is not usually recorded for managers or professional people at all. A successful method of reducing absenteeism is to introduce a bonus for regular attendance, though such schemes need to be introduced with the full participation of those involved (Steers and Rhodes, 1984).

Labour turnover is calculated as the number of workers leaving per year as a percentage of the number employed, and is typically 20–25 per cent. If it is high, it adds greatly to the expenses of selecting and training new personnel. Leaving a job is partly due to low job satisfaction, together with the discovery of a better alternative. Low commitment to the organisation is also a strong predictor. Turnover is higher for workers who are badly paid, and who do unskilled and boring jobs. It can be reduced by increased pay, by better training, by making greater efforts to fit individuals to jobs, and by the introduction of more rewarding and supportive styles of supervision (Mobley, 1982). Turnover is low when unemployment is high, and other jobs are harder to find; the correlation with job satisfaction is now *stronger* (-.50), because under these conditions people leave mainly because of dissatisfaction (Carsten and Spector, 1987).

Commitment to the organisation can be measured by questionnaire, and has two components – affective attachment and instrumental, or calculative, commitment. Affective attachment correlates with performance, while calculative commitment only correlates with intention to stay (Meyer *et al.*, 1989). Commitment correlates with job satisfaction, and causation is

Table 4.5   Occupational differences in job satisfaction, coronary heart disease and
social status

	Satisfied(%)	Coronary rate	Social status
University teachers	93	71	84
Biologists	89	69	80
Physicists	89	69	80
Chemists	86	100	79
Farmers	84	66	14
Lawyers	80	124	93
Managers	69	116	79
Sales	52	126	50
Skilled printers	52	110	49
Clerical	42	103	44
Paper workers	42	73	19
Skilled car workers	41	68	21
Skilled steelworkers	41	85	15
Textile workers	31	120	3
Unskilled steelworkers	21	125	4
Unskilled car workers	16	176	13

Source: Sales and House, 1971

in both directions. Organisational commitment is highest for those with some financial stake in the firm, or who have other 'investments', like tied pension plans or influencing instrumental commitment. Commitment is also high for those who participate in decisions and have been with the organisation a long time – probably affective attachment. It is very high among college athletes; Adler and Adler (1989) speculate on whether this is due to factors such as the work coinciding with a central life interest or the paternalistic and charismatic leadership. It could also be due to the intense public reinforcement for performance in the team.

Health and mental health. Some jobs are more stressful than others, and make people ill, in mind or body. Examples are jobs with severe time pressures, work overload, or with a lot of responsibility for others. These stresses can be offset by social support at work, and have less effect on 'hardy' personalities. We shall discuss methods of avoiding these effects of stress in Chapters 8 and 9. Job satisfaction may be part of the explanation, since it is correlated with poor mental health and physical health, and it has been found that job dissatisfaction leads to anxiety and depression, which in turn produce bodily complaints (French *et al.*, 1982). And there is a strong correlation between low job satisfaction and rate of coronaries; both are a function of occupation (Sales and House, 1971) (Table 4.5).

THE EFFECTS OF UNEMPLOYMENT AND RETIREMENT

Unemployment is a fact of life in most countries, and is now between 7 and 15 per cent in industrialised societies. It reached a peak of 13.1 per cent in Britain in 1986 but has fallen since then, partly by changes in definition; for example, of older, unemployed people as 'retired', younger ones as 'trainees'. Unemployment has risen in most industrialised countries as the result of automation and computers, which have abolished many manual jobs, and more recently many clerical ones. A rise in employment in service industries (education, entertainment, finance and so on) has generated more jobs, but now they too are becoming automated.

Unemployment has very undesirable consequences for most people. Many are unhappy, bored and apathetic, and have low self-esteem. Mental health is worse for many, with increased depression, alcoholism and suicide rate. Physical health is worse, with increased cholesterol, and the mortality rate is typically 36 per cent higher than average. These effects have all been shown to be caused by unemployment. For example, Banks and Jackson (1982) found that the General Health Questionnaire (GHQ) scores of school-leavers who did not find jobs increased, while for those who had jobs it decreased, over the two years after leaving school.

A comparison of the effects of unemployment in Britain and Spain found that the negative effects were much less marked in Spain. It was concluded that the most likely explanation is the much lower strength of PWE in Spain (Alvaro and Marsh, 1989).

It is interesting to examine the conditions under which unemployment does *not* have these negative effects.

1 *Social support from the family* is important because there is a loss of working relationships. Cobb and Kasl (1977) found that among men who lost their jobs as a result of factory closure 12 per cent became arthritic, while others had raised cholesterol. However, for those with good support from their spouse only 4 per cent became arthritic, while for those with low social support it was 41 per cent.
2 *Finding alternative activities*. Fryer and Payne (1984) discovered (with some difficulty, they tell us) 11 men who coped with unemployment in an unusually positive way. They preferred their own organisation of time and self-discipline to an imposed one; they had not liked hierarchical authority, and found enriched social support elsewhere; they chose their own goals in tune with their own values; they found their own identities, in one case as leader of a community project, who had as much opportunity as before for the daily exercise of competence and skill.
3 *Low work commitment*. Unemployment is worse for those who are committed to work. This is probably why unemployment is more distressing for middle-aged men than for young people or married

women. But even for those imbued with the PWE it should be possible to find satisfaction in some forms of serious leisure.

4 *Perception of impersonal causes of unemployment.* During periods of full employment, to be out of work was mainly due to personal incompetence. Recently Kelvin (1981) found when interviewing unemployed people the reply: 'And if you can't find any work to do, you have the feeling that you're not human. You're out of place. You're so different from all the rest of the people around you that you think something is wrong with you.'

Unemployment has now become very widespread, however, and includes people from all sections of society. The result is that many of the unemployed feel less responsible for their plight, and more accepting of it. If you know many other people who are also out of work, this part of the identity problem is greatly eased. It is found that satisfaction with the self is higher when the local level of unemployment is higher (Warr, 1984).

The unemployed appear to have limitless leisure, but it doesn't feel like that. Many just sit around, stay in bed, watch TV. Perhaps to enjoy leisure we need some work to contrast it with; a lot of leisure is related to work, either to relax or recover from it, or as an extension to similar activities. Some unemployed people keep up their skills – for example, setting up an office or workshop at home; this is good for the self-image as well as for filling time. Some take part in the informal or 'black' economy, which both helps financially (although illegally) and maintains a social network.

Retirement makes a very interesting contrast with unemployment, since the retired are also out of work. Most men in Britain retire by 65, women by 60, though a few work longer. Although the unemployed are less happy, the retired are somewhat happier on average, though some are bored or lonely. The main predictors of happiness for the retired are good health, enough income, active leisure interests and education. For those with strong work commitment it is good to find activities which are perceived as useful (Talaga and Beehr, 1989). (See p.294ff.)

There is little effect of retirement on mental health; 25–30 per cent have difficulty in adjusting to their new situation, but most do so during the first year. Physical health is the main reason for early retirement, which is why some retired people seem to be in poor health. Otherwise, carefully designed studies have found no overall effect of retirement on health. There is no immediate effect, and age of retirement has no effect on mortality rate or life expectancy; there is a slight improvement in the health of those who were in manual work, a slight decline for those in better jobs, but most show no change. Those in heavy, unskilled jobs benefit from the absence of strain and fatigue.

What is the explanation for the very different consequences of unemployment and retirement? It must be because retirement is an accepted and honourable social status, while unemployment is not. Retirement is seen as a proper reward for a hard life's work, while unemployment has the implication of failure, being unwanted, a scrounger, living on charity. 'For most men being retired seems to be a rather benign condition of life; being unemployed is a disturbing and often degrading experience' (Campbell, 1981).

Many retired people do seem to enjoy their leisure more than the unemployed; perhaps they feel more entitled to do so. Most keep up and extend previous leisure activities; a few take up new ones. Some pursue extensions to work: academics carry on writing, though the trend is to more television-watching and other 'passive' leisure occupations, and gardening, shopping and helping in the house. However, many retired people, if they are in good health and moderately well-off, do a great deal more than this.

THE FUTURE OF WORK

Much 'work' as it was experienced after the Industrial Revolution was hard and unpleasant. Most work has moved a long way from those conditions, and it may move a lot further still – depending partly on how much social scientists can influence things. Here is my contribution.

We have seen that automation and computers have increased unemployment. This is likely to become more extensive in the future, because machines are cheaper, don't go on strike, and can do some jobs more reliably and accurately. Could the human cost of unemployment be reduced? The most obvious solution is to spread work among more people, and there are several ways of doing this:

1 *Banning overtime* would create a quarter of a million jobs in Britain.
2 *A shorter working week*, perhaps 35 hours instead of 38 or 40, would have an even greater effect. This is planned in France.
3 *A shorter working life*, such as between ages 20 and 58, or with a flexible retirement age, or part-time work. Japanese firms have a retirement age of 55; many European firms are trying early retirement.
4 *More part-time jobs*. Already 20 per cent of the British work force is part-time, many of them women, but also some who are retired, and a number of professionals and managers.

The main difficulty with introducing any of these schemes is that they are resisted by those who are at work and enjoying it, or enjoying the pay.

Another consequence of technological change is that the whole nature of work is changing. The good side of this is that many routine, dirty, dangerous and heavy jobs can be eliminated. However, automation can easily lead to 'de-skilling', and workers may be relegated to jobs of a lower level of skill, needing less pay and less training, than those which were done before. This can certainly happen, and many kinds of white-collar work are coming to resemble factory work, with rows of workers sitting in front of

VDUs. But this appearance can be misleading, if there is a higher level of skill or autonomy. In the case of factory work itself, there can be a higher level of skill; for example, where machine operatives carry out maintenance, set the controls, and do some of the programming of the machines. Some sociologists have gloomily forecast a 'retreat from work', where work ceases to be a central life interest, because of these technological changes, but there is no real evidence yet that this is taking place.

The people who are likely to gain most power and influence from the new technology are those most closely involved with it, those with most access to the computers (Oborne, 1985). However, there can be de-skilling or redundancy at quite senior levels – if, for example, expert systems are designed which can do the work of bank managers.

Automation can also reduce the social joys of work. Instead of working in working groups that play games and gossip, workers can become isolated, tied to remote work stations.

Developments in technology have made home working more possible for many, by means of links to head office by telephone, computer or word processor. It is ideal for women with families and for the disabled, many of whom would otherwise not work at all. The jobs undertaken in the home are mainly typing, computing and sewing, but also include journalism, research, work for publishers and so on. However, home working has some serious disadvantages – loss of informal social contacts at work, less cooperation and joint problem-solving, less power and influence. A European survey asked samples of workers whether they would prefer to work from home for all or part of the week; 40.8 per cent of those surveyed in the UK were in favour of working from home.

It is now within the power of industrialists to create jobs which maximise job satisfaction, with its consequences for reduced absenteeism, turnover and accidents. Jobs could be designed which provide more intrinsic job satisfaction. There is no problem about professional, managerial, crafts or other highly skilled work; workers in these areas use skills, produce identifiable products, have an impact on others, and there is feedback on task performance. The difficulty comes with unskilled, repetitive manual and clerical work. These jobs can be improved by job enlargement, or can be partly computerised. We have seen that some workers don't want to do interesting or challenging jobs, but perhaps they should be educated and encouraged to do so. Machine-paced work is widely disliked, and it is possible to replace production lines by autonomous work-groups. It is very important to fit workers as far as possible to the work they do, in terms of ability, stressfulness and compatibility of goals; good personnel selection is the key to this.

The social context of work is very important; both automation and home working can create a lot of isolation. Most people like to work in small, cooperative teams. Supervisors should be trained in the correct use of initiating structure, consideration and participation. And organisations work better when they are small, with few levels, and allow consultation with workers at all levels.

Paid work, in a working organisation, is not the only kind of work, and alternative arrangements are becoming more widespread.

The 'Grey' economy. This consists of work which is done for ourselves or others but not paid for. It consists mainly of cooking and other housework, gardening, home maintenance, DIY and things done for others on the basis of friendship, neighbourliness or reciprocity. It has been estimated that 51 per cent of the total amount of work done is in the grey economy (Rose, 1983).

Informal, hobby-based work. This consists of part-time and self-employed activities which grow out of leisure activities such as carpentry, dressmaking, tutoring, vegetable-growing, decorating, typing, translating. For some this may develop into full-time work; for some, into larger concerns employing others.

Self-employed. About 7 per cent of the British work force are self-employed; that is, they run their own businesses – mainly shops, building, agriculture, and professional services. This has the advantage of autonomy and the possibility of wealth, usually involves long hours, and there is a risk of bankruptcy.

Voluntary work. About 10 per cent of the population do some unpaid or voluntary work once a week or more. This is mainly for the welfare of children, the elderly, the sick or disabled. It may also involve working for charitable organisations, raising money, selling things or doing clerical work.

It is clear that work involves more than working for wages, and can take other forms. Each brings special kinds of satisfaction: the grey economy strengthens social networks, informal work is closely based on leisure interests, the self-employed are autonomous, and voluntary work has the satisfaction of helping those in need.

Could work be made more like leisure – that is, the activities people perform simply because they want to? The distinction between work and leisure is quite subtle, since they may involve exactly the same activities; digging the garden, driving a car, decorating rooms, looking after other people, for example, may be either work or leisure. Work is usually paid (except for voluntary work), leisure usually yields no material gain (apart from gardening and crafts). Some work has a high degree of autonomy; some leisure involves regular hours and supervision, obligations to others, as in amateur drama and music. Work demands a competent standard of performance, but so does some leisure (music or sport). We shall explore the nature of leisure further in the next chapter.

CONCLUSIONS

Work is essential to life, to provide food, clothes, housing and the rest. In the modern world there are a number of problems, over work-stress, low job satisfaction and industrial conflict. The nature of work and work relationships depends on technology, and has taken very different forms historically. The motivation for work is partly economic, partly the need to achieve, partly social, and many like work for its own sake – the Protestant Work Ethic.

Most work is done in groups, under supervision. Work-teams can be effective and satisfying, but depend on informal relationships to establish cooperation, and rules to prevent friction. Larger groups become hierarchical organisations; these work better when smaller, flatter, more democratic, and fit the technology. Social skills are very important at work, especially supervisory and managerial skills, and the most effective styles are now known.

Different kinds of personality are more or less motivated, successful, satisfied, or stressed by work, as are men and women. Job satisfaction is greater for certain kinds of work and occupation, depends on social factors, and is a cause of (low) absenteeism and labour turnover, and (good) health.

Unemployment is a source of distress and ill health, but retirement is not, probably because it is perceived differently. More jobs could be created (for instance, by shorter working hours), and the nature of work could be further improved (such as by home-working and improved social grouping) to make it more satisfying.

REFERENCES

Adler, P.A. and Adler, P. (1989) The gloried self: the aggrandizement and constriction of self. *Social Psychology Quarterly, 52*, 299–310.

Alvaro, J.L. and Marsh, C. (1989) A cross-cultural perspective on the social and psychological distress caused by unemployment: a comparison of Spain and the United Kingdom. Unpublished. Madrid: Complutense University.

Argyle, M. (1983) *The Psychology of Interpersonal Behaviour*. 4th edition. Harmondsworth: Penguin Books.

—— (1989) *The Social Psychology of Work*. 2nd edition. Harmondsworth: Penguin Books.

—— (1991) *Cooperation: the Basis of Sociability*. London: Routledge.

Argyle, M. and Henderson, M. (1985) *The Anatomy of Relationships*. London: Heinemann; Harmondsworth: Penguin Books.

Arvey, R.D., Bouchard, T.J., Segall, N.L. and Abraham, L.M. (1989) Job satisfaction: environmental and genetic components. *Journal of Applied Psychology, 74*, 187–92.

Banks, M.H. and Jackson, P.R. (1982) Unemployment and risk of minor psychiatric disorder in young people: cross sectional and longitudinal evidence. *Psychological Medicine, 12*, 789–98.

Berkowitz, L., Fraser, C., Treasure, F.P. and Cochran, S. (1987) Pay, equity, job qualifications, and comparisons in pay satisfaction. *Journal of Applied Psychology, 72*, 544–51.

Blauner, R. (1960) Work satisfaction and industrial trends in modern society. *In* W. Galenson and S.M. Lipset (eds) *Labor and Trade Unions.* New York: Wiley.

Bluen, S.D., Barling, J. and Burns, W. (1990) Predicting sales performance, job satisfaction, and depression by using the achievement strivings and impatience-irritability dimensions of Type A behaviour. *Journal of Applied Psychology, 75*, 212–16.

Burke, M.J. and Day, R.R. (1986) A cumulative study of the effectiveness of managerial training. *Journal of Applied Psychology, 71*, 232–45.

Burns, T. and Stalker, G.M. (1961) *The Management of Innovation.* London: Tavistock.

Campbell, A. (1981) *The Sense of Well-Being in America.* New York: McGraw-Hill.

Caplan, R.D., Cobb, S., French, J.R.P., Van Harrison, R. and Pinean, S.R. (1975) *Job Demands and Worker Health.* Ann Arbor: Institute for Social Research, University of Michigan.

Carsten, J.M. and Spector, P.E. (1987) Unemployment, job satisfaction, and employee turnover: a meta-analytic test of the Muchinksy model. *Journal of Applied Psychology, 72*, 374–9.

Cobb, S. and Kasl, S.V. (1977) *Termination: the Consequences of Job Loss.* Cincinnati, OH.: U.S Department of Health, Education and Welfare.

Courtright, J.A., Fairhurst, G.T. and Roger, L.E. (1989) Interaction patterns in organic and mechanistic systems. *Academy of Management Journal, 32*, 773–802.

David, F.R., Pearce, J.A. and Randolph, W.A. (1989) Linking technology and structure to enhance group performance. *Journal of Applied Psychology, 74*, 233–41.

Derluga, R.J. (1988) The politics of leadership: the relationship between task-people leadership and subordinate influence. *Journal of Organizational Behavior, 9*, 359–61.

DeVore, I. (1965) *Primate Behavior.* New York: Holt, Rinehart & Winston.

Dreher, G.F. and Ash, R.A. (1990) A comparative study of mentoring among men and women in managerial, professional, and technical positions. *Journal of Applied Psychology, 75*, 539–45.

Eagly, A.H. and Johnson, B.T. (1990) Gender and leadership style: a meta-analysis. *Psychological Bulletin, 108*, 233–56.

Eysenck, H.J. (1967) Personality patterns in various groups of businessmen. *Occupational Psychology, 41*, 249–50.

Fiedler, F.E. and Garcia, J.E. (1987) *New Approaches to Effective Leadership.* New York: Wiley.

Fiedler, F. and House, R.J. (1988) Leadership theory and research: a report of progress. *In* C.L. Cooper and I.T. Robertson (eds) *International Review of Industrial and Organizational Psychology,* Chichester: Wiley.

Francis, A. (1986) *New Technology at Work.* Oxford: Clarendon Press.

French, J.R.P., Caplan, R.D. and Van Harrison, R. (1982) *The Mechanisms of Job Stress and Strain.* Chichester: Wiley.

Fryer, D. and Payne, R. (1984) Proactive behaviour in unemployment. *Leisure Studies, 3*, 273–95.

Furnham, A. (1990) *The Protestant Work Ethic.* London: Routledge.

Giorgi, L. and Marsh, C. (1990) The Protestant Work Ethic as a cultural phenomenon.

European Journal of Social Psychology, 20, 499–517.

Goldthorpe, J.H., Lockwood, D., Bechofer, F. and Platt, J. (1968) *The Affluent Worker: Industrial Attitudes and Behaviour*. Cambridge: Cambridge University Press.

Gooding, R.Z. and Wagner, J. (1985) A meta-analytic review of the relationship between size and performance: the productivity and efficiency of organizations and their subunits. *Administrative Science Quarterly, 30*, 462–81.

Goodman, P.S. and Garber, S. (1988) Absenteeism and accidents in a dangerous environment: empirical analysis of underground coal mines. *Journal of Applied Psychology, 73*, 81–6.

Goodnow, J.J. and Delaney, S. (1989) Children's household work: task differences, styles of assignment, and links to family relationships. *Journal of Applied Developmental Psychology, 10*, 209–26.

Guzzo, R., Jette, R.D. and Katzell, R.A. (1985) The effects of psychologically based intervention programs on worker productivity: a meta analysis. *Personnel Psychology, 38*, 275–91.

Hackett, R.D. (1989) Work attitudes and employee absenteeism: a synthesis of the literature. *Journal of Occupational Psychology, 62*, 235–48.

Hackman, J.R. and Oldham, G.R. (1980) *Work Redesign*. Reading, MA: Addison-Wesley.

Homans, G.C. (1951) *The Human Group*. London: Routledge and Kegan Paul.

Hoppock, R. (1935) *Job Satisfaction*. New York: Harper.

House, R.J. (1971) A path-goal theory of leader effectiveness. *Administrative Science Quarterly*, 16, 321–38.

Kelvin, P. (1981) Work as a source of identity. *British Journal of Counselling and Guidance, 9*, 2–11.

Kets de Vries, M. (1977) The entrepreneurial personality: a person at the crossroads. *Journal of Management Studies, 14*, 34–57.

Lawrence, P.R. and Lorsch, J.W. (1967) *Organization and Environment*. Boston, MA: Harvard Business School.

McClelland, D.C. and Boyatzis, R.E. (1982) Leadership motive pattern and long-term success in management. *Journal of Applied Psychology, 67*, 737–43.

Macholowitz, M. (1980) *Workaholics*. Reading, MA: Addison-Wesley.

Metcalfe, B.A. (1990) Women and management. Paper to BPS Social Psychology Section Conference.

Meyer, J.P., Pauroman, S.V., Gelatly, I.R. and Goffin, R.D. (1989) Organizational commitment and job performance: it's the nature of the commitment that counts. *Journal of Applied Psychology, 74*, 152–6.

Miller, K.I. and Monge, P.R. (1986) Participation, satisfaction, and productivity: a meta-analytic review. *Academy of Management Journal, 29*, 727–53.

Mirels, H. and Garrett, J. (1971) Protestant ethic as a personality variable. *Journal of Consulting and Clinical Psychology, 36*, 40–4.

Mobley, W.H. (1982) *Employee Turnover: Causes, Consequences and Control*. Reading, MA: Addison-Wesley.

Nelson, R.E. (1989) The strength of strong ties: social networks and intergroup conflict in organizations. *Academy of Management Journal, 32*, 377–401.

Neuman, G.A., Edwards, J.E. and Raju, N.S. (1989) Organizational development interventions: a meta-analysis of their effects on satisfaction and other attitudes. *Personnel Psychology, 42*, 460–89.

Newson, J. and Newson, E. (1976) *Seven Years Old in the Home Environment*. London: Allen & Unwin.

Oborne, D.J. (1985) *Computers at Work*. Chichester: Wiley.

Pasmore, W., Francis, C. and Haldeman, J. (1984) Sociotechnical systems: a North American reflection on empirical studies of the seventies. *Human Relations, 35*, 1179–204.

Petty, M.M., McGee, G.W. and Cavender, J.W. (1984) A meta-analysis of the relationships between individual job satisfaction and individual performance. *Academy of Management Review, 9*, 712–21.

Reid, I. (1989) *Social Class Differences in Britain*. 3rd edition. London: Fontana.

Rose, R. (1983) *Getting by in Three Economies*. University of Strathclyde, Glasgow: Centre for the Study of Public Policy.

Rosenberg, M. (1957) *Occupations and Values*. Glencoe, IL: Free Press.

Sales, S.M. and House, J. (1971) Job dissatisfaction as a possible risk factor in coronary heart disease. *Journal of Chronic Diseases, 23*, 861–73.

Schmitt, N. and Noe, R. (1986) Personnel selection and equal opportunity employment. *In* C.L. Cooper and I.T. Robertson (eds) *International Review of Industrial and Organizational Psychology*. Chichester: Wiley.

Schriesheim, C.A. and Hinkin, T.R. (1990) Influence tactics used by subordinates: a theoretical and empirical analysis and refinement of the Kipnis, Schmidt, and Wilkinson subscales. *Journal of Applied Psychology, 75*, 246–57.

Steers, R.M. and Rhodes, S.R. (1984) Knowledge and speculation about absenteeism. *In* P.S. Goodman, R.S. Atkin and associates (eds) *Absenteeism*. San Francisco: Jossey-Bass.

Sundstrom, E. (1986) *Work Places*. Cambridge: Cambridge University Press.

Sundstrom, E., De Meuse, K.P. and Futrell, D. (1990) Work teams: applications and effectiveness. *American Psychologist, 45*, 120–33.

Talaga, J. and Beehr, T.A. (1989) Retirement: a psychological perspective. *In* C.L. Cooper and I.T. Robertson (eds) *International Review of Industrial and Organizational Psychology*. Chichester: Wiley.

Thomas, K. (1964) Work and leisure in pre-industrial society. *Past and Present, 29*, 50–66.

Trist, E.L., Higgins, G.W., Murray, H. and Pollock, A.B. (1963) *Organizational Choice*. London: Tavistock.

Van Zelst, R.H. (1952) Validation of a sociometric regrouping procedure. *Journal of Abnormal and Social Psychology, 47*, 299–301.

Wall, T.D. and Lischeron, J.A. (1977) *Worker Participation*. London: McGraw-Hill.

Warr, P.B. (1984) Work and unemployment. *In* P.J.D. Drenth, H. Tierry, P.J. Willems and C.J. de Wolff (eds) *Handbook of Work and Organizational Psychology*. Chichester: Wiley.

Webber, R.A. (1974) The relationship of group performance to the age of members in homogeneous groups. *Academy of Management Journal, 17*, 570–4.

Wilson, E.O. (1971) *The Insect Societies*. Cambridge, MA: Belknap.

Woodward, J. (1965) *Industrial Organization: Theory and Practice*. Oxford: Oxford University Press.

Zahrly, J. and Tosi, H. (1989) The differential effect of organizational induction processes on early work role adjustment. *Journal of Organizational Behavior, 10*, 59–74.

Chapter 5

Leisure

Leisure occupies a lot of our time and money, and is a great source of satisfaction for many – more than work for some. Others, however, don't know what to do with it, as in the case of some unemployed people who lie in bed much of the time or watch TV. The amount of leisure we have is increasing, as the working week becomes shorter, people retire earlier, and unemployment remains high because of automation and computers. It is not for social scientists to say how people should spend their spare time, but at least we can show the effects on health and happiness of different life styles. It is essential that we should understand leisure – why people need it, what kinds of satisfaction it brings, for example. Yet psychologists have been slow in getting to grips with the subject. It is also a topic for which history and sociology are needed, since the forms of leisure and indeed the concept of leisure keep changing.

THE MEANING AND MEASUREMENT OF LEISURE

The history of the idea of leisure

Do animals have leisure? They certainly relax and socialise a great deal – for example, by grooming each other – while the young of some species play. In primitive societies, and in agricultural communities more recently, there was no clear demarcation of work from leisure, while both were combined with social life, such as ritual, music, story-telling and jokes. The number of hours of actual work was about 3–4 a day, and non-work activities were regarded as more important. For the Greeks leisure was definitely superior to work, which was mainly done by slaves, and leisure consisted of music, contemplation, politics, philosophy, ritual and athletics, activities performed for their own sake, and was believed to lead to truth and happiness. For Romans, on the other hand, the most celebrated form of leisure was entertainment by lions eating Christians and similar diversions. In the Middle Ages the monks taught that intellectual and religious work were superior to manual work, but later the idea of craftsmanship gave more dignity to manual work. In the thirteenth century it is estimated that people took about one day off in three for religious and other festivals and holidays. It is with the Industrial Revolution in the seventeenth century that people started to work much longer hours, and 'work' became clearly separated from 'leisure', which was often simply a period of resting and recovering from work. The Protestant reformers gave work top priority with their concept of the Protestant work ethic (see pp. 77, 151), thus reversing earlier religious ideas about the relative importance of work and leisure. Over the last 100 years the hours of work have dropped from over 70 to 38–40 hours per week, so that there is much more time for leisure. Opportunities for leisure have become commercialised and greatly expanded, so that millions of people do the same things, and go to the same places, though most leisure time is spent watching TV (Neulinger, 1981).

There are great cultural differences in leisure, but a number of basic forms are found in most cultures. Sitting around talking, eating and drinking are universal. So is dancing, often in quite frenetic forms of folk dancing. This may be part of carnivals or fiestas, and involve a lot of dressing up, excitement and drunkenness, or it may be connected with religious festivals. There are often competitive games, which may also be violent. There is often entertainment, from singing and theatre to cock-fighting. There are arts and crafts, but it is difficult to say whether these are work or play. Leisure follows similar themes in all cultures, but takes different, and often elaborate and exotic, forms in each. There are different games, different dances, different ceremonies. It depends on the material culture. In the modern world we have seen the rise of cars, air travel, TV, and the rise and fall of the cinema.

The meaning of leisure

What does leisure mean to people? Several research techniques have been used to investigate the subjective meaning of leisure. Research using the Semantic Differential has found that leisure (compared with work) is associated with play and free time, while workers see leisure as more active than do students (Neulinger, 1981). Iso-Ahola (1980) used an experimental procedure in which subjects imagined various leisure and non-leisure situations. The main variables which caused situations to be seen as leisure were perceived freedom, intrinsic motivation (that is, satisfying as ends in themselves) and lack of relation to work. Leisure activities are enjoyable in themselves, and produce little or no external reward, though they often lead to social rewards, such as the affection and respect of others.

As we saw above, the Greeks regarded leisure as activities which were freely pursued as ends in themselves and regarded as particularly worthwhile. We may want to extend the range of activities perceived as 'leisure'.

For a long time leisure was regarded as what was done in the time left over from work. It is now recognised that this is a mistaken emphasis, since some people are not at work, and for many people leisure is more important than work. A better approach is to define leisure as those activities which people do simply because they want to, for their own sake, for fun, entertainment or self-improvement, or for goals of their own choosing, but not for material gain.

The measurement of leisure

The main method of assessing leisure is by time-budgets, preferably for a whole week, or at least a weekday and the weekends. Subjects are persuaded to keep a diary of the way they spend their non-work time. Activities are then categorised. The hours of leisure in Britain in 1989, for different kinds of person, were as shown in Figure 5.1.

A further breakdown into leisure inside and outside the home shows:

Domestic work (inc. child care)   3 hours 42 mins
Personal care (inc. sleeping, eating) 10 hours 38 mins
Leisure outside home   1 hour 39 mins
Leisure at home   4 hours 3 mins

(Gershuny and Jones, 1987)

Both of these sets of results are taken from the British General Household Survey, which interviews about 20,000 households each year and sometimes asks about leisure activities. We shall draw on this source again in the course of this Chapter.

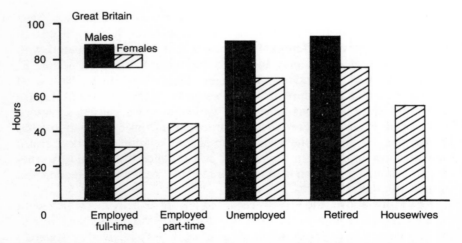

Figure 5.1 Leisure time in a typical week: by sex and employment status, 1988
Source: *Social Trends*, 1990

Table 5.1 Satisfaction with leisure

	Delighted	Pleased	Mostly satisfied	Mixed	Mostly dissatisfied	Unhappy	Terrible	Mean*
How do you feel about:								
The way you spend your spare time, your non-working activities?	11	32.5	36.5	11.5	6	1.5	1	5.25
The amount of time you have for doing the things you want to do?	6	24	33.5	16.5	13	5	2	4.7
The sports or recreation facilities you yourself use, or would like to use – I mean things like parks, bowling alleys, beaches? (14% chose not to answer this question)	9	32	33	12	7	4	3	5.0

* 1–7 scale; 'delighted' scores 7
Source: Andrews and Withey, 1976: 264

The amount of satisfaction with leisure can be obtained from direct questions, like those shown in Table 5.1, with the results from an American national sample. It can be seen that only 11 per cent were 'delighted', the top point of the scale, with their leisure activities; this compares with 15 per cent for work and 58 per cent for spouse, while only 6 per cent were delighted by the amount of leisure, and 5 per cent with their chances for relaxation.

Other measures have been used to find the degree of satisfaction with different kinds of leisure. Ragheb and Beard's scale (1980) measures satisfaction in the following areas: psychological (that is, using skills, gaining self-confidence), educational, social, relaxation, physical activity and aesthetic. Robinson (1977) asked an American national sample to rate their satisfaction with different kinds of leisure on 5-point scales (Table 5.2).

Table 5.2   Satisfaction with different leisure activities

Activity	Great satisfaction (%)
Your children	79
Your marriage	75
Your house (or apartment)	40
Religion	34
Being with friends	33
Helping others	33
Reading	32
Being with relatives	27
Making or fixing things	27
Relaxing, sitting around	27
Sports or games	26
Housework	25
Car	25
Cooking	23
Shopping	17
TV	17
Clubs	13
Politics	9

Source: Robinson, 1977

However, it is clear that the amount of satisfaction with different forms of leisure is not very closely related to the amount of time spent. The most frequent leisure activities are watching TV, walking, reading and listening to music; these are less fun than travel, mountain-climbing or skiing.

Another way of assessing leisure is in terms of its importance to those concerned, sometimes referred to as the 'quality of leisure'. Csikszentmihalyi and Kubey (1981) asked people to fill in a number of mood rating scales, while engaged in different leisure activities. They found that while watching most TV programmes people are generally found to be relaxed, cheerful and sociable; they are more drowsy, weak and passive than for reading or any other activity – for instance, work, other leisure, eating or talking. Other forms of leisure have a higher quality in terms of the greater intensity of joy, greater effort and use of skills, and experience of self-fulfilment.

Little (1987) introduced the concept of 'personal projects', most of which fall under leisure. Subjects were asked to produce a list of the various projects on which they are engaged, and then to rate them for importance, enjoyment and other scales. Certain dimensions were found to be correlated with life satisfaction: outcome (namely, success expected), feeling in control, time adequacy, and negatively with difficulty and stress.

THE PSYCHOLOGY OF LEISURE

Many 'theories' of leisure have been proposed. It has been suggested that leisure is a form of play, a source of self-fulfilment and personal growth, is for relaxation, a compensation for work or a continuation of work. It is obvious that each of these theories describes some kinds of leisure, but fails to fit others. Take play: party games are playful, serious leisure activities are not. Take relaxation: watching TV is relaxing, sport is not. Is there anything which all leisure activities have in common? Perhaps there is. By definition they are things people enjoy doing in their free time and which are rewarding in themselves (apart from some social rewards). During childhood and early life, people learn to find some activities enjoyable – certain kinds of sport, certain hobbies, for example. From this point onwards they will enjoy these activities, for their own sake, since they now provide their own rewards. An important factor in the process of developing an intrinsic interest is developing the skills, or discovering that one has the skills to perform the activity effectively.

Research on the socialisation of leisure has found that about 50 per cent of adult leisure activities began in childhood, under the influence of family (especially for girls), peer group (especially for boys) and school. These influences include passing on values; for example, that cooperation is good, or killing animals is wrong. On the other hand about 50 per cent of adult leisure activities were *not* begun in childhood but developed later. An important factor in deciding whether or not to stick with a form of leisure is perceived competence. And a number of changes of leisure are to other activities of the same type (such as games and sports, hunting and fishing), and can be regarded as substitutes which meet the same needs (Iso-Ahola, 1980).

There are a number of needs which seem to be met by leisure.

(1) Use and development of skills. Many leisure activities are experienced as intrinsically enjoyable. This is true of cycling, swimming and dancing, for example. Csikszentmihalyi (1975) found that the most satisfying elements

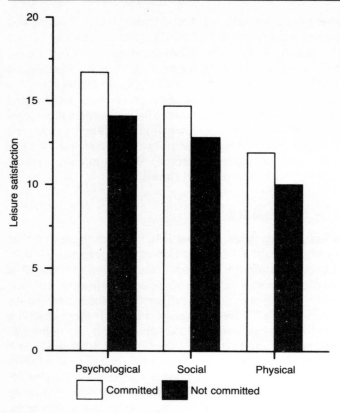

Figure 5.2 Satisfaction from serious leisure
Source: Lu and Argyle, unpublished

were enjoyment of the experience and use of skills, the activity itself (the pattern, the action, the world it provides), and development of personal skills. Similar conclusions came from a sociological study of amateurs in drama, archaeology and baseball, who were found to be deeply devoted to a disciplined and demanding form of activity which was the very opposite of relaxing (Stebbins, 1979). We have recently found that individuals who are seriously committed to a leisure activity are happier, have greater leisure satisfaction, and experience their leisure as more challenging, stressful and absorbing than those who are not (Lu and Argyle, unpublished).

(2) Social motivation. A great deal of leisure is carried out in the company of other people, and this is a major part of the satisfaction. Other people are necessary for many forms of leisure – most sports, clubs, dancing and talking, for example. We shall see that the company of friends generates immediate positive emotions, and provides help and other forms of social support.

(3) Leisure worlds. Some forms of leisure add greatly to an individual's

construction and experience of the world. Scottish country dancing, for instance, is very social, it involves the use and development of skills, and is relaxing in the sense that tensions can be discharged. But it is in addition a complete world of its own, with its calendar of events, network of relationships, music, repertoire of dances, special costumes and rituals, and it creates a great deal of joy.

(4) *Identity*. Taking up most forms of leisure adds to the self-image, and the image presented to others. Much leisure involves dressing up (even to go walking nowadays), acquiring new skills, membership of a new social group, and perhaps being an officer in it, sometimes putting on performances for others. For someone living in a house much like other houses, doing a job much like other jobs, it can be very important to be a member, even more an official, of an interesting club. It is not only punks and skinheads who put on fancy dress; Scottish country dancers, bowls players, musicians and many others have their special costumes. Mass forms of leisure do not help to give a sense of identity, with the exception of supporting sports teams, which certainly does. It is the more engrossing and less common forms of leisure that do most for identity.

(5) *Relaxation, drunkenness, and other reactions to work*. In the last century the main use of leisure was to recover from work, and relaxation is still important. It is one of the main reasons given for watching TV (60 per cent) or having holidays. It is still the case that unskilled manual workers are tired, and want to relax and watch TV at the end of the day; deep-water fishermen and some construction workers seek 'explosive compensation' for their demanding work, in drinking, fighting, drugs and promiscuous sex; advertising men and dentists play a lot of sport, perhaps to relax.

The opposite theory is that work spills over into leisure. People may take up leisure activities similar to their work – farm workers doing gardening, bank managers being treasurers of clubs, intellectuals reading or writing books. However, recent studies have found that reaction from work, and the extension of work only apply to a small section of the population, and that for most people work and leisure are unrelated. We found the same (see Figure 5.3).

A number of attempts have been made to classify leisure activities, or put them on dimensions, such as outdoor–indoor, relaxing–similar to work (Stockdale, 1987). What I shall do, however, is to discuss some of the most popular leisure activities (such as TV and sport) and group leisure activities based on the probable psychological processes involved (for example, serious leisure or social leisure).

Watching TV

This consumes more time on average than any other leisure activity. Almost everyone does it, for an average of $4^{1}/4$ hours a day for women

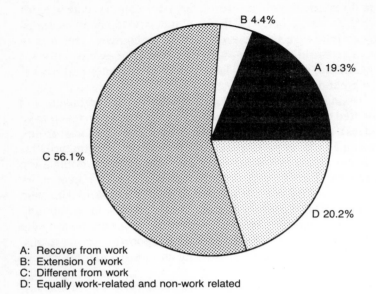

A: Recover from work
B: Extension of work
C: Different from work
D: Equally work-related and non-work related

Figure 5.3 Attitudes towards work–leisure relationship
Source: Lu and Argyle, unpublished

and 3³/4 hours a day for men. At peak times of the evening 55 per cent of the British population are doing it (Figure 5.4). There are some groups who watch more than average – women, the old and the young, those who are ill, housebound, unemployed or lonely, members of lower social classes and ethnic minority groups (Comstock *et al.*, 1978). As we showed earlier, TV is not regarded as a great source of satisfaction (Table 5.1), but is about the same as shopping and below housework. The state produced is rated as relaxed, drowsy and passive (p. 107).

Why do people spend so much time watching TV? Experiments have been done where different moods are induced, and subjects then asked to choose a TV programme to watch. Subjects who had been given a stressful puzzle to do chose a relaxing rather than an exciting film, while subjects who had been given a boring task mostly chose an exciting film (Bryant and Zillman, 1984). Evidently people can use TV to control their moods. This can be linked to the theory that leisure is a compensation for work, such as stressful work.

One of the most popular kinds of TV is 'soap opera', and it has been suggested that watching it is a kind of 'parasocial' activity – social behaviour at second hand. Livingstone (1988) carried out a content analysis of the reasons given by regular viewers for its popularity. The main ones were as follows:

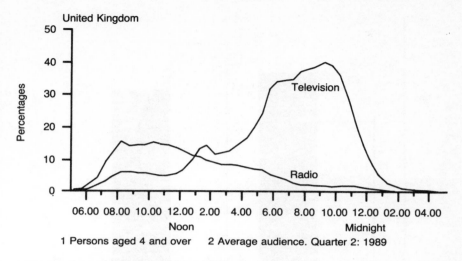

Figure 5.4 Radio and television audiences throughout the day, 1989
Source: *Social Trends*, 1990

1 *Entertainment and escapism* ('You can have a little romance, glamour, passion, love and hate in your life') (92 per cent);
2 *Realism* ('It [EastEnders] is very much a "soap of the 80s" dealing with the problems that occur in everyday life such as unemployment, racism, adultery, rape, alcoholism, and drugs') (89 per cent);
3 *Characters as extension of real-world social networks* ('I know that after a while the characters do become real people and we are concerned for their well-being just as we are for our friends and colleagues') (62 per cent);
4 *As an educational medium* ('We can relate to the situation and sometimes sort your own problems out through listening and doing what the character portrayed has done') (42 per cent);
5 *As part of daily life* ('After a while you watch it so much it becomes a regular thing to do. On Wednesdays you come home, have dinner, do your jobs, watch *Coronation Street*, wash up and then it's time for *Dallas*') (40 per cent);
6 *Emotional experience* ('When you're watching soap operas you can experience a full range of emotions from anger and despair to sheer joy, excitement and relief') (37 per cent);
7 *Keeping a critical distance* ('Many people like to watch them to laugh because we all know life is not really like that. However, even so, we like to get involved in their plots') (52 per cent).

We have found that regular watchers of soap opera have greater leisure satisfaction than irregular watchers. Frequent soap watchers are happier than infrequent watchers, but the reverse is true for frequent TV watchers in general (Figure 5.5).

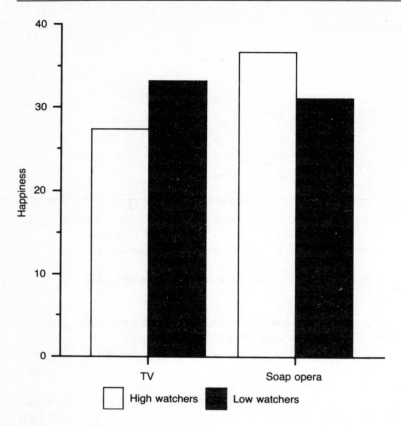

Figure 5.5 Effects of TV watching and soap opera watching on happiness
Source: Lu and Argyle, unpublished

Sport

Sport is the form of leisure which is most similar to the play of animals and children. Play, especially rough-and-tumble play, is found in the young of monkeys, cats and other species, though much less in the adults. Play and games are found in most, perhaps all, human societies, both primitive and developed, though they take different forms (Avedon and Sutton-Smith, 1971). In our own culture children are encouraged in fantasy play by mothers and older children, and also engage in rough-and-tumble play, and later in games with rules (Argyle, 1991).

Table 5.3 shows how many people take part in various kinds of sport, and how often. About 18 per cent do some outdoor sport regularly, not counting walking; 28 per cent do an indoor sport; and altogether 46 per cent do something regularly. The most common forms of sport or exercise are walking, dancing and swimming.

Table 5.3   Sport and exercise, Great Britain, 1986

	Percentages of population who participated in last 4 weeks	Days of participation per month for participants
Outdoor		
Walking 2 miles or more, inc rambling and hiking	19.1	8
Football	2.7	5
Golf	2.7	5
Athletics, inc. jogging	2.6	9
Swimming	2.4	7
Cycling	1.9	9
Fishing	1.7	4
Tennis	1.4	5
At least one outdoor, exc: walking	18.0	
inc: walking	32.0	
Indoor		
Dancing	11.0	3
Swimming	9.5	3
Snooker, billiards, pool	9.3	7
Darts	5.8	6
Keep fit, yoga	3.3	6
Squash	2.4	4
Badminton	2.1	9
Gymnastics, athletics	1.9	9
At least one indoor	28.0	
At least one indoor or outdoor	46.0	
Spectators		
At least one sport	8.0	
Football	3.1 (M 5, F 1)	

Source: Social Trends, 1986

Sport in the form of competitive games, like football and squash, is much less common. People can only engage in a sport if the facilities are available; for example, they are three times as likely to visit a park if it is within a quarter of a mile of where they live, than if it is between a half and three quarters of a mile (Burton, 1971). Skiing, mountaineering and surfing are only regularly accessible to a few. Individuals can only play a game if it has been invented, accepted into the culture, and accepted by their social class and regional sub-culture. Working-class boys in Britain do not play the Eton wall game, or Rugby Union football, and girls certainly don't. The historical development of these and other games has been studied by historians and sociologists. In Greek times sports were much more violent – the losers could be killed or mutilated. Since then sport has been civilised with elaborate rules developed, while maintaining the excitement, and later professionalised (Elias and Dunning, 1986).

Competitive games are found very enjoyable, and presumably meet psychological needs. Sport and exercise are major sources of joy (Argyle, 1987). The excitement – that is, arousal – is one such source, together with the pleasurable release of endorphins. The use of skills, especially when successful, is another. Where teams are involved there are the additional satisfactions of cooperation and leadership.

The most common forms of exercise are usually not competitive at all, as Table 5.3 shows: they are walking, dancing, swimming, jogging, cycling, keeping fit and so on. These are a little less exciting than competitive sports, but produce pleasurable bodily sensations through release of endorphins, plus the satisfaction of keeping fit, while some forms of exercise, like dancing, are highly sociable. More people watch football or tennis, and some other sports, than actually play. Watching sport is done by 8 per cent of people often once a week; 5 per cent of men and 1 per cent of women watch football, and the watching of football has been investigated most, because it has become a social problem. Spectators follow the action closely, turning their heads from side to side at tennis, and sharing bodily empathy with sports performers.

If watching TV is 'prosocial' activity, perhaps watching sport is 'parasport' – enjoying the play of others, without the need for physical effort, or the danger of getting hurt. However, there is still the danger of losing, for those closely identified with one side.

Football fans are closely identified with their teams, wear shirts or other symbols of these teams, and engage in mock-battles with supporters of rival teams. This is evidently a very important part of their lives, and an important part of their identity. The Canadian sociologist Gruneau (1983) suggested that part of what is happening is the excitement due to the symbolism of sport – 'dramatic utopian aspirations for human freedom, heroic actions and equality'. Turning to spectators of other sports, it is evident that inter-group loyalties are aroused when watching cricket and tennis, as well as football, and that great satisfaction is derived from high-level performances at any sport, perhaps especially when rare and heroic skills are involved – high diving, ski jumping and motor-racing, for example.

Social leisure

Most leisure is spent in the company of other people – friends, family, and others – who are seen only for a particular leisure activity. A lot of sport is social; indeed, it may take 2, or 22, to play at all. Some of the main social leisure activities are shown in Table 5.4.

As Table 5.4 shows, friends spend a lot of their time together talking. This takes place while walking, in one another's homes, at cafés and restaurants, while on outings together, and while taking part in shared leisure activities. Indeed, talking is an almost constant activity during the time friends are

Table 5.4   Social leisure, Great Britain, 1986

	% in last 4 weeks	Number of times
Going out for a drink	55.0	–
Going out for a meal	47.0	–
Visiting/entertaining friends or relations	94.0	–
Dancing	11.0	3.0
Cinema	8.0	2.0
Historic buildings/sites/towns	9.0	3.0
Visits to seaside	7.0	3.0
parks	4.0	3.0
countryside	3.0	3.0
Clubs and societies	12.3	3.6
Leisure classes	3.1	2.4
Amateur music/drama	4.0	11.0
Voluntary work	9.6	5.6
Bingo	9.6	5.6
Church (active members)	9.6	–
Spectators, at one sport	8.0	–
Spectators, at football	3.0 (M 5, F 1)	–

Source: Social Trends, 1986, Supplemented by Birch, 1977, for some items

together. Young people from 15 to 25 in particular spend a great deal of time together. Some conversation is sheer sociability, comparing notes about things, telling jokes or tall stories. There is also gossip and news, the discussion of common interests, which develops a common point of view, self-disclosure, and providing information and helping each other to solve problems. These conversations are usually accompanied by drinks, tea or coffee, or meals. Table 5.4 shows that 55 per cent of people had been out for a drink in the last 4 weeks; other studies show that 35 per cent of men between 18 and 24 are 'heavy' drinkers (that is, consume 7 or more glasses once a week or more (*Social Trends*)). Drinking alcohol is often a feature of social leisure. Part of the reason may be a reaction to the stresses of work. Another is that alcohol relaxes people and leads to easier social intercourse, more fun and a shared emotional state. Much drinking is governed by rules and customs, in connection with dinners and parties of various kinds.

Dancing is a highly sociable activity, and is enjoyed weekly by 11 per cent of the population. For the young it is part of courtship. At a later stage of life various forms of folk-dancing are less to do with sex, more about sociability in groups. The exercise, the use of skills, the music and the costumes contribute to a high level of joy.

Many people belong to clubs, classes and groups of a variety of kinds, from church to aerobics, chess to hang-gliding, and meet once a week or more. There is cooperation over the activities of the group, whether it is singing, praying, talking or dancing. There is cooperation over running the affairs of the club, and many people are, or have been, officials of some kind. There are a number of forms of social satisfaction here in addition to the joint activities – being a member of the in-group, being a leader, giving and receiving social support (Argyle, 1991).

Table 5.4 also shows the considerable number of people who attend clubs, classes and societies of various kinds. Another study found that 53 per cent of Londoners belonged to clubs, and that 16 per cent were officials in them. We show later that belonging to teams and clubs is a source of happiness, and so are parties and dances. Clubs are a major setting for leisure activities of a number of kinds. They are the main setting for most serious leisure, standards of excellence are sought, there is a high level of effort, and training or coaching is needed, so that a hierarchy of expertise and leadership develops.

Social leisure, of a variety of kinds, is a source of social support, and hence of health, mental health and happiness, as we shall see in later Chapters. Social support is partly derived from actual help, and from information. In the family it is derived from intimate relationships. Social leisure produces another kind of social support, based mainly on companionship, cooperation and coordination, acceptance and embeddedness in a group engaged in enjoyable activities (Argyle, 1991).

An impressive number of people in Britain engage in some kind of voluntary work; that is, do work for others that is unpaid. About 25 per cent of the population do some, 10 per cent once a week or more. There is advice and counselling, such as the Citizens' Advice Bureau and the Samaritans. There are emergency services, like the St John's Ambulance Association, Red Cross and the Royal National Life-Boat Institution; environmental organisations like the Royal Society for the Protection of Birds, and the Royal Society for Nature Conservation; for helping young people, like the YMCA; for helping old people, like Meals on Wheels; for the ill or disabled, like the Disabled Information and Advice Centre; and hundreds of others. The most active voluntary helpers are women, and 48 per cent of middle-class women are active in some way.

Home-based leisure

We saw on p. 104 that on average people spend just over 4 hours a day in leisure at home. Table 5.5 shows what they are doing. We saw in Table 5.2 that these are among the most satisfying leisure activities – children, marriage, houses, reading, making or fixing things.

Only about half the population read books at all, but those who do get through a large number, and enjoy this a great deal. Reading comes well above TV-watching, and above sport, in surveys of satisfaction with leisure activities (p. 106). Most of these books are about spies, detectives, love or adventure, and probably provide similar satisfaction to TV soap opera and watching dangerous sports. The public library is used mostly by more educated people.

Table 5.5 Participation in home-based leisure activities by socio-economic group, Great Britain, 1986 (persons aged 16 or over)

	Total
Watching TV	99
Visiting/entertaining friends or relations	95
Listening to radio	88
Listening to records/tapes	73
Reading books	60
Gardening	46
DIY	43
Dressmaking/needlework/knitting	27
Base = 100%	19529

Source: Social Trends, 1986

Many people do gardening, and like Scottish dancing it provides a variety of satisfactions. It is not very sociable, apart from chats over the garden fence. It is relaxing perhaps, but also hard work. It does involve the use of a variety of skills and the development of expertise. But it is a lot more; it is a world of its own, an enduring interest and concern. It also includes some sources of joy described in Chapter 11, of simply being in the garden on a nice afternoon. A similar story could be told about almost every leisure world – sailing, skiing, horse-riding, ballroom-dancing, greyhound-racing, pigeon-fancying, video games, ham radio and so on.

Holidays

In recent years 60 per cent of British people went away for a holiday each year, 20 per cent of them twice or more. Sixty-eight per cent of these holidays were in Britain, the remainder mostly in Spain and France. The most common places to stay were hotels, followed by friends' or relatives' houses, rented accommodation and holidays camps and others went camping and caravanning. Most people go with family or a friend, most want to relax, or to indulge themselves; the workaholics, however, are eager to get back to work, or they take it with them. While on holiday most people are in better physical and psychological health – they feel less tired, irritable, anxious and constipated, and are less likely to have headaches, insomnia or stomach trouble, and have more interest in sex (Rubenstein, 1980).

Outings are made to historical buildings and places (like Oxford), and to more or less serious walking and hiking, often in beautiful forest or mountain areas. This can be a source of aesthetic satisfaction, of agreeable exercise, and of social satisfaction, at the same time. There is a strong tendency for middle-class people, and of course those with cars, to enjoy the wilderness more.

GENDER, AGE AND CLASS

Gender

There are a number of interesting differences between the leisure of men and women. The sheer quantity of leisure time is greater for men. See Table 5.6.

Table 5.6   Leisure, minutes per day

	Males	Females
Outside the home	110	89
Inside the home	270	218
Total	380	307

(See also Figure 5.1.)

There are also differences in what they do. Men spend more time on:

sport, especially competitive sport,
clubs and pubs – the pub culture is important for many men,
drinking,
gardening and DIY.

Women spend more time on:

home-based leisure,
watching TV,
bingo (except professional women),
dressmaking, sewing and knitting,
watching sport (except football),
voluntary work (especially middle-class women).
(Gershuny and Jones, 1987; Smith, 1987)

However, for many women leisure is not entirely leisure, since it often consists of domestic work and child-care, or is combined with these. What sounds like the same activity may not be the same at all. 'Going swimming' for women may consist mainly of preventing children from drowning. The same is true of walking, watching TV, and all home-based leisure. Looking after children is a combination of work and leisure. Some of it is more like leisure (going to the zoo, playing games); sometimes it is work (such as feeding infants in the middle of the night). It has effects on the whole pattern of life, including making other leisure activities less accessible.

There is some evidence that men and women seek different kinds of satisfaction from leisure. Shamir and Ruskin (1983) compared Israeli husbands and wives: the men were interested in competitive sports, hard training and fitness, the women in getting to know people, the expression of artistic tendencies, relaxing and relieving tension.

Age

Leisure varies not so much with age as with the family life cycle. Hours of leisure are as follows:

Table 5.7   Leisure, minutes per day, 1983–84, Great Britain

	Younger, no children	Children < 5	Children 5 – 14	Older, no children
Outside the home	133	85	91	95
Inside the home	245	209	241	265
Total	378	294	332	360

Source: Gershuny and Jones, 1987

We shall look briefly at leisure for different points in the life cycle. Children like to play, but are often bored, don't know what to do and have to be entertained or put in front of the TV. This shows that to some extent we have to learn how to enjoy leisure.

Adolescents are interested in the opposite sex, the peer group and becoming independent of parents. Their main leisure pursuits include activities that are designed to cater almost exclusively for teenagers or are undertaken in groups: dancing, youth clubs, drinking, dating, going on the town, and 'hanging around' with friends (Hendry, 1989). There is a transition in this period of life, from clubs and other activities organised by adults, to commercially run establishments. There is still some interest in sports, though this drops sharply after leaving school.

Working-class youths often join noisy and sometimes aggressive sub-groups, such as football hooligans, punks and skinheads, regarded by sociologists as symbolic attempts to solve identity problems and the frustration of boring jobs or unemployment. Working-class youth is a distinctive sub-culture, quite different from other ages and classes, and it is mainly defined by its leisure activities. Middle-class youths are still in education, and have a wealth of leisure opportunities.

Young adults enjoy a lot of leisure before they have children. Then there is a sudden break, as the table above shows. There is less time for leisure, both inside and outside the home, especially for women. There are fewer outings of all kinds, though working-class men still go to the pub, middle-class men play golf and other sports, and working-class women play bingo. The pub forms another sub-culture, again based on leisure, this time mainly for working-class men. Some home-based leisure stays at the same level – TV, radio, friends, though often combined with child-care. Time spent reading and listening to records falls, perhaps because it is less easily combined with parenting (Smith, 1987; Rapoport and Rapoport, 1975).

Some activities, however, reach a peak in middle life: active sports and female voluntary work at 30–39, dancing and theatre-going at 40–59. Gardening and walking scarcely decline at all. Older people do less of most things, and especially:

> sport and exercise (16 per cent swim at 16–20, 1 per cent at 70),
> going out for a drink,
> going to the cinema,
> listening to records or tapes.

Older people do *more* TV watching: 37 hours 25 minutes per week at 65+, compared with 18 hours 34 mins for 4–15. For older adults, physical activity declines, and home-based leisure is important, such as TV and gardening.

Retired people have a great deal of time for leisure. However, the trend is towards more television watching, and other 'passive' leisure, and gardening, shopping and helping in the house. There is little increase after retirement in active leisure pursuits such as voluntary work and membership of clubs, although 48 per cent of retired men say they have time on their hands that they do not know what to do with, compared with 10 per cent of those of the same age still at work (Parker, 1983). Those who are above average in education, health and wealth usually enjoy themselves by pursuing leisure activities which had been developed before, and also by finding new activities. Others find retirement boring and frustrating, because they have lost the satisfaction of work and do not have leisure activities with which to replace them (Parker, 1983) (see p. 294ff).

Osgood and Howe (1984) reviewed a number of studies of the effects of age on leisure, and concluded that from ages 20 to 35 the main interest is in vigorous exercise and courtship, from 35 to 55 in home-based activities, spectating and clubs, and from 55+ in reading, gardening, handicrafts and contemplation.

Social class

Although the hours of leisure available are much the same in all social classes, working-class people engage less in most forms of leisure. This is partly because middle-class people spend more on leisure (18.5 per cent of their larger incomes versus 11.8 per cent for poorer people). They also have more space and facilities in their houses, and they have cars to get them to leisure facilities. Some forms of leisure are popular in all classes – watching TV, listening to the radio, reading the paper, gardening, walking, dancing.

Let us look first at the kinds of leisure which are pursued more by working-class individuals. They watch TV more (4 hours 52 minutes in classes DE versus 2 hours 49 minutes in AB), and they mainly watch ITV. Working-class people do the football pools more (46 per cent WC males v. 28 per cent MC males), bet more, the men play darts more (21 per cent versus 11 per cent), and fish more (D 10 per cent versus AB 5 per cent), and the women go to bingo more (15 per cent versus 1 per cent).

Middle-class people, however, engage in most leisure activities more.

Sport

There are some large class differences here: in the percentages saying that they played or took part in various sports:

	AB	E
Swimming	30	$12^1/_2$
Squash (males)	16	3
Hiking	14	$7^1/_2$
Tennis	12	$3^1/_2$
Golf (males)	20	5

Source: Reid, 1989

The reason middle-class people engage in so much exercise may be due to their more sedentary jobs, and because they have heard of the benefits of health; manual workers (though not clerical ones) get plenty of exercise at work.

The most popular forms of working-class sport are dancing and football (little class difference), darts and fishing. We needn't try too hard to explain all these differences. As a result of historical factors, only certain leisure activities are acceptable in each social class. And engaging in the right form of leisure is a form of self-presentation, of proclaiming one's class.

Social leisure

All classes go to pubs. Class I people are twice as likely to belong to clubs (17 per cent versus 9 per cent for class VI) and much more likely to go to restaurants regularly (77 per cent versus 28 per cent) or theatres. Working-class people are much less likely to engage in a lot of very cheap or free social leisure as well, like leisure classes, voluntary work, amateur music or drama, or going to church.

Home-based leisure

Middle-class people have more hobbies (Class I, 21 per cent; Class VI, 2 per cent), read and buy more books, use the public library more, do somewhat more gardening (61 per cent versus 38 per cent), but less dressmaking (10 per cent versus 28 per cent). The striking difference for hobbies may be due to costs or facilities needed.

Holidays and outings

Middle-class people of course have more holidays, and they are more likely to go abroad. Among DE people 42 per cent have no holiday at all versus 9 per cent of AB people. Middle-class people also go on more outings to beauty spots, stately homes and art galleries. This is partly because they have more cars; and middle-class folk with cars drive them a lot further (Reid, 1989).

The upper and middle classes of earlier times valued leisure above work; indeed, many of them did no work at all. Veblen, in his famous *Theory of the Leisure Class* (1899), showed how rich people engaged in conspicuous consumption and time-wasting, to show that they had no need to work, and had plenty of money and time to burn.

The unemployed, like the retired, appear to have a great deal of leisure, except that it doesn't seem like that to them. Here is how a sample of 1,043 unemployed British people said that they spent their time.

Table 5.8   How the unemployed spend their time, UK, 1982

	Morning		Afternoon		Total
	Men (%)	Women (%)	Men (%)	Women (%)	(%)
Housework	19	49	7	21	19
Shopping	20	26	9	17	16
Job hunting	22	16	12	13	16
Visiting friends or relatives	6	10	12	17	10
Gardening	14	2	13	3	11
TV	4	2	14	12	8.5
Reading	9	5	8	10	8
Decorating	7	3	7	2	5.5
Walking	5	3	8	2	5.5
Nothing/sitting around	3	3	9	6	5.5
Staying in bed	8	8	1	0	4.5
Visiting town	5	7	3	4	4.5
Playing sport	4	1	4	0	3
Drinking	2	1	3	1	2

Source: Social Trends, 1984

The main actual leisure activities were gardening (partly for material gain probably, therefore not true leisure), TV watching and reading. Very little time appears to be spent on any serious leisure. The unemployed drink and smoke more than others, and evidently have a lot of time on their hands 'hanging about' and staying in bed.

PERSONALITY

How far are choice and enjoyment of leisure due to individual differences in personality? Some dimensions of personality have been found to affect leisure. For example, Furnham (1981) found that extraverts are more likely to choose activities that are social or involve physical activity, or both, like dancing and sports. We found that if people are asked to discuss the most enjoyable recent events, extraverts mainly talked about social events, and to some extent physical activity, while introverts were more likely to mention solitary events such as 'parasocial' ones like watching TV. A related dimension is 'sensation-seeking'. This dimension describes those individuals who seek high levels of stimulation, sometimes by means of risky behaviour like motor racing, parachute-jumping and motor-cycling (Zuckerman, 1979). People also avoid situations which they can't cope with. Socially inadequate people, for example, commonly avoid parties or other social situations which cause them social anxiety.

Individuals differ in the strength of a whole range of needs or motivations which are related to leisure. Need for stimulation is one, need for social interaction is another, and many more have been proposed and measured (for example, Kabanoff, 1982). A number of studies have shown how different leisure activities meet different needs.

Leisure choice depends partly on abilities. People don't enjoy leisure activities unless they are reasonably good at them; this is necessary in order to enjoy using the skill, producing positive results and receiving the approval of others. Gardening is not very satisfying if nothing grows, nor is tennis if you miss the ball or it always goes into the net. Several studies have found that perceived ability is a strong predictor of taking up a leisure activity (Stockdale, 1987). Social skills are important here. Women who are socially competent are more likely to take up voluntary work and go to evening classes; those who are less competent are more likely to do sewing, knitting and crosswords (Paulhus and Christie, 1981). Ability is more important for some activities than others. Unless you are some good it is hard to play cricket or football at all; competence is important for tennis, squash and other competitive sports. Competence is less important for jogging, aerobics, walking or swimming – the most popular sports. The explanation for the enjoyment of activities requiring competence may be that a sense of control is a source of satisfaction and well-being (Propst and Kurtz, 1989). Or there may be a more basic satisfaction in the practice of skills which have been mastered.

Table 5.9   Factor analysis of 'Participation' scale

	Items	1	2	3	4	5
28	gardening	.75				
34	sleeping	−.72				
32	dressmaking/knitting	.65				
7	card games	.63				
1	chat with friend	−.62				
16	reading detective story	.61				
4	country walk	.56				
31	DIY	.56				
22	pottering about house	.52				
21	exercise	.51				
30	driving	.30				
9	quiet family evening		.56			
26	reading newspaper		.53			
35	walking by yourself		.51			
29	travelling		.51			
27	reading magazines		.48			
17	reading non-fiction		.47			
19	pop music		.47			
18	music (classic/jazz)		.47			
13	soap opera		.30			
24	film and video			.69		
36	social club			.55		
3	pubs			.52		
12	other sports			.46		
11	team sports			.44		
15	reading novel				.65	
14	TV				.58	
2	noisy party				−.55	
37	long bath				.48	
10	debates				−.47	
20	dancing				−.46	
5	meeting new people				−.40	
6	party games					.68
8	jokes/funny stories					.61
25	cinema					.59
33	sunbathing					.43
23	writing letters					.31
Reliability alpha		.80	.64	.60	.60	.57
Variance explained		14.2	9.5	7.7	6.5	5.3

Source: Argyle and Lu, 1990

It is probably a combination of motivation and skills which can result in a leisure activity becoming a 'central life interest' (Dubin, 1963) or a 'personal project' (Little, 1987), and thus an important part of the personality. When this happens leisure may become more important than work.

Another way of studying the relation of leisure to personality is to look for types of person as defined by their leisure activities. Argyle and Lu (1990) studied preferences for 39 leisure activities by 136 people, and found the factors shown in Table 5.9

There is a link with extraversion here: extraverts scored highly on factors 3 (teams and clubs) and 4 (dances, noisy parties, no long baths); these 2 factors also correlated with happiness, and partly explained the happiness of extraverts.

LEISURE AND WELL-BEING

Work is overall a greater source of satisfaction than leisure. However, 32 per cent of men and 36 per cent of women with jobs find leisure and work equally satisfying, and 19 per cent find leisure more satisfying (Veroff *et al.*, 1981). And of course housewives, the unemployed, the young and the old have *only* leisure to satisfy them. Retired people are on average happier than those at work. So it follows that individuals can be satisfied with leisure alone (Argyle, 1987). Does leisure affect overall happiness or well-being? The importance of leisure as a source of happiness has come out differently in different studies. In some of them, leisure was the most important predictor, more important than income or health, while these factors were important because of their effect on leisure. Leisure has been found to be particularly important in studies of old people (Stockdale, 1987). One problem with this research is that leisure is often carried out with family or friends, and it is difficult to separate the benefits from these relationships. When they *are* separated, leisure is found to be particularly important for the unmarried (Iso-Ahola, 1980).

We said earlier that certain kinds of leisure can be recommended, not from value judgements that poetry is better than drinking, but on the basis of which kind of leisure is found to be best for individuals. Certain kinds of leisure have specific benefits. Exercise and sport are very good for health, and also have a definite effect on positive mood, as many studies have shown (Wood, 1985). The effect appears to be partly physiological, through nor-adrenaline or the endorphins stimulating the pleasure centres. In addition there is usually social activity, and there may be satisfaction in achievement, or self-image gratification through dressing up in impressive sporting gear.

Leisure can be beneficial for mental health. Exercise relieves depression, and reduces anxiety, as well as benefiting physical health. Social leisure, such as spending time with friends and belonging to clubs, is a major source of social support. Relaxing forms of leisure, including TV watching and holidays, can relieve stress. We found that watching soap opera is related to a high level of happiness; a number of gratifications may be involved as shown above (p. 111). American studies have found that wilderness experiences are very good for relieving tension (Iso-Ahola, 1980). We have found that commitment to serious leisure activities is a cause of happiness and mental health.

These principles have led to a form of treatment for depression. In 'pleasant activities therapy' individuals keep a diary for a month, of pleasant events each day and their mood for each day. Computer analysis is then used to discover which activities have the greatest effect on mood for each person, and he or she is then encouraged to engage in these activities more often (Lewinsohn, Sullivan and Grosscup, 1982). Follow-up studies have reported positive results, for both patients and normals, especially when the treatment is combined with goal-setting or self-monitoring, and when the activities are freely chosen.

It is widely agreed that education for leisure should start in childhood, since leisure activities that become intrinsically rewarding in childhood continue to be enjoyed later in life. This can perhaps be done by helping and encouraging children to engage in a variety of leisure activities, but not with external rewards (Iso-Ahola, 1980). This can be continued in school if there is a wide liberal education, and extra-curricular activities, as well as training to pass exams.

Proposals, mainly in the USA, have been made for the development of 'leisure counselling'. Tests have been developed to assess, for example, whether individuals have an adequate conception of leisure, and how far they are enjoying it. Pleasant activities therapy is a special case of leisure counselling, and shows too that some people are not aware of what they enjoy doing most. Workaholics, who are only happy when working and do not enjoy holidays, are a group who have not found how to enjoy leisure. The largest group of all are the many individuals who just watch TV, which we have seen is a quite low-grade and not very satisfying leisure activity.

COULD LEISURE REPLACE WORK?

This is an important practical question for the retired, for housewives and for the unemployed. The retired are now living longer, and the unemployed are probably going to become more numerous. We have just seen that *some* people find leisure more satisfying than work, and that on average retired people are happier than those at work, though the unemployed are much less happy.

Fryer and Payne (1984, p. 93) located 11 people who had lost their jobs, and found more satisfying things to do while unemployed. McGoldrick (1982) studied 1,800 men who had retired early and their wives, who had found very interesting and satisfying things to do – serious hobbies and so on. Another group who seem to have had no problems with leisure were probably the 'idle rich' who lived on inherited wealth, before World War II, in Britain and elsewhere. As far as we can see they were perfectly happy, in part perhaps because they had never heard of the Protestant work ethic. Perhaps it was also because they led a fairly orderly way of life, undertook extensive duties (such as running estates) and country pursuits.

There is one feature of work which it is difficult for leisure to match, and that is pay. It seems to be necessary for those who are working to be given a financial incentive to do so: that is, they must be paid more than those who are not working, or many jobs would never be done at all. It follows that the 'working class' will inevitably be of higher status than the 'leisure class', contrary to earlier arrangements.

Work provides a range of satisfactions, as was shown in the last Chapter. Can leisure match them? Does it need to match them anyway if leisure can provide different satisfactions? For those who have internalised the PWE leisure will seem inferior and unimportant if it does not have qualities similar to work. Some kinds of leisure do have these work-like qualities. Leisure can be serious, of use to others, meet high standards, be done in a group, use skills and lead to recognition of excellence. Some of the activities of McGoldrick's retired sample certainly had these properties.

The alternative is to wean people away from the PWE – after all, it really is no longer necessary for everyone to work all the time, as it was once. They can learn the values of a 'leisure ethic' instead, perhaps. Scales have been constructed to measure acceptance of the leisure ethic. They contain items like 'the fewer hours one spends working and the more leisure time available, the better', and 'success means having time to pursue leisure activities'. Measures of leisure ethic by such scales reveal that it is accepted more by low-status and younger people; it is negatively related to the PWE and conservatism (Furnham, 1990).

While pursuing the goals of freedom, spontaneity, playfulness and relaxation may produce a lot of fun and relaxation, unless part of leisure is felt to be worthwhile and useful, and to be attaining certain standards there is a danger that life satisfaction will fall.

CONCLUSIONS

Leisure is a new field for psychology, though it takes up more time and is more important than work for many people. It has a complex history, and has been contrasted with work since the Industrial Revolution. People learn to enjoy certain leisure activities in childhood; these are satisfying because they use skills, are done with others, contribute to identity, open up new fields of experience, and for some compensate for work. Watching TV, especially soap opera, is now the most widespread leisure activity:

it relaxes and controls moods and provides a second-hand social life. Other home-based leisure is with children, DIY, reading and gardening. Many people engage in sport and in non-competitive exercise. There are a variety of social forms of leisure, eating, drinking, talking, clubs and voluntary work.

Women have a different pattern of leisure from men, much of it more child-care than leisure. Young people have a lot of leisure outside the home, but much leisure reaches a peak in middle age. Middle-class people have much more active leisure, such as exercise, hobbies and holidays. The unemployed make little constructive use of their free time.

Personality affects the choice and enjoyment of leisure; extraverts choose social activities more. People choose the sports and other activities they are good at. Leisure is a major source of satisfaction, more than work for many people. Certain kinds of leisure are good for happiness, health and mental health.

Much leisure is very similar to work, apart from not being paid. With the decline of work, its partial replacement by constructive leisure may be the shape of the future.

REFERENCES

Andrews, F.M. and Withey, S.B. (1976) *Social Indicators of Well-Being*. New York and London: Plenum.

Argyle, M. (1987) *The Psychology of Happiness*. London: Methuen.

——(1991) *Cooperation: the Basis of Sociability*. London: Routledge.

Argyle, M. and Lu, L. (1990) The happiness of extraverts. *Personality and Individual Differences, 11,* 1255–61.

Avedon, E.M. and Sutton-Smith, B. (eds) (1971) *The Study of Games*. New York: Wiley.

Birch, F. (1979) Leisure patterns 1973 and 1977. *Population Trends, 17,* 2–8.

Bryant, J. and Zillman, D. (1984) Using television to alleviate boredom as a function of induced excitational states. *Journal of Broadcasting, 28,* 1–20.

Burton, T.L. (1971) *Experiments in Recreation Research*. London: Allen & Unwin.

Comstock, G. (1980) *Television in America*. Beverly Hills, CA: Sage.

Comstock, G., Chaffee, S., Katzman, N., McCombs, M. and Roberts, D. (1978) *Television and Human Behavior*. New York: Columbia University Press.

Csikszentmihalyi, M. (1975) *Beyond Boredom and Anxiety*. San Francisco: Jossey-Bass.

Csikszentmihalyi, M. and Kubey, R. (1981) Television and the rest of life: a systematic comparison of subjective experiences. *Public Opinion Quarterly, 45,* 317–28.

Dubin, R. (1956) Industrial workers' worlds: a study of the central life interests of industrial workers. *Social Problems, 3,* 131–42.

Dunning, E. (1988) *The Roots of Football Hooliganism*. London: Routledge and Kegan Paul.

Elias, N. and Dunning, E. (1986) *Quest for Excitement*. Oxford: Blackwell.

Fryer, D. and Payne, R. (1984) Proactive behaviour in unemployment: findings and implications. *Leisure Studies, 3,* 273–95.

Furnham, A. (1981) Personality and activity preference. *British Journal of Social Psychology, 20*, 57–68.

——(1990) *The Protestant Work Ethic*. London: Routledge.

Gershuny, J. and Jones, S. (1987) The changing work/leisure balance in Britain 1961–1984. *In* J. Horne, D. Jary and A. Tomlinson. *Sport, Leisure and Social Relations*. London: Routledge and Kegan Paul.

Gruneau, R. (1983) *Class, Sports and Social Development*. Amherst: University of Massachusetts Press.

Hendry, L.B. (1981) *Adolescents and Leisure*. London: SSRC/Sports Council.

Iso-Ahola, S.E. (1980) *The Social Psychology of Leisure and Recreation*. Dubuque, IA: W. C. Brown Co.

Kabanoff, B. (1982) Occupational and sex differences in leisure needs and leisure satisfaction. *Journal of Occupational Behaviour, 3*, 233–45.

Lewinsohn, P.M., Sullivan, J.M. and Grosscup, S.J. (1982) Behavioral therapy: clinical applications. *In* A.J. Rush (ed.) *Short-term Therapies for Depression*. New York: Guilford.

Little, B.R. (1987) Personal projects analysis: a new methodology for counselling psychology. *Natcon, 13*, 591–614.

Livingstone, S. (1990) *Making Sense of Television*. Oxford: Pergamon.

Livingstone, S.M. (1988) Why people watch soap opera: an analysis of the explanations of British viewers. *European Journal of Communication, 3*, 55–80.

Lu, L. and Argyle, M. (unpublished).

McGoldrick, A. (1982) Early retirement: a new leisure opportunity. *Work and Leisure. 15*, 73–89.

Marsh, P. and Harré, R. (1978) The world of football hooligans. *Human Nature, 1*, 62–9.

Marsh, P., Rosser, E. and Harré, R. (1978) *The Rules of Disorder*. London: Routledge and Kegan Paul.

Neulinger, J. (1981) *The Psychology of Leisure*. 2nd edition. Springfield, IL: Thomas.

Osgood, N.J. and Howe, C.Z. (1984) Psychological aspects of leisure: a life-cyclle developmental perspective. *Society and Leisure, 7*, 175–95.

Parker, S. (1983) *Leisure and Work*. London: Allen & Unwin.

Paulhus, D. and Christie, R. (1981) Sphere of control: an interactionist approach to assessment of perceived control. *In* H.M. Lefcourt (ed.) *Research with Locus of Control*. Vol. 1. New York: Academic Press.

Propst, D.B. and Kurtz, M.E. (1989) Perceived control/reactance: a framework for understanding leisure behaviour in natural settings. *Leisure Studies, 8*, 241–8.

Ragheb, M.G. and Beard, J.G. (1980) Leisure satisfaction: concept, theory and measurement. *In* S.E. Iso-Ahola (ed.) *Social Psychological Perspectives on Leisure and Recreation*. Springfield, IL: Thomas.

Rapoport, R. and Rapoport, R.N. (1975) *Leisure and the Family Life Cycle*. London: Routledge and Kegan Paul.

Reid, I. (1989) *Social Class Differences in Britain*. London: Fontana.

Robinson, J.P. (1977) *How Americans Use Time*. New York and London: Praeger.

Rubenstein, C. (1980) Vacations. *Psychology Today, 13*, May, 62–75.

Shamir, B. and Ruskin, H. (1983) Sex differences in recreational sport behaviour and attitudes: a study of married couples in Israel. *Leisure Studies, 2*, 253–68.

Smith, J. (1987) Men and women at play: gender, life cycle and leisure. *In* J. Horne, D. Jary and A. Tomlinson (eds) *Sport, Leisure and Social Relations*. London: Routledge and Kegan Paul.

Stebbins, R.A. (1979) *Amateurs*. Beverly Hills, CA: Sage.

Stockdale, J.E. (1987) *Methodological Techniques in Leisure Research*. London: Sports Council and ESRC.

Suttler, G. (1972) *The Social Construction of Communities*. Chicago: University of Chicago Press.

Veblen, T. (1899) *The Theory of the Leisure Class*. New York: American Library.

Veroff, J., Douvan, E. and Kulka, R.A. (1981) *The Inner American*. New York: Basic Books.

Wood, C. (1985) The healthy neurotic. *New Scientist*, Feb., pp. 12–15.

Zuckerman, M. (1979) *Sensation-Seeking: Beyond the Optimal Level of Arousal*. Hillsdale, NJ: Erlbaum.

Chapter 6

Religious beliefs, behaviour and experience

For those involved, religion is another sphere of human quest and fulfilment, like relationships and work, or like health and happiness. Those not involved may see it in a more negative way. I shall treat religion in an empirical manner, and enquire later in the chapter about the effects of religion on other aspects of behaviour.

What is the point of studying religious activities psychologically? My aim is to extend our understanding of the whole of human life, including religion. If a psychological account can be found it does not follow that religion has been 'explained away'. The psychology of politics is a parallel case. The main causes of voting are known, so that it is possible to predict how others will vote. But psychologists also vote themselves – for the party which they think will bring about the kind of society they want, and about which they may have sophisticated ideas. The psychology of music is another example. In some universities music students have to take courses in physics, not to explain music away, but to help them understand better how sound is produced. Growing roses is another example. It takes an artist or poet to help us realise the beauty of the rose, but it needs a horticulturalist to grow them well. In each of these cases the subjective vision is quite separate from the scientific analysis of the causes of the experience. And in each case it is agreed that the experience is valuable in its own right. Other examples could be given, with different implications for religion, such as the psychology of dreams and optical illusions. I shall, however, adopt a 'non-ontological' point of view, and simply treat religion as a very interesting sphere of human activity.

Watts and Williams (1988) have recently tried to provide a psychological model for religious 'knowledge'. They suggest that it is like perceiving a work of art, like empathic knowledge of another person, and like the insights and understanding achieved by a patient in psychotherapy. This is an intuitive, partly emotional process, rather than a rational one, and is achieved by great effort.

THE MEASUREMENT OF RELIGIOUS ACTIVITY

There are a number of different ways in which people can be 'religious'; all are important, but they are not very highly correlated with one another.

Church membership looks like a useful measure, since it represents some degree of formal belonging and commitment. It can also be used to trace historical changes, the rise and fall of different churches. However, different churches count their members differently. The Roman Catholics count all baptised people in the area, the Church of England usually counts Easter communicants, while the non-conformist churches count those aged over 13 or 14 who have been placed on the roll of the church. And the criteria may change from time to time.

Frequency of church attendance is the most widely used index. It is usually obtained by asking questions, so there is some upward distortion of the true figure. The Roman Catholic Church exerts more pressure than others for sheer attendance. And although some regular attenders may believe little, nevertheless this is valuable as an objective measure, and it does correlate with other measures of religious activity.

Other religious behaviour. The saying of private prayers daily is a measure of a higher degree of devotion than going to church once a week. In the UK 44 per cent of people report daily prayers, compared with 14 per cent weekly attendance, but the nature and duration of such prayers is not known. About 11 per cent read the Bible daily. Donations to the church are another index. Members of the Church of England give 1.6 per cent of income, some people 'tithe', that is, give 10 per cent of income after tax.

Beliefs. About 75 per cent of people in Britain believe in a God of some kind, but only half of them believe in God as a kind of person who watches over them. About half the population believe in an after-life; we shall discuss later what they think it will be like. About 1 in 3 believe that Jesus can save them from sins, 25 per cent that the Bible miracles really happened, and 21 per cent believe in the Devil. Quite a lot of inconsistency is found here; for example, some do not believe in God but pray sometimes, others believe in the divinity of Christ but not in God, and so on.

Religious experience. These are usually assessed by questions like 'Would you say that you have ever had a "religious or mystical experience" – that is, a moment of sudden religious insight or awakening?' In this country about 35 per cent of people say that they have had such an experience. As we shall see later, there are quite a variety of such experiences, and this type of question biases the replies towards solitary experience.

Attitudes towards religion or the church have been measured by attitude scales. This has led to an important distinction between 'extrinsic' and 'intrinsic' religiosity. Examples of the intrinsic items are: 'My religious beliefs are what really lie behind my whole approach to life'; and 'The prayers I say when I am alone carry as much meaning and personal emotion as those said by me during services'. Examples of extrinsic items are: 'One reason for my being a church member is that such memberships help to establish a person in the community'; and 'What religion offers most is comfort when some misfortune strikes' (Allport, 1966).

We can now provide a picture of the state of religion in Britain in the late 1980s (Table 6.1).

Table 6.1   Religion in Britain, average of several surveys, late 1980s

	Gallup Poll, 1986	Gerard, 1985	Other sources
Believe in God	68	76	71[1]
Personal God	31	31	
Spirit or Life Force	41	39	
Atheists		4	
Heaven	52	57	
Hell	21	27	
The Devil	21	30	
Jesus was Son of God	48		
Weekly church attendance			19[1]
Monthly church attendance			27[1]
Have had religious or spiritual experience		19	34[2]
Daily Bible reading			11[3]
Daily prayer			44[3]
Belong to church group			22[3]
Donation to church (% of income)			1.6[3]

Other sources
1 NOP, 1985
2 Argyle and Beit-Hallahmi, 1975
3 Hay and Heald, 1987

RELIGIOUS BELIEFS

Max Weber (1922) thought that religion provides a solution to the irrational problems of life – suffering, illness, unfairness and evil. Others have developed this theme, and have suggested a longer list of problems which can be solved by religion: (1) Intellectual problems such as 'How did the world begin?', 'What is the purpose of life?' and others to which no answer is provided by science or common sense. (2) Unacceptable aspects of life, such as suffering and death. (3) Particular forms of frustration and unfairness, such as the lot of underprivileged individuals and groups. (4) Natural phenomena not yet explained by the local scientists, such as eclipses of the sun and lightning, for primitive tribes. (5) Natural phenomena perhaps inexplicable by science, as we know it: consciousness, creativity, aesthetic and mystical experiences. (6) Problems of identity and goals in life, phrased as cognitive issues.

Primitive religion sometimes provides an explanation for thunder, rain or eclipses of the sun. People in the modern world sometimes use religion to explain illness (in terms of punishment). Indeed, the finding that religion commonly comes into such lay explanations has increased interest among psychologists in the psychology of religion.

There is quite a lot of evidence that religious beliefs affect the way people think. For example, Thouless (1935) asked a sample of people whether they believed that 'Tigers are found in parts of China', and found the distribution shown in Figure 6.1.

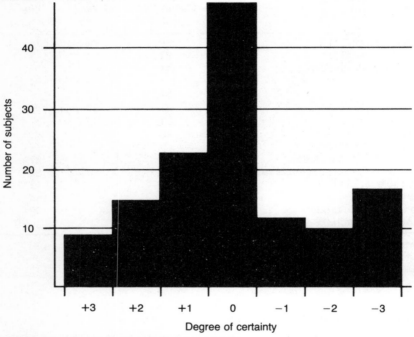

Figure 6.1 Tigers are found in parts of China
Source: Thouless, 1935

When they were asked whether or not they believed that 'Jesus Christ was God the Son', a quite different distribution was found – most were certain one way or the other (Figure 6.2).

Feather (1964) presented subjects with a number of syllogisms, some of them invalid. Religious subjects made errors in accepting some invalid syllogisms as valid, with conclusions favourable to religion; non-religious subjects, however, did not make errors in the opposite direction. Batson (1975) made up a bogus report on some new Dead Sea Scrolls, reporting how the body of Jesus was stolen from the tomb (and so did not rise from the dead). Beliefs of subjects were measured before and after reading this article. Non-believers believed even less afterwards. However, believers who believed the article had *stronger* beliefs afterwards.

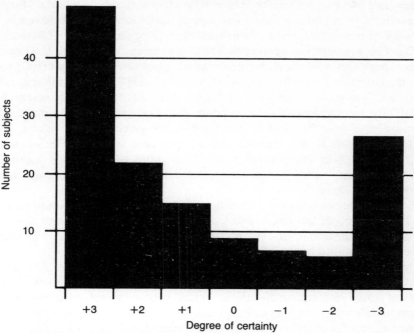

Figure 6.2 Jesus Christ was God the Son
Source: Thouless, 1935

Batson and Ventis (1982) argue that religion solves problems and provides benefits, but at the cost of loss of freedom to think or change our minds. They supported this view by a scale measuring 'bondage', with items like 'I do not think anything could make me change my present religious beliefs' and 'I would feel totally lost without my present religious beliefs'. Individuals high in intrinsic religiosity had high scores for bondage too (r = .48). However, people scoring high on another kind of religiosity, 'Quest', had low scores. 'This is an approach that involves honestly facing existential questions in all their complexity, while resisting clear-cut, pat answers. An individual who approaches religion in this way recognises that he or she does not know, and probably never will know, the final truth about such matters.' It may be objected that this is quite different from the usual kind of religious belief, and is akin to agnosticism, with an interest in religion.

There are some groups for whom religion as a source of meaning is important. Young people are often concerned with 'the meaning of life', and also with the meaning and purpose of their own lives. We shall suggest later that what the new sects and cults have to offer is a solution to the quest for inner meaning.

Can we explain the belief in God? Freud (1913) offered an explanation – that God is a projected and fantasy father figure, is modelled on the physical father, and becomes active when the real father ceases to be available. Many studies have found that images of God and attitudes towards God are similar to those of real fathers, and towards mothers (Argyle and Beit-Hallahmi, 1975). This research has been criticised on the grounds that both God and father inevitably contain elements of 'good' (and probably 'powerful') so that the correlation may be spurious (Spilka *et al.*, 1985). On the other hand there are a number of detailed findings within this tradition of research which give the hypothesis some support. For example, the percentage of children who describe God as like their father increases with age to 13 or 15, when it is 39 per cent for girls, 25 per cent for boys (DeConchy, 1967). It is found that Catholics see God more often as like mother than Protestants – this would be expected from the Catholic emphasis on the Virgin Mary.

Perhaps a better test of the Freudian projection hypothesis would be to see if young people become converted shortly after leaving home or after a parent died. There is some evidence that this occurs; for example, converts have been found to have absent or ineffective fathers more often.

Before we leave Freud, mention should be made of the negative relationship which has often been found between religion and sex. The rates of sexual intercourse and church attendance are negatively correlated among adolescents; virgins are stronger in intrinsic religiosity; and even among married people there is an inverse relationship (Woodruff, 1985). The lower rate of extra- and pre-marital intercourse among religious people could be caused by the church's prohibitions, but the effects for married people give some support to the theory that religion is some kind of substitute for sex (Argyle and Beit-Hallahmi, 1975).

Durkheim (1915) discussed one of the most primitive forms of religion – totemism, where a sacred animal is venerated as a spirit. His explanation is that the totem symbolises the society and its ideals, that society is the real object of veneration, and that the awe in which it is held produces respect for moral rules. This theory has led to interesting empirical research, through comparison of different tribes. Swanson (1960) proposed and found evidence that belief in monotheism occurred most often in societies with a hierarchy of decision-making bodies. Later work with 190 societies has found that economic as well as political hierarchies are associated with monotheism. 'A high god is a reflection of existing economic and social relationships, presiding at the ultimate level, over economic and political complexities' (Underhill, 1975).

Another widespread religious belief is in the after-life. About half the population believe in it. What do they think it will be like? Gorer (1955) once asked this question and received some surprising replies. Of those who believed in it 13 per cent referred to a scriptural heaven and hell, with judgement, plus another 9 per cent without judgement; 15 per cent had very material ideas of heaven as being like life here with the unpleasant features omitted and with endless leisure (for example, no sex, no washing-up, no dogs barking); 25 per cent believed in some kind of reincarnation; and 12 per cent looked forward to rejoining loved ones.

The belief in an after-life has a rather obvious explanation – it reduces anxiety about what is going to happen next. Fear of death is widespread – there is fear of going into the unknown, of loneliness, loss of identity, loss of loved ones and the other things of this world (Feifel, 1990). Belief in a pleasant after-life does much to relieve this anxiety: the older people are, the more they believe in it: in one study 100 per cent of those over the age of 100 did so. And more older people give 'reassurance of immortality' as their reason for going to church. Among those who are terminally ill, the religious have less fear of death and some are greatly looking forward to it – 'it will be wonderful' (Swenson, 1961). Hooper and Spilka (1970), in a study of 195 students, found that the more religious ones saw death as a rewarding after-life, and the expression of courage and values, but not as being fearful, punishing, lonely, or forsaking family.

There have been experiments – rare in the present field – in which awareness of death was aroused by tapes about accidents, dirge-like music, and slides of corpses. This was found to *reduce* fear of death for believers, but to increase it for others (Osarchuk and Tate, 1973). There is no doubt that death and religion are closely linked. In a British survey 64 per cent said that death made them think about religion, compared to 2 per cent each for holidays, work, or making love (ITA, 1970).

There is a problem about hell; this belief is likely to increase anxiety rather than reduce it. In Britain 20–27 per cent believe in it, and in the USA, 65 per cent. There are several possible explanations – the belief in a just world and the need to balance things up, a feeling of guilt and desire for punishment, and the after-effects of evangelical preaching on sin and hell.

RELIGIOUS RITUAL

By rituals are meant standardised patterns of behaviour, usually bodily behaviour, which are mainly symbolic, rather than affecting the material world. Marriage services and religious healing are 2 examples – they produce changes of relationships or states of mind rather than any immediate physical effects. Religious rituals involve both verbal and non-verbal behaviour, and are presided over by a priest. Attending church services is one of the main kinds of religious activity, and services are ritualistic in form. Some are more ritualistic than others; the Roman Catholics and High Anglicans have more set prayers, candles, bells and other symbolic events. Protestant churches have fewer, and other sects are much more freely expressive.

Freud (1907) had a theory about religious ritual; he thought that it was a kind of obsessional neurosis, when the patient has compulsions (for example) to keep washing his hands to get rid of his guilt, and becomes very anxious if he or she can't. It is true that some ritualistic individuals are very concerned over the minutiae of religious observances, with the correct sequence of bowing, kneeling, making the sign of the Cross, and so on; orthodox Jews appear to be very obsessional over food regulations, and how not to work on the Sabbath. On the other hand there are some important differences: religious ritual is social and public, not individual. And obsessional neurotics really are neurotic, whereas most church attenders are not (see below).

We shall look at ritual from some other points of view – as a case of non-verbal communication, and as examples of rites of passage and other ceremonies studied by anthropologists. To start with, most religions, and not only Christianity, make a lot of use of a certain kind of non-verbal signal – silence, rhythmic chanting, dim lighting, candles, bells, incense, bowing and laying on of hands. Somehow, in a way we do not yet understandd, these things have the power to evoke a religious response. Other non-verbal signals have a clearer meaning. In Christianity wine stands for blood, the cross for the Cross, gothic arches point up to heaven, the font is near the door, and so on. The altar is in a specially sacred, taboo area; the priest is raised up and wears an impressive costume.

Non-verbal communication often has greater effect than language because of its power to produce emotional effects, through its use of bodily symbolism, and its capacity to communicate below the threshold of conscious understanding.

However, words are used in ritual, and rituals derive meanings partly through verbalised sets of ideas, such as Christian theology. Rituals can be described in words and initiated in words, but as Firth (1970) said, gestures 'have a significance, a propriety, a restorative effect, a kind of creative force which words alone cannot give'. Words add to the meanings of the NV signals, and religious ritual thus consists typically of a combination of verbal and non-verbal, where the two kinds of meaning are combined. This adds the precision of words to the emotive power of bodily signals.

Healing services are a widespread kind of religious ritual. At Lourdes about 3 per cent of visitors are cured; in primitive healing the recovery rate may well be much higher, since more powerful rituals are used, and Lourdes patients include many who were previously incurable. Very few of these cures are claimed to be miraculous. They are cases of 'psychosomatic' influences; for example, via the impact of positive emotions on the body (p. 242). I witnessed healing at an Africanised Christian church in Ghana. Several hours of singing and dancing in a very crowded hall resulted in 75 conversions. The converts were then treated by the casting out of devils, each representing one bodily ailment; elders pressed their hands on the converts' heads and shouted at the devils to come out. Probably important here is the very powerful social pressure, and a high level of excitement, or perhaps exhaustion. However, the symbolism is important too. In a ceremony for barren women in Zambia red clay represented menstrual blood, carved figures stood for babies (Turner, 1967). In rituals for mental healing in Haiti, washing the head with water stands for cleanliness, fig leaves for the holy tree with magical virtue (Huxley, 1966).

Other services appear intended to influence the deity. There are prayers for rain, peace, sick people and the departed. Often sacrifices are made of animals, perhaps in the hope of reciprocity. Yet other services simply express religious beliefs and devotion, by singing hymns, and by appropriate symbolic behaviour. Attitudes of humility and repentance can be expressed by bodily postures such as bowing the head, kneeling or lying flat on the floor. Attitudes of joy can be expressed by singing and dancing, attitudes of aspiration by looking and reaching upwards.

Religion plays a role in rites of passage like marriage and funerals; indeed, more people engage in these forms of religious activity than in any other. In primitive societies there are many more of them, marking transitions from one stage of life to another. This 'ritual work' enables those concerned to feel that a change of condition has taken place. The ritual is performed primarily by priests or senior members of the group. They also use spoken words which have the character of 'performative influences'; that is, the act of saying 'I marry you' accomplishes this change in social state. The emotive power of the ritual is needed to bring about the changed attitudes, cognitions and pattern of behaviour, and public affirmation is given to the change of state.

Funerals are ostensibly rites of passage for the departed, but are also important for the bereaved. Our human capacity for love and attachment means that we are ill equipped to deal with bereavement and need help. Rituals of mourning together with the provision of social support, and a period of cathartic grief, a time for readjustment, all help. At the end of a period of withdrawal the bereaved can return to normal life.

RELIGIOUS EXPERIENCE

Many people report experiences of a religious nature. Surveys have asked about these in several ways. We gave one version earlier (p. 132). However, this kind of question tends to produce reports of intense and solitary experiences, rather than the quite common, and often intense, experiences during religious services, or at evangelical meetings. The results of a British survey of a national sample, who were asked these questions are shown in Table 6.2. This shows the percentages of the population who report, for example, awareness of a sacred presence in nature (16 per cent), and also the proportion of those who gave this a religious interpretation (61 per cent). I have multiplied these together to give, in the third column, the population of the percentage who had a religious experience from nature (9.8 per cent).

There are several different kinds of religious experience, and they are triggered in different ways. We shall discuss four of the main varieties.

Table 6.2   Religious experience in Britain

Type of experience	(1) Those reporting this (%)	(2) Those interpreting religiously (%)	Religious experience (1×2) (%)
Awareness of the presence of God	27	80	21.6
Awareness of receiving help in answer to prayer	25	79	19.8
Awareness of a guiding presence not called God	22	58	12.8
Awareness of a sacred presence in nature	16	61	9.8
Awareness of patterning in synchronicity	29	32	9.3
Awareness of the presence of someone who has died	18	35	6.3
Awareness of an evil presence	12	38	4.6
Experiencing that all things are one	5	55	2.75

Source: Hay and Heald, 1987

1 Awareness of a sacred presence in nature

This reflects the impact of the European Romantic tradition, in which poets like Wordsworth and painters like Turner 'discovered' in the eighteenth century the beauty of the natural world of mountains, lakes and other features of the landscape. Before that time people thought that mountains, for example, were simply a nuisance. Research into the causes of joy has found that experience of nature, and sunny days, are common sources of this emotion (Argyle, 1987). Research in the psychology of religion has found that mountains, deserts and wilderness are sources of religious experience (Rosegrant, 1976). Environmental psychologists have pinpointed the precise features which evoke positive (though not necessarily religious) reactions. These are settings which are green with grass or trees, where there is water, and depth of view. These features, together with sunshine, are obviously of biological importance, suggesting that there may be a biological basis for these reactions.

2 Music

Music is not mentioned in Table 6.2, since it occurs in group rather than solitary settings. Music is one of the main methods used to generate emotions in the laboratory, it has been described as 'the language of emotion', and it plays a central part in most religious services. In the laboratory, it has been used to produce elation and depression but it can produce more complex emotions than this: the second part of Beethoven's 'Eroica' symphony was described by subjects as 'sadness, despair or grief' (Hampton, 1945), and the same composer's 'Pastoral Sonata' as 'the joyful uplifting of the oppressed soul that finds itself released from depths of anguish' (Valentine, 1962). Susanna Langer (1942) suggested that music and emotional experience have the same temporal structure; both have periods of 'motion and rest, attention and release, of agreement and disagreement, preparation, fulfilment, excitation and sudden change'. In Europe there has been a long tradition of church music, of which Bach's is the most renowned. While music can generate any emotion, religious music has a special quality, a kind of deep joy, triumph over tragedy.

Religious ideas are often expressed in music and other non-verbal ways, perhaps because religion is more a matter of emotion, to which words cannot do justice. Common non-verbal symbols here are architecture (soaring to heaven), posture (submission), bells (announcing the holy presence), dark blue stained glass (sombre mood), impressive costumes (the status of the priest), touch (laying on of hands), and water (cleansing in baptism). Ritual acts are used which symbolise important facts of life, such as birth and death, relations with parents, the seasons, and to influence other people as in healing, rites of passage, funerals, or the deity as in sacrifice. Research has revealed the operation of two different kinds of thinking. People with dominant left hemispheres engage primarily in rational and verbal thinking, those with dominant right hemispheres prefer metaphor and are concerned with music and the arts, and other non-rational activities (Bakan, 1971).

3 Mystical experience – 'all is one'

This is the classic mystical experience, often regarded as archetypical, though as Table 6.2 shows, it is actually quite rare – only 2.75 per cent of people report it. It is, however, more typical of Eastern pantheistic mysticism. Hood (1975) factor-analysed statements representing the 8 aspects of religious experience described by Stace. The main factor consisted of the items about unity, transcendence of time and space, ego loss and related topics.

This classic type of experience, though rare, can be produced by means of drugs. Pahnke (1966) reports an experiment in which theological students were given the drug psilocybin, and others a placebo. Those who had the drug reported what appears to be the classic mystical experience, of unity, timelessness and the rest (Table 6.3). This experiment has been criticised on the grounds that the subjects realised whether they were in the experimental or control groups, and that the only categories which they were given in which to describe their experiences were mystical ones. Nevertheless it is impressive that six months later the psilocybin subjects reported strong benefits, such as feelings of strengthened commitment to the religious life (Batson and Ventis, 1982).

Table 6.3   The effects of psilocybin on mystical experience

| Category | Percentage of maximum possible score for 10 subjects | | |
	Experimental	Control	p*
1 Unity	62	7	0.001
(a) Internal	70	8	0.001
(b) External	38	2	0.008
2 Transcendence of time and space	84	6	0.001
3 Deeply felt positive mood	57	23	0.020
(a) Joy, blessedness and peace	51	13	0.020
(b) Love	57	33	0.055
4 Sacredness	53	28	0.020
5 Objectivity and reality	63	18	0.011
6 Paradoxicality	61	13	0.001
7 Alleged ineffability	66	18	0.001
8 Transiency	79	8	0.001
9 Persisting positive changes in attitude and behaviour	51	8	0.001
(a) towards self	57	3	0.001
(b) towards others	40	20	0.002
(c) towards life	54	6	0.011
(d) towards the experience	57	31	0.055

* Probability that the difference between experimental and control scores was due to chance
Source: Pahnke, 1966

However, not all experiments with drugs have been so successful, and mescaline and LSD have simply produced strange and unpleasant experiences for many. The percentage who report a religious experience is far higher (75–90 per cent) for those individuals with a strong religious background.

The explanation for this variability may lie in the two-factor theory of emotion. This says that the experiencing of an emotion requires the combination of physiological arousal and cognitions which suggest a particular emotion (Schachter, 1964). In the case of mystical experience a special kind of physiological arousal may be needed, such as is provided by hallucinogenic drugs, and religious beliefs and setting.

But why should certain drugs produce these experiences? This is far from clear. Of course the drugs do occur in nature, and some Mexican Indians chew peyote for religious purposes, not realising that it contains mescaline. Perhaps similar bodily states can be achieved in other ways, such as by fasting, loss of sleep and other monastic practices.

Another experimental approach to religious experience was used by Hood *et al.* (1990): subjects were placed in an isolation tank – in total silence and darkness and 10 inches of warm water. After 20 minutes they were asked to reply 'yes' or 'no' to questions on a mysticism scale. Intrinsically religious subjects gave positive responses, extrinsically religious subjects did not, while the indiscriminately pro-religious did so only if they had been given instructions suggesting that they might have a religious experience.

It is interesting that religious experience often has positive effects – it 'makes men stronger', as Durkheim said, it produces positive attitudes towards others, and it creates a feeling of unity with others, as is seen in Table 6.3. We shall show later that church membership leads to better health, mental health, happiness and concern for others. These findings give some support to those who have argued that there is an evolutionary basis for religion.

4 Experiences of God and others

In mystical experiences the individual feels merged into a larger whole. We now turn to encounters with God as a separate entity. Table 6.2 shows that this is much more common – awareness of the presence of God (22 per cent), of receiving help or answer to prayer (20 per cent), or of another guiding presence (10 per cent).

These experiences may be unexpected or they may be worked for. Meditation of various kinds involves concentrating the mind, in silence, in one of a number of ways imported from India. Meditation on a vase for 15-minute periods is one way. Prayer can also produce powerful physiological and experiential effects. In American surveys many religious experiences were reported which had taken place during prayer, but for some reason the proportion is much lower in Britain (Hay, 1985).

There is a psychological explanation for hearing voices and receiving guidance. Small children can sometimes be heard talking to themselves in the voice of a parent, saying things like 'don't touch', 'naughty' and so on. Often, repeated interaction sequences result in the child's learning how the parent responds in a number of situations. If people often address God in prayer, the typical human responses could be activated. The Freudian theory is that God is an internalisation of parent images, a theory which was discussed earlier (p. 136). A different version of the theory was put forward by Sunden (1965) to account for hearing the voice of God. He suggests that religious people become familiar with biblical events, with the roles involved

(God included), and the pattern of interaction between them. They then see analogies between their own life situations and those of biblical characters and have expectations of how the others will respond. The voice of God would be derived from the voice of a parent. Buber (1936) described the encounter with God as an 'I–Thou relationship', in which He is known in prayer as we know real persons. This must consist of a kind of dialogue, mainly one-sided, but where the responses of the other are included.

There are similar encounters and relationships with the Virgin Mary, Jesus, the saints and with the dead. This happens in bereavement, and could be because of the often-repeated interaction sequences in the home, where the reactions of the other are very familiar and so become aroused in fantasy after their death. We discussed Sunden's explanation of hearing the voice of God above. Another theory of religious voices is due to Jaynes (1976), who suggested that the Greeks at the time of Homer, and the Jews in Old Testament times, had a 'bicameral mind'. The right cerebral hemisphere may have been responsible for auditory hallucinations which the left hemisphere interpreted as the voices of the gods. The right hemisphere told people what to do in times of stress, the left hemisphere carried it out. Hearing such voices is less common now, and Jaynes argues that the bicameral mind broke down between 2000 and 1000 BC, as a result of increased trading with other peoples and the discovery that different gods said different things. As a result of these cultural changes the left hemisphere became dominant, concentrating on cognitive activity, problem-solving and controlling events. However, the right hemisphere is still there, and is responsible for religious experiences today and also for the experience of love, as described by poets and others.

THE EFFECT OF SOCIAL INFLUENCE

All beliefs, values, opinions and attitudes which have been studied by psychologists have been found to be affected by social influences. These may be the shared norms of groups to which individuals belong, the personal influence of friends, or the effects of leaders. In the case of religion there is a special reason for this: we cited Max Weber earlier as saying that religion provides a solution to irrational life problems; he and other sociologists also proposed that religion provides a socially shared solution to these problems. Berger and Luckmann (1966) described it as the 'social construction of reality'. Religious beliefs cannot be verified scientifically, but they can be supported by the beliefs of other people. As well as solving problems about death and so on, religion provides a guide to life, supports discipline and the restraint of egocentric impulses, and encourages concern for others.

Conversion involves substantial changes in individuals' subjective worlds. They see themselves as radically changed, they see their own past differently, may reject their former self, reconstruct their biography, use different language and undergo a process of self-transformation, as has been shown in depth interviews with converts (Staples and Mauss, 1987).

Friends and groups of friends are an important source of influence. An early study of religious converts found that 42 per cent said they had been converted mainly as a result of social pressure or imitation. In many marriages between individuals of different faiths one partner changes to the beliefs of the other. There is a high correlation (over .60) between the religious beliefs and attitudes of students and those of their parents, especially if they are still living at home, and if they like their parents, especially between mothers and daughters. An individual will be influenced most by a social group if he or she is attracted by the group, and wants to be accepted by it. There may be a continuous process of change of ideas through exposure to the group and its way of talking and thinking, and its practices; this is sometimes described as 'gradual conversion'.

'Sudden conversion' – for example, at evangelical revivals – is rather different. John Wesley was a very effective preacher. An example of his message is

> I preach hell because it arouses their fears, arrests their consciences and causes them to reform their lives and habits . . . Hell has been running for six thousand years. It is filling up every day. Where is it? About eighteen miles from here. Which way is it? Straight down – not over eighteen miles, down in the bowels of the earth.

(Sargant, 1957)

The emotions were further stirred by the singing of very moving hymns. The result was often devastating. Hundreds of those present would speak with tongues or bark, display violent jerking and twitching, while many collapsed senseless on the ground (Davenport, 1906). Nowadays evangelism is more restrained. Billy Graham's three campaigns in Britain attracted about $5\frac{1}{2}$ million attenders, some more than once. About 120,000 came forward and made 'decisions for Christ', of whom 75 per cent were making their first public decision and 61 per cent were not already church members. How long does it last? From follow-up studies it seems that over 50 per cent of genuine converts were still going to church a year later. John Wesley formed his converts into Methodist groups; the Graham organisation put converts in touch with the local vicar; such continuing social influence is probably crucial.

How does this social influence work? It is found that emotional messages have more impact than rational ones – no one ever ran a successful evangelical campaign with arguments for the existence of God. One theory is that a high level of emotional arousal makes people suggestible, and that when combined with powerful social pressures, it leads to religious change. Emotions are aroused at the Graham meetings by the mass singing of emotional hymns, and a highly charged message, saying, for example, that 'In 10 years' time a quarter of you will be dead' (demographically incorrect, since the average age of his audience was under 20). The social pressure is created both by the large and enthusiastic audience, and by up to 2,000 counsellors who come forward to greet those making decisions (Argyle and Beit-Hallahmi, 1975).

Social pressures can be seen at work on those occasions when empirical support for religious beliefs has been reduced, 'when prophecy fails'. This happened in 1843 to the Millerites in the USA, when the world did not end as they predicted. There was actually an increase in fervour and membership over the next 18 months, presumably an attempt to increase social support. In 1955 a small group in Minnesota also expected the end of the world, but that they would be saved, and were closely studied by psychologists who had infiltrated the movement. After the first failure the leader announced that 'your faith has saved the world', and revised the date by a year. During that time there was increased publicity and proselytising, and the membership grew, but fell after the second failure of prophecy (Festinger *et al.*, 1956). In small sects social pressures can be very strong, as will be described below. If a sect is physically isolated, and cut off from outside opinions, from physical not social reality, there can be 'belief escalation', whereby absurd and destructive ideas become shared. In the Jonestown sect the Revd Jim Jones ordered all the 913 members to commit suicide by taking poison, and they did so.

Hayden (1987) put forward an interesting evolutionary explanation of shared religious ecstasy in groups. He argued that among primitive men it was important to establish strong emotional bonds to hold groups together in times of stress. Ecstatic states, in which individual identities were suppressed, enabled such bonds to form, and rituals developed to generate them. He showed that there was more belief in celestial gods in tribes of gatherers suffering environmental stress, and in animal gods in hunting tribes.

SECTS, CULTS AND COMMUNES

We have just seen that religion is usually a social phenomenon, where beliefs are sustained by religious groups, and their services. In the modern world many people belong to 'churches'; that is, large, organised bodies, with a hierarchy of leaders, and a large number of rather similar, local groups, directed by salaried clergy. Such churches developed over the centuries from much smaller, less formal bodies, very similar to what are regarded as 'sects' today. There are still a large number of sects, some formed by breaking away from churches, because some members did not feel that the church met their needs, others formed spontaneously from individuals who may or may not have been church members before. By 'sects' I mean groups such as Adventists, Assemblies of God, Pentecostalists and other, more or less Christian bodies.

Sects are started by a single charismatic leader, who is a powerful preacher and able to attract and convert a number of followers. John Wesley and William Miller (originator of the Seventh Day Adventists and Jehovah's

Witnesses) are good examples. The followers who are drawn to such leaders are mostly underprivileged, or from ethnic minority groups. The sect aspires to an intense kind of spirituality, and makes strict demands for behaviour, such as 'tithing' (giving 10 per cent of income to the sect). The services are usually noisy, with rousing sermons and loud hymn-singing, many 'Alleluias', and in earlier times members barking like dogs or rolling on the floor (Sargant, 1957).

Some of the practices may separate the sect from its mother church, and may have been the occasion for splitting, though often they are quite minor, such as objecting to organs. The result is that the members see themselves as separate from the rest of the world, as a kind of spiritual elite.

A common explanation of sects is that they offer compensations for the frustrations of deprived sections of the community. This is supported by: (1) their belief in the speedy ending of this world and the coming of the next where the rich shall be cast down and the humble and meek raised up; (2) their puritan morality in which a virtue is made of frugality, humility and industry, while luxuries and worldly amusements are vices; (3) the stress on simplicity of worship and opposition to expensive equipment – the Churches of Christ opposed missionary activity because of the cost involved; (4) a defined purpose: for example, the Church of the Nazarene, which openly states that its mission is to the poor – others have missions to blacks.

This does not explain the concern with sin and salvation, the 'extreme Protestantism' of most sects, or their great emotionality. Sects are only one possible way of coping with deprivation – left-wing politics is a more common one. The emotionality probably reflects the tensions of deprived people. The tight membership is perhaps a response to social isolation and disorganisation produced by rapid social change. The concern with sin and salvation may simply be due to the traditional approach of evangelists, stirring up emotions by arousing guilt feelings (Argyle and Beit-Hallahmi, 1975).

Since World War II a number of new 'cults' have appeared in all Western countries – such as the Moonies, the Jesus cult, followers of the Bhagwan, and others. These are different from the traditional sects. Instead of ecstatic services there is meditation. This is because of the origins of most cults in Indian ideas, though some are Christian as well. The members are mostly middle class and in their twenties, but have often been in trouble, with drugs and alienation from family and the wider society. While some cults make moral demands, others encourage sexual promiscuity. All make great efforts to attract and convert new members, and some have developed high-pressure techniques, like the Moonies' 'love-bombing', which have been compared to brain-washing.

The cults have been widely attacked on a number of grounds. Although they have been accused of inducing mental disturbance in young people, there is little evidence that they are bad for people, and sometimes the results have been found to be positive, largely because many members were in considerable distress when they joined, and many have been cured of drugs (Richardson, 1985). There are also costs of belonging – especially loss of freedom of thought and separation from family, though in defence it is clear that the young members were often alienated from their families already. In some cases there has been loss of more basic freedoms, even to leave the sect premises, resulting in some families kidnapping and 'deprogramming' their children. There is clearer evidence that leaving the sect is often traumatic. Members become disillusioned, but can't leave without breaking their emotional bonds to the group, and even more to the charismatic leader. After leaving they often have nightmares or hallucinations, or produce violent outbursts, especially in those who have been deprogrammed (Lewis and Bromley, 1987).

The psychological interpretation of these cults is not clear. The attractions of a close and supportive community to drop-outs in trouble are easy to understand. Perhaps Indian ideas and meditational practices offer a source of peace and what looks like a deeper source of wisdom than the rejected mores of the home. One theory is that these cults are an aftermath to the widespread alienation of young people during the seventies – when the cults became popular. If this theory is correct, the prediction is that the cults will all fade away, or change their nature.

Another kind of cult is psychological rather than religious – Transcendental Meditation, EST, Exegesis, Rebirthing, and a variety of similar movements, partly from India via California, partly re-hashed popular psychology. They promise psychological benefits, and longer life, rather than spiritual goals. The practices are not 'services', but occasions for meditation, or the practice of psychological techniques. There is, however, a high level of emotional arousal, sometimes involving screaming, shouting at and insulting the members, or 'flying' (in TM). The clientele are mostly well educated and affluent people in their twenties. Surprisingly large fees are charged. What do the members hope to gain? What they do gain is some reduction of tension, together with, for example, reduced blood pressure, as happens with any form of relaxation. They also gain membership of a congenial middle-class club. The services offered are quite similar to group therapy, or to relaxation therapy, but the members are not like patients. It may be suggested that what they are seeking is some higher level of fulfilment, perhaps the achievement of a more positive identity. Slugoski *et al.* (1984) distinguished several stages of identity formation, and found that many young people have failed to achieve the higher levels, and that coming to a decision about religious issues was central to identity achievement.

Since World War II, many residential communes and Utopian communities have been established in the USA and Britain, some of them religious. In the USA there have been perhaps as many as 100 at any one time, involving over 100,000 people. The Shakers had 6,000 members in 18 groups; other well-known ones were the Hutterites and the Oneida community. In

Britain there have been a smaller number including Findhorn, Beshara and Kingsway. More recently there have been a number of cult communities, attached to the Moonies, the Jesus Movement, the Bhagwan, and TM. As well as being larger than the communes described earlier, the religious communities last longer – an average of 50 years, some over 100, with 50 per cent lasting more than 20 years (Figure 6.3). There is a strong ideology in these communities, usually Christian (though not attached to any church), mystical, occultist, Buddhist or communist, often with some rather strange ideas as well. The Oneida community abolished marriage, while others have demanded asceticism.

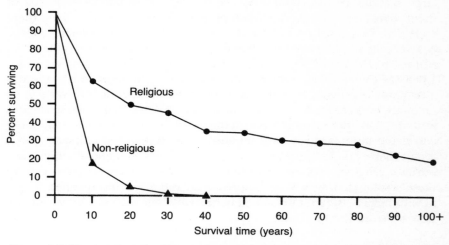

Figure 6.3 Percentage of religious and non-religious communes surviving first
            hundred years
Source: Stephan and Stephan, 1973

There has been some research into the conditions under which such communities are successful. We have already seen that religion is a major positive factor. Kanter (1968) compared 9 successful and 21 unsuccessful ones, and concluded that a number of 'commitment mechanisms' were important, such as various kinds of abstinence, renunciation and morti-fication. Hall (1988) re-analysed this data, and concluded instead that the most important predictors for success were having a common ethnic background and homogeneity, as well as instituting confession and a spiritual hierarchy. Abrams and McCulloch (1976) are critical of Kanter's emphasis on commitment mechanisms, which they see as similar to brain-washing, and inducing too much conformity and personality change. This has been widely reported to happen in some of the new cults like the Moonies.

Quite a lot has been learnt about the conditions under which such communities succeed. As we have seen, they do better if there is a clear religious basis; members need to share beliefs and ideals. And there must be clear leadership and rules, which are accepted by the members. A problem with many small non-religious communes has been that the members were often rebels and drop-outs who refused to accept any authority or keep to rules.

RELIGION AND PERSONALITY

Do religious people have a certain kind of personality? Do members of particular denominations or sects have special kinds of personality? Since large sections of the community are involved it would be surprising if there were very strong relationships here. Indeed, at first sight there appear to be almost no effects of personality at all. For example, there is a very small tendency for religious people to be introverts rather than extraverts. Francis (1985) found a correlation of $-.15$ with extraversion for 1,088 15–16-year-olds, and .10 with neuroticism. In other words, there is a very weak tendency for a greater proportion of neurotic introverts to be religious, at that age. A later study with 1,745 children found that irreligious attitudes had little relationship with the sociability side of extraversion, but correlated more strongly with impulsiveness. Baker and Gorsuch (1982) found that while extrinsic religiosity was stronger in anxious individuals, intrinsic religious attitudes correlated with lack of anxiety. However, all these results are rather weak, unpredicted, and as yet unexplained. I turn now to links between religion and personality that *were* predicted, and do have a theoretical rationale.

Religion and conflict

A number of psychoanalytic writers have suggested that religion relieves guilt feelings, sometimes interpreted as aggression directed towards the self. It follows that people with strong internal conflicts and guilt feelings should be attracted to Protestantism, with its emphasis on sin and salvation. Clark (1929) found that 55 per cent of sudden converts at a revival had suffered from a sense of sin, compared with 8.5 per cent of all those converted. Heinrich (1973) studied 310 Catholics, half of whom had joined a Pentecostal group. More of the latter said that they had experienced personal stress before being converted to Pentecostalism. A number of studies have compared Protestants and Catholics, and found that Protestants have somewhat stronger guilt feelings, direct anger inwards and have a higher suicide rate (Argyle and Beit-Hallahmi, 1975).

Batson and Ventis (1982) argue that religious experience involves creative problem-solving to deal with personal crises, and that there is a surrender to a new vision of life. This is helped by drug-induced or other kinds of religious experience, since there is a loosening of cognitive structures, and a shift to right-hemisphere activity. A number of studies support this view. Brown *et al*. (1978) studied 192 Christians who reported mystical experiences. Correlations were found between self-dissatisfaction and evidence of personal re-creation, measures of positive and fundamental change and enlightened and new knowledge.

A number of studies have found that one kind of religious person or another is rather suggestible (Argyle and Beit-Hallahmi, 1975). Spanos and Moretti (1985) for example, found that students who reported religious experiences also had high scores on questionnaire measures of 'absorption' (that is, capacity for total attention to an imagined object), and hypnotisability. Those reporting diabolic experiences scored high on suggestibility and neuroticism.

The Protestant work ethic (PWE)

Max Weber (1904) thought that Protestantism led to capitalism because the reformers taught that people would be judged individually, and would be judged on the basis of their whole life's work, of which their 'calling' was the most important part. The PWE, on the other hand, held that money should not be spent on oneself. This led to a life of hard work, self-discipline, asceticism and concern with achievement; it also led to the accumulation of money which could not be spent on luxury, but which could be put into one's own business.

McClelland (1961) offered a social-psychological explanation for the link between Protestantism and capitalism. The theory is that Protestant ideas and values produce, first, a certain way of bringing up children, which, secondly, leads to the children acquiring strong achievement motivation, and thirdly that high achievers become entrepreneurs and create an expansion of business.

In previous times there was a tendency for more entrepreneurs to be Protestant, including some of the leaders of the Industrial Revolution. McClelland found that Protestant countries were more prosperous than Catholic ones, and Protestants have often been found to be of higher social class or occupational status within countries. However, these differences have now all but disappeared.

Questionnaire measures of the PWE have been constructed – for example, by Mirels and Garrett (1971) – and there are also measures of achievement motivation. It has sometimes been found that Protestants scored a little higher than Catholics, but the difference is now small, and that Jews score even higher (Argyle, 1989; Furnham, 1990).

AGE, GENDER AND SOCIAL CLASS

Age

Religion takes a different form at different ages. Children learn a simple version of whatever their family believes, with little difficulty. God is like a fairy-tale person, prayers are for simple childish needs. Adolescence is a more stormy period, and is the time for conversions, often part of rebellion or seeking independence from parents, typically at ages 14–16. Beliefs become less literal, more abstract or metaphysical, but there is often great interest in religion at this time; there may be doubts over earlier beliefs, or loss of faith or a watered-down faith. Many studies, though not all, have found a decline in religious activity between 18 and 30, and may be due to the effects of World War II and later recovery on different age groups. Probably there *is* a decline, certainly in emotional intensity, and in the urgency of questioning religious doctrines.

During middle age there is an increase in religious activity, according to many studies, including church attendance, prayer, holding orthodox beliefs, religious values, and playing a role in the organisational side of the church. Old age brings some decline in church attendance, because of reduced mobility, but increase in private prayer, belief in God, and the after-life, and the importance of religion.

The heightened religion of age is very different from the heightened religion of adolescence. In adolescence there is a great intellectual perplexity and doubt coupled with emotional turmoil: young people suddenly change their whole orientation one way or the other. In old age, when both intellect and emotions are dimmed, there is no worry about the niceties of theology, nor is there any emotional excitement about religious matters (Argyle and Beit-Hallahmi, 1975). As we reported earlier, *all* people over the age of 100 believe in God and the after-life.

Gender

One of the strongest empirical findings about the psychology of religion, in Christian countries at least, is that women are on average more religious than men. They are more active on all criteria, but more so for some criteria than others. The differences can be expressed as ratios between (for example) the percentages of women who believe in God and the percentages of men. The greatest difference is in the percentages reporting private prayer, 1.7:1, or 70 per cent more women than men. In Britain the ratios for basic beliefs, church attendance and reporting religious experiences are about 1.5:1, while for church membership there is no difference.

There are striking denominational variations in these gender differences. The greater activity of women is most marked in Protestant, especially extreme Protestant, groups, where it approaches 2:1 in the membership of American churches. The difference is least for Roman Catholics. Women also hold a rather more positive image of God, as healer, creator, friend, father and redeemer (Nelsen, Cheek and Au, 1985).

Can we explain these interesting gender differences? The conflict theory is one possibility. Women do have more guilt feelings, so this could explain why they are attracted to Protestant churches. The father-figure theory of belief in God could explain why more women are drawn towards Christianity with a male father-figure, and why men are attracted towards Catholicism, where there is also a mother figure. It is found that working women are less active in religion than non-working women, possibly because they have less time or energy. This could explain the difference between men and women. A careful statistical analysis of 476 women, by Ulbrich and Wallace (1984), found that the working women went to church 34.4 times per year, and the non-working women 42.8 times. These explanations seem the most plausible, but there are a number of other theories (Argyle and Beit-Hallahmi, 1975).

Social class

There are interesting class differences in religious behaviour and beliefs, and these are of great theoretical interest. It has often been suggested that religion is a fantasy compensation for frustration. Marx (1964) said,

> Religious suffering is at the same time an expression of real suffering and a protest against real suffering. Religion is the sigh of the oppressed creature, the heart of a heartless world, and the soul of soulless conditions. It is the opium of the people.

Davis (1948) added, 'The greater his [man's] disappointment in this life, the greater his faith in the next.'

Such theories lead us to expect that those of lowest social status or income would be the most religious. If we look at the number of people claiming to belong to some denomination, there is no class difference. But for frequency of church attendance there is a large class difference: twice as many AB people in Britain go to church once a week or more (17 per cent), compared with 9 per cent for C2, D and E. This has been the case for a long time, and the same is found in the USA. However, on an index of overall commitment (the subjective importance of God, and orthodoxy of beliefs), working-class people in Britain score *higher* (Gerard, 1985). In American studies it is found that middle- and upper-class people hold more liberal beliefs, working-class people more traditional and fundamentalist ones.

Different denominations attract different social classes. For a long time in Britain the Church of England was mostly middle class, while non-conformist churches were less so, and the Roman Catholics succeeded in attracting people from all classes. The differences are smaller now, though middle-class people support the Church of England more, while the non-conformists have declined in all classes. In the USA the Congregationalists, Episcopalians and Presbyterians are at the top. In both countries the sects appeal most to working-class individuals, and members of ethnic minority groups.

It is only the sects which fit the deprivation theory, as explained earlier. Why do middle-class people support their churches so much? It may be because these churches are respectable, conventional, aspects of normal middle-class establishment life, and that middle-class people join groups like this. The formal cerebral, form of worship appeals to them. Working-class people prefer more informal, emotional, spontaneous forms of worship, seen more strongly in the small sects.

THE BENEFITS OF RELIGION – TO THE INDIVIDUAL

Does religion do people any good? Fortunately there has been good research which can tell us the answer.

Health

The best-known study, by Comstock and Partridge (1972) studied mortality rates for the population of part of Maryland in 1960–64, about 55,000 in all. Those who went to church once a week or more had much lower death rates than those who went less often, or not at all (Table 6.4). Other studies have shown that church attenders also have lower rates of chronic bronchitis and of fatal one-car accidents. No correlation with church attendance has been found for cancer of the colon.

Table 6.4   Mortality rates of regular church-goers and others (per 1,000 over 5 years in most cases)

	Once a week or more	Less than once a week
Heart disease	38	89
Emphysema (3 years)	18	52
Cirrhosis (3 years)	5	25
Cancer of the rectum	13	17
Suicide (6 years)	11	29

It has been pointed out that the relation between church attendance and health could be due to people who are ill not being able to get to church. However, a statistical comparison of 3,063 American counties found that there were lower rates of cancer, especially respiratory and digestive cancer, in areas of higher church membership (Dwyer *et al.*, 1990). Another explanation could be that church attenders drink and smoke less. However Spilka (cited by Gorsuch, 1988) found that religious people were still in better health when smoking and drinking had been taken account of statistically. As Comstock and Partridge suggest, peace of mind and release of tensions could affect pulse and blood pressure, and so could the effects of a supporting group. Most of the ailments studied affect the elderly in particular, and the effects of religion on psychological health are strongest for this group.

Religious groups have traditionally been concerned with health, and prayers for the health of members and faith healing are widely practised. Do these prayers work? There is a certain amount of evidence that faith healing has some effect, at any rate for psychosomatic ailments. About 3 per cent of the many thousands of visitors to Lourdes are cured or partly cured (McComb, 1928).

Mental health

Are religious people also in better mental health than others? There have been many investigations of this topic; mostly in the USA, using different measures and yielding different results. A meta-analysis of 24 studies, using nearly 10,000 subjects in all, produced a small positive correlation of .09, between measures of religious activity or attitudes, and mental health (Bergin, 1983), though some studies produced the opposite result. Batson and Ventis (1982) showed that a relationship between religiosity and mental ill health is only found for measures of extrinsic, or instrumental, religiosity, 10 out of 13 studies. For 23 analyses using measures of intrinsic or quest religiosity (see p. 135), 12 found a positive correlation between religion and mental health, 8 no relation, and only 3 a negative relationship.

Religious activity correlates with particular aspects of mental health. The extrinsic, means orientation appears to have a rather pervasive negative relationship to mental health, regardless of how mental health is conceived. An intrinsic, end orientation is positively associated with reports of greater freedom from worry and guilt and reports of greater personal competence and control, but not with greater open-mindedness and flexibility. A quest orientation is positively associated with greater open-mindedness and flexibility, greater personal competence and control, and greater self-acceptance, but not with greater freedom from worry and guilt (Batson and Ventis, 1982).

Maton (1989) found that perceived support from God had a positive effect in reducing depression, and sustaining self-esteem and emotional adjustment, in people who were under high stress, but it had no such effects on those not under stress. This is a 'buffering' effect similar to the effect of an intimate relationship (p. 265). We can see how religion can help people in trouble: Pargament et al. (1988) found 3 kinds of coping religious individuals: (1) collaborating with God to solve the problem, (2) waiting for solutions from God, and (3) emphasising the freedom God gives to direct their own lives.

Religious events and experiences can have definite positive or negative effects on mental health. The Millerite revival in New England, for example, produced many admissions to mental hospitals of patients suffering from 'religious excitement' – the meetings were evidently too exciting for them, and the same has been reported for other revivals (Argyle, 1958). But for other people conversion has had positive effects – 'personal recreation', and joining sects has more positive than negative effects for mental health (p. 147ff).

What about psychosis, schizophrenia and the rest? There is no doubt that some mental patients are very religious (13.5 per cent in one study), and that religion sometimes plays a central role in their disturbance. For example, Rokeach studied the 'Three Christs of Ypsilanti' (1964). He put them all in the same hospital ward to see what would happen: each denounced the others as imposters. Religious delusions are most common in paranoid schizophrenics and depression, especially in working-class women. Furthermore many saints, mystics and other important religious figures in the past are recognised to have displayed symptoms of schizophrenia, hysteria, epilepsy and so on. What exactly is the difference between such religious leaders and religious lunatics? There are two obvious differences. First, religious leaders must have been more in touch with other people, and been more skilful organisers than are regular psychotics. Secondly, the ideas which they proclaimed must have had a far wider appeal and have been able to solve other people's problems, compared with the usual psychotic delusions (Argyle and Beit-Hallahmi, 1975).

One sphere in which religion does appear to do some good is in reducing the rate of suicide. Durkheim thought that this was because of the social integration provided by religion, but Stark et al. (1983) found that in 214 cities suicide rates were substantially lower for those with large numbers of church members, with social integration held constant (measured by the rate of population turnover), ($r = -.36$). There was no effect of Catholicism as opposed to Protestantism.

Happiness

Are religious people any happier than other people? Large-scale surveys of happiness and satisfaction have found modest positive correlations of about .17 (Campbell et al., 1976). Stronger effects than this have been found for people over 65, especially if they are fully retired or single, suggesting that social support from the church community is responsible (Moberg and Taves, 1965). St George and McNamara (1984) found that among black Americans church attendance was the best predictor of well-being; they benefited from the religious community. But for white Americans religious *attitudes* predicted well-being better; the authors suggested that the key factor is 'the *degree of engagement* of individuals' beliefs with the way they look at life and feel about it'. Marital happiness is considerably higher for church members, and the rate of divorce much lower. Agreement over religion is even more important, and a very strict religious upbringing can lead to sexual problems in marriage.

Other research suggests that it is not so much going to church, or holding particular beliefs, that makes people happy. It is feeling that life has some meaning and purpose, and confidence in guiding values (Freedman, 1978). In Britain, religious people are less likely to experience life as meaningless. Religion can provide a sense of meaning and purpose, and the church community can provide social support for beliefs and values.

THE BENEFITS OF RELIGION – FOR OTHERS

Religion may be good for those who practise it, but do they behave any better to other people? Do they love their neighbours?

Racial prejudice

There have been many studies in the USA and elsewhere, showing that religious people are *more* prejudiced than others. However, if different measures are compared, it turns out that this result is entirely due to the intolerance and prejudice of extrinsically religious individuals, and that the intrinsically religious are not at all prejudiced. However, this is a tricky research question, since giving unprejudiced answers and giving intrinsic religious answers may both be due to social desirability bias – trying to look good. Attempts to overcome this problem led Batson and Ventis (1982) to conclude that 'a quest orientation to religion is related to low prejudice, while an intrinsic, end orientation is related to only the appearance of low prejudice'.

Helping behaviour

Self-report measures of helping behaviour and altruism show a positive effect, but perhaps this should not be taken too seriously either. Experiments in which people have the opportunity to engage in real help have shown very little effect of religion. However, these were mostly rather trivial acts of help, like posting lost letters, and also should not be taken very seriously. Better measures of helpfulness, perhaps, are ratings by other people, and studies using these have all shown positive results, the correlations with church attendance coming in the range .20 to .50 (Batson and Ventis, 1982). Francis (1987) found a clear relationship, of 33, between religious attitudes and empathy for 560 children aged 11–17. This could explain the helpfulness: religious influences encourage an empathetic concern for others.

Attitudes to 'sinners' (tolerance of deviates)

Christians are supposed to accept, forgive and help 'sinners', but do they do so? Many of them do not. Not only are many church-goers unsympathetic to racial minority groups, but also to criminals, homosexuals, unmarried mothers, conscientious objectors, drug addicts and political dissenters. While this finding is ironic, its explanation is simple. Church members feel that at least they are trying to be good, and they exaggerate the differences between their in-group and out-groups which are not even trying.

CONCLUSIONS

Religious beliefs can be interpreted as providing solutions to human problems; belief in an after-life can be so explained; God may be a projection of parents or of society. Rituals use the power of shared non-verbal signals to produce solidarity and healing, and to cope with major transitions. Religious experience can be produced by nature or drugs and in other ways; a number of evolutionary and other explanations have been put forward. Social influence is important, and much religious activity takes place in groups, including conversions, and services. There has been a recent growth of sects and cults, as a product of social conditions and charismatic leaders.

The correlation between religious activity and personality is weak, though conversion is associated with personal crises, and the Protestant work ethic is still important. Religious activity is greatest among adolescents and the elderly, women and higher social classes, though lower classes are more fundamentalist and join sects more.

Church membership produces greater health and mental health; the belief that life has a meaning and purpose makes people happy. And church members have greater concern for others and help more, though some are ethnocentric.

REFERENCES

Abrams, P. and McCulloch, A. (1976) *Communes, Sociology and Society*. Cambridge: Cambridge University Press.

Allport, G.W. (1966) The religious context of prejudice. *Journal for the Scientific Study of Religion*, 5, 447–57.

Argyle, M. (1958) *Religious Behaviour*. London: Routledge and Kegan Paul.

——(1987) *The Psychology of Happiness*. London: Methuen.

——(1989) *The Social Psychology of Work*. 2nd edition. Harmondsworth: Penguin.

Argyle, M. and Beit-Hallahmi, B. (1975) *The Social Psychology of Religion*. London: Routledge and Kegan Paul.

Bakan, P. (1971) The eyes have it. *Psychology Today, 4*, April, 64–7.

Baker, M. and Gorsuch, R. (1982) Trait anxiety and intrinsic-extrinsic religiousness. *Journal for the Scientific Study of Religion, 21*, 119–22.

Batson, C.D. (1975) Rational processing or rationalization? The effect of disconfirming information on a stated religious belief. *Journal of Personality and Social Psychology, 32*, 176–84.

Batson, C.D. and Ventis, W. (1982) *The Religious Experience: a Social–Psychological Perspective*. New York: Oxford University Press.

Berger, P.L. and Luckmann, T. (1966) *The Social Construction of Reality*. New York: Doubleday.

Bergin, A.E. (1983) Religiosity and mental health: a critical re-evaluation and meta-analysis. *Professional Psychology: Research and Practice, 14*, 170–84.

Brown, G.A., Spilka, B. and Cassidy, S. (1978) The structure of mystical experience and pre- and post-experience lifestyle correlates. Cited by Batson and Ventis (1982).

Buber, M. (1936, 1958) *I and Thou*. New York: Scribner.

Campbell, A., Converse, P. and Rodgers, W.L. (1976) *The Quality of American Life*. New York: McGraw-Hill.

Clark, E.T. (1929) *The Psychology of Religious Awakening*. New York: Macmillan.

Comstock, G.W. and Partridge, K.B. (1972) Church attendance and health. *Journal of Chronic Diseases, 25*, 665–72.

Davenport, F.M. (1906) *Primitive Traits in Religious Revivals*. New York: Macmillan.

Davis, K. (1948) *Human Society*. New York: Macmillan.

DeConchy, J.P. (1967) *Structure génétique de l'idée de Dieu*. Brussels: Lumen Vitae.

Durkheim, E. (1915) *The Elementary Forms of Religious Life*. London: Allen & Unwin.

Dwyer, J.W., Clarke, L.L. and Miller, M.K. (1990) The effect of religious concentration and affiliation on county cancer mortality rates. *Journal of Health and Social Behavior, 31*, 185–202.

Feather, N.T. (1964) Acceptance and rejection of arguments in relation to attitude strength, critical ability and intolerance of inconsistency. *Journal of Abnormal and Social Psychology, 69*, 127–36.

Feifel, H. (1990) Psychology and death: a meaningful rediscovery. *American Psychologist, 45*, 537–43.

Festinger, L., Riecken, H.W. and Schachter, S. (1956) *When Prophecy Fails*. Minneapolis: University of Minnesota Press.

Firth, R. (1970) Postures and gestures of respect. *In* J. Pouillon and P. Marande (eds) *Échanges et Communications*. The Hague: Mouton.

Francis, L.J. (1985) Personality and religion: theory and measurement. *In* L.B. Brown (ed.) *Advances in the Psychology of Religion*. Oxford: Pergamon.

Francis, L.J. and Pearson, P.R. (1987) Empathic development during adolescence: religiosity, the missing link? *Personality and Individual Differences, 8*, 145–8.

Freedman, J.L. (1978) *Happy People*. New York: Harcourt Brace Jovanovich.

Freud, S. (1907) Obsessive acts and religious practices. *Collected Papers, 2*, 25–35.

——(1913) *Totem and Taboo*. London: Hogarth Press.

Furnham, A. (1990) *The Protestant Work Ethic*. London: Routledge.

Gerard, D. (1985) Religious attitudes and values. *In* M. Abrams, D. Gerard and N. Timms (eds) *Values and Social Change in Britain*. London: Macmillan.

Gorer, G. (1955) *Exploring English Character*. London: Cresset.

Gorsuch, R.L. (1988) Psychology of religion. *Annual Review of Psychology, 39*, 201–21.

Hall, J.R. (1988) Social organization and pathways of commitment: types of communal groups, rational choice theory, and the Kanter thesis. *American Sociological Review, 53*, 679–92.

Hampton, P.J. (1945) The emotional element in music. *Journal of General Psychology, 33*, 237–50.

Hay, D. (1982) *Exploring Inner Space*. Harmondsworth: Penguin Books.
——(1985) Religious experience and its induction. *In* L.B. Brown (ed.) *Advances in the Psychology of Religion*. Oxford: Pergamon.
Hay, D. and Heald, G. (1987) Religion is good for you. *New Society*, 17 April.
Hayden, B. (1987) Alliances and ritual ecstasy: human responses to reduce stress. *Journal for the Scientific Study of Religion*, 26, 81–91.
Heinrich, M. (1973) Change of heart: a test of some widely held theories about religious conversion. *American Journal of Sociology*, 83, 653–80.
Hood, R.W. (1975) The construction and validation of a measure of reported mystical experience. *Journal for the Scientific Study of Religion*, 14, 29–41.
Hood, R.W., Morris, R.J. and Watson, P.J. (1990) Quasi-experimental elicitation of the differential report of religious experience among intrinsic and indiscriminantly pro-religious types. *Journal for the Scientific Study of Religion*, 29, 164–72.
Hooper, T. and Spilka, B. (1970) Some meanings and correlates of future time and death among college students. *Omega*, 1, 49–56.
Huxley, F. (1966) The ritual voodoo and the symbolism of the body. *In* J.S. Huxley (ed.) *A Discussion of Ritualization of Behaviour in Animals and Men*. Philosophical Transactions of the Royal Society of London.
ITA (1970) *Religion in Britain and Northern Ireland*. London: Independent Television Authority.
Jaynes, J. (1976) *The Origins of Consciousness in the Breakdown of the Bicameral Mind*. Boston, MA: Houghton Mifflin Co.
Kanter, R.M. (1968) Commitment and social organization: a study of commitment mechanisms in utopian communities. *American Sociological Review*, 33, 499–517.
Langer, S.K. (1942) *Philosophy in a New Key*. Cambridge, MA: Harvard University Press.
Lewis, J.R. and Bromley, D.G. (1987) The cult withdrawal syndrome: a case of misattribution of cause? *Journal for the Scientific Study of Religion*, 26, 508–22.
McClelland, D.C. (1961) *The Achieving Society*. Princeton, NJ: Van Nostrand.
McComb, S. (1928) Spiritual healing in Europe. *Mental Hygiene*, 12, 706–21.
Marcia, J.E. (1966) Development and validation of ego-identity status. *Journal of Personality and Social Psychology*, 3, 551–8.
Marx, K. (1964) *Early Writings*. New York: McGraw-Hill.
Maton, K.I. (1989) The stress-buffering role of spiritual support: cross-sectional and prospective investigations. *Journal for the Scientific Study of Religion*, 28, 310–23.
Mirels, H. and Garrett, J. (1971) The Protestant ethic as a personality variable. *Journal of Consulting and Clinical Psychology*, 36, 40–4.
Moberg, D.O. and Taves, M.J. (1965) Church participation and adjustment in old age. *In* A.M. Rose and W.A. Peterson (eds.) *Older People and their Social World*. Philadelphia: F.A. Davis.
Nelsen, H.M., Cheek, N.H. and Au, P. (1985) Gender differences in images of God. *Journal for the Scientific Study of Religion*, 24, 396–402.
Osarchuk, M. and Tate, S.J. (1973) Effect of induced fear of death on belief in afterlife. *Journal of Personality and Social Psychology*, 27, 256–60.
Pahnke, W.H. (1966) Drugs and mysticism. *International Journal of Parapsychology*, 8, 295–314.
Pargament, K.I., Kennell, J., Hathaway, W., Grevengoed, N., Newman, J. and Jones, W. (1988) Religion and the problem-solving process: three styles of coping. *Journal for the Scientific Study of Religion*, 27, 90–109.
Pearson, P.R., Francis, L.J. and Lightbown, T.J. (1986) Impulsivity and religion.

Personality and Individual Differences, 7, 89–94.

Reid, I. (1989) *Social Class Differences in Britain*. 3rd edition. London: Fontana.

Richardson, J.T. (1985) Psychological and psychiatric studies of new religion. *In* L.B. Brown (ed.) *Advances in the Psychology of Religion*. Oxford: Pergamon.

Rokeach, M. (1964) *The Three Christs of Ypsilanti*. New York: Knopf.

Rosegrant, J. (1976) The impacy of set and setting on religious experience in nature. *Journal for the Scientific Study of Religion*, 15, 301–10.

St George, A. and McNamara, P.H. (1984) Religion, race and psychological well-being. *Journal for the Scientific Study of Religion*, 23, 351–63.

Sargant, W. (1957) *Battle for the Mind*. London: Heinemann.

Schachter, S. (1964) The interaction of cognitive and physiological determinants of emotional states. *Advances in Experimental Social Psychology*, 1, 49–80.

Slugoski, B.R., Marcia, J.E. and Koopman, R.F. (1984) Cognitive and interactional characteristics of ego identity statuses in college males. *Journal of Personality and Social Psychology*, 47, 646–61.

Spanos, N.P. and Moretti, P. (1985) Correlates of mystical and diabolical experiences in a sample of female university students. *Journal for the Scientific Study of Religion*, 27, 105–16.

Spilka, B., Hood, R.W. and Gorsuch, R.L. (1985) *The Psychology of Religion*. Englewood Cliffs, NJ: Prentice-Hall.

Staples, C.L. and Mauss, A.L. (1987) Conversion or commitment? A reassessment of the Snow and Machalak approach to the study of conversion. *Journal for the Scientific Study of Religion*, 26, 133–47.

Stark, R., Doyle, D.P. and Rushing, J.L. (1983) Beyond Durkheim: religion and suicide. *Journal for the Scientific Study of Religion*, 22, 120–31.

Stephan, K.H. and Stephan, G.E. (1973) Religion and the survival of Utopian communities. *Journal for the Scientific Study of Religion*, 12, 89–100.

Sunden, H. (1965) What is the next step to be taken in the psychology of religion? *The Harvard Theological Review*, 58, 445–51.

Swanson, G.E. (1960) *The Birth of the Gods*. Ann Arbor: University of Michigan Press.

Swenson, W.M. (1961) Attitudes towards death in an aged population. *Journal of Gerontology*, 16, 49–52.

Thouless, R.H. (1935) The tendency to certainty in religious beliefs. *British Journal of Psychology*, 26, 16–31.

Turner, V.M. (1967) *The Forest of Symbols*. Ithaca, NY: Cornell University Press.

Ulbrich, H. and Wallace, M. (1984) Women's work force status and church attendance. *Journal for the Scientific Study of Religion*, 23, 341–50.

Underhill, R. (1975) Economic and political antecedents of monotheism: a cross-cultural study. *American Journal of Sociology*, 80, 841–61.

Valentine, C.W. (1962) *The Experimental Psychology of Beauty*. London: Methuen.

Watts, F. and Williams, M. (1988) *The Psychology of Religious Knowing*. Cambridge: Cambridge University Press.

Weber, M. (1904) *The Protestant Ethic and the Spirit of Capitalism*. London: Allen & Unwin.

——(1922) *The Sociology of Religion*. Boston, MA: Beacon Press.

Woodruff, J.T. (1985) Premarital sexual behavior and religious adolescents. *Journal for the Scientific Study of Religion*, 24, 343–66.

Chapter 7

Aggression and conflict between groups

Social psychologists have been very interested in the milder forms of inter-group conflict, such as people liking other groups less than they like their own, and holding negative beliefs about them. And psychologists have of course studied these mild forms of conflict in a scaled-down way, when subjects express small degrees of favouritism to imaginary groups which they are told they belong to. Meanwhile the world is being torn apart by real conflicts, where people hate and kill one another on an enormous scale. It may be between communist and capitalist nations, Israelis and Arabs, blacks and whites in Africa, and in numerous 'civil' wars. Although psychology's contribution to these matters has so far been meagre, I feel that we should at any rate confront the issues.

THE EXTENT OF AGGRESSIVE CONFLICT

Racial prejudice

Prejudice against other racial groups is very widespread in the world. In Israel there is intermittent violence between Jews and Palestinians. In South Africa there is hostility between blacks and whites, especially on the part of Boers, and also between different tribal groups. In many countries there is a racial minority group which is disliked – Turks in Germany, Koreans in Japan, for example.

The state of racial attitudes in the USA has been closely monitored in many surveys. These show a great improvement in white attitudes towards blacks; acceptance of desegregated schools increased from 31 per cent in 1942 to 90 per cent in 1985. However, there is still a minority of whites who dislike blacks: the percentage of whites who would be unwilling for more intimate social contacts such as coming home to dinner is about 25 per cent, and indirect and deceptive measuring methods uncover quite a lot of prejudiced attitudes (Myers, 1990). The situation in Britain is similar, and some of the population think that 'they should go home', and a lot more think that native whites should be given jobs, promoted, or given housing ahead of coloured immigrants.

Violence in crowds

There have been a number of race riots in Britain in recent years – in Bristol (1980) and Toxteth, Liverpool (1984), for example. In the USA lynchings were a common feature of life in the Southern states in the 1930s, as were riots in cities during hot summers after World War II, culminating in the 1965 Watts riot in Los Angeles. Inter-tribal and black–white riots are so common in South Africa that this is better described as a civil war. At the time of writing the main conflict is between two black groups – the African National Congress and Zulus.

Other violent crowds have a political origin – miners versus police, and the storming of the Bastille, for example. During the 1960s some student riots were very aggressive, like the Grosvenor Square riot, and the confrontations at Berkeley.

Football hooliganism

Britain invented football, and later invented football hooliganism, exporting it to many other countries. This has become increasingly violent, and resulted in many deaths, for example at the Huyssel stadium in Brussels (1985) where the behaviour of English fans led to the deaths of 38 others, mainly Italians.

This is a form of violence on the part of a minority of those attending, who in turn comprise about 5 per cent of the male adult population, and are mostly young, working-class males.

Wars

The number who were killed in wars during the nineteenth century has been estimated as about 5,817,000; in the twentieth century, up to 1986, about 84 million have been killed so far (Sivard, 1983). At the time of writing there are wars in the Middle East, South Africa, Liberia, Lebanon and Central America.

At an earlier historical period the majority of the population were relatively unaffected by wars, which were fought by standing armies, often foreign mercenaries and professional soldiers. Now wars are different, and the entire civilian population becomes involved and at risk. Terrorists threaten and use violence against military and civilian targets for political motives. During recent years terrorism has become increasingly widespread in Britain and the rest of Europe. As well as the IRA, there are a number of Palestinian and other Arab groups, revolutionary communists, and other political organisations based in Germany, Italy, France and Spain. They are notable in the aggressiveness of those involved, and the risk to the civilian population (Giddens, 1989).

BIOLOGICAL AND PSYCHOLOGICAL ORIGINS OF AGGRESSION

The evolution of aggression

Aggression is found in most species of animals, and plays a key role in evolution. It is used to compete for food, shelter, territory or females, and male animals in particular are equipped with horns, teeth and claws with which to do it. Fighting within the group is mainly for dominance, is ended by submission signals, and by the loser accepting a lower place in the hierarchy. Aggression towards other groups and other species is more violent and more risky. It is onnly underttaken if the expected gains, in access to scarce resources, for example, are greater than the risks. Complex strategies are used, such as adopting a threatening posture and baring the teeth, but withdrawing if the other retaliates. Males are much more aggressive than females, and often fight over females. Males attack males, females attack females. But males rarely attack pre-pubertal males, or males who have been castrated.

Since successful aggression leads to survival, there is an evolutionary trend towards the development of aggressive powers, such as size and strength in males. However, in the non-human primates things are more complicated, and status depends on the intelligence and social skills needed to establish coalitions. The dominant animal is not usually the most aggressive.

Animals do not have wars. The only exception is in insects; in the case of ants, different nests may fight and take prisoners which are made into slaves. There can be fights between groups of rats, or hyenas, but our closest relatives, the primates, keep to their own territories, and rarely fight; if different groups meet they simply engage in aggressive displays (Huntingford, 1989).

How far have humans inherited these aggressive dispositions? We do have similar aggressive displays, in facial expression. We are less friendly to members of out-groups, including different racial groups. And, as with animals, it is young males who are the most aggressive.

Archaeological studies show that, from about 2 million years ago, primitive men started to eat large animals, and had tools and weapons. Groups of males cooperated over hunting animals, and had the capability for fighting other groups. But for humans the role of socialisation is more important – and it may increase or reduce aggressiveness. And the role of cognition, ideas, strategies and plans is far more important than for animals.

The physiology of aggression

Twin studies in humans show that individual differences in aggressiveness have a strong genetic component, about 50 per cent. In addition, males with the XYY chromosome are usually very aggressive, and often go to prison, though this is at least partly because of their irritability and hyperactivity, and consequent rough treatment by parents. Experiments have been done in which mice or dogs have been bred to develop aggressive or unaggressive strains.

Body chemistry plays a role in aggression. Injecting male animals with the male sex hormone, testosterone, increases their territory-marking with urine or other odours, and increases aggressiveness; treating females with female sex hormones does the same. Castration reduces marking, sexuality, dominance and aggressiveness, and also makes animals less often targets of aggression.

Aggression is produced by certain parts of the brain – the hypothalamus and other areas of the limbic system. Damage to the hypothalamus reduces aggression, while electrical stimulation increases socially appropriate aggression, such as to lower-ranking animals. Delgado (1969) carried out spectacular experiments in which bulls were caused to charge and stop charging by radio-transmitted signals to implanted electrodes. Damage to the amygdala, on the other hand, leads to socially *in*appropriate violence.

Gender differences in aggression

In all modern societies and most primitive ones, men are more aggressive than women; only men fight in wars, men commit most violent crimes, all football hooligans are males. Most physical aggression is by adolescent males; male aggression is intended to inflict pain; female aggression is mostly verbal, and is intended to inflict psychological pain. This gender difference is probably innate in part: sex differences are found in very young children, from age $2^1/2$; and there is a rise in testosterone in adolescent males; males are more aggressive among non-human primates and other animals. The difference may be partly the result of socialisation. Women feel more guilt and anxiety about aggression; it is likely that maternal prohibitions have a greater impact on them (Geen, 1990).

However, females do fight sometimes, especially with one another. Campbell (1981) found that among female delinquents it was sufficiently common for rules to develop, controlling the nature of this aggression (Table 7.1, see page 170).

The social learning of aggression

Experiments have shown that aggression can be learnt – or unlearnt. Geen and colleagues (1990) showed that the size of electric shocks which subjects would give to another person increased if they were rewarded by verbal approval. Bandura (1973) found that nursery-school children of both sexes behaved more violently towards a Bobo doll if they had seen a film of another child doing the same, especially if that child was seen to be rewarded afterwards. Learning by observation and modelling is one of the main forms of social learning here.

It has been widely found that aggressive boys come from homes where they were rejected, and received irregular discipline and a lot of physical punishment. But are they aggressive because they were punished, or vice versa? Olweus (1986) carried out a causal analysis, which shows the sequence of events (see Figure 7.1). This shows that the boys' (aggressive) temperament affects mother's permissiveness for aggression, but that mother's negative attitude and use of power assertive methods were independent causes of aggression.

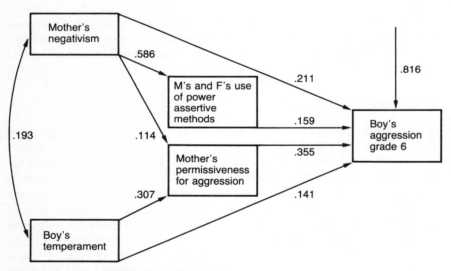

Figure 7.1 Causal model of aggression
Source: Olweus, 1986

Aggression is also learned from experience, and practice, with siblings. Patterson (1986) found that brothers especially had very frequent conflicts, more in the case of problem children, and that this could be controlled by parents if they monitored and disciplined this behaviour, and rewarded for cooperative behaviour, though they were often attacked themselves.

Do children learn aggression from TV? There is certainly a correlation between aggressiveness and frequent watching of violent films. It is estimated that the average American has seen 25,000 people 'killed' on TV by the time they are 18. But does watching violent TV *cause* aggression? There have been a number of attempts to find out. One of the best was by Eron and Huesmann (1980) who found that viewing violence among 8-year-old boys predicted aggressiveness at age 19, while aggressiveness at 8 did not predict violent viewing at 19. There have been a number of realistic experiments. For example, Leyens *et al.* (1975) in Belgium exposed delinquent boys in an institution for a period to films which were rated high or low in aggressiveness. There was more physical violence between the boys who had been exposed to the more violent films. From these and other studies it seems very likely that aggressive films do increase aggressive behaviour.

Cultural differences in aggression

There are cultural differences between tribes in aggressiveness; some are very peaceful and never fight anyone. Cross-cultural studies have been able to show not only which socialisation practices are responsible, but also what causes these practices to occur.

The most important point is that societies which expect to be at war, and need aggressive young men to fight, encourage aggression compared with more peaceful societies. In a comparison of 6 cultures, Lambert (1971) found that aggression towards peers was less if people lived surrounded by close kin, as with Mexican Indians – because peers were mostly kin, and inter-kin aggression was prevented. There was less aggression towards mothers when the latter retaliated, which they did when there were often adults living in the same building, and there was fear of the aggression generalising, as in a Kenyan tribe.

There may be differences in aggressiveness between developed countries too. It has been found that the effects of violent TV on aggression are less in Australia, Finland, Israel and elsewhere than in the USA, perhaps because cultural norms and socialisation restrain it more (Segall, 1989). Surveys in the USA have found a lot of support for aggressive values. For example, 70 per cent agreed that 'when a boy is growing up, it is important for him to have a few fist fights' (Mulvihill and Tumin, 1969).

In Britain and in most modern countries there has been a long-term trend towards the restraint of aggression, in everyday life and also in sports (Elias and Dunning, 1986). However, within some working-class, ethnic and delinquent sub-cultures, aggression is widely used and valued as a mark of masculinity.

The immediate causes of aggression

It is now generally agreed that aggression is a response to certain situations. It is not a need like hunger which builds up and has to be satisfied.

In *instrumental aggression* there is another goal, not injury of the other person, and there is no anger or hostility. This happens when it is judged that the likely benefits will be greater than the costs, and there are weak internal restraints for aggression. Crimes like mugging are an example. Football hooligans and members of other sub-cultures give peer-group approval for acts of violence, which may then be mainly instrumental.

Physical *attacks* and verbal insults are the most powerful instigators of angry aggression, if the aggressor is believed to have had hostile intentions. In laboratory experiments subjects retaliate with electric shocks to others who they think have shocked them. In the real world one has to decide whether another person has been aggressive, or whether it was an accident, playfulness or something else. The criteria used are intention to harm, actual harm and norm-violation (Mummendey, 1988). There can easily be an escalation, if, for example, A thinks that B is looking at him or behaving in a hostile or insulting way, and then speaks angrily to him, whereupon a real fight may start.

Pain is often produced by attacks, and is itself a stimulus for aggression; Berkowitz *et al.* (1981) found that simply having a hand in unpleasantly cold water made subjects more aggressive.

A classical theory of aggression was that its main cause is *frustration*; that is, the blocking of a sequence of goal-directed behaviour, so not reaching an expected goal. Frustration is not the *only* cause of aggression, as we have seen. And it leads to aggression only under certain conditions, especially when it is due to intentional, arbitrary, unfair and illegitimate behaviour by another. So 'frustration', or pain, produced by doctors or dentists does not lead to aggression, nor usually do accidents. Frustration is an important cause of real-life aggression such as race riots, though the frustration involved may be due to rising expectations which are not fulfilled. Feierabend and Feierabend (1972) compared 84 countries, and found that in politically unstable countries with a lot of violence there is less provision of desired and expected services. And there is often displacement of aggression from the true cause to attacking some more visible and usually weaker target person. There were more lynchings of black Americans in the American South when the value of cotton was low, with consequent economic deprivation (Hovland and Sears, 1940).

Arousal, from any source, makes people more likely to be aggressive, and frustration is one source of arousal. Zillman *et al.* (1972) carried out experiments in which arousal was induced by riding on an exercycle; later, annoyance was met with heightened aggression. In other experiments he found that excitation of one kind can transfer to another, so that sexual arousal can transfer to aggression and vice versa. Schachter and Singer (1962) induced anger or euphoria, by contact with a confederate, and both states were amplified by an adrenaline injection, showing that general arousal can enhance aggression, if other conditions suggesting aggression are also present. Another formulation is in terms of *negative affect* (negative emotions), which can be generated by a variety of stresses. One which has been much studied is *heat*. Violent crimes and race riots are more common in the USA on days when the temperature is over 90°. Aggression is also increased by noise, overcrowding and atmosphere pollution (Geen *et al.*, 1990).

Social influence: people may be aggressive because they are ordered, or paid, to be so, or will be punished if they are not. This is an important feature of armies and delinquent sub-cultures. It was modelled by Milgram (1974) who found that 65 per cent of his subjects would give what appeared to be very dangerous electric shocks to another subject, because the experimenter told them that they 'had to', and threatened disapproval if they didn't.

The important of anonymity was developed in theories of '*de-individuation*'. Zimbardo (1969), in a rather bizarre experiment, dressed subjects up in baggy overalls and hoods, Ku-Klux-Klan style, and in a dim light; in this condition subjects gave longer electric shocks to confederates who had behaved in an annoying way. It has been argued that lack of self-awareness is the key factor in producing more spontaneity, less concern with norms or evaluation by others.

Alcohol is an important factor in everyday violence. Sixty-four per cent of violent crimes are carried out under the influence of drink, and it appears to be a major factor in football hooliganism. Laboratory experiments have shown that alcohol makes people more aggressive when threatened, more difficult to restrain from violence, and less concerned with social restraints, but this is true only of people with an aggressive disposition (Geen, 1990).

Drugs are a major cause of aggression, especially in parts of American cities, mainly because of the need to steal money to pay for the drugs.

Individual differences in aggressiveness

Some individuals are much more aggressive than others – terrorists, violent offenders and school bullies, for example. Are they too simply responding to attacks or suffering from frustrations and so on? Not entirely, since some of them start such attacks. Bullies usually start fights by attacking smaller children (Olweus, 1979). They don't do it all the time; it is only in a certain range of situations that it happens. Such aggressiveness is partly inherited – about 50 per cent of it, according to twin studies. Aggressive offenders are often found to have had a family history of rejection and physical punishment.

Some violent offenders have been found to be 'overcontrolled', to have too much internal restraint against aggression. If frustration builds up too far they break out with an abnormally violent response (Megargee, 1966). Others feel anxious or guilty over the use of aggression and have strong internal controls, the opposite of irritability and impulsiveness. Socialisation experiences can develop internalised restraints against aggression, especially by exhortation, and other kinds of rewards, punishments and social pressure from parents, short of the use of physical punishment (Krebs and Miller, 1985).

Restraints on aggression

Although most individuals are frequently frustrated, sometimes insulted, occasionally attacked, and often in a state of negative affect, aggression is quite rare – because there are powerful restraints.

Social norms, in most groups, are against it, especially aggression towards members of the group. On the other hand, delinquent and other deviant groups encourage aggression towards other people. However, there are still norms controlling the nature and level of such aggression; the rules for fighting between women found by Campbell (1981) are shown in Table 7.1. Society imposes formal punishments, and there is evidence that these have some deterrent effect. Figure 7.2 shows that the

Table 7.1   Rules for fighting among females

1	Should not use a bottle to hit the other person schoolgirls 85% (borstal girls 58%)
2	Should not ask friends to call the police borstal girls 85%
3	Should not use a handbag to hit the other person 69%
4	Should not use a knife on the other person schoolgirls 89% (borstal girls 52%)
5	Should not report it to the police later 86%
6	Should not ask friends to join in 81%
7	Should not tell the school later 85%
8	It is OK to kick the other person borstal girls 78%
9	It is OK to slap the other person prison women 85%
10	It is OK to punch the other person borstal girls 90%

Source: Survey of 251 schoolgirls, borstal girls and prison women, from Campbell, 1981

numbers of murders per week in England fell by 35 per cent for 3 weeks around the time of well-publicised executions in London in the period 1858–1921, when capital punishment was still in force.

In addition to fear of punishment by the law there is also *fear of retaliation*. Laboratory experiments with electric shocks have found that subjects are less likely to give shocks to another who had provoked them, if he would be in a position to retaliate later, unless the subjects were very angry (Baron, 1973).

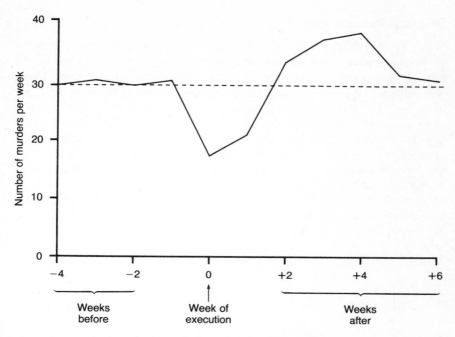

Figure 7.2 The effect of capital punishment on the murder rate
Source: Phillips, 1980

Empathy for the victim is an important restraint. Experiments by Geen (1990) found that subjects who had been provoked by another used less aggressive retaliation if the other winced, groaned or showed other non-verbal signs of distress. This effect is stronger if the victim is similar to the angered subject, and is presumably due to the arousal of a state of empathy.

Making people *self-aware*, self-conscious, imagining themselves as observed from outside, makes them behave more responsibly and conform to norms. This can be done by placing them in front of a mirror, or a TV camera, or by making them look distinctive. Zimbardo (1969) 'individuated' subjects by giving them prominent name labels and bright illumination; they gave shorter shocks than subjects in hoods and a dim light (see p. 169). But if people are in favour of punishment, individuation causes them to give *more* shocks.

CONFLICT BETWEEN GROUPS

We turn now to conflicts between groups of people. There have been many laboratory experiments here, but few involving actual aggression.

Do groups enhance aggression?

Sherif *et al*. (1961) ran a celebrated experiment in a summer camp for 12-year-old boys. New groups were formed by putting boys together in huts so that most of each boy's friends were in the other group. There was evidence of some in-group favouritism as a result of being in the same huts, but this was greatly increased when tug-of-war and other contests were arranged between 2 groups, and there was real hostility when 1 group appeared to have frustrated the other. But is there *more* hostility when groups are involved? Rabbie (1989) says that there is, because group norms are formed which support more extreme, risky attitudes towards the other group. We shall see below that football hooligans in large groups behave in ways in which no individual would behave alone. Analysis of lynchings has found that the larger the lynching group, the more vicious the violence to the victim (Mullen, 1986).

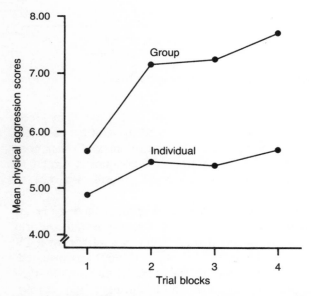

Figure 7.3 Escalation of physical aggression for individuals and groups
Source: Jaffe and Yinon, 1983

Minnix (1982) found that group discussion about a possible crisis in the Persian Gulf (which came true in 1990) led to more hostile proposals in groups of American officer cadets and RUTC members; however, groups of students became more cautious – their initial norms were different. Laboratory experiments with electric shocks have confirmed this effect. Jaffe and Yinon (1983) found that students in groups who had been angered by another subject gave increasingly large shocks, much more than individuals gave (Figure 7.3).

Categorising and stereotyping

Part of the explanation of hostility to other groups is that negative beliefs are held about them. To begin with, there is a strong tendency to categorise people as members of the in- or the out-groups. In the case of racial out-groups, these are often thought to be 'dirty', 'aggressive', 'oversexed' and so on. Members of different groups are clearly recognisable (even in Northern Ireland), by accent or appearance, and it is easy to categorise people by their obvious group membership, and apply stereotypes to them. There is a tendency to exaggerate the homogeneity of the out-group, and its differences from the in-group, partly since there is little contact with out-group members, who may all 'look the same'. Often these stereotypes include the idea that members of the other group are sub-human, like animals, or have no soul. These negative views provide justification for aggression or other negative behaviour towards that group. However, the other group often holds very similar stereotypes, indeed they often form mirror-images. Bronfenbrenner (1961) pointed out that the Russian view of the Americans at the time was similar to the American view of the Russians – aggressive, untrustworthy, irresponsible, and ruled by governments which exploited and deluded them.

An important way of countering this cognitive categorising of them and us is the introduction of 'cross-cutting categories'. Experiments have shown that there is less discrimination against another group if they belong to a different category on one criterion and to a similar category on another (Deschamps and Doise, 1978). In practice this could consist of similar occupational, social class or religious categories to offset different racial categories, for example.

The search for a superior identity

Social identity theory offers an explanation of why stereotypes of other groups are usually negative, and why people think so highly of their own groups. Tajfel (1970) carried out a 'minimal group' experiment in which schoolboys were allocated to arbitrary groupings on the basis of their apparent preference for Klee or Kandinsky. Although subjects never met the other members of their 'group' they allocated slightly larger sums of money on special matrices to unknown members of their own group. Rabbie and Horwitz (1969) in a similar experiment had found that the 'blue' subjects rated the 'green' subjects less favourably than they rated other blue subjects, and vice versa. Tajfel (1978), in his 'social identity theory', suggested that it is because our self-image and self-esteem depend partly on the groups to which we belong that we do our best to see our groups as distinctive and superior in some way to other groups.

It is often the case that one group is, in worldly terms, of higher status or power than another group. The low-status group can deal with this in a number of possible ways. Several kinds of 'social creativity' are possible, and have been found in experiments. These are: discovering new dimensions for comparison, on which the in-group does better, deciding that certain attributes which the group possesses are good rather than bad (such as 'black is beautiful'), and selecting different out-groups for comparison purposes. This opens the way to a kind of cooperation, where each side selects for emphasis the dimensions where it does well. An example is that South African Hindus see themselves as superior to the whites in spiritual, social and practical spheres, though the whites no doubt see the Hindus as inferior in wealth and social status (Mann, 1963). Two groups can cooperate and be interdependent while recognising each other's different qualities; that is, while keeping their stereotypes.

One revision of the theory is needed. Positive attitudes to the in-group are often not correlated with negative attitudes to the out-group as expected, and probably have different causes. Rabbie (1989) suggests that in-group feelings are produced by 'common fate, physical proximity, and a shared territory, positive independence . . ., cooperative intragroup interaction, and shared success experience'. Out-group hostility, on the other hand, is mainly due to illegitimate frustration caused by the other group.

Cultural differences

Another fundamental source of conflict between groups derives from cultural differences – in language, beliefs, rules and general way of life. Deviates within a group are often rejected, so it is not surprising that whole groups of deviates are similarly rejected. Dijker (1987) reports a study of the effects of physical proximity in Amsterdam. He found that proximity led Dutch residents to like Indonesians but not Turks. Presumably the cultural differences between Dutch and Turks were too great.

Several aspects of culture are important here. One of the reasons why people dislike other racial and cultural groups is that it is believed that they hold different beliefs and values, think differently, and are therefore incomprehensible, not quite human. Rokeach et al. (1960) found that similarity of beliefs was a more important factor than similarity of race, when subjects were asked for their attitudes towards various target persons, presented by verbal descriptions or by photographs.

We shall discuss later a number of other aspects of culture, which apply particularly to racial and national conflicts:

Language
Non-verbal communication
Rules of situations
Relationships
Social skills
Ideas and concepts.

Inter-cultural training can take account of these differences, and train people, for example, in the rules of the other culture.

Real conflict between groups

Bad relations between groups are often based on real conflict. In the Sherif experiment there was real competition between the groups, and later there appeared to be real frustration. Sherif proposed that realistic conflict is the main cause of inter-group conflict. This theory fits the hostility felt towards the other side during wars, and for some years afterwards.

On a larger scale war leads to great hostility and prejudice against members of the other side; in the case of British against Germans and Japanese in World War II it took several years before these attitudes subsided. There is a great deal of conflict in industry, between workers and unions on the one side and owners and managers on the other. There is real conflict here; for example, over levels of wages, and laying off workers when work is short. This conflict is manifested in strikes, stoppages, go-slows and even sabotage. There are also conflicts between different groups of workers, who may see themselves as competing for pay and status. There is real conflict today between blacks and whites, Israelis and Arabs, and others. Rupert Brown (1986) found that hostile as opposed to friendly attitudes towards other departments in a factory were primarily the result of perceived conflict with them, and not of in-group identification (as the theory discussed above predicted). This theory has the attraction that it suggests a solution to inter-group conflict – the discovery of 'superordinate goals' which appeal to both groups (p. 184ff).

There is a special kind of conflict in which there are differences of power or status (usually both) between two or more groups. The reason is simple: where there is unequal status the superior group is able to regard the other group or groups as inferior; the low-status groups resent their low position and feel hostile towards higher-status groups. When there are power differences too, low-status groups resent the capacity of other groups to control them.

The most obvious case of status difference is in relations between different racial groups. Usually there are status differences between black and white, or there can be a complex pecking order of ethnic groups, as in the USA and South Africa. In South Africa the status differences between races have been sustained by an elaborate set of laws, and large differences in wealth and housing.

Experiments have thrown further light on antipathy as a result of different power or status. It is found that in-group bias increases the more power one group has. In several experiments it has been the high-status or high-power group which showed the most bias. The effect is greater if the status difference is 'illegitimate' (that is, undeserved), which is quite irrational in the case of high-status groups. Low-status groups show little in-group bias in experiments, if the status differences are believed to be legitimate and stable (not likely to change). But if the differences are seen as illegitimate and unstable, low-status groups 'may start to assert themselves by displaying in-group favouritism and a rejection of the dominant group's "superiority"' (Brown, 1988).

REAL INTER-GROUP AGGRESSION

In this section we shall look at five cases of real aggression between groups.

Tribal wars

Most hunters and gatherers fought neighbouring groups at times, in short raids by young men, in a formal, ceremonial way, to avenge wife-stealing or witchcraft, rather than for economic gain. Among more settled farming communities, economic gain or conquest became factors, and led to peace and the integration of groups into larger tribes. War became more serious, and more dangerous. The exceptions are such peaceful peoples as the Zuni Indians and Eskimos (Wright, 1968). Brewer and Campbell (1976) carried out a survey of 50 members each of 30 tribes in East Africa. Most tribes gave more favourable ratings to their own tribes on scales with some evaluative content, such as 'honest', 'peace-loving', 'virtuous' and 'liking'. On the whole tribes liked adjacent tribes more than non-adjacent ones, and gave them higher ratings – a clear case of social contact leading to liking, perhaps because there would be more trading links. On the other hand, more conflict was also reported with these adjacent tribes – more contact also produces more scope for friction. In a study of 48 primitive societies, Naroll (1966) found that being prepared for war, by means of weapons, fortification and prepared tactics, had no relationship with frequency of wars: it did not have a deterrent effect or increase the likelihood of war. It looks as if aggressiveness and war have little relationship here.

Tribal war is still common in the world, especially in Africa. In 1990 there was severe conflict in South Africa between Zulus and others, mainly armed with spears and clubs. Such tribal hostility could be explained by the inclusive fitness model, of concern for kin because of their shared genes.

At a higher stage of civilisation, especially in large empires, there have been standing armies of professional soldiers, often well equipped. In the eleventh century the Chinese government arsenals produced 32,000 suits of armour a year (Giddens, 1989).

Racial prejudice in modern society

We have seen that there is widespread prejudice against racial minority groups in modern society. This leads to discrimination in jobs and housing, and some violence both by police and members of delinquent groups – 'Paki-bashing' has been a British version.

The sociological causes of prejudice are competition for jobs, housing and social status. For example, there was almost no prejudice in Britain towards black immigrants until there was an economic recession, and consequent competition for jobs. In Lancashire the unemployment of whites was blamed both on black immigrants taking jobs and on cheap imports of textiles from Pakistan and other parts of Asia. The competition for social status is shown by the finding that 67 per cent of working-class whites could recognise class differences within the black population, while only 6 per cent of middle-class whites could do so (Abrams, 1969). In the USA there is most anti-black prejudice amongst downwardly mobile whites. This is a clear case of frustration leading to aggression. We saw earlier that there were more lynchings during periods of economic depression. Housing is a traditional source of friction: immigrants have great difficulty finding accommodation; when they do so a number of immigrant families occupy a house, making a great deal of noise and mess, and driving out the neighbours, until the whole road 'goes black'. It is those who feel they are being driven out who cause race riots.

Prejudice and discrimination can lead to the very behaviour for which a minority group is blamed – poverty, aggressiveness, delinquency and so on – which has been called a 'self-fulfilling prophecy'. Laboratory experiments have shown that this can happen with social interaction. Word et al. (1974) found that when students interviewed blacks they sat further away, ended the interview sooner and made more speech errors. When this style was used with white interviewees, the latter behaved in a more nervous and less effective way – just as the black interviewees had done. So discrimination strengthens negative aspects of behaviour in the minority group, and this validates negative stereotypes, which in turn can be used to rationalise or provide an excuse for unfair treatment.

Once prejudice is established in a community, it is passed on to children in a number of ways. American children pick up their parents' racial attitudes by the age of 3; it is age 7 in New Zealand. Children hear what their parents say, and may be punished if they play with the wrong children. There can be very strong conformity pressures – those who have too much contact with the other group may themselves become targets for violence towards themselves or their property, verbal abuse, social ostracism or losing their jobs. This is one of the ways in which racial attitudes are a feature of the community rather than of the individual.

Further roots of social prejudice have been found in personality dynamics. Prejudiced people often have an authoritarian personality. These are individuals who despise weaker people, especially members of minority groups, are submissive to authority, and have very rigid and punitive attitudes. The psychoanalytic ideas which lay behind the original formulation have not been confirmed – 'sexual projectivity' and the like – but one mechanism has been confirmed: displaced aggression. Authoritarians are also found to have been reared under harsh discipline, by authoritarian parents who demanded obedience without explanation. Pettigrew (1958) found that people in South Africa and in the Southern American states were more prejudiced, but not any more authoritarian, so national differences cannot be explained in terms of individual authoritarianism. However, individual differences in racial prejudice within these areas *can* partly be explained in this way.

Violence in crowds

Le Bon (1895) based his account of crowds on the behaviour of mobs during the French Revolution. He thought that crowds regressed to primitive and irrational behaviour, and that this was due to three factors – anonymity, contagion and suggestibility. Later theories have underplayed the emotionality of crowds, but it does seem that 'the massing of large numbers of people together, in some circumstances, can generate a collective emotionalism which leads to unusual types of activity' (Giddens, 1989: 622).

The ideas of contagion and suggestibility have been taken up by a number of social scientists. If the members of a crowd already have a shared emotional state, whether of anger or some other emotion, this could well be amplified by mutual influence and stimulation, or it could be that this influence results in convergence towards a shared emotional state (Milgram and Toch, 1969).

Reicher (1984) studied the race riot in Bristol in 1980, and he argues that in a crowd there is a shift to salience of social identity as a member of the crowd, so that there is heightened conformity to crowd norms, which are already known. At the Bristol riot, the main goal of the crowds was to attack the police, their identity was 'the St Paul's community', traffic was allowed to flow smoothly, and there was no damage to domestic property, supporting the idea that the mob was rational rather than emotional or uncontrolled. There was, however, quite a lot of random damage to cars and shop windows.

Some kinds of crowds become frenzied and violent, as at some sports events. The question is, when do crowds become frenzied and violent, and when do they not? Some become emotional but not violent – at pop concerts and religious services, for example – and some don't become emotional at all – at Ascot, air shows, motor races and athletic events, for instance. Benewick and Holton (1987) describe the crowds of up to 100,000 during the Pope's visit to England, which were extremely peaceful, but where the participants experienced a strong feeling of unity.

Violent crowds may appear spontaneously, as the result of a build-up of frustration and grievance, but more often they are organised by leaders, and may be completely stage-managed. The aim may be to attack members of a racial minority group, the police or a rival group; the aim may be primarily a 'demo', to impress onlookers, and for consumption by TV. However, crowds are unpredictable and the aims may change; football fans may try to kill the referee, a crowd gathered to greet a political leader may turn on the police. There are usually leaders, who are the focus of the crowd's attention, have loud-hailers and the skills of arousing crowd emotions, and who may lead the crowd in a march or an attack. Most crowds are composed of members of a group which already has agreed goals and norms. They know the slogans and songs, may have banners, and many know others within sub-groups, which may have their own banners (Milgram and Toch, 1969).

There were tremendous civil disturbances in pre-industrial times. Since 1900 violent disturbances of most kinds in Britain have declined (see Figure 7.4). There has been much less industrial violence, much less political

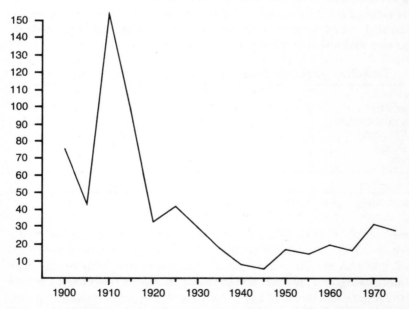

Figure 7.4 Reported rate of violent disturbances in England, Wales and Scotland in the *Leicester Mercury*, 1900–75
Source: Waddington *et al.*,1987

violence and less violence in the community (for example, much less gang violence) since World War II. The one sphere in which violence has increased is in connection with sport (Dunning *et al.*, 1987).

The background conditions for crowd violence are the feelings of deprivation and grievance of disadvantaged groups (miners, ethnic minorities and so on) where violence is legitimated by political ideas, or by political leaders, though it can be sparked off by quite minor annoying incidents. Often there has been a history of conflict with the police. Sometimes the media make things worse by describing the rioters as anti-social, 'animals' or 'the enemy within'. Often the physical setting is important; for example, attack or defence of a symbolically important building. And the violence is often against buildings or the police rather than the real enemy (Waddington *et al.*, 1987).

Football hooliganism

This has been an increasing problem during recent years, first in Britain and later in other countries. It takes the form mainly of the supporters of the two teams threatening and insulting each other inside the ground, sometimes charging and attacking each other in large groups, invading the pitch, attacking members of the other side outside the ground, and doing miscellaneous damage. The fans are more or less restrained by large numbers of police. And there is a hard core of violent individuals who go mainly for the fighting rather than the football. What is unusual here is that the battles are between very similar groups of people who have not frustrated each other, and are not obviously competing for anything.

Table 7.2   The social class of football hooligans, percentages

Professional	0.4
Intermediate	2.5
Skilled, non-manual	5.6
Skilled, manual	18.9
Semi-skilled	25.4
Unskilled	47.2
Total	100.0

Source: Dunning, 1989

Marsh *et al.* (1978) offered an interesting interpretation of these phenomena. They said that it is ritual, symbolic aggression, in which no one gets seriously hurt, because there are rules against injuring people. The aim is more to frighten the other side and make them look ridiculous. The fans enjoy the reputation, invented by the media, of being dangerous and violent. Evidence for shared rules against injury was obtained from interviews with hooligans, and supported by the very small number of injuries at the Oxford

United ground. However, this view has been disproved by events – a series of disasters – at which English fans have been responsible for large numbers of deaths, especially at international matches, as at the Huyssel stadium in Brussels. And in fact there always was quite a lot of real violence, outside the ground if not inside, especially at more important games than those with Oxford United.

The inter-group psychologists (see p. 173) have not yet turned their attention to football hooligans, who appear to be a very good example of this theory. The fans are closely identified with their teams, wear scarves, flags and other badges, and have ritual chants to display their allegiance. This group membership and the identity it gives are evidently very important to them. The main activity of these groups is pursuing their rivalries and vendettas with other groups. Status is gained by the team winning, or by the humiliation of the other team's supporters. The insults are to the effect that the others are weak, non-masculine, 'wankers' and so on. However, contrary to inter-group theory, football hooligans are trying to establish a satisfying social identity in relation to very similar groups, not in relation to economically and occupationally more successful ones.

Elias and Dunning (1986) point out that nearly all football hooligans – such as the ones convicted of violence at matches – are unskilled or unemployed working-class young men (Table 7.2). They come from lower-working-class estates where parents do not restrain aggressive behaviour, the children often see violence between adults, and macho behaviour and 'hardness' are valued as one of the main sources of reputation and status, among young people who have failed to achieve any success in the educational or occupational spheres. In terms of inter-group theory, they have discovered a new dimension of achievement and in-group superiority. The real football hooligans enjoy fighting, as the following interview quote shows:

I go to a match for one reason only: the aggro. It's an obsession, I can't give it up. I get so much pleasure when I'm having aggro that I nearly wet my pants . . . I go all over the country looking for it . . . every night during the week we go around the town looking for trouble. Before a match we go round looking respectable . . . then if we see someone who looks like the enemy we ask him the time; if he answers in a foreign accent, we do him over; and if he's got any money on him we'll roll him as well.

(Elias and Dunning, 1986: 246)

There are feuds and vendettas between families, neighbourhoods and street-corner gangs; it is suggested that in these communities there is 'segmental bonding' – that is, close bonding within local and kinship groups – and rejection of outsiders. This explains why there can be such aggressive rivalry between fans from different clubs, especially if they come from London versus the North, England versus Scotland, or even more in international games.

Elias and Dunning suggest that there has been a progressive civilising of society, elaboration of manners and standards, and increased control of emotions since the Middle Ages. All sports have become less violent and better controlled, and people no longer get pleasure from violent spectacles. However, as we have seen, football hooligans come from sections of society which such civilising processes and better manners have not yet reached.

An important aspect of football is the amount of alcohol drunk, and one of the main steps taken to deal with violence here has been to prevent drinking at the grounds, though it is impossible to prevent earlier drinking.

War and aggression

Attempts to explain war in terms of individual aggressiveness are generally judged to have failed (for example, Groebel and Hinde, 1989). But there is no doubt that war involves a very high level of aggressive behaviour. So what causes wars?

Economic factors

Economic factors are often assumed to be the main cause, and Marxists have supposed that economic competition between capitalists is the main root. Countries seek more land for farming, and to relieve population pressure, raw materials, slaves to do the work, or more recently cheap labour, or a population to provide soldiers. On the other hand, wars are very expensive, and do not make a profit (except for the armaments manufacturers). Richardson (1960) carried out a statistical analysis of wars between 1820 and 1949 and found that economic factors were directly relevant in only 29 per cent of them, and then mainly in small wars. Capitalist problems were usually settled by diplomacy or arbitration rather than war. Most students of war have come to believe that political and ideological issues are more important than economic ones (Wright, 1968).

Political factors

Many wars have been the result of nations trying to expand, to establish empires, in the search for glory and security, in addition to any economic advantages. Other wars are caused by suppressed minorities or colonial peoples seeking their freedom. There are wars over territory, as between Israelis and Arabs. Revolutions and civil wars arise from a suppressed group trying to get the upper hand. Wright (1968) analysed 278 wars between 1484 and 1945; of these he describes 135 as balance-of-power wars to maintain national sovereignty against imperial encroachments, 78 were revolutionary civil wars, and 65 were between people of different civilisations, some for colonial expansion.

Ideology and leaders

Most wars are inspired by ideological differences, but in some cases this is the main factor. Many wars have been religious ones – the Crusades, and Muslims versus Hindus in India, for example. Wars have been fought to defend European civilisation, against the Turks, or against Africans in South Africa. The Cold War was between the rival ideologies of communism and capitalism. World War II was partly due to concern about the tyrannical, anti-Semitic regime inside Germany, and the wish to avoid such a regime spreading.

Ideologies are usually promoted, and sometimes created, by leaders. When the origins of specific wars are analysed it often turns out that leaders mobilise their people and rationalise the war by ideas – the Kaiser told Germans in 1914 that they were surrounded by enemies; Hitler told them in 1939 that Germany had been humiliated at Versailles, needed more *Lebensraum* and was doing badly economically because it was being undermined by Jews and other inferior races (Winter, 1989). Hitler and his followers were very skilled propagandists and manipulators of public opinion, via mass meetings, the youth movement, and general terror. Real or re-written history often plays an important role here. The Afrikaners in South Africa keep alive the memory of the Voortrekkers who first settled the country. The Israelis keep up many ancient biblical sites proving that they are the true owners of the land.

Political leaders sometimes start aggression towards another country or group in order to unite their own, divided nation behind them. It has been suggested that Hitler integrated Germany by focusing hatred on Jews and communists. The Argentinians suddenly pulled together during the Falklands War, and Mrs Thatcher's popularity was enhanced at the same time. Rabbie (1989) found that leaders of laboratory groups opted for inter-group competition rather than cooperation when threatened with loss of their elected leadership position.

However, wars are not fought because a lot of individuals feel frustrated and want to be aggressive. They are fought by armies, some of whom are professional soldiers, all of whom are trained, paid, led and disciplined. Aggression in armies is managed in special ways. Not many people kill one another normally, so soldiers have to be trained to do so.

Marshall (1947) interviewed many American soldiers after World War II, and found that only 15 per cent had fired their guns at all, even when under attack. Aggression training may include bayonet practice at sacks, accompanied by blood-curdling shrieks. Such training is particularly intense in special groups like the Commandos and British SAS, some of whom have had difficulty in adjusting to unaggressive civilian life afterwards. There is an emphasis on strict obedience and standard routines, with the intention that if a soldier is ordered to shoot, jump or kill he does so. Leadership is authoritarian, and uses the sanctions of fear of punishment (soldiers may be shot for running away) and moral commitment – to national victory, the honour of the regiment, and belief in the ideology for which the war is being fought. Soldiers are paid nowadays, but this is hardly a incentive – there is no bonus for winning, though there is for promotion. Mercenaries, who are important in parts of Africa today, only fight for the pay, and don't pretend to believe in anything; they are usually paid rather well.

Most of the actual fighting is done by young men, of working-class origins, and the physical conditions of life are primitive, the life style is that of earthy, lower-class masculine sexuality. The life of the officers is totally different; they live the lives of an artificial elite, and a social gulf separates them from the men (Van Doorn, 1990).

At the higher levels of leadership are senior officers and political leaders, who decide on the strategy of the war, and decide whether to have a war at all. Clausewitz said that war was a rational, limited instrument of national policy. Since then war has changed in being less limited: 'total war'. And it is less clear that war is based on rational decisions. If war is due to aggression at all, it is aggressiveness on the part of individual leaders – Hitler, Mussolini, Saddam Hussein, Gaddafi and others. It may also be due to aggression on the part of senior officers; when the generals have a lot of power war is more likely.

THE PREVENTION OF INTER-GROUP AGGRESSION

These are very serious social problems, the most serious faced by the world. Can psychology make any contribution to solving them? The problems and the possible solutions are different in the different cases we have discussed.

Racial prejudice, tribal wars and similar conflicts

This is the general case when there are two or more groups, with distinctive characteristics, whose members do not like one another. Research has led to the development of a number of methods of reducing hostility.

Creating superordinate goals

This was first used by Sherif (1961) to resolve the conflicts which he had created in boys' camps. The water supply was interfered with, so that both groups had to cooperate in pulling a water cart – using the same rope which had recently been pulled in opposite directions in a tug-of-war. This was successful in resolving the hostility between the groups. Laboratory experiments in which groups cooperate with each other find that the groups like each other more than when the groups compete. However, if the enlarged group is then unsuccessful, there is a danger that one sub-group may blame the other (Worchel, 1979).

Moving further into real-life inter-group problems, Brown (1978) asked workers in an engineering factory what they would do if the management declared 10 per cent redundancy. He expected that as active trade unionists they would favour a cooperative strategy, but only 20 per cent of workers did, the majority being primarily concerned with defending their own group. Brown later noted a similar failure of large-scale groups to cooperate among the centre parties in British politics in the 1980s. On the other hand, as we have seen, some political leaders have succeeded in integrating their countries by directing aggression against another group – a clear case of a superordinate goal. A number of nations cooperated in 1990 with the superordinate goal of defending themselves against Iraq, but this required extensive diplomatic effort. It looks as if positive shared goals only work readily on a small scale, while aggressive ones may work on a much larger national scale.

Sheer contact with the other group

The 'contact hypothesis' states that sheer contact between members of two groups is all that is needed to produce positive attitudes between them. Impressive evidence to this effect appeared to be provided from studies of the effects of belonging to platoons in mixed black and white companies in the US Army in World War II. Among those who had been in these platoons, 64 per cent of white soldiers thought this was a good general policy, compared with 18 per cent of those who had not (Star *et al.*, 1965); 51 per cent of black soldiers felt less hostile to whites than before. The recent situation in the US Army, however, is that extensive race-relations training is needed to make desegregation work. Desegregated housing is moderately successful. Deutsch and Collins (1951) found that there were usually regular and intimate contacts and relationships between black and white neighbours in the USA, in mixed communities; however, most communities are *not* mixed. The effects of desegregation of American schools have been very disappointing; there has been no overall improvement of attitudes on either side, mainly because black children do not do well in desegregated schools.

However, we now know the conditions under which sheer contact is successful in reducing prejudice. It is important that the out-group members should be of equal status, or of higher status, though either may be difficult to arrange, and may make them seem atypical. There should also be cooperation, intimacy and a climate of external support. These conditions were realised in Aronson's 'jig-saw classroom' (1978). Groups of 6 children are formed, including Anglo, Mexican-American and black. Each pupil is taught part of the materials needed for a group project, and then teaches the others; the teachers just help. There is no competition between groups, they meet 3 times a week for 6 weeks, and the pupils are marked individually. The results of several follow-up studies were that the jig-saw pupils increased in liking for the other ethnic groups more than those in ordinary classes. They also liked school more and increased in self-esteem. However, these effects were actually quite small, and there is a danger that a team may lose because of the lack of ability of a member, and this can lead to increased prejudice towards the group to which he belongs.

Sometimes contact results in people liking the members of the other group whom they meet, but thinking they are 'exceptional' and not generalising this attitude to others. Wilder (1986) did experiments in which members of one college met pleasant members of another, who were manipulated to appear to be 'typical'; this led to some generalisation. It is even better if varied members of the other group are met, because this disrupts stereotypes, and if those met are seen to be leaders, or otherwise socially integrated members of the other group (Hamburger, in press).

Education, propaganda, and inter-cultural training

Many people are trained successfully for working abroad in another culture, so it should be possible to use such training more widely. Many follow-up studies have been carried out to test the success of films, lectures and other educational methods in improving racial and other inter-group attitudes. A film followed by lecture or discussion is quite successful, lectures are better in small groups and with a prestigious speaker, using several methods is best. Attitude changes have been found in most studies, though the effects are often small and people can easily avoid such propaganda (Stephan, 1985). Propaganda could be designed better – to show the basic similarities of the other group, to show its achievement and contributions, or to show the range of individuals in it, for example.

Education is potentially very important here. Prejudice is correlated with ignorance and misinformation about the other group. Stephan and Stephan (1984) conclude that it is necessary to provide knowledge and understanding of both similarities and differences with the other group. Neither should be overdone. However, to produce a change in attitudes and behaviour needs more than correcting misinformation; more active methods of education are required, such as role-playing or actual contact with the other group.

A specialised form of teaching which has been devised for inter-group education is the Culture Assimilator. A 'critical incidents' survey is carried out first of a large sample of difficulties experienced with the other group. This leads to locating 40–100 types of incidents, which are then embodied in a tutor text which takes 6–8 hours to work through: each incident is presented as a problem.

One day a Thai administrator of middle academic rank kept two of his assistants about an hour from an appointment. The assistants, although very angry, did not show it while they waited. When the administrator walked in at last, he acted as if he were not late. He made no apology or explanation. After he was settled in his office, he called his assistants in and they all began working on the business for which the administrator had set the meeting.

(Brislin and Pederson, 1976: 90–1)

Several explanations are offered, of which the correct one is: 'In Thailand, subordinates are required to be polite to their superiors, no matter what happens, nor what their rank may be.' A number of Culture Assimilators have been constructed, mainly to teach Americans about other cultures, including black Americans, also for Australians and Aboriginals. The contents convey a lot of information about the rules, ideas and social relationships of the other culture. Follow-up studies have found positive, though modest, improvements – for example, in behaviour in mixed racial groups – though not much change in prejudice (Brislin and Pederson, 1976).

Non-verbal communication

It is possible to include training in NVC in inter-cultural training. For example, Collett (1971) trained a number of English males to use the NV style of Arabs – closer proximity, touch, high level of gaze, and so on. Arabs who met them liked them much more than members of a control group who had merely learnt about the River Nile. At the very least trainees need to know which gestures, or other aspect of NVC, will cause offence, and prevent them taking unnecessary offence themselves.

If the other group speaks a different language, this is a colossal barrier. Knowing another group's language is a matter of degree, and it has been found in the USA that the adjustment of overseas students is greatly affected by competence in the language, and in Canada that lack of interaction between English- and French-speaking Canadians is partly due to lack of language skills. Languages vary in their polite, colloquial usage. Most cultures have a number of forms of polite usage, which may be misleading. These may take the form of exaggeration or modesty. Americans ask questions which are really orders or requests ('Would you like to . . .?'). And in every culture, in many situations, there are special forms of words, or types of conversation, which are thought to be appropriate – for example, to ask a girl for a date, to disagree with someone at a committee, to introduce people to each other and so on.

War

We have seen that war is not caused by the aggressiveness of populations, though it may be affected by the aggressiveness of political and military leaders. The contribution of psychology may lie at the level of negotiation procedures between politicians, diplomats and senior officers. Pruitt (1981) has argued that negotiators should aim for 'integrative agreements', which reconcile the interests of both sides, and give maximum benefit to each, and that this can be achieved by adopting a problem-solving approach. The others are more likely to make concessions and move towards an agreement if there are going to be advantages for them too. There is usually an informal phase in any negotiations, and it is here that a problem-solving approach can be adopted. It is a much more cooperative process than bargaining proper, and both sides consider the other's point of view. Often a new solution can be found which is acceptable to both sides. One type of problem-solving has been described as 'log-rolling', where there is an exchange of quite different concessions. One side gives way on X, the other on Y. Negotiation is much easier if a positive relationship can be established between some of those on opposite sides. Sometimes quite junior individuals are able to do this, since they can consider more radical concessions and solutions. This is said to have happened during the Cuban missile crisis.

Different bargaining strategies can be used. Osgood (1962) proposed a strategy designed to resolve hostilities between two countries. This is intermediate between military action and unilateral disarmament. It goes as follows:

1 Announce the intention of reducing tension by making a number of concessions.
2 Announce each move in advance.
3 Invite the other side to reciprocate.
4 The concessions are continued for some time regardless of reciprocation.
5 Initiatives are risky but do not reduce the capacity to retaliate if necessary.
6 If there is reciprocation, the level of concessions is increased.

It seems likely that GRIT (Graduated and Reciprocated Initiatives in Tension-Reduction) has actually been used in international affairs; for example, between the USA and the USSR. Concessions made by Kennedy during the Cuban missile crisis in 1962 were reciprocated by the Russians (Lindskold, 1986). Baron (1973) found that industrial negotiators were rated most positively and produced larger concessions and greater collaboration when their actions seemed to be based on sincere beliefs about the value of their departments. Negotiators are also successful if they can reduce anger or other negative feelings on the other side (Kabanoff, 1985).

Cultural differences can make negotiation very difficult. Language difficulties can be solved to some extent by skilled interpreters, but the same word may have different meanings, through being part of different ideologies, as with 'freedom', 'democracy', 'hostage' and so on. Different non-verbal styles can cause problems; for example, Arabs shout to show sincerity rather than aggression. Asians are very concerned with saving face, and it may be particularly important for the other side to make concessions. The troubles in the Persian Gulf in 1990 provide many examples of how the different sides saw things differently. The Americans saw themselves as international peace-keepers, the Arabs saw them as interfering with an internal Arab problem, and supporting an illegitimate regime in Israel.

Control of crowds

We have seen that violent crowd behaviour is not just individual aggressiveness, but a phenomenon at the level of the group. The usual solution is to use the police to control crowds, but this very easily leads to violent confrontation with the police themselves. However, if crowds are not controlled there is a danger of violence against whatever other groups they don't like, or feel aggrieved about.

Football hooligans

The Marsh interpretation had a clear implication: do nothing because there isn't really a problem. As violence increased this has turned out to be wrong. Other steps have already been taken – preventing the sale of alcohol in grounds, TV surveillance, and heavy police presence, segregating rival groups of fans, and replacing the old open terraces by seats. These methods will probably reduce or remove violence inside the ground, but may fail to deal with trouble outside. If the Elias and Dunning theory is correct, inter-group aggression is endemic in the lower-working-class sub-culture, so the basic roots of the problem may be difficult to eradicate.

CONCLUSIONS

Aggressive conflict between groups is widespread. Aggression is partly an innate response to attack, with a physiological basis and it is stronger in males. It is also the product of socialisation, there are cultural differences, it is provoked by a variety of situational stresses and restrained by social norms and empathy.

Conflicts can be enhanced by groups, because they form negative stereotypes of one another, seek for a superior in-group identity, and because there is often conflict between them.

Real aggression between groups is found in tribal wars, and in racial prejudice, which has roots in economic stress and competition for jobs, as well as in socialisation and personality. Some crowds are violent, others are not; it depends on grievances and leaders, and the traditions of the crowd.

Football hooliganism has become worse, and is partly just an aggressive ritual, but it also involves some real aggression, caused by the search for a macho identity from youths from some working-class areas.

War is partly due to economic and political causes, such as seeking independence, and is partly inspired by leaders with a convincing ideology. It is not due to the aggressiveness of soldiers, though it may be due to aggressive leaders.

Attempts to prevent or resolve conflicts between groups include the presentation of superordinate goals, which works only on a small scale. Sheer contact with the other group under the right conditions can be effective. Education, propaganda and inter-cultural training can make good use of research on cultural differences, and there can be training in negotiation for leaders.

REFERENCES

Abrams, M. (1969) The incidence of racial prejudice in Britain. *In* E.J.B. Rose (ed) *Colour and Citizenship*. Oxford: Oxford University Press.

Aronson, E., Stephan, W., Sikes, J., Blaney, N. and Snapp, M. (1978) *Cooperation in the Classroom*. Beverly Hills, CA: Sage.

Bandura, A. (1973) *Aggression: A Social Learning Analysis*. Englewood Cliffs, NJ: Prentice-Hall.

Baron, R.A. (1973) Threatened retaliation from the victim as an inhibitor of physical aggression. *Journal of Research in Personality*, 7, 103–15.

Benewick, R. and Holton, R. (1987) The peaceful crowd: crowd solidarity and the Pope's visit to Britain. *In* G. Gaskell and R. Benewick (eds) *The Crowd in Contemporary Britain*. London: Sage.

Berkowitz, L., Cochran, S. and Embree, M. (1981) Physical pain and the goal of aversively stimulated aggression. *Journal of Personality and Social Psychology*, 40, 687–700.

Brewer, M.B. and Campbell, D.T. (1976) *Ethnocentrism and Intergroup Attitudes: East African Evidence*. New York: Halsted Press.

Brislin, R.W. and Pederson, P. (1976) *Cross-cultural Orientation Programs*. New York: Gardner Press.

Bronfenbrenner, U. (1961) The mirror image in Soviet–American relations: a social psychologist's report. *Journal of Social Issues*, 1, 45–56.

Brown, Rupert. (1988) *Group Processes*. Oxford: Blackwell.

Brown, Rupert J., Condon, S., Mathews, A., Wade, G. and Williams, J. (1986) Explaining intergroup differentiation in an industrial organization. *Journal of Occupational Psychology*, 59, 273–86.

Campbell, A. (1981) *Girl Delinquents*. Oxford: Blackwell.

Collett, P. (1971) On training Englishmen in the non-verbal behaviour of Arabs: an experiment in intercultural communication. *International Journal of Psychology*, 6, 209–15.

Delgado, J. (1969) *Physical Control of the Mind*. New York: Harper & Row.

Deschamps, J.C. and Doise, W. (1978) Crossed category memberships in intergroup relations. *In* H. Tajfel (ed.) *Differentiation Between Social Groups*. London: Academic Press.

Deutsch, M. and Collins, M.E. (1951) *Interracial Housing: A Psychological Evaluation of a Social Experiment*. Minneapolis: University of Minnesota Press.

Dijker, A.J.M. (1987) Emotional reactions to ethnic minorities. *European Journal of Social Psychology*, *17*, 305–25.

Dunning, E.G., Murphy, P.J. and Williams, J. (1987) *The Social Roots of Football Hooliganism*. London: Routledge and Kegan Paul.

Elias, N. and Dunning, E. (1986) *The Quest for Excitement*. Oxford: Blackwell.

Eron, L.D. and Huesmann, L.R. (1980) Adolescent aggression and television. *Annals of the New York Academy of Science*, *347*, 319–31.

Feierabend, I.K. and Feierabend, R.L. (1972) Systemic conditions of political aggression: an application of frustration-aggression theory. *In* I.K. Feierabend, R.L. Feierabend and T.R. Gurr (eds) *Anger, Violence, and Politics*. Englewood Cliffs, NJ: Prentice-Hall, pp. 136–83.

Geen, R.G. *et al.* (1990) *Human Aggression*. Milton Keynes: Open University Press.

Giddens, A. (1989) *Sociology*. Oxford: Polity Press.

Groebel, J. and Hinde, R.A. (eds) (1989) *Aggression and War*. Cambridge: Cambridge University Press.

Hovland, C. and Sears, R. (1940) Minor studies in aggression. VI. Correlation of lynchings with economic indices. *Journal of Psychology*, *9*, 301–10.

Huntingford, F.A. (1989) Animals fight, but do not make war. *In* J. Groebel and R.A. Hinde (eds) *Aggression and War*. Cambridge: Cambridge University Press.

Jaffe, Y. and Yinon, Y. (1983) Collective aggression: the group–individual paradigm in the study of collective antisocial behavior. *In* H.H. Blumberg, A.P. Hare, V. Kent and M.H. Davies (eds) *Small Groups and Social Interaction*. Vol. 1. Cambridge, MA: Wiley.

Kabanoff, B. (1985) Potential influence structures as sources of interpersonal conflicts in groups and organizations. *Organizational Behavior and Human Decision Processes*, *36*, 113–41.

Krebs, D.L. and Miller, D.T. (1985) Altruism and aggression. *In* G. Lindzey and E. Aronson (eds) *Handbook of Social Psychology*, 3rd edition, *2*, New York: Random House, pp. 1–71.

Lambert, W.W. (1971) Cross-cultural background to personality development and the socialization of aggression: findings from the six culture study. *In* W.W. Lambert and R. Weisbrod (eds) *Comparative Perspectives on Social Psychology*. Boston, MA: Little, Brown.

Le Bon, G. (1895) *Psychologie des foules*. Translated as *The Crowd*. London: Unwin, 1908.

Leyens, J.P., Camino, L., Parke, R.D. and Berkowitz, L. (1975) Effects of movie violence on aggression in a field setting as a function of group dominance and cohesion. *Journal of Personality and Social Psychology*, *32*, 346–60.

Lindskold, S. (1986) GRIT: reducing distrust through carefully introduced conciliation. *In* S. Worchel and W.G. Austin (eds) *Psychology of Intergroup Relations*. 2nd edition. Chicago: Nelson.

Mann, J.W. (1963) Rivals of different rank. *Journal of Social Psychology*, *61*, 11–28.

Marsh, P., Rosser, E. and Harré, R. (1978) *The Rules of Disorder*. London: Routledge and Kegan Paul.

Marshall, S.L.A. (1947) *Men Against Fire*. New York: Marrow.

Megargee, E.I. (1966) Undercontrolled and overcontrolled personality types in extreme antisocial aggression. *Psychological Monographs, 80* (3).

Milgram, S. (1963) Behavioral study of obedience. *Journal of Abnormal and Social Psychology, 67,* 371–8.

——(1974) *Obedience to Authority*. New York: Harper & Row.

Milgram, S. and Toch, H. (1969) Collective behavior: crowds and social movements. *In* G. Lindzey and E. Aronson (eds) *The Handbook of Social Psychology*, 2nd edition, *4*. Reading, MA: Addison-Wesley, pp. 507–610.

Minnix, D.A. (1982) *Small Groups and Foreign Policy Decision Making*. Washington, DC: University Press of America.

Mullen, B. (1986) Atrocity as a function of lynch mob composition: a self-attention perspective. *Personality and Social Psychology Bulletin, 12,* 187–97.

Mulvihill, D.J. and Tumin, M.M. (1969) *Crimes Violence: A Staff Report Submitted to the National Commission on the Causes and Prevention of Violence*. Washington, DC: US Government Printing Office.

Mummendey, A. (1988) Aggressive Behaviour. *In* M. Hewstone, W. Stroede, J-P. Codol and G.M. Stephenson (eds) *Introduction to Social Psychology*. Oxford: Blackwell.

Myers, D.G. (1990) *Social Psychology*. New York: McGraw-Hill.

Naroll, R. (1966) Does military deterrence deter? *Trans-Action, 3,* 14–20.

Olweus, D. (1979) Stability of aggressive reaction patterns in males: a review. *Psychological Bulletin, 86,* 852–75.

——(1986) Aggression and hormones: behavioral relationship with testosterone and adrenaline. *In* D. Olweus, J. Block and M. Rodke-Yarrow (eds) *Development of Antisocial and Prosocial Behavior*. Orlando: Academic Press.

Osgood, C.E. (1962) *An Alternative to War or Surrender*. Urbana, Ill.: University of Illinois Press.

Patterson, G.R. (1986) The contribution of siblings to training for fighting: a microsocial analysis. *In* D. Olweus *et al*. (eds) *Development of Antisocial and Prosocial Behavior*. Orlando: Academic Press.

Pettigrew, T.F. (1958) Personality and sociocultural factors in intergroup attitudes: a cross-national comparison. *Journal of Conflict Resolution, 2,* 29–42.

Phillips, D.P. (1980) The deterrent effect of capital punishment: new evidence on an old controversy. *American Journal of Sociology, 86,* 139–48.

Pruitt, D.G. (1981) *Negotiation Behavior*. New York: Academic Press.

Rabbie, J.M. (1989) Group processes as stimulants of aggression. *In* J. Groebel and R.A. Hinde (eds) *Aggression and War*. Cambridge: Cambridge University Press.

Rabbie, M. and Horwitz, M. (1969) Arousal of ingroup–outgroup bias by a chance win or loss. *Journal of Personality and Social Psychology, 13,* 269–77.

Reicher, S. (1984) St Paul's riot: an explanation of the limits of crowd action in terms of an identity model. *European Journal of Social Psychology, 14,* 1–21.

Richardson, L.F. (1960) *Statistics of Deadly Quarrels*. London: Stevens.

Rokeach, M. (1968) *Beliefs, Attitudes, and Values*. San Francisco: Jossey-Bass.

Rokeach, M., Smith, P.W. and Evans, R.I. (1960) Two kinds of prejudice or one? *In* M. Rokeach (ed.) *The Open and Closed Mind*. New York: Basic Books.

Schachter, S. and Singer, J. (1962) Cognitive, social, and physiological determinants of emotional state. *Psychological Review, 69,* 379–99.

Segall, M.H. (1989) Cultural factors, biology and human aggression. *In* J. Groebel and R.A. Hinde (eds) *Aggression and War*. Cambridge: Cambridge University Press.

Sherif, M., Harvey, O.J., White, B.J., Hood, W.R. and Sherif, C.W. (1961) *Intergroup Cooperation and Competition: The Robbers Cave Study*. Norman, OK: University Book Exchange.

Singer, J.D. (1989) The political origins of international war: a multi-factorial review. *In* J. Groebel and R.A. Hinde (eds) *Aggression and War*. Cambridge: Cambridge University Press.

Sivard, R.L. (1983) *World Military and Social Expenditures*. Washington, DC: World Priorities.

Star, S.A., Williams, L.M. and Stouffer, S.A. (1965) Negro infantry platoons in white companies. *In* H. Proshansky and B. Seidenberg (eds) *Basic Studies in Social Psychology*. New York: Holt, Rinehart & Winston.

Stephan, W.G. (1985) Intergroup relations. *In* G. Lindzey and E. Aronson (eds) *Handbook of Social Psychology*. 3rd edition, 2. New York: Random House.

Stephan, W.G. and Stephan, C.W. (1984) The role of ignorance in intergroup relations. *In* N. Miller and M.B. Brewer (eds) *Groups in Contact*. New York: Academic Press.

Tajfel, H. (1970) Experiments in intergroup discrimination. *Scientific American*, *223*, 96–102.

Tajfel, H. (ed.) (1978) *Differentiation Between Social Groups: Studies in the Social Psychology of Intergroup Relations*. London: Academic Press, European Monographs in Social Psychology.

Van Doorn, J. (1990) War, the theory and conduct of: modern armed forces. *Encyclopaedia Britannica*, *29*, 699–708.

Waddington, E., Jones, K. and Critcher, C. (1987) Violent disorders in twentieth-century Britain. *In* G. Gaskell and R. Benewick (eds) *The Crowd in Contemporary Britain*. London: Sage.

Wilder, D.A. (1986) Social categorization: implications for creation and reduction of intergroup bias. *Advances in Experimental Social Psychology*, *19*, 291–355.

Winter, J.M. (1989) Causes of war. *In* J. Groebel and R.A. Hinde (eds) *Aggression and War*. Cambridge: Cambridge University Press.

Worchel, S. (1979) Cooperation and the reduction of intergroup conflict: some determining factors. *In* W.G. Austin and S. Worchel (eds) *The Social Psychology of Intergroup Relations*. Monterey, CA: Brooks/Cole.

Word, C.O., Zanna, M.P. and Cooper, J. (1974) The nonverbal mediation of self-fulfilling prophecies in interracial interaction. *Journal of Personality and Social Psychology*, *10*, 109–20.

Wright, Q. (1968) The study of war. *International Encyclopedia of the Social Sciences*, *16*, 453–68.

Zillman, D., Katcher, A.H. and Milavsky, B. (1972) Excitation transfer from physical exercise to subsequent aggressive behavior. *Journal of Experimental Social Psychology*, *8*, 247–59.

Zimbardo, P. (1969) The human choice: individuation, reason, and order versus deindividuation, impulse and chaos. *Nebraska Symposium on Motivation*, vol. 17. Lincoln, NB: University of Nebraska Press.

Chapter 8

Social class

Social class is one of the main sources of variation in behaviour and life style in society. The idea of class is familiar: society is seen as composed of a number of layers of people in a hierarchy. Within each layer individuals accept one another on equal terms, and are more likely to intermarry, for example. There are no clear boundaries between the layers, but a number of distinct classes are generally recognised – 'middle class' and 'working class', for example. The hierarchy reflects, and is partly based on a number of hierarchical organisations, especially working organisations, where those at higher levels have more power and money than those lower down.

As we shall see in this chapter, most people recognise that there is a class system, and are able to say to which class they belong (p. 197). Many people think that there is conflict between the classes, that the differences are greater than they should be, that the rich earn too much, that it is difficult to move to another class, and say that most of their friends come from their own class (p. 206).

Social scientists in Britain usually assess class from the occupation of the family's main earner. Class defined in this way has a statistical but far from perfect correspondence with self-rated class. This is because people use other criteria besides occupation, especially 'the way they speak, where they live, the friends they have, the sort of school they went to, the way they spend their money, the way they dress, and the car they own' (Reid, 1981). In American research, income and education are often used as indices of socio-economic status.

Since members of the public agree on the relative status of different occupations, it is possible to obtain a measure of this component of social class. The scheme which has been most often used in research in Britain is the one used by the Census, which has 5 divisions, as follows:

I   Professional, such as doctors, solicitors, accountants, university teachers.

II   Intermediate, such as schoolteachers, nurses, managers.

III(n)   Skilled non-manual, such as clerical workers, estate agents, shop
         assistants.
III(m)   Skilled manual, for example, cooks, bricklayers, hairdressers.
IV   Partly skilled, for instance, farm workers, bus conductors.
V   Unskilled, such as office cleaners, labourers.

The proportions in each social class, defined in this way, in Britain are
shown in Table 8.1.

Table 8.1   Percentage distribution[1] of the social classes in Great Britain

	I	II	IIIn	IIIm	IV	V	All
			Social class (RG 80)				
Males	5	22	12	36	18	7	100
Females	1	21	39	9	22	7	100
Both	4	22	22	26	19	7	100
As % of each class							
Males	90	63	33	87	57	62	63
Females	10	37	67	13	43	38	37

1 Of economically active, retired or permanently sick who were classified.
Source: Calculated from Table 16A, *Economic Activity, Census 1981, Great Britain*, 1984

There are other, and probably better schemes. Goldthorpe and Hope
(1974) placed 36 categories of occupation in order in terms of their social
standing, and then collapsed them to smaller numbers of categories. A
3-category version is 'service' (I, II above), 'intermediate' (III), and
'working' (IV, V). A 5-category version has been found to be predictive
of voting, since it is based on a division of classes which reflects the different
economic interests of (for example) employers and salaried professionals
(p. 213). In the following section we shall describe the main classes as
discerned by sociologists, the main social divisions of society, based on
shared social life, culture, education and wealth, as well as on occupation.

DESCRIPTION OF THE MAIN SOCIAL CLASSES

Upper class

This class falls outside occupational scales – many of its members don't
have regular jobs (and probably don't reply to social surveys). However,
in 1987 the richest 0.1 per cent of the population (43,000 people) owned 7
per cent of shares and property, and the top 1 per cent owned 21 per cent
of it (*New Society*, 1987). The upper class consists of a distinctive group of
families who know one another, intermarry, and have directorships in one
another's firms. Many of them have inherited wealth, and often titles from
several generations back, though there are also newcomers who have made

their own fortunes. Wealth makes possible an expensive and gracious life style and leisure activities from which others are excluded (such as polo and yachting), and the provision of very good education for children. Their control of industrial capital and their status and connections give them access to influential positions in industry and commerce, and in other spheres, including government.

Upper middle class

This corresponds roughly to occupation class I, and some of II, management, though at the top end it merges into the upper class. The 'old' middle class consists of independent professionals and the owners of businesses. The new middle class is made up of salaried individuals with higher education who have been successful in their careers. We shall see later that they vote differently from the old middle class. Upper-middle-class families are concerned with success in careers, and the life style which this creates, and plan for this to be continued by their children.

Lower middle class

This consists of the skilled, non-manual group (class IIIn), together with the lower ranks of class II. They are distinguished from the upper middle class by their lower occupational status, and their lower incomes. They have a quite different life style and values from working-class people, and are concerned with respectability, despite earning less than better-paid manual workers.

Working class

This corresponds to a wide range of manual jobs, classes III(m) to V. The old, or traditional, working class consists of manual workers who live in council property, accept their place in society, and are not interested in education, work or careers. The 'new' working class consists of affluent skilled workers, many of whom own their own houses, and who quite often vote Conservative, but who still belong to trade unions and have a working-class life style. Some sociologists think that there is also an 'underclass' of the long-term unemployed, including a lot of members of ethnic minority groups, people who have no aspirations or ability to join normal society, and who have a high rate of crime, homelessness, drug use and illegitimacy (Haralambos and Holborn, 1990).

THE EXPERIENCE OF SOCIAL CLASS

Most people accept that there are social classes, and in 1979 in Britain people described themselves, unprompted, as shown in Table 8.2 (Reid, 1989).

Table 8.2   Unprompted self-ratings of social class (percentages)

	Upper/ upper middle	Middle	Lower middle	Upper working	Working	Other	Rejected class	No/hazy concept
Men	1.7	32	5	1.6	50	5	4	1.3
Women	1.5	39	4	1.4	43	5	4	1.6
All	1.6	36	4	1.5	46	5	4	1.5

Source: Reid, 1989

There is a strong, but far from perfect, correlation between these self-ratings and objective class, as defined by occupation.

If people are asked about their social distance or willingness for intimate relationships, with a range of occupations, they prefer those of similar social status, but they also have a preference for occupations of higher rank (Laumann, 1966).

Table 8.3   Rank order of social class criteria

(a)	Men and women	(b)	Women only
1	The way they speak (33)	1	Appearance and behaviour (53)
2	Where they live (28)	2	Family background (50)
3	The friends they have (27)	3	Attitudes, beliefs and political views (45)
4	Their job (22)	4	Style of life (42)
5	The sort of school they went to (21)	5	Education (38)
6	The way they spend their money (18)	6	Occupation (31)
7=	The way they dress (12)	7	House/area in which they live (13)
8=	The car they own (5)	8	Income (13)
		9	Prestige/standing in community (11)

(c)	Men	Women	Men and Women
1	Way of life (29)	1 Way of life (33)	1 Way of life (31)
2	Job (22)	2 Family (21)	2 Family (18)
3	Money (17)	3 Money (16)	3= Job (17)
4	Family (15)	4 Job (12)	4= Money (17)
5	Education (10)	5 Education (11)	5 Education (10)

Note: figures in brackets denote the percentages of respondents using each criterion.
Source: Reid, 1989

If people are asked what they understand by 'middle class', and so on, they are able to respond in terms of groups of occupations. However, they normally use criteria other than job for deciding to which class they or others belong. In a 1972 British survey the criteria which people used to decide someone's class were as shown in Table 8.3.

In an earlier American study it was found that the criteria used varied with the class of the judge. Upper-class people emphasised family, leadership and good character, and attitudes and beliefs as criteria for upper-class membership more than other classes did. Working-class people emphasised 'working for a living' as the criterion of being working class much more than others did (Centers, 1949).

In Britain it has been found that several rather different models, or images, of the class system are held by different groups. Many industrial workers see society as divided into 'us' and 'them', with a power difference and conflict between those two groups. Prosperous workers often see class mainly as a matter of money, while middle-class people see it as a ladder of opportunity and prestige (Reid, 1989).

It is widely felt that class differences in wealth and other benefits are unfair and too great. In Britain 71 per cent of people think that the distribution of wealth and income is not fair, with surprisingly little class difference (class I, 69 per cent; class VII, 78 per cent). A majority think that the gap between haves and have-nots is too great (Marshall et al., 1988). In a sample of English workers, 56 per cent thought that the main difference between classes was wealth; 53 per cent thought this should be less; 48 per cent, that the rich have not deserved it; 68 per cent, because it was inherited; 28 per cent, through exploitation, or fraud; and 60 per cent that there is a great difference in living standards, and that this inequality is seen in salaries and conditions of work (27 per cent), in the street and housing (22 per cent), and in treatment in shops and restaurants (5 per cent) (Gallie, 1983).

Many people feel that there is a 'class struggle' – 66 per cent in Britain in 1986 (Reid, 1989). It is in industry, in the conflicts between managers or owners and workers that this conflict is most apparent. It is interesting that French workers feel this very strongly, that there is a higher degree of resentment about class inequality, and a stronger identification with the working class. Gallie (1983) explored various explanations for this, and concluded that it was due to the hierarchical and authoritarian structure of French industry, with less industrial democracy than in Britain, together with a stronger revolutionary tradition and Communist Party.

People are often rather pleased when high achievers, 'tall poppies', fail, especially if the latter's previous success was not the result of ability, effort or fair competition, but rather of help or influence – in Australia, at least (Feather, 1989). This suggests considerable envy and hostility to some of those further up the scale.

THE ORIGINS OF SOCIAL CLASS

I shall not begin with Marx and Weber, as is the custom of sociologists, but with smaller models of the class system. Groups of 80 or so monkeys have a hierarchical order, with a single dominant male at the top, who takes the lead – in matters of defence, for example. Other males take their places in the hierarchy, established by fights, and their females and their children have the same rank as their mates. In small human groups, especially of males, a similar informal hierarchy develops; among working-class male youth fighting is a factor here, but more often position depends on skills and ability to help the group reach its goals. There is a widespread desire, especially among men, to occupy positions of power and status.

A functionalist explanation of the emergence of hierarchies in small groups is supported by several kinds of evidence. Hierarchies emerge more readily and are more accepted when there is a task, when the group is large, and when decisions must be made quickly; groups with leaders are more effective (Argyle *et al.*, 1981).

When human groups become larger than about 15, they divide into 2 or more sub-groups, each with their leader, so that a second level of authority is needed to supervise these leaders. Because the span of control – the number of individuals one person can supervise – is limited, in large organisations there are many levels in the hierarchy, creating a miniature class system. The class system is partly based on these power and status hierarchies in working organisations. Marx thought that the basic division in society was between owners and employers, on the one hand, and workers, on the other. However, there are now several levels of managers in between, and similar hierarchies are found when there are no owners at the top, such as in the church, universities, hospitals and the civil service.

Later sociologists recognised other sources of power in addition to ownership – expertise leading to authority, and the collective power of trade unions. Max Weber accepted the idea that social class depends on economic power, but thought that status is different: it is how individuals are valued by others; this is correlated with and partly depends on economic power, but can be out of step with it. For example, newly rich people have lower status in the group in which they have just arrived.

Functional sociologists, from Durkheim onwards, have argued that social classes have the functions of filling all the different roles in society, and of rewarding those which demand more training, responsibility or other difficulties, with status and money. It is claimed that classes promote social stability, because people are rewarded and adjusted to their position in society. But Merton (1949) observed that any hierarchical society is bound to produce tensions at the lower levels, because the culturally prescribed goals and rewards are found to be unattainable – at least by legitimate means. As a result, lower-class and minority group members are likely to turn to crime or rebellion. Marx of course predicted that the proletariat would overthrow the capitalists by revolution. It has been questioned whether an unequal division of economic rewards is necessary for a stable society, or whether this is a source of instability. The actual discrepancies of wealth and income in modern societies are very large, as we shall see next, and perhaps smaller differences would do the job – after all, there are the rewards of power and status as well. The Israeli kibbutz is an interesting example here, since there are (reluctantly) appointed administrative leaders, but no pay differentials at all. In our own society something similar can be found in sporting and voluntary organisations.

THE DIFFERENCES BETWEEN SOCIAL CLASSES

Income and wealth

'The rich are different from us, they have more money.' As we have seen, differences in wealth are not the only source of class differences, but they are certainly an important one. How great are they?

Income

The average household incomes, after tax, and including social security allowances, in Britain (1986) are shown in Figure 8.1.

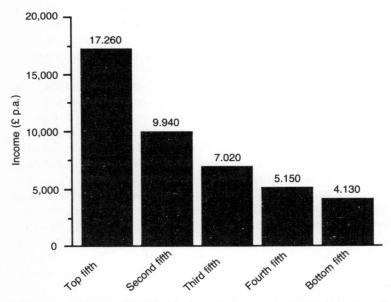

Figure 8.1 Average household incomes, after tax and including social security
allowances, Great Britain, 1986
Source: *Social Trends*, 1990

The best-paid occupations for men included doctors (£22,115), and finance and tax specialists (£20, 996); the lowest were farm workers (£6,292) and barmen (£6, 422). There are some higher salaries than these – those of some financiers and a small number of managing directors. However, within the main occupations the top ones are paid less than four times as much as the bottom ones.

There is another important difference: working-class people are in greater danger of losing their jobs, as factories are closed and workers laid off; the level of unemployment is much higher for working-class people.

Wealth

The story here is completely different: the top 0.1 per cent of wealth-holders in Britain owned about 7 per cent of property and wealth of other kinds in 1986, about £740,000 each, and the top 1 per cent owned 21 per cent – about £190,000 each. For the top 5 per cent the corresponding figure is £73,600 each, and for the bottom 50 per cent of the population it was only £845 each (*New Society*, 1987).

However, wealth is much more equally distributed than earlier in the century, when the top 1 per cent owned 69 per cent (as opposed to 18 per cent in 1987). Changes towards greater equality of incomes have been much smaller, and during the Thatcher years salary differentials became greater again (Heath *et al.*, 1991).

Are people aware of these class differences? Runciman (1966) found that only about 20 per cent of manual workers compared their incomes with those of businessmen or professionals, and many could not think of any group of people who were doing better than themselves.

Work

Social class is often assessed from occupation, and occupational status is at the heart of the class system. Those with high-status jobs own the place of work, or manage it, or have professional, technical or social skills. Those in different jobs within class I perform a variety of jobs – compare the activities of doctors, managers, university teachers, and others. What they have in common is that they supervise and control others, they are paid well and have freedom to do the work as they like. They usually have the best offices, and they undertake varied activities, some of which are challenging and interesting. However, they need to have long amounts of education or training, pass a lot of exams, and may have stressful amounts of responsibility and large work loads. At lower levels the work is less interesting, less challenging, and can be physically hard, dirty and dangerous, and takes place in a less pleasant environment. At senior levels there are no set hours of work, and competence is assessed once or twice a year or less; at lower levels people are paid by immediate results or by the hour.

Middle-class people have careers, and expect to have a series of promotions. For many manual jobs there is little chance of promotion; the next step is more often starting a new small business. Middle-class people are often ambitious, have a high need for achievement, Type A personalities, and are high in Protestant work ethic; some manual and clerical workers just work for the money, and do as little as they can get away with. Senior members of organisations are deeply committed to the organisation. Many at lower levels are alienated and don't care what happens to it. Many manual workers belong to trade unions, which in Britain (though not in Sweden) heighten conflict with managers, with constant efforts to increase wages, shorten hours and improve conditions. Manual workers and others at lower levels have less job security, in the private sector at least, and were often laid off when there was a fall in business. During recent years managers have been almost equally at risk, while in many organisations there have been improvements in security of tenure for many.

The effect of these differences between the nature and conditions of work at different levels is that there is a much higher degree of job satisfaction at higher levels and for middle-class people generally. There is also a higher degree of involvement with and attachment to the working organisation (Argyle, 1989: and Chapter 4).

Education

Class and educational success

Children from higher social classes are more successful at school and college, and receive more years of education. Table 8.4 shows some of the figures for Britain in 1985–86.

Upper- and middle-class people also send their children to different kinds of school (such as fee-paying schools), and, if they can, to better colleges afterwards.

What is the explanation of the greater educational success of upper- and middle-class children? Are they more intelligent? They do score higher, on average, on intelligence tests, and this is probably part of the explanation. However, Douglas (1964) compared the success at 'O' level of children of similar ability but different class. Among the most intelligent group 77 per cent of upper-middle-class and 37 per cent of lower-working-class children obtained good 'O' levels. The explanation of this class difference is probably that the different sub-cultures support educational achievement differently. Upper- and middle-class families value education more; middle-class careers lead to willingness to prepare for the future and postpone immediate gratifications; working-class children in school often join a counter-culture which rejects the aims of school education. Better-off parents, if their children do badly, can arrange for private coaches or crammers to repair the damage.

Table 8.4   Class and education

	I	II	III	Men IV	V	VI	VII
Degree or equivalent	51	22	27	17	7	5	3
No qualifications (CSE, 'O' level, etc.)	6	17	13	20	35	46	55
				Women			
Degree or equivalent	25	12	16	5	3	2	1
No qualifications	7	19	15	28	46	55	68

Source: General Household Survey, 1986

Education is one of the main routes to success in life, and to achieving a higher social class, though not the only one. Table 8.5 shows the educational backgrounds of members of different classes.

Table 8.5   Education and later social class (1984–5), males and females

	I	II	III	IV	V	VI
Degree or equivalent	63 (80)	14 (11)	18 (8)	1 (2)	1 (0)	1 (0)
Higher education below degree	18 (5)	17 (17)	18 (17)	5 (1)	2 (2)	1 (1)
No credentials (inc. CSE)	2 (2)	24 (30)	21 (29)	49 (56)	69 (71)	82 (84)

Source: General Household Survey, 1985

Table 8.5 shows very clear differences in the later social class following different levels of education. Education also affects later income, though the effect is not very great, since there are a lot of well-paid jobs in finance and business which do not require degrees, and skilled manual jobs which are well paid, compared to those of schoolteachers and clergymen, for example. Part off the explanation is obvious; many class I jobs actually require a degree or equivalent – doctors, lawyers, university teachers, for example. Other jobs require lower educational qualifications.

Some educational theorists have argued that schools simply reproduce the 'cultural capital' of parents in their children. They reproduce the existing class system. Halsey, Heath and Ridge (1980) found that social class had a big effect on whether children stayed on at school after 16 (70 per cent of classes I and II, 17 per cent for working class) or to 18 and beyond (28 per cent versus 3 per cent), but for those who did stay on, the level of success at

'A' level was much the same. So a proportion of working-class children were receiving middle-class cultural capital from school, and the family cultural climate had no effect at this stage.

In Britain, public schools seem to confer some advantage – going by the high proportions of bishops, judges, Conservative MPs and company directors who went to them (Reid, 1989). Oxford and Cambridge have a similar effect – but at least it takes a high level of secondary-school success to get in. Public school and Oxbridge graduates are acceptable to employers of similar background. They may have acquired some cultural capital – self-confidence, social skills and accent, for example. The same principle could apply to all levels and types of education: polytechnics, art colleges, agricultural colleges – all have their special sub-cultures and outlooks.

Family and socialisation

American and British studies have found similar differences in a number of areas. Middle-class families are smaller, with fewer children and fewer other family members. They are more often stable, with a father. Middle-class mothers are less often under 20 when the first child is born (6 per cent versus 38 per cent for class V), and fewer middle-class children are conceived pre-maritally (6 per cent versus 26 per cent). Mothers of all classes love their children, but middle-class fathers are home more and have a warmer relation with them. Middle-class parents talk and read to, interact and play with, their children more. Different kinds of discipline are used: working-class parents use much more physical punishment, as Table 8.6, from a study in Nottingham, shows.

Table 8.6　Social class and discipline

	I & II	III(n)	III(m)	IV	V
Smacks once a week to once a day (at 4)	61	68	70	66	79
Frequent use of corporal punishment (at 7)	21	27	34	31	40

Source: Newson and Newson, 1968, 1976

Middle-class parents use more persuasion and explanation. And the aim of discipline is different: for middle-class parents it is internalisation, self-control, consideration for others. For working-class parents it is more a matter of respectability and conformity, and they have been found to be more authoritarian in their handling of the children. Middle-class parents put on more pressure for educational achievement, encourage children to tackle intellectual tasks and teach them more. An interesting difference is that working-class parents in Britain give their children more pocket money.

In lower-working-class circles, in the so-called 'underclass', there is a high rate of teenage pregnancies, and of single mothers. This results in less adequate supervision and discipline, and children who do not have a role model of a working, responsible father (Murray, 1989).

What is the source of these differences in parental practices? As we show below, middle-class culture places great value on educational achievement, which is seen as essential for later careers. The greater use of physical punishment by working-class parents reflects the higher level of violence in working-class culture, itself perhaps due to greater frustration. Some of the differences may be due to cultural lag: middle-class parents hear first about the latest fashions of recommended child-rearing (Argyle and Henderson, 1985; Zigler and Child, 1969).

THE EFFECT OF CLASS ON SOCIAL BEHAVIOUR

Social relationships

Friendship

In the traditional working class, in the East End of London, and similar areas of industrial towns, people had few 'friends'. They had 'mates', whom they met in connection with particular activities, or in particular places – the pub, church, football and so on. Mates were not invited into the home, which was reserved for family, and was too small for easy entertaining. Husbands and wives had mainly different friends (40 per cent versus 9 per cent, for the middle class; Willmott, 1986). Middle-class people meet a wide variety of other people through work and leisure, from a wider geographical area, and through having cars, and make a deliberate effort to strengthen these links into friendship by meeting them in a variety of settings. They have homes which are better equipped for entertaining, and thus introduce friends and potential friends to one another, and to the family at dinner parties; the homes and the dinners are used for display and self-expression. The 'new' working class, those who have moved out of cramped Victorian terraces into new estates, often own their homes. Their pattern of friendship is similar to the middle-class one – friends are invited into the home rather than met in a pub – the homes are better and the pubs fewer. Husbands and wives are more likely to share the same friends (Allan, 1989). Middle-class people, when they need help, are more likely to call on their friends, while working-class people usually call on their kin (Willmott, 1987).

Table 8.7   Help from relatives and friends in different classes

	Middle class	Working class
Main source of help in child's illness		
Relatives	56	77
Friends	39	19
Main source of advice on a personal matter		
Relatives	34	58
Friends	64	39

Source: Willmott, 1987

Table 8.8(a)   Good friends and social class

Subject's class	Friends from each class (%)		
	I – II	III – V	VI – VII
I	81	14	5
III–V(nm)	30	44	26
III–V(m)	29	45	26
VI and VII	17	25	55

Source: Goldthorpe, 1987

Table 8.8(b)   Occupational status of all friends reported, by respondents' occupational status

Friends' occupational status	Respondents' occupational status					
	Top prof., business	Semiprof., middle bus.	Clerical, small bus.	Skilled	Semi- and unskilled	Total
	DISTRIBUTION (%)					
Top prof., business	74.2	22.9	19.0	9.0	3.9	24.4
Semiprof., middle bus.	17.1	47.9	26.3	16.2	11.1	22.4
Clerical, small bus.	2.5	13.1	19.6	13.1	12.2	11.8
Skilled	3.8	8.9	21.8	34.8	22.8	18.3
Semiskilled, unskilled	2.5	7.2	13.4	26.7	50.0	23.1
Total	100.0	100.0	100.0	100.0	100.0	100.0

Source: Laumann, 1966

In all classes people choose most of their friends from the same class, and the same level of prosperity. Table 8.8 gives the results of a British and an American study. It can be seen that there is a strong tendency to choose friends from the same class, and that this tendency is stronger at the top and at the bottom; class I people can only choose from class I or below, the middle classes have a wider choice. Within-class preference is stronger for friends than for neighbours or kin (Laumann, 1966).

Marriage

Working-class couples marry younger – typically when the bride is aged 21, compared with 26 in class I – are more often pregnant when they marry (43 per cent in class V), and have children earlier. The level of divorce is much higher – 51 per cent in class V compared with 22 per cent in class I – and they are less happily married on average. There are a number of factors here: working-class couples still do fewer things together, have fewer shared friends, confide less in each other, and are not such companions as middle-class couples (Argyle and Henderson, 1985).

However, working-class marriage in Britain has been changing. In the traditional East End type of family the husband came home to eat, sleep and recuperate, and then went to the pub; his wife ran the house; they had separate leisure and friends. In the new working class, the home is more comfortable, the husband spends more time in it, and families have become more 'symmetrical' and companionate, more like the middle-class (Young and Willmott, 1975).

Most people marry someone from the same social class; it is evidently desirable that they should do so, since mixed-class couples are less happy and more likely to become divorced, especially when the wife is of higher social class. In one study it was found that 45 per cent of husbands were violent when the wife was better educated, compared with 9 per cent when he was better educated or if they were equal (O'Brien, 1971).

Kinship

In the traditional working class, kinship was very important, as a source of social support and mutual help, with money and with the family. Working-class people are still more likely to have married children or siblings in the same house or living very near (Willmott and Young, 1960). Working-class people still call on kin more often for help, while middle-class people more often ask friends or neighbours; kin are also chosen more often as companions for leisure (Goldthorpe, 1987). Kin are invited into the house (unlike friends), and are the main confidants for wives – working-class husbands are not very good at this. Middle-class people live in smaller, nuclear families, and are less likely to have kin living near, because of geographical mobility due to education and careers. The new working class again are moving towards the middle-class pattern. However, when working-class families move out to the suburbs they do not go alone: one family goes first and then the rest follow, so that part of the previous pattern is maintained (Allan, 1989).

Most kin are of the same class. However, they can drift apart when (for example) one sibling does better or worse than the others, or than the parents. This leads to strains within the family and reduced interaction. There is least effect on the bonds between sisters and between mothers and daughters, but more effect on relations between siblings than on parent–child relations. Middle-class families are disappointed if the children move down; working-class families are not always happy about daughters who move up (Willmott and Young, 1960).

Neighbours

People from higher social classes know more neighbours well or meet them fairly often (average 3.2 versus 1.4 for classes VI–VII). They see more work colleagues outside work fairly regularly: 2.4 (I, II) versus 0.7 (III–V), and 1.2 (VI and VII). They also belong to more clubs (see p. 121). However, working-class networks of neighbours and others are more interlocking; that is to say, different friends and neighbours also know one another (Goldthorpe, 1987). Neighbours tend to be of similar social class, but the effect is considerably weaker than for friends (Laumann, 1966). For the traditional working class, neighbours lived very close and were a major source of help and support; for example, lending money and food, or minding children.

Neighbours included friends and kin, there was very little privacy from them, and there was close identification with this local community. Middle-class people don't bother to know most of their neighbours, and don't recognise those of a different class as neighbours at all. Their friends are drawn from much further afield. They keep on friendly but distant terms with immediate neighbours, may ask them in for a drink though not for a meal, and don't need to borrow things from them. They are less likely to use local pubs, but do play a role in neighbourhood organisations and clubs, and are likely to be officers or committee members (Argyle and Henderson, 1985).

The material culture of different classes

By 'culture' we mean the complete way of life, including the material conditions, patterns of behaviour, ideas and values. We shall start with the material culture.

Houses

The higher the social class the larger the house, with more rooms per person. More families in classes I and II live in detached houses, more in IV–VI in terrace houses; semi-detached are almost equally common in all classes. Many more people in higher classes own their houses, many more in lower classes rent them, mainly from the local council. Similarly, in higher classes a greater percentage own cars, telephones, dishwashers and other equipment, though nearly all have TV (Reid, 1989).

The furnishing and decoration of houses varies with social class. Chapin (1935) produced one list of 17 items and another of 50 items of living-room equipment which could be used as an index of social class. The items (at that time in the USA) included radio, newspapers, a fireplace and hardwood floor. These scales correlated with both income and occupational status.

Clothes

Until about 200 years ago in England there were laws prescribing the clothes that members of different classes could wear; you had to have a certain status to wear silk, for example. There are still class differences today, though these are much less clear than they used to be. Clothes are used to send signals about the self, as 'self presentation', and can do so better than words, which are often disbelieved; for example, 'I am very rich and important'. Veblen's *Theory of the Leisure Class* (1899) was that rich people engaged in conspicuous consumption, with expensive clothes and jewellery, which proclaimed their wealth and which were obviously unsuitable for work. Social class is still signalled by clothes and general appearance. Sissons (1971) did an experiment at Paddington Station in which an actor dressed up as an obvious member of social class I or of social class V, and was readily recognised as such. However, the finer class divisions are more difficult to recognise and are partly a matter of quality and cost of clothes as well as fashion.

Clothes affect the behaviour of others towards the wearer, as a result of signalling social class. Experiments in which an experimental confederate wore different clothes have found that respectable clothes lead to more help and cooperation from most strangers, though this effect is weaker for younger people. If a newsreader does not wear the proper respectable clothes, viewers believe and remember the news less. So there is some basis for the 'dress for success' doctrine.

Fashions in clothes keep changing; the 'trickle-down' theory was revised since the initiators of fashion are not so much the upper class as pop singers, film stars and others in the public eye. However, the fashion scene is now quite different, partly because the fashion industry now produces new styles at all levels simultaneously, so that the fashion lag is much less marked. Indeed, fashion is really trickling horizontally here; people are trying to keep up with current mass fashions as opposed to imitating anyone in particular (Argyle, 1988).

Speech styles

This and other aspects of speech associated with social class was discussed in Chapter 2.

Leisure

The leisure activities of different classes were described in Chapter 6. Large differences were reported; for instance, middle-class people engage in more sport, reading, voluntary work, and cultural and community activities, while working-class people wanted more TV, follow football and play bingo (p. 121).

Religion

More middle-class people go to church; this has been the case for some time, and is also true in the USA.

	AB	C1	C2	DE	(%)
Once a week or more	17	11	8	9	

Source: Reid, 1989

This and other aspects of class differences in religion were discussed in Chapter 6.

The explanation of these class differences in religion is that the main denominations, such as the Church of England, are definitely part of middle-class culture: they are formal, traditional and intellectual, normal and respectable; the smaller Protestant sects at the other extreme are informal, emotional and spontaneous, and reflect the interests of the underprivileged. They believe that only members of their group will go to heaven, and that rich people will not; they offer acceptance and status in the church, and emotional release (Argyle and Beit-Hallahmi, 1975).

Law-breaking

The percentage of working-class people who break the law, and are caught, is much higher than for middle-class people. Table 8.9 shows the percentages of boys who had been found guilty of various offences by the age of 17.

It can be seen that the lower working-class rates are far higher (17 times greater for serious offences). A classic study of delinquent sub-cultures in Chicago found that the percentages of delinquents rose from 1.8 per cent in the outer suburbs to 11.9 per cent in the inner city (Shaw and Mckay,

1942). Recent studies in London have found that in working-class areas the percentages of convicted delinquents are 20–25 per cent (West and Farrington, 1973).

Table 8.9   Delinquency rates and social class, percentages

	U.M.	L.M.	U.W.	L.W.
Any offence	2.7	8.3	9.7	18.7
One or more serious offence	0.8	4.2	6.1	13.8

Source: Reid, 1989

However, if self-report methods of locating delinquents are used, rather different results have been obtained. To begin with, the level of self-reported law-breaking is far higher, but this is mainly based on minor offences like riding a bicycle without a light (c. 80 per cent), trespassing on railway lines or private gardens (65 per cent), or smoking under the age of 15 (c. 40 per cent). Some surveys have found very small class differences, or no class differences at all, using self-reports. However West and Farrington (1973) used careful interviews, rather than questionnaires, and found that self-reports located many of the same people who had also been caught, and that self-reported crime was more common among boys from poorer homes. It is possible that use of questionnaires invites exaggeration. In this and other studies delinquency was found to be predictable from: low family income, large family size, parental criminality, low intelligence and poor parental child-rearing.

The explanation of lower-class law-breaking is not difficult to find. Juveniles from poor homes are short of pocket money and are deprived in many ways; poor adults may find it difficult to cope economically. They share the goals of other people, but lack the means to attain them. Parental discipline is less well carried out in lower-working-class homes, partly because of larger family size. Whole deprived areas become 'delinquent sub-cultures' where law-breaking is the norm. These sub-cultures are passed on from one generation to the next. In a re-analysis of the West and Farrington study it was found that delinquency was predictable both from bad homes and inadequate child-rearing, and also from labelling produced by the conviction of a parent or the early conviction of a child (Hagan and Palloni, 1990).

However, there does seem to be some bias against poorer people and those from ethnic minorities. This has been shown in many American studies. In California 46.5 per cent of young people who are arrested go to juvenile court, but in the Lafayette district only 17 per cent – 'For the same offense, a poor person is more likely to be arrested, and if arrested charged, than a middle- or upper-class person' (Reiman, 1984: p. 82). Poor, black and young defendants are more likely to be found guilty by the courts, partly because they have less competent lawyers, perhaps also because judges or juries are biased against them. In addition, there is a class difference in the types of crime committed. Middle-class people go in more for 'white-collar crime', poorer people for theft and violence. The sentences for the latter tend to be longer. In the USA the average number of months in prison for the crimes of the poor are:

robbery	131.3
burglary	63.4
larceny/theft	31.0

The sentences for white-collar crime were much shorter:

embezzlement	18.8
fraud	22.0
tax evasion	15.5

(Reiman, 1984)

Middle-class people go in more for business fraud, but working-class people engage in more theft and violence, and trouble at football grounds.

Health and mental health

Class differences in health were discussed in Chapter 1. We showed that working-class health is much worse than that in the middle class. This is partly because working-class people engage in worse health behaviour (such as more smoking and less exercise), have worse living conditions, and less access to medical services.

Working-class mental health is also much worse for most mental disorders. This is because working-class people have more everyday hassles (such as financial problems, drunken husbands), have fewer resources (money, social networks) to deal with stresses, and adopt passive forms of coping (p. 259).

Social class has quite a strong effect on self-esteem. However, in an American study it was found that among men for whom work was central to their self-image, job status and other aspects of social class had a stronger effect on self-esteem; for men for whom family was more central there was very little effect (Gecas and Seff, 1990).

THE RELATIONSHIPS BETWEEN CLASSES

Political attitudes and class

In all Western countries there is a strong tendency for working-class people to vote for left-wing parties. By 'left-wing' is meant parties favouring more equal distribution of income and wealth, the nationalisation of industry, and state provision of health, education and welfare. The extent of this tendency is shown from the results of the 1959 and 1987 elections in Britain (Table 8.10).

Table 8.10   Class and voting in 1959 and 1987 in the UK

		1959	1987
Manual	Labour	62	42
	Conservative	34	36
	Centre parties	4	22
Non-manual	Labour	22	18
	Conservative	69	55
	Centre parties	8	27

Source: Haralambos and Holborn, 1990

Although there is a clear effect of class, there is also a lot of 'deviant' voting: 36 per cent of manual workers voted Conservative, and 18 per cent of non-manual workers voted Labour. This table also shows that the effect of class on voting appears to be declining. However, Heath et al. (1985) divided up the classes more in accord with their economic interests and found a stronger link with class (Table 8.11).

Table 8.11   Voting and social class (percentages)

Class	Conservative	Labour	Alliance	Others	
Petty bourgeoisie	71	12	17	0	100
Salariat	54	14	31	1	100
Foremen/technicians	48	26	25	1	100
Routine non-manual	46	25	27	2	100
Working class	30	49	20	1	100

Source: Heath, Jowell and Curtice, 1985: 20

The most conservative were the 'petty bourgeoisie'; that is, owners of small businesses, farmers and self-employed manual workers. The most strongly labour were manual workers employed by others. Most Alliance support came from the 'salariat', managers and professionals.

The most obvious explanation of the influence of class on voting is that the Labour Party represents working-class interests, while the Conservative Party represents middle-class interests. A more elaborate version of this was developed by Himmelweit et al. (1981), who proposed that people make rational 'consumer' choices and select the party whose policies best match their political views. This was supported by evidence that from 21 political attitude statements voting could be predicted with about 85 per cent accuracy – though much less than this for Liberal voters. However, later and more rigorous tests of this approach have not confirmed it (for example, Heath *et al.*, 1985). Nevertheless there are clear ideological differences between parties, and there are similar differences between classes. So, for example, both the Labour Party and working-class people favour more income re-distribution and are against trade-union reform. Such differences must be part of the explanation of class differences in voting.

The other main theory is that people in different classes identify with certain parties, so that working-class people see themselves as Labour Party supporters. Butler and Stokes (1974) found that 95 per cent of people identified with a party, most of them strongly, and that those who did so voted accordingly. When asked why they voted as they did, 69 per cent of Labour supporters, but only 32 per cent of Conservatives, said that it was because of the class links with their party; another 32 per cent of Conservatives said that they generally approved of the party. These authors also argue that people are 'socialised' into their party, mainly by influence from parents. However, this theory has not been able to explain the large changes in voting between successive elections, and party identification in Britain has declined since 1974 (Heath *et al.*, 1991).

What is the explanation for the sections of the population who apparently do not vote in accordance with their class interests? Several theories have been put forward. There is some evidence that some working-class people defer to and accept upper-class leadership; older, female, working-class voters have been found to prefer such leaders when given hypothetical choices. Another explanation is that the more prosperous working-class people are more satisfied with their incomes and more likely to vote Conservative. They have undergone 'embourgeoisement'; that is, they have become in some ways middle class. Sarlvik and Crewe (1983) found that the 'new' working class, who own their houses, work in the private sector, and live in the South, are much more likely to vote Conservative (47 per cent of owner-occupiers versus 19 per cent of council tenants). Butler and Stokes (1974) found that working-class individuals (as defined by occupation) who regard themselves as middle class are much more likely to vote Conservative, and that people who own their homes see themselves as middle class.

Another cause of deviant voting is that many people come under social influences that pull them away from the view of their class. Middle-class Labour Party supporters more often have fathers who voted Labour (60 per cent versus 37 per cent for all salaried workers), or who were working class (47 per cent versus 33 per cent); they are also more likely to have

degrees (48 per cent versus 28 per cent) (Heath and Evans, 1988).
They tend to be teachers, scientists or social workers, who have no
economic stake in the success of business enterprises, but rather an
idealistic concern for the welfare of the community. Some working-class
Conservatives have no contact with the world of industrial trade unions,
but work in small firms or organisations with middle-class people (Parkin,
1972).

Personality factors also affect right–left voting. Evans (1988) found that
individuals who felt themselves to be 'powerless', unable to influence
events, were stronger Labour supporters if they were working class, but
stronger Conservative supporters if they were middle class.

What about the centre party supporters? They tend to be middle class,
and again are more often teachers, scientists or social workers than in
business. They do not have a very distinctive ideology – between Labour
and Conservative, sharing some of the views of each. There is a tendency
to be 'tender-minded' on issues such as punishment and the environment;
they do have a distinctive image, however, as 'fair' and 'good for all
classes' (Heath *et al.*, 1991). Himmelweit *et al.* (1981) and others have
found that political attitudes are basically two-dimensional, and that
Liberal, or Liberal Democrat views are on a dimension orthogonal to
the left–right dimension.

Explanation of wealth and poverty

Many studies have asked people how they explain why some are rich and
others are poor. It is found that middle-class people and Conservative
voters place more emphasis on individual factors to explain success – hard
work, intelligence, money management. Working-class people think that
certain individual factors are important – ruthlessness, inherited wealth
and educational advantages. They also favour societal explanations more:
that the economic system is unfair; for example, taxation favours the rich
and high wages in certain jobs, and the belief that the economic system
automatically creates inequality.

Explanations for unemployment also vary between different classes. The
majority of people in Britain during recent years think that societal factors
are the main explanation – government policies, inefficient industries going
bankrupt, incompetent management, for example. However, employed
people, and those strong in the Protestant work ethic, believe that these
societal factors are less important than the unemployed themselves think.
Instead they think that people are out of work because of individual
factors such as lack of ability, being unable to adapt to new conditions,
or move to other places of work, and not trying hard enough to get
jobs. A third kind of explanation for unemployment is bad luck, such
as illness, world-wide recession and the introduction of automation; the

unemployed thought these were more important than did those at work (Furnham, 1988).

This pattern of explanations follows a familiar pattern, in that people tend to attribute their own success to their competence or hard work, and their failures to external factors or bad luck, and the failures of others to lack of competence.

Social interaction between classes

What happens when members of different classes meet; do they meet at all, and if so when? They may meet in public places, in the street and shops, and on public transport. In the experiment at Paddington Station an actor dressed up either as a manual labourer or as upper middle class and asked 100 people the way to Hyde Park. Interactions were longer with the actor in his middle-class role with both MC and WC subjects. MC subjects smiled at him more when he was MC (Sissons, 1971). Many studies have been carried our in which an experimental confederate, dressed to look tidy or untidy, respectable or disreputable, stopped people in the street to request an interview or other help. Nearly all these studies found that a conventionally or tidily dressed person elicited more help or cooperation (Argyle, 1988). This suggests that most people have respect for, or are prepared to defer to, middle-class people.

Another setting where different classes meet is leisure groups of various kinds. In Britain, class I individuals belong to more clubs (3.6 each) than classes VI and VII (1.5). Working-class people belong more to social clubs (28 per cent versus 2 per cent for class I), mainly working men's clubs and trade unions. Middle-class people belong instead to a variety of sporting, educational, cultural, and other groups. Middle-class people have more often been an officer of a club (52 per cent versus 19 per cent for classes VI and VII) (Goldthorpe, 1987). How far do the different classes meet in such clubs? Warner (1963) in his studies of 'Yankee City' found that many leisure groups spanned 3–4 of his 6 classes, though some were drawn exclusively from one or two adjacent classes, and women favoured this kind of group. He found that many of these groups were quite small, 28 per cent had under 10, 54 per cent had up to 20 members, and so the contact would be quite close. Laboratory studies of groups find that informal leaders tend to be older, male and middle class; this has been found in juries selecting foremen, and is probably a common phenomenon.

Perhaps the most frequent contact between classes is at work, and between doctors and other professionals and office workers, and their clients. Doctors find that their consultations with working-class patients are more difficult, and report communication problems in 21 per cent of them (Jaspars and Pendleton, 1983). However, many cross-class encounters in work settings go quite well. With different racial groups it is found that work contacts go easily, because they are formal, programmed and not intimate, but the same people do not choose to spend their leisure together. The same is probably true of different classes.

There is little friendship across class lines. In one survey 56 per cent of English workers thought this would be unlikely, though 14 per cent thought it was very likely and 29 per cent quite likely (Gallie, 1983). Most people marry someone from the same class, or failing this from an adjacent class, and as we have seen marriages are happier when they do.

Can we describe in more detail the nature of the social interaction between classes? First, there is a greater 'social distance' than for in-class encounters; that is, there is less immediate liking or prospect of friendship. Another social class is a different social group, so it would be expected that there would be some rejection of the out-group, and negative stereotypes about it. We have seen that there are such negative stereotypes about the rich, the poor and the unemployed. These stereotypes would be expected to be especially strong for people who have little social contact with the other class.

There may also be some degree of deference, acceptance of the higher status of higher-status groups. This probably varies with different sections of each class. The traditional working class, as we have seen, had a strong 'us' and 'them' view of society, and were probably both deferential and hostile to those of higher social class; other workers, like those in small farms and small firms are more deferential; the 'new' working class are less deferential, though they do not see themselves as middle class (Goldthorpe et al., 1969). Similarly, the traditional middle class of owners of businesses probably take a more superior and distant view of workers than the new middle class of teachers, social workers and professionals.

The emergence of status differences in small social groups provides an interesting model of the class system. Informal hierarchies emerge in various ways. A major factor is real contribution to the work and goals of the group. However, leadership can also appear before this has had a chance to happen. Simply being or appearing to be middle class is one way, because it creates expectations of competence. In some experiments a stronger factor has been non-verbal signals of dominance and assertion – by posture and tone of voice. These may be the ways in which deference is brought about in the class system.

Social mobility

How much do people move upwards or downwards from the class that they were born into? The Oxford mobility study in 1972 studied 10,000 men in England and Wales, and some of the findings are shown in Table 8.12. The figures in the top right hand corner of each square show 'outflow', or destinations. Thus of fathers in class I, 45.7 per cent of sons were in class I, 19.1 per cent in class II, etc. The figures in the lower left hand corners show 'inflow' or origins. Thus of all the sons in class I, 25.3 per cent had fathers in class I, 13.1 per cent had fathers in class II, etc. (Goldthorpe, 1987). Clearly there was quite a lot of mobility, but mainly to the next class, and more rarely to a more distant class. The two percentages above show that it is 6^1/$_2$ times more likely that a person born into class I will end up there than that a class VII person will.

Table 8.12   Social mobility: fathers and sons

		\multicolumn{8}{c}{Son's class in 1972}
		1	2	3	4	5	6	7	Total
	1	45.7	19.1	11.6	6.8	4.9	5.4	6.5	100.0
		25.3	12.4	9.6	6.7	3.2	2.0	2.4	(680)
	2	29.4	23.3	12.1	6.0	9.7	10.8	8.6	100.0
		13.1	12.2	8.0	4.8	5.2	3.1	2.5	(547)
Father's	3	18.6	15.9	13.0	7.4	13.0	15.7	16.4	100.0
		10.4	10.4	10.8	7.4	8.7	5.7	6.0	(687)
class	4	14.0	14.4	9.1	21.1	9.9	15.1	16.3	100.0
		10.1	12.2	9.8	27.2	8.6	7.1	7.7	(886)
	5	14.4	13.7	10.2	7.7	15.9	21.4	16.8	100.0
		12.5	14.0	13.2	12.1	16.6	12.2	9.6	(1,072)
	6	7.8	8.8	8.4	6.4	12.4	30.6	25.6	100.0
		16.4	21.7	26.1	24.0	31.0	41.8	35.2	(2,577)
	7	7.1	8.5	8.8	5.7	12.9	24.8	32.2	100.0
		12.1	17.1	22.6	17.8	26.7	28.0	36.6	(2,126)
Total		100.0	100.0	100.0	100.0	100.0	100.0	100.0	
		(1,230)	(1,050)	(827)	(687)	(1,026)	(1,883)	(1,872)	(8,575)

Classes

No.	Description
1	Higher professionals, higher grade administrators, managers in large industrial concerns and large proprietors
2	Lower professionals, higher grade technicians, lower grade administrators, managers in small businesses and supervisors of non-manual employees
3	Routine non-manual – mainly clerical and sales personnel
4	Small proprietors and self-employed artisans
5	Lower grade technicians and supervisors of manual workers
6	Skilled manual workers
7	Semi-skilled and unskilled manual workers

Source: Adapted from Goldthorpe, 1987 by Haralambos and Holborn (1990)

However, class I here refers to quite a large group, including 10–15 per cent of employed males. If a really upper-class group is examined – people in *Who's Who*, or company chairmen, for example – a much more closed circle appears. The chance of getting your name in *Who's Who* is 75 times greater if your father did, and your chance of being the director of a bank is 200 times more if father was one (Heath, 1981).

Many people change their social class as assessed by social scientists – they move into better (or worse) jobs, earn higher incomes, become educated. But many of them do not feel any different or that their class has changed. Richardson (1977) interviewed a sample of socially mobile people in London and South-east England. Many said things like 'I don't think you can change class', 'It's just not possible', 'It's easier to become rich than to change class', 'I like me as I am', or thought that they could never be accepted by another class, and didn't want to be.

Has society become more open over the years? Education has become more widely available and there has been much talk of the development of a 'meritocracy'. On the other hand, successive sociological studies have not detected much change in the amount of mobility in Britain. There have, however, been general changes in society, in particular a reduction in the number of manual workers, and an increase in white-collar workers, so that there has been a general trend 'upwards', except that the gain in salary involved may be minimal. Social mobility has been compared in different countries, and it is found that Britain and the USA have intermediate levels; Australia and Sweden are higher: the other European countries have lower rates (Heath, 1981). Women have a somewhat different pattern from men, in that women from classes I and II tend to be downwardly mobile since there are so many women's jobs in class III (non-manual); women in class V–VII are often upwardly mobile for the same reason (Heath, 1981).

It is interesting to find which individuals move up and down. Sociologists have succeeded in providing part of the explanation. The occupations (and hence the class) of some are partly predictable ($r = .33$) by their educational level, and also by their father's occupation. The educational level of the sons is also partly predictable from their father's occupation and education (Halsey *et al.*, 1980). It looks as if the abilities and social position of fathers are able to influence their sons' careers, but particularly via influencing their education. However, it is familiar that the sons in the same family may have quite different degrees of educational and occupational success. Jencks (1972) found that sons' IQ also predicted sons' jobs, particularly by leading to a higher educational level (see Figure 8.2).

The predictions made from these models leave much to be explained, and Jencks thinks that a lot of mobility is due to luck, such as meeting chance acquaintances who get you a good job. However, personality variables are important too, and have not been studied by sociologists. The most obvious one is that mental disorder, such as schizophrenia, leads to downward mobility. For upward mobility, achievement motivation is an obvious candidate. It has been found that individuals who are strong in this kind of motivation work very hard, with persistence and are more upwardly mobile than others; they are successful in a variety of occupations, especially in sales and business (McClelland, 1987).

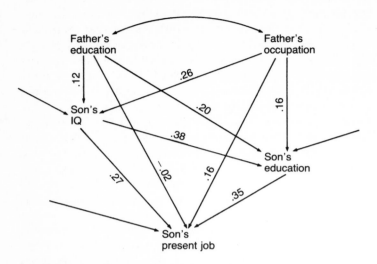

Figure 8.2 IQ and other sources of social mobility
Source: Jencks, 1972

Another personality characteristic which leads to mobility is social skills. Many jobs require social skills of some kind, so that both selection for the job and success in it are affected by social competence. Physical appearance is also relevant. American experiments have found that physically attractive candidates for jobs, of either sex, are offered substantially larger salaries, as are taller men; fat people are less likely to get the job at all (Argyle, 1988).

CONCLUSIONS

Most people are agreed that there is a class system, and can place themselves in it; social scientists usually assess it from occupation. Each class forms a sub-culture, with a distinctive way of life, and differing in income, wealth, power and education, as well as occupation. Children of higher classes do better in the educational system, which in turn leads to better jobs. Middle-class families apply more pressure for, and help with, such achievement.

Middle-class people make more use of friends, less of kin or neighbours, and traditionally had a different style of marriage. There are class differences in houses, clothes, speech style, leisure and religion. Working-class youths break the law more, though the law may be biased against them.

Political attitudes and voting are related to class, especially for employers compared with manual workers, though there is a lot of 'deviant' voting.

There are predictable class differences in the explanations given for wealth, poverty and unemployment. Social interaction between classes is restricted and constrained, but occurs in social clubs and at work.

There is a lot of social mobility, especially via education, but it is difficult to move into the highest levels. There is most upward mobility for people of high intelligence and achievement motivation.

REFERENCES

Allan, G. (1989) *Friendship*. Brighton: Harvester Wheatsheaf.
Argyle, M. (1988) *Bodily Communication*. 2nd edition. London: Methuen.
——(1989) *The Social Psychology of Work*. 2nd edition. Harmondsworth: Penguin.
Argyle, M. and Beit-Hallahmi, B. (1975) *The Social Psychology of Religion*. London: Routledge and Kegan Paul.
Argyle, M., Furnham, A. and Graham, J.A. (1981) *Social Situations*. Cambridge: Cambridge University Press.
Argyle, M. and Henderson, M. (1985) *The Anatomy of Relationships*. London: Heinemann; Harmondsworth: Penguin.
Butler, D. and Stokes, D. (1974) *Political Change in Britain*. London: Macmillan.
Census (1971) England and Wales General Report (1979). London: OPCS and HMSO.
Centers, R. (1949) *The Psychology of Social Classes*. Princeton, NJ: Princeton University Press.
Chapin, F.S. (1935) *Contemporary American Institutions: A Sociological Analysis*. New York: Harper.
Douglas, J.W.B. (1964) *The Home and the School*. London: McGibbon & Kee.
Evans, G.A. (1988) Causal explanation, perceived efficacy and social class. Unpublished D.Phil. thesis, Oxford University.
Feather, N.T. (1989) Attitudes towards the high achiever: the fall of the tall poppy. *Australian Journal of Psychology*, *41*, 239–67.
Furnham, A. (1988) *Lay Theories*. Oxford: Pergamon.
Gallie, D. (1983) *Social Inequality and Class Radicalism in France and Britain*. Cambridge: Cambridge University Press.
Gecas, V. and Seff, M.A. (1990) Social class and self esteem: psychological centrality, compensation, and the relative effects of work and home. *Social Psychology Quarterly*, *53*, 165–73.
General Household Survey (1985, 1986, 1989) London: OPCS and HMSO.
Giddens, A. (1989) *Sociology*. Oxford: Polity Press.
Goldthorpe, J.H. (1987) *Social Mobility and Class Structure in Modern Britain*. 2nd edition. Oxford: Clarendon Press.
Goldthorpe, J.H. and Hope, K. (1974) *The Social Grading of Occupations: a New Approach and Scale*. Oxford: Clarendon Press.
Goldthorpe, J.H., Lockwood, D., Bechofer, F. and Platt, J. (1969) *The Affluent Worker in the Class Structure*. Cambridge: Cambridge University Press.
Hagan, J. and Palloni, A. (1990) The social reproduction of a criminal class in working-class London, circa 1950–1980. *American Journal of Sociology*, *96*, 265–99.
Halsey, A.H., Heath, A.F. and Ridge, J.M. (1980) *Origins and Destinations*. Oxford: Clarendon Press.
Haralambos, M. and Holborn, M. (1990) *Sociology*. 3rd edition. London: Unwin Hyman.

Heath, A. (1981) *Social Mobility*. Glasgow: Fontana.
Heath, A. and Evans, G. (1988) Working class conservatives and middle class socialists. *In* R. Jowell, S. Witherspoon and L. Brook (eds) *British Social Attitudes, the Fifth Report*. Aldershot: Gower.
Heath, A., Jowell, R. and Curtice, J. (1985) *How Britain Votes*. Oxford: Pergamon.
Heath, A., Jowell, R., Curtice, J., Evans, G., Field, J. and Witherspoon, S. (1991) *Understanding Political Change*. Oxford: Pergamon.
Himmelweit, H.T., Humphreys, P. and Jaeger, M. (1981) *How Voters Decide*. London: Academic Press.
Hurlock, E.B. (1929) Motivation in fashion. *Archives of Psychology III*.
Jaspars, J.M.F. and Pendleton, D. (1983) The consultation: a social psychological analysis. *In* D. Pendleton and J. Hasler (eds) *Doctor–Patient Communication*. London: Academic Press.
Jencks, C. (1972) *Inequality: a Reassessment of the Effect of Family and Schooling in America*. Harmondsworth: Penguin.
Laumann, E.O. (1966) *Prestige and Association in an Urban Community*. Indianapolis, IN: Bobbs-Merrill.
McClelland, D.C. (1987) *Human Motivation*. Cambridge: Cambridge University Press.
Marshall, G. (1988) *Social Class in Modern Britain*. London: Hyman.
Marshall, G., Newby, H., Rose, D. and Voglen, C. (1988) *Social Class in Modern Britain*. London: Hutchinson.
Merton, R.K. (1949) *Social Theory and Social Structure*. New York: Free Press.
Murray, C. (1989) Underclass. *Sunday Times* 26 Nov.
New Society (1987) Database: personal wealth. 24 April.
Newson, J. and Newson, E. (1968) *Four Years Old in an Urban Community*. London: Allen & Unwin.
——(1976) *Seven Years Old in the Home Environment*. London: Allen & Unwin.
O'Brien, J.E. (1971) Violence in divorce-prone families. *Journal of Marriage and the Family, 33*, 692–8.
Parkin, F. (1972) *Class Inequality and Political Order*. St Albans: Paladin.
Reid, I. (1981) *Social Class Differences in Britain*. 2nd edition. Oxford: Blackwell.
—— (1989) *Social Class Differences in Britain*. 3rd edition. London: Fontana.
Reiman, J.H. (1984) *The Rich get Richer, and the Poor get Prison*. New York: Wiley.
Richardson, C.J. (1977) *Contemporary Social Mobility*. London: Pinter.
Runciman, W.G. (1966) *Relative Deprivation and Social Justice*. London: Routledge and Kegan Paul.
Sarlvik, B. and Crewe, I. (1983) *Decade of Dealignment*. Cambridge: Cambridge University Press.
Shaw, C.R. and McKay, H.D. (1942) *Juvenile Delinquency and Urban Areas*. Chicago: University of Chicago Press.
Sissons, M. (1971) The psychology of social class. *In Money, Wealth and Class*. Milton Keynes: Open University Press.
Social Trends (1987, 1990) London: HMSO.
Veblen, T. (1899) *The Theory of the Leisure Class*. New York: Viking.
Warner, W.L. (1963) *Yankee City*. New Haven, CT: Yale University Press.
West, D.J. and Farrington, D.P. (1973) *Who Becomes Delinquent?* London: Heinemann.
Willmott, P. (1987) *Friendship Networks and Social Support*. London: Policy Studies Institute.
——(1988) Urban kinship past and present. *Social Studies Review*, Nov.

Willmott, P. and Young, M. (1960) *Family and Class in a London Suburb*. London: Routledge and Kegan Paul.

Young, M. and Willmott, P. (1975) *The Symmetrical Family*. Harmondsworth: Penguin.

Zigler, E. and Child, I.L. (1969) Socialization. *In* G. Lindzey and E. Aronson (eds) *The Handbook of Social Psychology*. 2nd edition, vol. 3. Reading, MA: Addison-Wesley.

Chapter 9

Health

The traditional view was that illness is due to infectious or other biological sources, and could sometimes be cured by medicine or operations. Certain complaints were later thought to be 'psychosomatic' – headaches and ulcers, for example. It was then discovered that heart disease, and later cancer, were also like this, and it is now realised that *all* illnesses have psychological as well as physical causes, and are partly due to stresses of various kinds.

Instead of trying to account for illness only in terms of low-level processes, like disorders of cells or the contents of the blood, the importance of higher-level processes such as emotions, personality and social support is now recognised. It is found, for example, that some people are more or less likely to fall ill than others, when exposed to exactly the same germs or stresses. This is partly because they have different personalities, or have different degrees of social support. They may also have different beliefs about health, and this affects their 'health behaviour' (smoking, drinking, eating, exercise and so forth). And the effectiveness of doctors in persuading their patients to comply with their suggestions depends on doctor–patient skills, which can now be taught.

Health psychology has become a very active field, and knowledge has been increasing fast. Is there still a Type A personality? How about Type C? How does social support really work? And why are individuals of higher status in better health? Why are women in worse health but live longer?

THE DISTRIBUTION OF HEALTH IN THE POPULATION

The measurement of health

The best measure of an individual's health is a complete medical examination by a doctor, supported by a number of medical tests. This method has been used in surveys of GP lists, but there is a problem: 30 per cent of people or more have not seen a doctor in the last year, and over

10 per cent never see one at all (Wadsworth, Butterfield and Blaney, 1971). There is also the problem of different doctors applying different standards of 'good' health.

There is some advantage in using social-survey methods to assess health, in order to sample those who do not go to the doctor, and to find out how ill people feel. Several surveys have asked questions like 'Would you say your state of health in the past 14 days was . . .?' (average of several surveys.):

	%
excellent	28
good	39
fair	24
poor	9

Source: Dunnell and Cartwright, 1972

One can ask people whether they have any of a list of possible symptoms. They average about 3 for males and $4^{1}/_{2}$ for females on any particular day. The most common symptoms experienced in a two-week period are coughs (28 per cent), trouble with nose (27 per cent) and feet (21 per cent) (Hannay, 1979). Many of these symptoms are of course trivial, and are reported by people who regard themselves as being in perfect health.

The General Household Survey asked a number of other questions:

	Yes
Do you have chronic health problems?	33%
Do you have a limiting long-standing illness?	20%

To what extent do these subjective reports of ill health and symptoms reflect genuine ill health? It has recently been found that subjective reports correlate quite highly, .30 to .50, with unhappiness, neuroticism and negative mood. However, in a number of studies subjective symptoms had little relationship with cholesterol, blood pressure or immune functioning. Subjective reports of ill health may be due to negative emotions causing people to attend more to bodily symptoms, to be more sensitive to them, while important bodily conditions such as blood pressure go unnoticed (Watson and Pennebaker, 1989).

There are some aspects of self-reported health which are more objective, like taking medicine and going to the doctor, but these too may be the result of negative moods. For example:

| How many days were you off last year? | 17.6 days |
| How often did you see the doctor in the last year? | 3.5 times |

Another measure is the amount of medicine taken. Over a two-week period 80 per cent of people have taken some medicine, most of it not prescribed, with an average of 2.2 doses each. The commonest medicines are aspirins, indigestion remedies, skin ointments, cough medicines, sleeping pills, tranquillisers, and laxatives (Dunnell and Cartwright, 1972). People also take a lot of other 'medicines' – tonics, vitamin pills and so on.

A more important measure of health is simply staying alive, and we shall use this to look at the effects of some social variables.

The numbers who die in Britain at different ages are shown in Table 9.1. It can be seen that 6 per cent of men die before they are 40 and 10 per cent before the age of 50, while 31.5 per cent do not live to collect their pensions at 65.

Table 9.1   Life expectancy tables, by social class for males and by sex

| | | Social class (RG 70) | | | | | | |
	At age	I	II	IIIn	IIIm	IV	V	All
Male expectation	15	57.2	57.0	56.0	55.7	55.1	53.5	55.6
of life in years	45	28.5	28.3	27.5	27.2	27.0	26.2	27.4

		Female	Male
Expectation of	0	77.0	71.0
life in years	10	68.0	62.2
	20	58.1	52.5
	30	48.3	42.9
	40	38.7	33.3
	50	29.4	24.3
	60	20.9	16.4
	65	NA	13.0
	70	13.4	10.1

Source: Reid, 1989

The most common causes of death, taking all age groups together, are: coronary thrombosis, cancer, stroke, bronchitis, other heart diseases, pneumonia and hypertension. The most common causes of early death are: heart disease, cancer (especially lung cancer), cirrhosis of the liver, accidents, suicide, and (in the USA) homicide (*Social Trends*, 1983). It is obvious that several of these causes of death are largely avoidable.

Gender differences

Women are in somewhat worse health than men. (See table on p.227.)

Why do women have worse health? If self-report surveys are compared with clinical data, it is found that women over-report their illnesses (or men under-report them) and, having decided they are ill, seek medical help at a lower level of illness. Other studies have found that women take more medicine than men, for the same symptoms (Dunnell and Cartwright, 1972). However, this does not apply to women with jobs. It is partly that women are more concerned about health. And women do suffer from female disorders related to menstruation and pregnancy.

	Men (%)	Women (%)
Limiting long-standing illness	18	20
Days of restricted activity per year	20	28
Average number of symptoms	3.2	4.5
Average number of visits to doctor per year	3	5
Took prescribed medicine	22	37
Reported health in last year was good	64	54

Sources: GHS, 1988, and other sources

Nevertheless, women on average live longer than men: 7–8 years, paradoxically. The explanation is that most female illnesses are minor ones, while men suffer from heart disease and lung cancer in particular, also from a number of other potentially fatal conditions. There is a biological explanation for women's lower rate of heart attacks – oestrogen gives protection; oestrogen therapy lowers the rate (Rodin and Ickovics, 1990). In addition, most of these diseases are avoidable, and result from unwise health behaviour on the part of men. Heart attacks are made more likely by smoking, drinking, bad diet and stress, lung cancer by smoking, cirrhosis of the liver by drinking, and accidents are due to dangerous work, fast driving or alcohol. It is now clear that the main explanation for the shorter lives of men relates to behaviour which is encouraged in men – smoking, drinking, fast driving, competitiveness, all part of the traditional masculine way of life (Waldron, 1976). Women have a better diet than men because they try to keep their weight down. On the other hand they take less exercise.

It is also possible that women benefit from the stronger social support networks which they establish with family and kin, friends and neighbours. The benefits which women receive from these networks include medical advice – health is one of the main things women talk about – as well as material help and social and emotional support. The one relationship in which women benefit less than men is marriage.

Are women with jobs in better health? Yes, despite the pressure of family plus work, women with jobs are mostly in better health (Rodin and Ickovics, 1990), though partly because only those who are well

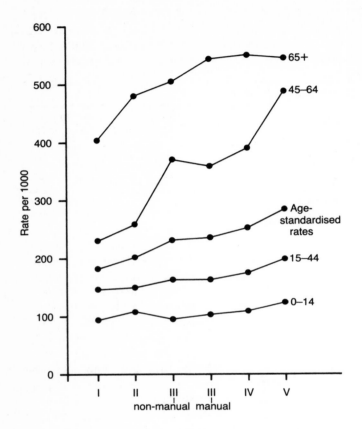

Figure 9.1 Long-standing illness: males, 1974−6
Source: Black, 1980

enough go to work. It also depends on the job: highly educated women in good jobs have fewer chronic illnesses and live longer, while women in clerical jobs have a high rate of heart attacks (Haw, 1982). And women at work who have young children at home are under more stress.

Class differences

There is a strong correlation between health and social class. Table 9.2 shows some British data.

Table 9.2   Illness and social class (UK)

| | Classes | | | | | |
	I	II	III	IV	V	VI
Long-standing illnes(%)	13.0	16.8	19.2	19.2	26.5	31.7
Limiting long-standing illness(%)	6.5	9.0	10.4	11.3	16.2	20.8
Number of working days lost per year	3	6	6	9	11	18

Source: General Household Survey, 1980

	I	II	III(n)	III(m)	IV	V
Number of repeated symptoms	3.4	3.7	3.6	4.0	4.0	4.6
Percentage rating health fair or poor	17	28	28	36	37	43

Source: Dunnell and Cartwright, 1972

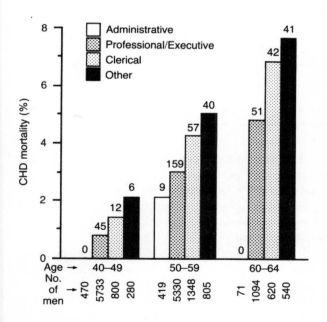

Figure 9.2 Coronary heart disease mortality (and number of deaths) in seven and a half years by civil service grade and age

Note: The figures on top of the histograms are the numbers of CHD deaths

Source: Marmot et al., 1978

It can be seen that, for example, 6.5 per cent of people in social class I have limiting long-standing illness, compared to 20.8 per cent in social class VI. And in class I, 15-year-olds can expect to live to age 57.2 compared with 53.5 in class V (using a slightly different division of the classes). The differences are particularly great in middle age, as Figure 9.1 shows.

Most illnesses affect working-class people more, and more die from heart disease, lung cancer and other kinds of cancer, pneumonia and other respiratory diseases, ulcers, cirrhosis of the liver and other digestive problems, and they have more accidents, at work and elsewhere. Coronaries are no longer more common for middle-class males, since they take more exercise; leukaemia is, however, more common in the middle classes, because they have more X-rays.

On the other hand, as Table 9.1 showed, class differences in longevity are fairly small: class I males can expect, at age 15, to live only 3.7 years longer than class V males; differences in health are greater than differences in length of life.

Why do working-class people have worse health? Partly, it is assumed, because of worse housing, food and other conditions of life, together with more dangerous work, and certain occupational diseases.

In addition, there are large differences in health behaviour. In particular there is clear evidence, using other classification systems, that middle-class people:

Smoke less	2.63:1	V and VI:1
Are less obese	2.54:1	
Take more exercise (at least one sport)	2.44	class I: classes V and VI

Source: Reid, 1989

What is the reason for these class differences? It is partly that new ideas, such as keeping fit and having a proper diet, start among better educated and informed people, and filter through to the others later, as fashions in clothes did once. It may also be because the unemployed, and those doing unsatisfying jobs and living in bad areas, simply seek whatever sources of gratification are most easily obtained.

In addition, middle-class people often succeed in obtaining more medical attention. They make more use of preventive services – antenatal clinics, vaccination, cervical screening and the dentist (Black, 1980). And doctors spend more time with them. There is evidence that National Health Service expenditure on middle-class people is 41 per cent higher than on those in classes IV to VI – because classes I and II know how to make better use of the system, and manage to get better attention (Le Grand, 1978). However, it has also been estimated that only about 10 per cent of the class differences in health are due to such differences in medical care (Williams, 1990).

A study of 17,530 British civil servants found that the lower grades had 3.6 times as many deaths as the highest grades from heart attacks over a 7½ year period. This could partly be explained by the lower ranks having higher blood pressure, smoking more, having less active leisure, and shorter and heavier physique. However, 60 per cent of the variance was still unexplained and must be due to some other effects of status, such as differences in autonomy or self-esteem (Marmot *et al.*, 1978).

Age

Ill health increases with age, as Figure 9.1 showed. The figures for women are similar. It can be seen that the percentage of people aged 65 or over with long-standing illness is over 50 per cent for most social classes, though only about half this is 'limiting'. Only 7 per cent of those aged 15–44 stated that their health in the last year was not good; this increases considerably among older people. The number of days of restricted activity per year shows a similar steady rise. The frequency of going to the doctor more than doubles between childhood and old age.

The probability of dying is small until the age of 50, and then increases rapidly (see Table 9.1). It can be seen that there is a steadily increasing number who die in each period, so that of males born in 1960, 10.4 per cent will probably die between the ages of 60 and 65; 13.7 per cent between 65 and 70; and so on. Forty-two per cent of the females and 23 per cent of the males will still be alive at the age of 80, in 2040, assuming that there are no nuclear or other catastrophes.

Health behaviour changes a lot with age, some for the better, some for the worse. Drinking declines – only 4 per cent of men over 65 drink 7 or more units of drink once or twice a week or more, compared with 37 per cent of those between 18 and 24. Smoking falls off a little. However, exercise also declines a lot – much less swimming or football, but slightly fewer people walk 2 miles or more once a week.

Living or dying is partly dependent on the will to live, which can be assessed by asking people to rate their keenness to carry on living. The will to live is much reduced in those who are socially isolated, who are in poor health, or who feel that they have lost their usefulness (Ellison, 1969).

THE EFFECTS OF STRESS ON HEALTH

Stress is a familiar source of *mental* illness, and this will be discussed in the next chapter. Here we are concerned with the effect of stress on physical health – because cancer, heart disease and the rest result not only from infections or biological causes, but also from the effects of stress.

By 'stress' we mean external conditions which produce feelings of discomfort and tension, since they are seen as threatening or frustrating, or they exceed the individual's capacities to deal with them. Stress is not just an objective state of affairs, but depends on an individual's perception and interpretation of it – how harmful it is likely to be and whether he thinks he is able to cope with it.

The immediate reaction to stress is physiological – increased arousal, with higher blood pressure, heart rate, speed of breathing and the rest. There are emotional reactions, fear leading to flight, anger leading to confrontation, depression and so on.

How does stress make people ill? In a number of ways. Frequent physiological arousal can produce increases of blood pressure, disrupt digestion or produce fatigue, for example. Stress may result in poor health behaviour; people who are widowed often fail to have proper meals, are likely to drink more, and take more pills. Stress may lead to 'taking the sick role' more readily – staying at home or going to the doctor as a result of interpreting the physiological consequences of stress as symptoms of illness (Taylor, 1986).

Stress has another general effect: it suppresses the immune system. This consists of organisms in the blood which defend the body against biological invasions, by killing the invading cells. It has been found that the level of these immune organisms is reduced by stress, such as loud noises, shocks and examinations. The same stresses then produce higher rates of infectious diseases. There are a number of biological routes between stress and the immune system (Jemmott and Locke, 1984). In a series of studies Kiecolt-Glaser and colleagues have found lower immune-system activity in people who have recently been separated or divorced, especially if the spouse initiated this, and among those who are lonely or are taking examinations (for example, Kennedy et al., 1990). We shall see later that certain kinds of personality have weak immune systems, and that social support strengthens immunity.

Let us look at some concrete examples of how stress causes illness.

Headaches. Anxiety leads to contracting the muscles in the head and neck, and this causes pain in the head. Headaches are produced by daily hassles at work, in the home or with other relationships, and can be relieved by psychological methods such as biofeedback and relaxation.

Ulcers have been produced experimentally in monkeys. Anxiety or hostility can produce acids in the stomach, which damage the mucous stomach lining. This is more likely in monkeys and rats when unexpected and uncontrollable shocks are received, so that the animal is helpless.

Hypertension (high blood pressure). Raised blood pressure can be produced in the lab by stresses like noise, mental arithmetic, and putting a hand in cold water. The effect is greater in hypertension, and lasts longer. Hypertension is found in people who have been exposed to stress such as low social status or unemployment, and at work. One possible route is through the kidneys retaining more salt, and this happens to individuals with strongly reactive sympathetic nervous systems, such as neurotics.

Heart disease is more common among those under certain kinds of stress – bereavement, unemployment or low-status jobs. We shall see later that individuals with something like Type A personality have a high rate of sympathetic nervous activity, which raises the blood pressure and heart rate, and this leads to more heart attacks.

Cancer. The likelihood of getting cancer is increased by stressful life events, lack of social support, and having a 'Type C personality' – that is, passive and unassertive (p. 241). The intervening mechanism is probably suppression of the immune system in response to stress, as described above, allowing cancerous cells freedom to multiply.

Infectious diseases, like colds, coughs and flu, have also been found to be more common in people under stress, though the effect has sometimes been more on subjective than on objective illness. Suppression of the immune system has been found to occur in a number of studies (Cohen and Williamson, 1991).

Stressful life events

In the next chapter we shall describe inventories of stressful life events which have been used in the study of mental illness to tot up how much stress individuals have been exposed to. These include such events as bereavement, divorce, prison and debt and so on. Such inventories have also been used to predict physical illnesses. It is found that those people who have been exposed to more of these events over the past 6 months are more likely to become ill. Totman *et al.* (1980) gave volunteers a weak dose of cold infection, and found that more of those with higher stress scores caught colds than did the others. A number of American studies have found a consistent, though rather small, correlation of about .3 between illness and stress scores. However, these effects of stress are usually temporary, after which individuals return to base-line. Illnesses which are particularly susceptible to stress are heart disease, ulcers and headaches.

So far we have been talking about major stressful life events – divorce, prison and so on. However, lesser, daily hassles are also important – such as worrying about weight, noisy neighbours and travel problems – and these will be discussed further in connection with mental health later (p. 263). It has now been found that the extent of such daily hassles predicts ill health better than major life events (DeLongis *et al.*, 1982).

Stress at work

Table 9.2 shows that there are huge differences in subjective health between different occupational groups. There are also large differences in actual rates of heart-attacks, hypertension, ulcers, and the rest.

There seems to be little evidence that the stresses of work overall are bad for people. On the contrary, work seems to be good for us. Nevertheless some jobs are clearly more stressful than others. Karasek *et al.* (1987), in a study of 8,700 Swedish white-collar workers, examined the effect of demographic, work and family variables on indices of health; work variables accounted for 60 per cent of the variance that could be explained.

Job status is a major factor, but this is at least partly due to the different kinds of work done. *Job overload* is another – as in machine-paced work on assembly-lines. Managers who work longer hours, have more telephone calls, visitors and meetings, have been found to smoke and drink more and to have more coronaries (Cooper and Marshall, 1978). During periods of overload, cholesterol levels and blood pressure rise; for example, in accountants as tax deadlines approach, and in air-traffic controllers when there is a lot of traffic (Kasl, 1978).

Lack of control. Things are worse for those who have little freedom to do things in their own way and in their own time, who have less 'autonomy', or who participate less in decisions. A number of studies have compared the health of people in jobs with high autonomy (such as doctors) and those with low autonomy (e.g. waiters), or have rated the degree of control in different jobs, or asked people to rate their perceived control. It is found that low control is clearly associated with high blood pressure and other physiological measures, and is a risk factor for heart disease (Steptoe and Appels, 1990). The position seems to be deteriorating as the result of new technology.

Repetitive work involves both overload and lack of control. In earlier periods some workers repeated exactly the same operation every few seconds, but such jobs have mostly been automated, or modified by 'job enlargement'.

Responsibility for others. Managers and supervisors have worse health than professional people of a similar level. French and Caplan (1970) found that responsibility for others was associated with smoking, high blood pressure and high cholesterol levels. It involves a lot of extra tension and worry and sustaining many, sometimes difficult, relationships, coping with pressure from above and below, making decisions about subordinates, dealing with frictions, taking the blame for others' failures, and attending endless meetings and consultations.

Role conflict occurs when an individual is under different pressures from different people, from supervisors and subordinates, clients and colleagues, for example. This has been widely found to produce increased blood pressure and other somatic complaints.

Danger. Some jobs are very dangerous – those of the armed forces, police, firemen, miners and divers, for example. Danger produces very high adrenalin, heart rates and blood pressure and, if prolonged, illness. There is probably a high degree of self-selection for dangerous jobs, and those who like excitement and who are low in anxiety will be attracted. Nevertheless, prolonged exposure to danger in wartime produces high levels of 'war neurosis' among those involved.

Environmental stress. There are serious physical stresses at work: for example, the heat and atmosphere in steel works, and the dust in coal mines and quarries. Noise, shiftwork, loss of sleep, and commuting also act as stresses and can be causes of ill health (Argyle, 1989).

Bereavement

Death of spouse is rated as the most stressful life event in stress inventories (p. 264). Many studies have found that there is a greater death rate for the widowed than for married people of the same age or for those who have never married. For men, the danger period is the first 6 months, after which their mortality rate is no longer raised. For women, according to some studies, the first 6 months, but in others the second year after bereavement, are the worst. Most of this increased mortality is due to heart attacks, though the causes of death which show the largest differences

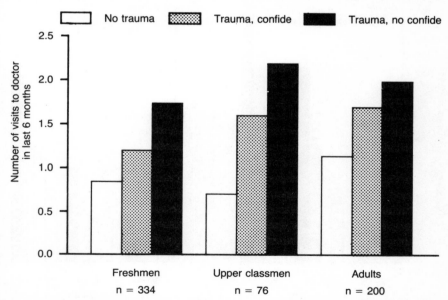

Figure 9.3 Effect on measures of health of traumatic events, confided and not confided
Source: Pennebaker, 1989

between the widowed and others are the rarer ones of cirrhosis of the liver, accidents and TB.

Studies comparing the physical health of the widowed with controls find that they suffer more from a wide range of illnesses during the first year. The widowed are also depressed; in one study it was found that if depression was held constant there was no difference in health, suggesting that depression may be the cause of illness among the widowed. These effects of bereavement are greater for men, probably because they do not have other close relationships from which they can obtain the right kind of social support. And the effects are greater for younger people, probably because their bereavement is so unexpected (Stroebe and Stroebe, 1987).

Traumatic experiences

People who have survived concentration camps, seen their friends or relations killed at close quarters or have experienced similar violent and terrible events tend to have worse health than others. Figure 9.3 shows the effect on measures of health. This study also showed that those who had not confided their experiences to anyone were in worse

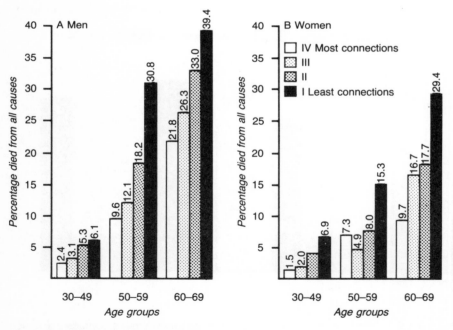

Figure 9.4 Social networks and mortality
Source: Berkman and Syme, 1979

health. In a series of experiments Pennebaker (1989) found that 5-minute tape-recorded confessions induced in the lab, about rather less extreme experiences, resulted in a lower rate of visits to the doctor, fewer days of restricted activity, and increased immune function activity.

THE EFFECTS OF SOCIAL SUPPORT ON HEALTH

Stress is bad for health, but social support can prevent these ill-effects. In a famous study in California Berkman and Syme (1979) followed up 6,900 people over 9 years, and found massive differences in the mortality rate of those who initially had strong or weak supportive social networks. It can be seen that for men in their fifties, of those with the weakest networks 30.8 per cent had died, compared with 9.6 per cent for those with the strongest networks. There have been many further studies of this effect, and a meta-analysis has been carried out of 55 such studies, involving altogether 32,739 people (Schwarzer and Leppin, 1989). This analysis showed that overall the effect of social support on health is greatest for women, from support by family or friends, emotional support and when they are under stress. Other studies have found that social support leads to fewer complications during pregnancy, a lower incidence of cancer, and of arthritis and cholesterol among workers who have lost their jobs. Some studies, especially of intimate relationships, have found a 'buffering effect', that is, social support has an effect only when there is stress; but other studies, especially of networks of friends, have found a main effect, which operates whether there is stress or not (Cohen and McKay, 1984).

Three different kinds of support have been distinguished – emotional (providing comfort and esteem), cognitive (giving information and advice) and material. There is some evidence that they should be provided in this order, corresponding to three phases of a stress – crisis, transition and deficit – as, for example, in unemployment or bereavement (Jacobson, 1986).

Intimate relationships

We saw above that family support has the greatest effect on health, especially for women. Many studies have shown the importance of close relationships for both physical and mental health. Married people have lower rates for a range of illnesses (Table 9.3). This shows, for example, that single men are 5.7 times as likely to die of TB during a given period than married men, and divorced men 10 times more likely. Having children also leads to a lower death rate, especially among parents under 45.

The family is a special kind of social group, engaging in a kind of biological cooperation, in which the members eat and sleep together, and look after each other, in a high degree of intimacy (Argyle, 1991). It is found that in close or 'communal' relationships, those involved are much concerned

Table 9.3 Marital status and mortality: males

Cause of death	Death rates for white men				Death rates for non-white men			
	Married	Single	Widowed	Divorced	Married	Single	Widowed	Divorced
Coronary disease and other myocardial (heart) degeneraton	176	237	275	362	142	231	328	298
Motor vehicle accidents	35	54	142	128	43	62	103	81
Cancer of respiratory system	28	32	43	65	29	44	56	75
Cancer of digestive organs	27	38	39	48	42	62	90	88
Vascular lesions (stoke)	24	42	46	58	73	105	176	132
Suicide	17	32	92	73	10	16	41	21
Cancer of lymph glands and of blood-making tissues	12	13	11	16	11	13	15	18
Cirrhosis of liver	11	31	48	79	12	40	39	53
Rheumatic fever (heart)	10	14	21	19	8	14	16	19
Hypertensive heart disease	8	16	16	20	49	68	106	90
Pneumonia	6	31	25	44	22	68	78	69
Diabetes mellitus	6	13	12	17	11	18	22	22
Homicide	4	7	16	30	51	79	152	129
Chronic nephritis (kidney)	4	7	7	7	11	18	26	21
Accidental falls	4	12	11	23	7	19	23	19
Tuberculosis, all forms	3	17	18	30	15	50	62	54
Cancer of prostate gland	3	3	3	4	8	7	15	12
Accidental fire or explosion	2	6	18	16	5	15	24	16
Syphilis	1	2	2	4	6	10	14	15

Source: Carter and Glick, 1970: 345

with the needs and welfare of one another, and that doing things to help the other is a source of joy (Williamson and Clark, 1989). People who have children, as well as those who are married, consume less drink and drugs, take fewer risks, and have a more orderly life style: they are taking more responsibility for their own health because of their family (Umberson, 1987). And there is evidence that the immune system is stronger for people with strong affiliative needs, who are more likely to be in love or form close relationships (McClelland, 1987). It looks as if there are direct biological advantages from intimate relations.

Friends and work-mates

A second kind of social support is provided by groups and networks of friends and work-mates. These relationships are usually less intense or intimate than those discussed above. Friends engage in leisure activities together, and talk a lot; work-mates cooperate and help one another over work, and also engage in quite a lot of talk, games and fooling about. These relationships have been found to have benefits for health whether stress is present or not.

Friends have been found to benefit health, though not so much as family. This has been found for old people in particular, many of whom have lost other relationships. It has also been found for young people, of student age, especially if contacts with friends are found to be intimate, pleasant, and involve self-disclosure, and especially with female friends (Reis *et al.*, 1984).

We saw that stresses at work are an important source of illness. However, these effects are greatly reduced, or abolished, if there is social support from work-mates or supervisors (Figure 9.5). This kind of social support is more useful than family support for difficulties at work. Overall, work is good for people: those at work are in better health than those who are not, and the unemployed are in quite poor health, including an increased cholesterol level and mortality rate (Argyle, 1989).

How social support influences health

More than one process is probably responsible. First, the best-documented is the effect of social support on health behaviour. People who are married, and who have children, are found to drink less, drink and drive less, take drugs less, and engage in less risky behaviour. Those who live with others look after themselves better, either because others keep them up to scratch in matters of health behaviour, or perhaps because they feel responsible for others. However, with health behaviour held constant, there is still a relation between isolation and ill health.

Second, family members certainly look after one another, but in addition, as we shall see, affiliative needs are associated with greater activity of the immune system. Married women who are more closely attached to their spouses have more active immune systems (Kiecolt-Glaser *et al.*, 1987). This may explain why married people and those with children live longer.

Third, the benefits of friends are rather different. Leisure activities shared with friends are one of the main sources of joy, and this displaces negative emotions such as depression and anxiety, which can have damaging bodily effects. Taking part in enjoyable cooperative activities produces a sense of social embeddedness; acceptance of others leads to self-acceptance.

Fourth, work-mates operate partly like friends, but in addition they can provide help at work, while their potential help and support renders threatening events less stressful. Low status and powerlessness are sources of ill-health, but a supportive group or network is a source of power.

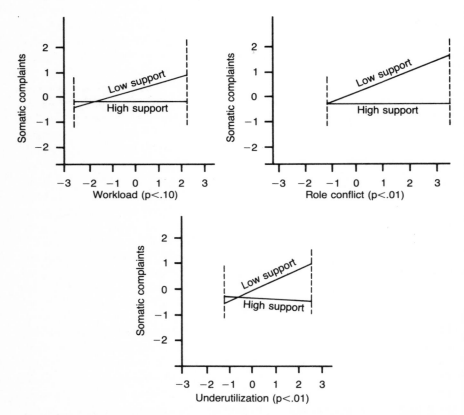

Figure 9.5 Buffering effects of co-worker support on relationships between perceived job stress and somatic complaints
Source: House, 1981

PERSONALITY AND HEALTH

There are a number of aspects of personality which have been found to be linked to health.

Type A personality and heart attacks

The famous Type A personality was a person with strong competitive achievement strivings, a sense of time urgency, and easily aroused hostility. It was measured either by questionnaire or, better, by interview, since there are non-verbal components, such as a rapid, loud and explosive speech pattern. Type As work extremely hard and ignore fatigue, though they may damage their prospects by ill health and by not keeping up good relationships with their colleagues.

Earlier research showed a clear connection between this kind of personality and heart disease: 2.92 deaths per 1,000 per year, compared with 1.32 for Type Bs. However, recent prospective studies have found that Type A did not predict death from heart attacks, but that hostility and anxiety are the effective predictors (Matthews, 1988). These have some overlap with Type A, since hostility is one of its three components, and some of the theory surrounding Type A may still be correct. It was widely surmised that the sympathetic nervous systems of Type As are very reactive, so, for example, their blood pressure goes up a lot under stress. They are also very concerned about being able to control events, and become disturbed when they cannot.

Type C personality and cancer

Is there a 'Type C' personality? There is a lot of evidence that a certain kind of person is more likely to get cancer – those who are unassertive, unaggressive, compliant, and passive patients. They suppress emotions, especially anger. They are upset by interpersonal problems, but do nothing about them, and become hopeless and depressed. There have now been several prospective studies that have found that if people are tested while they are still healthy, this kind of personality predicts the development of cancer over the next 10 years (Dattore et al., 1980). Personality also predicts the speed at which the illness develops, and whether patients survive or not, but it has little effect once the illness is well advanced. Depression is a further aspect of personality that is related to cancer, and has been found to be predictable in long-term follow-up studies. The kind of personality who is most likely to survive either has a 'fighting spirit' or denies the existence of the disease, rather than patiently accepting it.

Hardiness

Some people are made ill by stress, while others are not. Those who are not are said to possess the quality of 'hardiness'. The original work was done by Kobasa (1982) who was working with managers. She found that the hardy ones scored higher on internal control (they believed that they could influence things that happened to them), were strongly committed to their work and other activities, and saw changes as challenges and opportunities for growth. Later research has found that, of these three components, internal control is the most important. Those with high internal control know more about health, seek more information about diseases to which they are susceptible, engage in more relevant health behaviours, believe that they can control their own health, and become less ill (Lau, 1988). Associated aspects of personality that have been found to affect hardiness include happiness, optimism, assertiveness and self-confidence. Internal control is increased by social support, and in turn strengthens the immune system (Kubitz et al., 1986). This may be because 'internals' engage in more physical exercise.

Another component in hardiness has been identified as 'toughness', which consists of having a low base-rate of adrenalin and activity of the sympathetic nervous system, combined with a capacity for rapid increase, followed by a rapid return to normal, so that stresses can be dealt with. This is produced in part by frequent experiences of stresses such as cold shocks and exercise, which all strengthen the immune system (Dienstbier, 1989).

Neuroticism is the other end of the scale, and makes for lack of hardiness. Those high on neuroticism are easily upset by stress, suffer from a wide range of complaints, especially 'psychosomatic' ones like headaches and ulcers, but also from heart disease. They also complain more of being ill for the same level of symptoms.

Mood. We said above that negative moods correlate with reported ill health, more strongly than with physiological measures of ill health. Experiments have been done in which different moods were induced in subjects: those in the sad condition reported twice as many aches and pains as those in the happy condition. Subjects in the happy condition also felt confident of being able to carry out good health behaviours and believed that these would work, and that serious illness was less likely to happen to them. There are several possible explanations for this, including the known effect of mood on the immune system (Salovey et al., 1991).

Strength of the immune system

The body has a number of biological defences against invasion by germs. The lymphatic system plays an important role in immunity, by draining off foreign bodies from the spaces between cells, partly through the actions of a type of white blood cell. A measure of its strength can be obtained from saliva, S-I_gA, salivary immunoglobulin. Using this measure it has been found that stress, such as taking exams, lowers the level of immunity. It is also found that its strength varies with personality. McClelland and Jemmot (1980) found that individuals with a strong need for affiliation (greater than their need for power), had much higher S-I_gA scores. In other studies McClelland (1987) found that people with a high need for affiliation had lower blood pressure, and reported less illness – probably because of their more active immune systems. And just as stress reduces S-I_gA, it was also possible to increase it, temporarily at least, by showing a film about Mother Teresa caring for the sick. Low levels of S-I_gA were found in people with a strong need for power, greater than their need for affiliation, especially if they were experiencing stress in relation to their power needs. These individuals also had high blood pressure and reported more severe illness.

There is evidence that depression lowers immunity, as in the cancer-prone personality. And we showed earlier that this kind of hardiness can be increased by exposure to physical stresses in the past.

Health beliefs and health behaviour

People are often very ill informed about health matters, about the causes of illness and the appropriate treatment. They may be misinformed about how colds are caught, or about the causes of heart attacks. They may label their own symptoms wrongly. They may think that high blood pressure is an acute (that is, temporary) condition. They may believe that their illness is due to divine punishment.

What people believe about health matters has an important effect on what they do about health; namely, their health behaviour. Many studies have been carried out to try to predict when individuals will go to the dentist, stop smoking, have a health check-up, a flu injection, a polio vaccination or take prescribed medicine. The best predictors are (1) beliefs about the severity of the illness (for example, lung cancer), together with beliefs about the likelihood of getting it, and general interest in and concern about health; and (2) belief that the health behaviour in question will be effective, and that the benefits will exceed the costs. Although this model has been widely confirmed, it must be admitted that the predictive power is not very great: it explains about 22 per cent of the variance in health behaviour (Bush and Iannotti, 1988) – though it works better for middle-class people, who know more about health.

Another way of predicting health behaviour is from intentions – for example, to stop smoking – which in turn can be predicted from (1) beliefs about the outcome, and evaluation of the outcome, and (2) the social norms of family and other groups, and the desire to conform to them

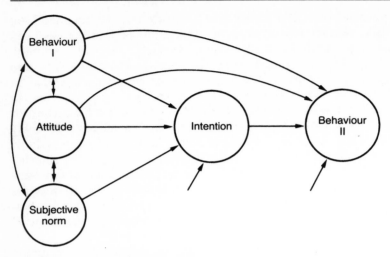

Figure 9.6 A model of the attitude–behaviour relation incorporating previous
         behaviour
Source: Bentler and Speckart, 1979

(Ajzen and Fishbein, 1977). This model too is predictive of a wide range of
health behaviours. However, there is an interesting further development,
that often people say that they intend to give up smoking, keep fit or keep
to a diet – and then they don't do it. However, some health behaviours can
be predicted from past behaviour and from attitudes, and these influences
are not channelled entirely via intentions (Figure 9.6). This is most familiar
in the cases of addiction to drugs (Bentler and Speckart, 1979).

An important part of health beliefs is the belief that illness can be
controlled. We saw above that such inner control leads to relevant health
behaviour, and the belief that one is able to carry out the recommended
action (such as giving up smoking; Seydel *et al.*, 1990). The most important
source of health behaviour and beliefs in young adults has been found to
be their parents, whose effect is long-lasting, though it may be modified
by exposure to new influences during vulnerable periods, such as just after
leaving home, or setting up a new home (Lau *et al.*, 1990).

There have been considerable changes in health beliefs, probably as
the result of health education, and these are reflected in substantial age
differences. In a British survey of 9,003 people it was found that more
younger people were aware that heart attacks are influenced by smoking,
drink and exercise, more middle-class people knew that heart attacks are
influenced by stress. Many more young people were engaging in active
sports to keep fit, and more women were attending to diet (Cox, 1987).

Studies of individual differences in smoking, drinking, exercise, diet and
sleeping do not find that people are very consistent in adopting good or
bad health behaviours. However, there is an overall relationship with

personality – an unhealthy life style is correlated with neuroticism, hostility and low self-esteem (Vingenhoets *et al.*, 1990).

THE CONTRIBUTION OF PSYCHOLOGY TO PREVENTIVE MEDICINE

The main contribution of psychology is in persuading people to adopt healthier forms of behaviour. How successful is this?

Smoking

Stopping people from smoking is more likely to improve their health prospects than any other kind of health-related behaviour. Smoking is a major cause of lung cancer, which produces about 30 per cent of all deaths from cancer; it also leads to emphysema, and is an important contributory cause of heart attacks, the most common cause of death. The overall percentage dying per annum for men aged 55–64 is 6.8 per cent for smokers and 4 per cent for non-smokers (Rogot, 1974). The overall rates of illness are higher for smokers than non-smokers, especially for respiratory illnesses, and especially for older people (*GHS*, 1988).

In Britain in 1988 40 per cent of men and 31 per cent of women smoked; 33 per cent of men and 30 per cent of women smoked cigarettes, an average of 17 and 14 a day. There has been a sharp fall since 1972. The percentage of professional men smoking cigarettes fell from 33 per cent in 1972 to 17 per cent in 1986. The figures for unskilled men fell from 64 per cent to 44 per cent. As these figures show, there is a large social class difference: working-class people smoke a lot more, especially manual workers, and those with fewer educational qualifications.

The percentage of smokers is less for married people, but more for the ex-married, and of young married people those with children smoked more.

The number of people who have given up smoking has greatly increased: the percentage of ex-smokers among those who had ever smoked increased from 31 per cent in 1972 to 49 per cent in 1988 for men and 19 per cent to 38 per cent for women. The individuals who were most likely to give up smoking were older men, of higher social class, who were married (*GHS*, 1988).

Different methods have been used in the 'treatment' of individuals to stop them smoking, and to change the habits of whole populations. We shall take large-scale methods first. A BBC film showing a heavy smoker dying from lung cancer, and bins of cancerous lungs, had no effect. A single session and provision of nicotine gum was more successful in that 12 per cent of those attending stopped smoking (Sutton and Hallett, 1988).

To treat individuals – namely, those who want to change their own behaviour – more powerful methods are possible. Self-monitoring has had some success – clients simply keep a record of each occasion that they smoke; this gives some insight into the situations that elicit smoking. Various kinds of aversion therapy have been used, such as smoking and inhaling in a small, unventilated room, and thinking about the negative aspects of this experience. Operant conditioning has been used – the client has to light up whenever a buzzer is sounded; this detaches smoking from the normal situational cues – drink, coffee, conversation and so on (Taylor, 1986).

Many people stop smoking without treatment. The main reasons that they give for doing so are illness, fear of future illness and expense. They are often affected by social influence, especially from doctors, spouse or relatives.

Drinking

Alcohol can lead to death from cirrhosis of the liver, it increases the rate of heart disease, of cancer in men, of accidents, especially in cars and of brain damage, and for pregnant women it can damage the foetus.

Nine per cent of men drank 1 glass a week or less in 1988, 33 per cent drank 1–10 glasses, 25 per cent 11–21, and 34 per cent 22 glasses plus, including 9 per cent who drank over 51 glasses. For women the corresponding figures were 33 per cent, 40 per cent, 14 per cent and 13 per cent, with only 2 per cent consuming over 51 glasses a week (*GHS*, 1988). So men drink a lot more than women, three times as much on average. Those between the ages of 18 and 44 drink most, older people least, and heavy drinking declines greatly with age. In 1988 in Britain the higher social classes drank more, poorer people drank less, especially women (*GHS*, 1988), though earlier studies had found more heavy drinking in the lowest classes (Reid, 1989). In Britain there has been some fall in the amount of alcohol consumed since 1961. For young men it has fallen from an average of 26 to 21 half-pint units per week.

Married people drink least, the widowed, divorced or separated most; married people without dependent children drink more. Heavy drinkers are also heavy smokers. A longitudinal study found that problem drinking is made more likely by feelings of powerlessness, job stress, unemployment and weak engagement with social networks; some drinkers are encouraged by their drunken friends, others drink alone (Seeman *et al.*, 1988).

Drinking can be a major problem for employers, who usually prefer their staff to be sober and not suffering from hangovers; most industrial accidents are drink-related and take place after 'lunch'. In one American firm 6 per cent of employees were found to have a serious drinking problem, while in Britain 35 per cent of young men can be regarded as heavy drinkers – defined as drinking 7 units (at a sitting) once a week or more (*Social Trends*, 1987). This is sometimes dealt with by offering a counselling service, and an American firm which did this was successful with 41 per cent out of 990 who asked for help. The counselling can take various forms; the learning of controlled drinking is one: the client sets a goal of consumption, monitors his amount and rate of drinking, and rewards himself accordingly. Individual treatment by behaviour therapy methods has used sessions in which the client drinks after an injection of Antabuse, which produces nausea and vomiting. This is very unpleasant, but high success rates have been reported.

A widely followed procedure is to join Alcoholics Anonymous, the first of many kinds of self-help groups – now extended to groups of widows, the recently divorced, parents of handicapped children, families of prisoners, neurotics, gamblers, obese people and others. These groups sometimes have an inspirational, almost religious, air about them. About $6^1/_4$ million Americans belong to such groups, which threaten to rival psychotherapy as the preferred treatment for a number of problems, partly because they are much cheaper. They can also be seen as a replacement for the family, as a source of social support, and hence of health and mental health. A curious feature of the groups is that many members never leave (Jacobs and Goodman, 1989). In addition to providing practical help and advice they provide new, non-drinking norms: it can be very difficult to stop drinking if all the other members of the social circle are heavy drinkers.

Social skills training has also been used successfully with alcoholics, since many of them drink because of their social anxiety. Increasing social competence leads to reduction of such anxiety.

Exercise

The benefits of exercise for health have been well documented in a number of excellent large-scale studies. For example, Paffenbarger *et al.* (1978) followed up nearly 17,000 Harvard alumni over 6–10 years. The effects of exercise on heart attacks are shown in Figure 9.7. This suggests that 20,000 k cal of exercise per week are optimal – which could be expended in 200 minutes' strenuous activity. Exercise also reduces the risk for a whole range of other illnesses, such as hypertension, diabetes and arthritis, and, as we shall see in the next chapter, mental illness too. Exercise promotes the level of health – lower heart rate and blood pressure, greater lung capacity, less obesity; and these effects are greater for older people (Cox, 1987).

Most people in Britain take part in some kind of exercise, especially walking, dancing and swimming; fewer take part in sport, such as football, tennis or squash. Health education and popular books on fitness have had their effects. There has been a jogging movement, especially in the USA, for some years, and marathons have recently attracted a very large attendance in Britain. *Social Trends* (1990) reveals a considerable increase in the numbers of people engaging in several forms of exercise.

Young people are a lot more active than older ones, men more than women, and middle class compared with working class. (We discuss class

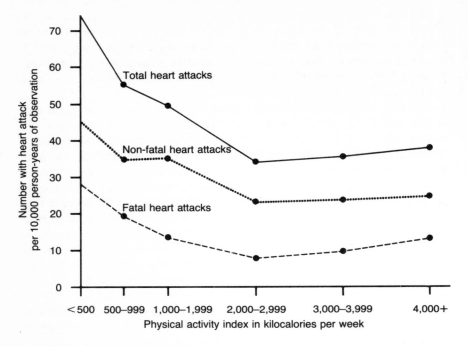

Figure 9.7 Age-adjusted first heart-attack rates by physical activity index in a six- to ten-year follow-up of male Harvard alumni
Source: Paffenbarger *et al.*, 1978

differences in sport and exercise on p. 121.) Middle-class people engage in far more squash, tennis, golf, swimming, hiking and jogging, but working-class people take part in just as much football and dancing.

Many industrial firms have found that exercise is good for business. The most extensive follow-up to be reported was of two North American insurance companies, where a fitness programme was introduced to the 1,125 employees of one company but not to the employees of the other. Following the introduction of the programme absenteeism fell by 22 per cent after a year, and labour turnover decreased (Melhuish, 1981). Other similar studies have found that exercise schemes in firms can result in improved health, greater energy and stamina, improved work performance, weight reduction and less tension. The problem with exercise is persuading people to keep it up. About half those who start an exercise programme give up after 6 months, and only 20 per cent are still exercising after 3 years. Exercise takes effort and time, and competes with other activities. However, those who do keep it up enjoy it enormously, and may become 'addicted' in the sense that when deprived of it they feel tense and out of sorts (Feist and Brannon, 1988). Fit people have a certain kind of personality – they are self-confident, self-disciplined and competitive (Hogan, 1989).

Diet

This is very important for health. Those who are overweight are at risk for heart attacks, strokes and diabetes, in particular. Too much fat or sugar, too little fibre, affect heart attacks and cancer.

Diet in Britain has improved a lot in recent years. Since 1961 butter consumption has fallen to a third, and eggs by a third, while brown and wholemeal bread consumption has increased by a factor of 2½, while fruit, salad and soft margarine have all increased. There are large class differences: 49 per cent of professional men eat brown bread versus 17 per cent of unskilled males; for women the figures are 72 per cent and 30 per cent – women have a better diet than men. Working-class people and men eat more chips and fried food. Younger people have a better diet in most respects, except that they eat more chips (Cox, 1987). Americans diet as much to improve their appearance as for their health; Germans, on the other hand, diet mainly for health reasons (Cockerham et al., 1988).

The main large-scale method which has been used for persuading people to improve their diet is through education – pamphlets, schools and TV commercials. Behaviour therapy has been used for individuals, mainly to help them reduce their weight. The methods used include self-monitoring and reinforcement, either for losing weight or for good eating habits. Dieting can be successful without formal therapy. Schachter (1982) found that 29 out of 46 fat people at Columbia University were successful: they lost an average of 30 lb.

The other kinds of health behaviour that we have discussed are also relevant to weight loss. Exercise makes people leaner, whereas drinking does not, especially drinking large quantities of beer.

Prevention of illness

One of the largest experiments carried out on health education was the Stanford Heart Disease Prevention Program. Two communities were subjected to a massive media campaign, about diet, smoking and exercise, for two years, by TV, radio, newspapers, posters and mail leaflets. One community, in addition, received face-to-face instruction for those most at risk for heart attacks. In this community there was a substantial improvement in health behaviour, mainly in reduced smoking, but in the media-only community there was very little difference from a third, control community (Meyer et al., 1980).

We have seen that certain kinds of person are less at risk from stress – those who are low in neuroticism and Type A qualities but who are high in internal control and toughness. Some studies have succeeded in modifying Type A personalities by teaching stress management methods (see p. 273). Friedman et al. (1986) did an experiment with 862 cardiac patients. Those given stress management training in groups of 10 over 4½ years had 12.9 per cent heart attacks and 3.4 per cent deaths, while in a control group who were simply given good cardiac care there were 21.2 per cent heart attacks and 6.4 per cent deaths. And it has been found that increasing internal control produces general benefits. Langer and Rodin (1976) gave old people in a nursing home control over the care of plants. This experience of control produced general benefits such as increased activity, positive mood, better health and a lower mortality rate than in another control group.

DOCTOR–PATIENT INTERACTION

This is a social event, in a social relationship. Increasingly doctors are now being trained in the social aspects of their skills.

Compliance

A major problem is that patients often do not do what the doctor says they should do. On average patients carry out 50 per cent of the instructions – for example, in taking a series of pills – but some patients scarcely carry out the doctor's instructions at all. This is most likely to happen in the case of less severe illness, when there are unpleasant side effects of the treatment, if the symptoms disappear, or if the treatment is complex. Sometimes they simply forget the instructions. Some people are less likely to comply than others – those who are male, young, lower class, or who belong to ethnic minority groups. Non-compliance is more likely in those who live alone than for people who have social support.

Research also suggests what can be done to improve compliance. The relationship with the doctor is important: there is greater compliance if patients have a good relation with him, find him warm and competent, and if he explains clearly what the treatment requires. Some degree of persuasion helps, explaining the advantages of carrying out the treatment. Techniques derived from behaviour therapy have been found to work. These include self-monitoring – keeping a record of treatment, reinforcement by members of the family, linking treatment to regular events such as meals, and gradual approximation, as in the cases of exercise and diet (Feist and Brannon, 1988).

Doctor skills

Several aspects of doctor behaviour have been found to be important. The affective, socio-emotional side of the relationship influences both compliance and patient satisfaction – the doctor should express warmth and interest, be a sympathetic listener. His task behaviour is equally important – providing information, asking questions, reassuring, and providing evidence of medical competence. Social skills training for doctors has often included history-taking skills, especially looking for hidden fears and psychiatric problems; this leads to more accurate diagnosis. There are often communication problems, because patients don't understand medical terms, and working-class people in particular feel that their doctor has not explained things very well. In fact doctors spend less time with working-class patients, though in this respect their need is greater (Pendleton and Hasler, 1983).

CONCLUSIONS

There are great variations in health and mortality, due to social variables, stress and personality. Women are in worse health than men, but live longer. Working-class people have worse health, partly because of unwise health behaviour. Health is affected by stress, through impairing the immune system, increasing blood pressure and in other ways. This includes stressful or traumatic life events, such as bereavement and work stress. Social support prevents the effects of stress, via better immune system functioning and people looking after one another, with resultant improved health behaviour.

Some kinds of personality are more at risk for stress: hostility and anxiety make heart attacks more likely, passivity is a risk factor for cancer. People less at risk are those low in neuroticism, but high in internal control and physiological toughness. The immune system is stronger in those with strong affiliative motivation, and health beliefs lead to corresponding health behaviour.

Psychologists can influence health mainly through developing techniques for modifying the health behaviour of individuals or whole communities, and several large-scale projects have been carried out. Several techniques are successful in modifying smoking and drinking. It is possible to modify the behaviour of individuals at risk for heart disease by relaxation training, and to change health behaviour by behaviour therapy. In addition, it is possible to increase network support. The skills of doctors can be identified and improved by means of social skills training; this leads to better diagnosis, and more compliance by patients.

REFERENCES

Ajzen, I. and Fishbein, M. (1977) Attitude – behavior relations: a theoretical analysis and review of empirical research. *Psychological Bulletin, 84*, 888–918.

Argyle, M. (1989) *The Social Psychology of Work*. 2nd edition. Harmondsworth: Penguin.

——(1991) *Cooperation : the Basis of Sociability*, London: Routledge.

Bentler, P.M. and Speckart, G. (1979) Models of attitude–behavior relations. *Psychological Review, 86*, 452–64.

Berkman, L.F. and Syme, S.L. (1979) Social networks, host resistance, and mortality: a nine year follow-up study of Alameda county residents. *American Journal of Epidemiology*, *109*, 186–204.

Black, D. (1980) *Inequalities in Health*. London: DHSS.

Bush, P.J. and Iannotti, R.J. (1988) Pathways to health behavior. *In* D.S. Gochman (ed.) *Health Behavior*. New York: Plenum.

Carter, H. and Glick, P.C. (1970) *Marriage and Divorce: a Social and Economic Study*. Cambridge, Mass.: Harvard University Press.

Cockerham, W.C., Kunz, G. and Lueschen, G. (1988) On concern with appearance, health beliefs, and eating habits: a reappraisal comparing Americans and West Germans. *Journal of Health and Social Behavior, 29*, 265–9.

Cohen, S. and McKay, G. (1984) Social support, stress and the buffering hypothesis: an empirical and theoretical analysis. *In* A.Baum, J.E. Singer and S.E. Taylor (eds) *Handbook of Personality and Health*, Vol. 4. Hillsdale NJ: Erlbaum.

Cohen, S. and Williamson, G.M. (1991) Stress and infectious diseases in humans. *Psychological Bulletin, 109*, 5–24.

Cooper, C.L. and Marshall, J. (1978) Sources of managerial and white-collar stress. *In* C.L. Cooper and R. Payne (eds) *Current Concerns in Occupational Stress*. Chichester: Wiley.

Cox, D. (1987) *The Health and Lifestyle Survey*. London: Health Promotion Research Trust.

Dattore, P.J., Shontz, F.C. and Coyne, L. (1980) Premorbid personality differentiation of cancer and noncancer groups: a test of the hypothesis of cancer proneness. *Journal of Consulting and Clinical Psychology, 48*, 388–94.

DeLongis, A., Coyne, J.C., Dakof, A., Folkman, S. and Lazarus, R.S (1982) Relationship of daily hassles, uplifts, and major life events to health status. *Health Psychology, 1*, 119–36.

Dienstbier, R.A. (1989) Arousal and physiological toughness: implications for mental and physical health. *Psychological Review, 96*, 84–100.

Dunnell, K. and Cartwright, A. (1972) *Medicine Takers, Prescribers and Hoarders*. London: Routledge and Kegan Paul.

Ellison, D.L. (1969) Alienation and the will to live. *Journal of Gerontology, 24*, 361–7.

Feist, J. and Brannon, L. (1988) *Health Psychology*. Belmont, CA: Wadsworth.

French, J.R.P. and Caplan, R.D. (1970) Psychosocial factors in coronary heart disease. *Industrial Medicine, 39*, 383–97.

Friedman, M. *et al*. (1986) Alteration of type A behavior and its effects on cardiac recurrences in post myocardial infarction patients: summary results of the recurrent coronary prevention project. *American Heart Journal, 112*, 653–65.

General Household Survey (1980, 1983, 1988, 1990) London: HMSO.

Hannay, D.R. (1979) *The Symptom Iceberg*. London and Boston: Routledge and Kegan Paul.

Haw, A.H. (1982) Women, work and stress: a review and agenda for the future. *Journal of Health and Social Behavior, 23*, 132–44.

Hogan, J. (1989) Personality correlates of physical fitness. *Journal of Personality and Social Psychology, 56*, 284–8.

House, J.S. (1981) *Work Stress and Social Support*. Reading, MA: Addison-Wesley.

Jacobs, M.K. and Goodman, G. (1989) Psychology and self-help groups: predictions on a partnership. *American Psychologist, 44*, S36–45.

Jacobson, D. (1986) Types and timing of social support. *Journal of Health and Social Behavior, 27*, 250–64.

Jemmott, J.B. and Locke, S.E. (1984) Psychosocial factors, immunology mediation, and human susceptibility to infectious diseases: how much do we know? *Psychological Bulletin*, *95*, 78–108.

Karasek, R.A., Gardell, B. and Lindell, J. (1987) Work and non-work stress. *In* C.L. Cooper and R. Payne (eds) *Stress at Work*. Chichester: Wiley.

Kasl, S.V. (1978) Epidemiological contributives to the study of work stress. *In* C.L. Cooper and R. Payne (eds) *Current Concerns in Occupational Stress*. Chichester: Wiley.

Kennedy, S., Kiecolt-Glaser, J.K. and Glaser, R. (1990) Social support, stress, and the immune system. *In* B.R. Sarason, I.G. Sarason and G.R. Pierce (eds) *Social Support: An Interactional View*. New York: Wiley.

Kobasa, S.C. (1982) The hardy personality: toward a social psychology of stress and health. *In* G.S. Sanders and J. Suls (eds) *Social Psychology of Health and Illness*. Hillsdale, NJ: Erlbaum.

Kubitz, K.A., Peavey, B.S. and Moore, B.S. (1986) The effect of daily hassles on humoral immunity: an interaction moderated by locus of control. *Biofeedback and Self Regulation*, *11*, 115–23.

Langer, E.J. and Rodin, J. (1976) The effects of choice and enhanced personal responsibility for the aged: a field experiment in an institutional setting. *Journal of Personality and Social Psychology*, *34*, 191–8.

LaRocco, J.M., House, J.S. and French, J.R.P. (1980) Social support, occupational stress and health. *Journal of Health and Social Behavior*, *21*, 202–18.

Lau, R.R. (1988) Beliefs about control and health behavior. *In* D.S. Gochman (ed.) *Health Behavior*. New York: Plenum.

Lau, R.R., Quadrel, M.J. and Hartman, K.A. (1990) Development and change of young adults' preventive health beliefs and behavior: influence from parents and peers. *Journal of Health and Social Behavior*, *31*, 240–59.

Le Grand, J. (1978) *The Strategy of Equality*. London: Allen & Unwin.

Lynch, J.J. (1977) *The Broken Heart*. New York: Basic Books.

McClelland, D.C. (1987) *Human Motivation*. Cambridge: Cambridge University Press.

McClelland, D.C. and Jemmott, J.B. (1980) Power motivation, stress and physical illness. *Journal of Human Stress*, *6(4)*, 6–15.

Marmot, M.G. Rose, G., Shipley, M. and Hamilton, P.J.S. (1978) Employment grade and coronary heart disease in British civil servants. *Journal of Epidemiology and Community Health*, *32*, 244–9.

Matthews, K.A. (1988) Coronary heart disease and Type A behaviors: update on and alternative to the Booth-Kewley and Friedman (1987) quantitative review. *Psychological Bulletin*, *104*, 373–80.

Melhuish, A.H. (1981) The doctor's role in educating managers about stress. *In* J. Marshall and C.L. Cooper (eds) *Coping with Stress at Work*. Andover: Gower.

Meyer, A.J., Nash, J.D., McAlister, A.L., Maccoby, N. and Farquhar, J.W. (1980) Skills training in a cardiovascular health education campaign. *Journal of Consulting and Clinical Psychology*, *48*, 129–42.

Paffenbarger, R.S., Wing, A.L. and Hyde, R.T. (1978) Physical activity as an index of heart attack in college alumni. *American Journal of Epidemiology*, *108*, 161–75.

Pendleton, D. and Hasler, J. (eds) (1983) *Doctor–patient Communication*. London: Academic Press.

Pennebaker, J.W. (1989) Confession, inhibition, and disease. *Advances in Experimental Social Psychology*, *22*, 211–44.

Reid, I. (1989) *Social Class Differences in Britain*. London: Fontana. 3rd edition.

Reis, H.T., Nezlek, J., Kernis, M.H. and Spiegel, N. (1984) On specificity in the impact of social participation on physical and mental health. *Journal of Personality and Social Psychology, 48*, 456–71.

Rodin, J. and Ickovics, J.R. (1990) Women's health: review and agenda as we approach the 21st century. *American Psychologist, 45*, 1018–34.

Rogot, E. (1974) Smoking and mortality among US veterans. *Journal of Chronic Diseases, 27*, 189–203.

Salovey, P. O'Leary, A., Stretton, M.S., Fishkin, S.A. and Drake, C.A. (1991) Influence of mood on judgements about health and illness. *In* J.P. Forgas (ed.) *Affect and Social Judgments*. Oxford: Pergamon.

Schachter, S. (1982) Recidivism and self-cure of smoking and obesity. *American Psychologist, 37*, 436–44.

Schwarzer, R. and Leppin, A. (1989) Social support and health: a meta-analysis. *Psychology and Health, 3*, 1–15.

Seeman, M., Seeman, A.Z. and Budros, A. (1988) Powerlessness, work and community: a longitudinal study of alienation and alcohol use. *Journal of Health and Social Behavior, 29*, 185–98.

Seydel, E., Taal, E. and Wiegman, O. (1990) Risk-appraisal, outcome and self-efficacy expectancies: cognitive factors in preventive behaviour related to cancer. *Psychology and Health, 4*, 99–109.

Social Trends (1982–90) London: HMSO.

Steptoe, A. and Appels, A. (1990) *Stress, Personal Control and Health*. Chichester: Wiley.

Stroebe, W. and Stroebe, M.S. (1987) *Bereavement and Health*. Cambridge: Cambridge University Press.

Sutton, S.R. and Hallett, R. (1988) Smoking intervention in the workplace using videotapes and nicotine chewing gum. *Preventive Medicine, 17*, 48–59.

Taylor, S.E. (1986) *Health Psychology*. New York: Random House.

Totman, R., Kiff, J., Reed, S.E. and Craig, J.W. (1980) Predicting experimental colds in volunteers from different measures of recent life stress. *Journal of Psychosomatic Research, 24*, 155–63.

Umberson, D. (1987) Family status and health behaviors: social control as a dimension of social integration. *Journal of Health and Social Behavior, 28*, 306–19.

Vingenhoets, A.J.J.M., Croon, M., Jeninga, A.J. and Menger, L.J. (1990) Personality and health habits. *Psychology and Health, 4*, 333–42.

Wadsworth, M.E.J., Butterfield, W.J.H. and Blaney, R. (1971) *Health and Sickness: The Choice of Treatment*. London: Tavistock.

Waldron, I. (1976) Why do women live longer than men? *Journal of Human Stress, 2*, 19–30.

Watson, D. and Pennebaker, J.W. (1989) Health complaints, stress, and distress: exploring the role of negative affectivity. *Journal of Personality and Social Psychology, 96*, 234–54.

Williams, D.R. (1990) Socioeconomic differentials in health: a review and redirection. *Social Psychology Quarterly, 53*, 81–99.

Williamson, G.M. and Clark, M.S. (1989) Providing help and desired relationship type as determinants of changes in moods and self-evaluations. *Journal of Personality and Social Psychology, 56*, 722–34.

Chapter 10

Mental health

WHAT IS MENTAL HEALTH?

The simplest definition of mental health is that it is the absence of anxiety, depression or other symptoms commonly found in mental patients. A definition of positive mental health has been suggested by Marie Jahoda (1958) as success or adaptation in the areas of love, work, play, interpersonal relations, situational requirements, ability to adapt and problem-solving.

It is possible to make some assessment of mental health in the population by one question: 'Did you experience unpleasant emotional strain yester-day?' In a recent British survey the extent of such distress was as follows:

	%
All of the time	4
Most of the time	5
About half the time	4
Some of the time	7
Just a little of the time	13
Not at all	65

Source: Warr and Payne, 1982

Psychological distress consists of negative emotions and related conditions: depression, anxiety and worry; minor physical symptoms such as headaches, sleeplessness and exhaustion; feelings of personal inadequacy, or of impending nervous breakdown. There is extensive evidence that such feelings are found in the same individuals, and that this forms a 'general factor' of personality. This general factor corresponds to the 'neuroticism' factor of the Eysenck Personality Questionnaire, and is also measured by the General Health Questionnaire (GHQ), both of which have been widely used in research. The short (12-item) version of the GHQ is set out in Table 10.1.

Table 10.1   The General Health Questionnaire (GHQ) (12-item version)

Have you recently
* 1   been able to concentrate on whatever you're doing?
  2   lost much sleep over worry?
* 3   felt that you are playing a useful part in things?
* 4   felt capable of making decisions about things?
  5   felt constantly under strain?
  6   felt you couldn't overcome your difficulties?
* 7   been able to enjoy your normal day-to-day activities?
* 8   been able to face up to your problems?
  9   been feeling unhappy and depressed?
  10   been losing confidence in yourself?
  11   been thinking of yourself as a worthless person?
*12   been feeling reasonably happy all things considered?

* These items are scored in reverse
Source: Goldberg, 1978

Each item is scored from 'agree strongly' to 'disagree strongly' on a 4-point scale. There is a second aspect of mental disorder, corresponding to psychotic disturbance as in schizophrenia, and this can be measured from Eysenck's psychoticism factor.

Probably the most valid measure of psychological disorder is an examination by a psychiatrist. There is a lengthy standard form used in Britain known as the Present State Examination (PSE), and a shorter version for community studies (Wing, 1976). Although this is more valid, it is much less convenient for research purposes.

How many people are mentally disturbed, at a given time? There is no clear cut-off point; it is like asking how many people are tall or intelligent. About 14–17 per cent of the people who see a GP are diagnosed as having a psychiatric problem. The *General Household Survey* finds that about 1 person in 3 reports some kind of psychological distress – severe headaches, exhaustion, sleeplessness, anxiety or depression; only 17 per cent went to see their doctor about it (*General Household Survey*, 1979). A survey of psychological symptoms over a 2-week period found that some kinds of distress are very widely reported (see Table 10.2).

Evidently, symptoms of psychological distress are very widespread – like coughs and colds in the sphere of physical health. Recent American interview surveys have found that 17–23 per cent of adults were affected by psychological disorders, 7–15 per cent by anxiety, with lifetime prevalence rates of 29–38 per cent (Santer *et al.*, 1990). Being sufficiently distressed to see the doctor, or to be regarded by the doctor as a psychiatric patient, applies to about 15 per cent of the population. Clinical psychologists cite 8–10 per cent as being suitable for treatment: e.g. in university clinics.

Table 10.2   Psychological symptoms recorded by GPs over a 2-week period

	%
Irritability	24
Severe headaches	20
Exhaustion	19
Sleeplessness	19
Depression, severe	9
mild	17
Obsessions	13
Pains in chest	13
Anxious, worried	10
Puzzled, hear voices	5

Source: Hannay, 1979

THE DISTRIBUTION OF MENTAL ILL HEALTH

Social class

There are quite large class differences in the distribution of mental ill health. In modern society, working-class people in general tend to be in worse mental health. Table 10.3 shows a British and an American survey.

Table 10.3   Class differences in strain and worry

	UK – class		
	ABC1	C2	DE
Reported unpleasant emotional strain yesterday: most or all of the time	7	8	14
Had experienced strain for more than a month		14.5	23.5

Source: Warr and Payne, 1982

	USA – education		
	College	High school	Grade school
Worry a lot	30	38	40
Feelings of impending nervous breakdown	16	19	20

Source: Bradburn, 1969

Many studies in Britain, the USA and elsewhere have found that there are much higher rates of schizophrenia, depression, alcoholism, drug addiction and crime among the working classes. Middle-class people, on the other hand, are more prone to anxiety disorders and psychotic affective disorders (Dohrenwend, 1975). One of the best-known studies of depression was carried out among women in London (Brown and Harris, 1978). It was found that working-class women were much more depressed than middle-class women, especially if they had young children at home.

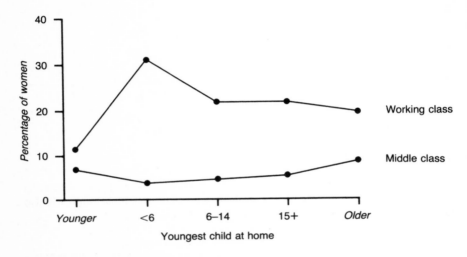

Figure 10.1 Female depression as a function of social class and age of children
Source: Brown and Harris, 1978

Are these differences caused by working-class people having more stressful life-events? They are exposed to more stress, especially stressful events for which they are not responsible (75 per cent versus 38 per cent for middle class), and involving loss of status (61 per cent versus 38 per cent) (Dohrenwend, 1975). More important perhaps, working-class people do have more everyday hassles: health problems in the family, financial problems, drunken husbands, inconvenient hours of work and so on were cited for 61 per cent of the working class and 38 per cent of the middle-class women in the Brown and Harris study.

This does not explain all the class differences: working-class people are upset more by the *same* amount of stress. They do have smaller financial resources to deal with stress, but lack of education and low job status also predict vulnerability to stress (McLeod and Kessler, 1990). It is possible that supportive social networks are weaker. There is clearer evidence that lower-status individuals use more passive forms of coping, as opposed to seeking help, or trying to solve the problem – probably the result of socialisation in a low-resource sub-culture, as is shown in a study by Gurin *et al.* (1960) (Table 10.4).

Table 10.4   Class differences in ways of coping with worries and unhappy periods (US national sample, percentages)

	Education		
	Grade school	High school	College
Passive reactions	41	31	28
Prayer	21	14	11
Direct coping reactions	8	15	24
Informal help-seeking	17	32	27

Source: Gurin, Veroff and Feld, 1960

Gender differences

Women report more symptoms of psychological distress than men, and their doctors agree with them (Table 10.5). The difference varies with the disorder: women report depression twice as often as men, but on the other hand men are more likely to become alcoholics or criminals (Table 10.6).

Table 10.5   Sex differences in strain and mental health (UK surveys, percentages)

	Males	Females
Experienced unpleasant emotional strain yesterday for about half of the time or more	13	18
Worried a lot or all the time	26	37
Felt about to have a nervous breakdown	12	25
Report nerves, depression or irritability	14	27
Report sleeplessness	12	20
Take tranquillisers, sedatives or sleeping pills	6	13
Scored over 12 on GHQ	13.5	18.7
Diagnosed by GP as having mental disorder	7.4	14.9

Source: Argyle, 1987

The explanation for these differences is not agreed. It is partly a cultural phenomenon, as is shown by the fact that these differences between the

Table 10.6   Typical sex ratios for mental illness, etc. (male: female)

Depression	1:2
Neurosis, anxiety, etc.	1:1.5
Mental disorder, all kinds	1:1.7
Schizophrenia	1:1
Alcoholism	3:1
Crime	8.5:1

Source: Argyle, 1987

sexes are becoming less all the time. Recent studies of American students and of the Amish culture have found no difference at all. It is partly that women are more willing than men to admit to emotional disturbance and to 'take the sick role'; however, this has been estimated to account for only 25 per cent of the difference. Women who have jobs are as reluctant as men to go sick. One theory is that such roles keep people going; it is curious that looking after a family does not produce the same benefits.

Women seem to be exposed to additional stresses whether they are at work or at home. If they are at work they feel they ought to be at home, and in any case have the additional load of doing the domestic work. If they are not at work, they are liable to become isolated and frustrated. Brown and Harris (1978) found that depression was very high for women without social support at home, without jobs and with small children.

Kessler and McLeod (1984) carried out an intricate analysis of the effect of stressful life-events for men and women. They found that women were not more upset by loss of income or marital disruption, but they were more upset by death of a loved one, and other crises in the social network. Part of the greater amount of distress experienced by women is due to their greater emotional involvement in social relationships, making them more vulnerable to a whole class of stressful events.

The greatest difference is for depression. A recent study suggests a possible explanation. Subjects were asked, 'What do you do when you feel depressed?' Women were most likely to cry, talk to other people about it – a 'ruminating' style – while men engaged in physical activity and avoided thinking about the causes of their depression (Nolen-Hoeksema, 1987).

Cultural differences

It is difficult to analyse cultural differences in mental health, because mental disorders take somewhat different forms in different cultures. The Neuroticism dimension is well-established, however, and has been carefully translated into a number of languages. There is a problem about how comparable the samples are who have been tested, except that samples of students have often been used. There have been two interesting differences. Germany, Italy and Japan, which suffered massive social disorganisation after World War II, showed a marked increase in average neuroticism for 10 years, and then returned to normal. And today, the Arab countries of the Middle East have high scores, though whether this is a cause or an effect of political instability we do not know (Lynn, 1981).

Depression is found all over the world, but in Africa and in parts of India, where there has been little contact with European ideas, it takes a different form. There is no sense of guilt, sin or inadequacy; instead, those affected feel tired, weak, have headaches and have no interest in food, sex or social life. It may be that people have to learn Jewish–Protestant ideas of sin and guilt before they can be depressed in the Western style (Marsella, 1980).

THE SOCIAL BEHAVIOUR OF MENTAL PATIENTS

Mental patients of different kinds have distinctive patterns of social behaviour. These are part of the condition, and may be the cause of other symptoms.

Neurosis

A proportion of neurotic patients are identified by psychiatrists as socially incompetent. We found that about 27 per cent of out-patients had difficulty in social situations, as a result of their inadequate social behaviour; probably many other neurotics share the same problems in lesser degrees, since neurotics are found to have only a quarter as many friends as controls. Their non-verbal communication is less positive – less smiling, gaze and proximity, with gestures of self-touching rather than communication. They are anxious in social situations, often tense, with strained faces and trembling hands, and they make many speech errors. A number of studies have recently found that neurotic patients of all kinds have an abnormal degree of self-attention or 'self-absorption' (Ingram, 1990). As a result, they are often found to be very self-centred, taking little interest in other people, and take no account of others' point of view. They are often very poor conversationalists, speaking little, not introducing new materials, so that the conversation soon dries up.

Other kinds of neurotic social behaviour apply to special sub-groups. Depressives tend to be in a depressed mood, with gloomy facial expressions and tone of voice, drooping posture, speaking very little. They are found very unrewarding by others and are avoided. Hysterics are more cheerful, often flamboyant, though their egocentric self-presentation and devious manipulation of others can be irritating. Another deviant kind of self-presentation is found when a person presents a quite misleading identity, as when a psychologist looks like a patient, or a student like a professor.

Schizophrenia

Here the failure of social performance is far worse. Non-verbal communication can be very deviant: the face may be blank with some grimaces, the gaze is averted with strangers, spatial proximity is avoided and much more space is needed, gestures are irrelevant and self-directed, posture is immobile, sometimes symbolic, the voice is flat and monotonous, the appearance very untidy. There is little conversation, and there is a general withdrawal from other people, with no cooperation or relationships. These patients are found very unrewarding, 'socially bankrupt', and are made anxious by supervision or criticism. They often behave in an eccentric way, seen by others as rule-breaking, perhaps due to disturbed thought processes (Argyle, 1983, 1988).

We shall pursue later the idea that failure of social skills is central to some forms of mental disorder, the cause of the rest of the trouble.

THE EFFECTS OF STRESS ON MENTAL HEALTH

We discussed the meaning and measurement of stress in the last chapter, in connection with its effect on physical health. The first inventory of stressful life-events to be widely used was by Holmes and Rahe (1967), where death of spouse was rated 100, death of a close friend 37, Christmas 12, and so on. The total score for the previous 6 months gives some prediction of mental ill health. A number of later investigators have concluded that it is better to measure stressful events by means of an interview, so that the seriousness of the events can be assessed. There is a further problem in the case of mental ill health, that the 'life-events' may really be caused by the patient, as for example in the cases of trouble with spouse, other family members or at work. It is necessary to show that the stressful event was outside the control of the person affected. This too can be assessed in an interview. Brown and Harris (1978) did interview their subjects, and eliminated stressful events which were the results of the patients' state. The massive effect on depression rate is shown in Table 10.9 (see p. 265).

As well as such serious but isolated events, repeated daily 'hassles' are also important. Kanner *et al.* (1981) asked subjects to keep records of the frequency and intensity of 117 kinds of hassle. These predicted psychological symptoms better than major stressful events did, the most common being those listed in Table 10.7.

How important are stressful events or daily hassles as causes of mental disorder? Rabkin and Struening (1976) concluded that there was typically a correlation of about .30, or only 9 per cent of the variance. The effect is greatest for depression, and the most stressful event is loss of a social relationship. This effect is quite strong, as in the Brown and Harris study. Another estimate is that the risk of becoming depressed is increased up to 6:1 by stressful events. Other mental disorders are affected too: suicide is also increased by relationship loss; for schizophrenia the effect is weaker, and mainly due to quite recent events; anxiety is sometimes found to be affected by crises, failure, danger or threatening events (Paykel, 1985).

Table 10.7   The ten most frequently reported hassles and uplifts

Item[a]	% of times checked
Hassles	
1 Concerns about weight	52.4
2 Health of a family member	48.1
3 Rising price of common goods	43.7
4 Home maintenance	42.8
5 Too many things to do	38.6
6 Misplacing or losing things	38.1
7 Yard work or outside home maintenance	38.1
8 Property investment, or taxes	37.6
9 Crime	37.1
10 Physical appearance	35.9
Uplifts	
1 Relating well with your spouse or lover	76.3
2 Relating well with friends	74.4
3 Completing a task	73.3
4 Feeling healthy	72.7
5 Getting enough sleep	69.7
6 Eating out	68.4
7 Meeting your responsibilities	68.1
8 Visiting, phoning or writing someone	67.7
9 Spending time with family	66.7
10 Home (inside) pleasing to you	65.5

[a]   Items are those most frequently checked over a period of nine months. The '% of times checked' figures represent the mean percentage of people checking the item each month averaged over the nine monthly administrations

Source: Kanner *et al.*, 1981

Stressful events are only part of the explanation, since much mental disorder is chronic; that is, it persists over long periods, regardless of events. The best predictor of disturbance is previous disturbance. However, this may be partly due to continued stress, such as unemployment, marital discord or illness (Depue and Monroe, 1985).

An example of a stressful event which has powerful effects on mental health is war experience. Hobfoll (1988) studied Israeli soldiers who had different degrees of exposure to combat during the war with Lebanon. He used a measure of Combat Stress Reaction (CSR), based on ratings of various aspects of psychological disturbance – agitation, hysterical blindness, waxy immobility, talking to dead comrades, acute apathy. CSR correlated .26 with measures of battle intensity. Millions of servicemen in World War II suffered from 'war neurosis'. It was estimated that if men were kept in action for 60 days, all would break down, but that about 60 per cent of these would recover at once after removal from the scene and rest.

Death of spouse is rated as the most stressful event in stress inventories. The main effect is to produce depression. In one study 42 per cent of widows were in the mild-to-severe range of the Beck Depression Inventory, compared with 10 per cent of the married. The numbers ill enough to be hospitalised are affected similarly: the bereaved are 2.5–6 times as likely to become in-patients as the married, according to different studies. The effects of being widowed fall off after 1–2 years, and faster for women. For those who are hospitalised the depression rate is higher for women, alcoholism for men (Stroebe and Stroebe, 1987).

Unemployment is another stress which is externally imposed, especially when a whole factory closes, or when the whole area has a high rate of unemployment. The general mental health, as measured on the GHQ, deteriorates, while among school-leavers who find jobs it improves. Depression increases and becomes worse with time, in one study to an average score of 11 on the Beck Inventory, compared with 5.5 for those at work. Alcoholism increases; there are twice as many heavy drinkers. Attempted suicide is 8 times more common, especially during the first month (Argyle, 1989). In several of these studies it was possible to demonstrate that unemployment caused the mental ill health rather than vice versa.

Work can be a serious source of stress, resulting in mental ill health. Some jobs are more stressful than others. We discussed the features of jobs that make them stressful in a previous chapter – job overload, repetitive work, responsibility for others, and so on. How far a job is found to be stressful depends partly on the personality of the individual doing it – some people have a need for excitement. It is the mismatch between person and job which causes the stress, as Figure 4.1 (p. 88) shows.

An interesting form of stress response caused by work is 'burn-out', found among people in the medical and caring professions, and administrators who have to deal with a lot of people. It is a form of emotional exhaustion, which may lead to withdrawal, depression, alcoholism and even suicide. Patients and other clients can be very stressful, if they are aggressive, demanding, upset, dirty and so on, if they have to be given bad news, or if they fail to show any improvement (Maslach and Jackson, 1982).

THE EFFECTS OF SOCIAL SUPPORT ON MENTAL HEALTH

We saw in the last chapter that social support, from family, friends or work-mates, can reduce the effects of stress on physical health. The overall effects there were modest, but greatest for women, helped by family, and receiving emotional support (p. 236). Social support also affects mental health, and here the effects are stronger.

Simply being married, whether happily or not, produces benefits for mental health (Table 10.8). However, the quality of the relationship is also important. A number of studies have found that an intimate relationship has a buffering effect; that is, it counters the effects of stress when needed. Brown and Harris (1978) in their study of depression in south London found a powerful buffering effect, as Table 10.9 shows.

Table 10.8   Mental hospital admissions and marital status (England, 1981)

Marital status	Mental hospital admissions per 100,000
Single	770
Married	260
Widowed	980
Divorced	1,437

Source: Cochrane, 1988

Table 10.9   Depression, stress and social support (percentage depressed)

	Support		
	High	Mid	Low
Women who had stressful life event	10	26	41
Women with no such events	1	3	4

Source: Brown and Harris, 1978

However, there can also be direct benefits from social support that occur whether there is stress or not, and this is found with support in the form of social embeddedness in a wider social network, of friends, work-mates and neighbours, as well as family (Cohen and Wills, 1985). In a study of a Chinese-American community in Washington, support from friends and neighbours had as much effect as being married, and as much effect, though in the opposite direction as the (damaging) effects of stress (Lin et al., 1979).

Williams et al. (1981) studied 2,235 people in Seattle, measuring social support by a questionnaire about community attachments and close personal ties, and found main effects on mental health at all stress levels (Figure 10.2).

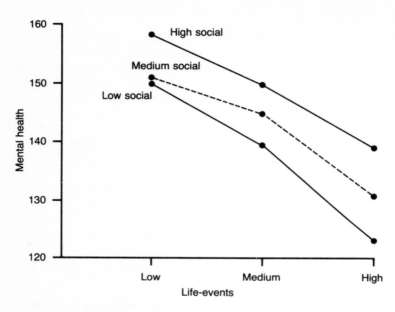

Figure 10.2 Plot of mean mental health scores for nine groups differing in levels of social support and life-events
Source: Williams *et al.*, 1981

A number of different kinds of social support have been distinguished, and measures devised for each of them. For example, Cohen *et al.* (1988) produced scales for (1) appraisal, the perceived availability of someone to talk to about one's problems, (2) self-esteem, (3) belonging, the perceived availability of material help. There are quite high correlations between these scales at .30 and .50. Wellman (1985) studied the entire social networks of 29 people in Toronto, involving 336 social ties, and found 5 factors, as shown in Table 10.10.

Comparison of these factors with the scales by Cohen *et al.*, shows that there are two kinds of material help and an informative factor, but no self-esteem.

The different sources of social support probably function in rather different ways. The *family* produces direct biological effects on health (p. 237ff); it is a little group which cooperates over mutual care, the sharing of food and property, and in the rearing of children. The benefits for physical health come from family members looking after one another, with the result that there is better health behaviour; in addition, the immune system is strengthened by intimate attachments.

Table 10.10   Clustering of types of social support

Cluster	Variable	Correlation with own cluster	Correlation with next highest cluster
1	*Information*		
	Job opening information	.78	.02
	Job contacts	.80	.01
	Housing search aids	.13	.02
2	*Services*		
	Minor household aid	.64	.07
	Minor services	.45	.06
	Major household aid	.42	.13
	Organisational aid	.20	.04
	Household items	.50	.14
3	*Companionship*		
	Doing things together	.45	.03
	Discussing things	.70	.01
	Sociability	.39	.02
	Formal group activities	.24	.01
4	*Emotional*		
	Major services	.25	.09
	Family advice	.65	.12
	Minor emotional support	.66	.06
	Major emotional support	.53	.12
5	*Financial*		
	Small $	.60	.16
	Big $	.58	.04
	Housing $	.39	.02

Source: Wellman, 1985

Close relationships may affect mental health in rather different ways. Why is the buffering effect particularly due to this kind of relationship? When people are in real trouble, with serious illness, money or the law, they need real help, and usually it is only families and kin who are prepared to do this. And when a person is in serious emotional trouble, it is only those in close family relationships in whom he is willing to confide, from whom he has no secrets. Another theory is that simply being loved is the key, derived from the early and innate dependence of infants on their mothers' love and protection. Another theory is that this kind of support increases self-esteem and feelings of mastery. And of course in the case of spouses, sex may be important.

Friends are an important part of the wider social network, which produces direct effects on mental health, whether there is stress or not, though they don't have much effect on physical health. Friends produce tangible help and information through the social network, and the larger and more varied this is the better. And friends enjoy helping one another, especially in close or 'communal' relationships. Friends spend a lot of time when they are together just talking, and above all engaging in joint leisure. We saw earlier the characteristic things that a sample of Oxford friends said that they did together (Table 3.2, p. 46). It can be seen that these are all very enjoyable activities, most of which require the cooperation of others. Studies of happiness, which will be discussed in the next chapter, find that being with friends is the most common source of joy.

Groups of friends cooperate over joint leisure activities, and it may be this which produces the feelings of belonging and embeddedness. Doing things together with friends is a major source of joy, thus banishing negative emotions. However, talking to friends about one's troubles can make things worse; this has been described as 'negative buffering'. We saw that women can become more depressed if they have a moan with their friends (p. 259), and it has been found that those people who talk to their friends most about their troubles become more depressed, although those with strong social support become less so (Ross and Mirowsky, 1989). It follows that for social support to be effective it must take other forms. Bolger and Eckenrode (1990) found that social integration did more than social support for examination stress. Providing material help or advice could add to resources and control. And some kinds of talk can be successful when it solves problems, when it produces a more constructive outlook or allows catharsis (p. 235), as in psychotherapy. It seems very likely that cooperation leads directly to positive relations between people and to positive emotions (Argyle, 1991).

As to *work-mates*, we saw in the last chapter that work relationships can buffer the effects of work stresses on physical as well as mental health. This source of support is more effective than social support at home – the wife usually can't do much to help with work difficulties, but work-mates and supervisors can. Research on social support at work has often found a buffering effect, as the study by House (1981) showed.

There has been some disagreement over how important work relationships are. We thought that this might depend very much on the closeness of the relationship. We compared work relationships at four levels of closeness. The closest level was of people who became friends in the usual sense; for example, asking one another home, and meeting outside work. These helped one another a lot at work. They also engaged in many non-work activities – gossip, games, discussing personal life, having coffee or meals together, joking and teasing. Work-mates, like friends, are part of a cooperative group, feel accepted and embedded, and derive self-esteem from it. People who become unemployed experience both a loss of status and loss of the wider social contacts and activities provided by work. However, the work network is different from friendship, since help and cooperation over the work is central; work-mates can be relied upon to help with difficulties, and this results in work stresses being perceived as less stressful (Argyle, 1989).

There are quite strong sex differences in the benefits received from social support. Women have more intimate relationships, with both family and friends, are more comfortable with intimacy than men are, and benefit more from social support (Hobfoll, 1988). On the other hand, women also give more social support than men, so that in marriage it is the husbands who benefit more – wives are better confidantes than husbands (Vanfossen, 1981).

PERSONALITY FACTORS IN VULNERABILITY

There are genetic predispositions to be vulnerable to stress and hence to become mentally ill. Twin studies have shown that schizophrenia is strongly affected in this way. Depression, and the general personality factor of neuroticism, are about 50 per cent due to inheritance. Unfavourable childhood experiences can add further to vulnerability. Here the evidence is less clear, because correlations between parental behaviour and later mental disorder in the children may be due to the parents reacting to early manifestations of disorder in the child. Schizophrenics are often found to have had dominant and rejecting mothers, and delinquents to have been beaten and rejected especially by their fathers, but we are not entirely sure that the parents' behaviour was the cause rather than the effect. Loss of parents by death or divorce has sometimes been found to lead to later depression, which looks like a true case of causation, but this effect is a very weak one. For what it is worth, a number of studies suggest that the best kind of home to have for future mental health (1) is complete, with two parents, (2) is warm and cohesive, with joint family activities and outings, (3) has firm discipline with standards and limits set, reasons given and discussion of them allowed (Baumrind, 1980).

Both genetics and socialisation have effects on the adult personality, and the characteristics of personalities which make them more or less vulnerable to stress have been extensively studied, and to these we now turn. To start with, vulnerability depends on a number of factors, past and present, as Brown and Harris (1978) found.

The general factor of neuroticism describes vulnerability to stress. Individuals with high scores on this dimension are more easily upset, and tend to be anxious, depressed, and complain of a variety of minor health problems, such as headaches and other pains though, as we have seen, there is a smaller relationship with serious illness.

How about the people who are *less* upset by stress? The concept of 'hardiness' was introduced by Kobasa (1982) in a study of managers, as we described earlier (p. 242). The component of hardiness which correlates best with the capacity to cope with stress is internal control. Lack of internal control correlates with depression and other adverse responses to stress, but it fails to predict (that is, act as a causal agent) (Steptoe and Appels, 1990). Type A personalities (the ones prone to heart attacks) are more upset by stress than others, probably because they are upset by events which they can't control.

A second component of hardiness is self-esteem: Cronkite and Moos (1984) studied married couples and found that self-esteem predicted lower depression at a later date, especially when the spouse also had high self-esteem, this time as a main effect, not interacting with level of stress. Self-confidence is also a factor in responding well to stress. A sense of mastery includes confidence in being able to cope with difficulties, that problems can be solved; this is strongly linked to ability to deal with stress, and with positive mental health (Hobfoll, 1988).

Social interest, a dimension of positive concern for and interest in others, is sometimes used as a measure of cooperativeness. Those scoring high on social interest are found to have stronger social support and to be less upset by stress (Crandall, 1984). Other studies have found that vulnerability is less in individuals who look on the bright side and think positively, a factor we shall discuss further in the next chapter as a source of happiness. Religious beliefs may help, and have certainly helped many people to cope well, e.g. prisoners of war and others. How religion helps was discussed in Chapter 6.

Individuals differ in coping styles, and this affects their vulnerability to stress. On the whole people use problem-focused coping for situations over which they think they have some control, and emotion-focused coping for situations which have to be accepted. In addition, there is quite a wide variation in styles of coping, and while internal controllers adopt this flexible pattern, externals cope in less adaptive ways – for example, using suppression for situations which could be changed. Less direct or less problem-solving coping leads to a higher level of mental disturbance in response to stress, and a higher level of disturbance when social support is low, as found by Parkes (1990) in a longitudinal study of trainee teachers. For controllable situations, problem-solving is better for mental health than emotion-focused coping or avoidance and denial (Lazarus and Folkman, 1984). Depressed individuals use less problem-solving and more emotional coping, but coping style and depression probably influence each other (Hobfoll, 1988). Parkes (1986) found that direct coping is more common in extraverts and those with social support; perhaps their possession of greater internal and external resources makes such coping more possible.

Differences in coping style can explain some of the demographic differences reported earlier. Why are women twice as likely to become depressed as men?

It may be because of differences in coping styles. Some of the differences between men and women in coping styles are shown in Table 10.11. Class differences in mental health may also be partly due to differences in coping styles. Working-class people are more likely to react passively to stress, while middle-class people use more problem-solving and help-seeking (Gurin *et al.*, 1960). This may be because middle-class people usually have better resources and are thus able to tackle their problems more directly.

Table 10.11   Sex differences in methods of coping with worries

	Males	Females
UK (1982)[1]		
Take medicine or tablets	13	18
Eat a bit more than usual	6	13
Drink a bit more than usual	8	5
USA (1976)[2]		
Positive coping (do something)	19	9
Passive methods (do nothing)	27.5	21.5
Prayer	16.5	29.5
Seek informal help	43.5	52.5
(Of these) From spouse (married only)	73	58
Friends	32	34
Children	2	6

Sources: [1] Warr and Payne, 1982
          [2] Veroff *et al.*, 1981

Social competence is an important area of personality with implications for mental health. The model which inspired a great deal of social skills training is as follows: individuals who are unable to make friends, deal with relationships at work or in everyday life, or have difficulty or experience anxiety in common social situations, will experience a lot of stress. They are likely to be rejected and isolated, and this is liable to cause anxiety and depression. The reason that they have poor social skills in the first place lies mainly in socialisation in childhood and adolescence; for example, having poor models in the family, or being isolated for some reason, or maybe never meeting the opposite sex (Trower, Bryant and Argyle, 1978). In the same tradition Libet and Lewinsohn (1973) suggested that depressives are so unrewarding to other people that others avoid them; it is this rejection that produces depression.

We described the social behaviour of some kinds of patients earlier; it can be seen how social difficulties could arise in each case. However, the forms of social failure are partly more specific. A number of studies have found different clusters of, for example, depressives, with different social behaviour deficits (Phillips, 1978).

We showed earlier that the social performance of schizophrenics is extremely disturbed and inadequate. However, the causal story here may be different: it seems likely that the entire personality of schizophrenics is disturbed, including their social performance. This may in turn cause further difficulties and exacerbate their condition.

It was shown above how social support creates some immunity to stressful events. However, some people are less able to profit from social support because they are socially isolated, or are unable to obtain support for other reasons. This is a second model relating lack of social competence to mental disorder, very similar to the social skills model just described, but placing the emphasis on skills related to social support. Those high on neuroticism receive a lot less social support, extraverts somewhat more (Costa *et al.*, 1985). Sarason and Sarason (1985) found that people who had little social support had rigid, authoritarian attitudes, low tolerance for deviance and a negative, alienated, pessimistic view of life; these authors argue that such views would not be conducive to the formation of close, supportive ties. Jones (1985) found that lonely people lack social skills in a number of ways: they are less rewarding, are shy and unassertive, hostile and pessimistic, and are self-centred, taking little interest in others. This whole negative syndrome is also found in unhappy people. Heller and Lakey (1985) compared people who reported high and low levels of social support. Those with high social support talked more and disclosed more to a friend or a sibling in a laboratory setting.

We showed above that many mental patients are chronically disturbed. One reason for this may be that they continually create stresses for themselves; for example, by their inadequate social behaviour. Such people may be in perpetual conflict with their associates, or alternate between dependence, abuse and neglect, with the result that others withdraw and become alienated. As we have seen, loss of social support is a major cause of depression (Depue and Monroe, 1985).

THE SOCIAL PREVENTION AND TREATMENT OF MENTAL ILLNESS

If social factors play such an important part in the causation of mental illness, it seems likely that social factors might be useful in prevention and treatment.

Prevention

The main applications of social methods have been on the part of employers, to make their employees more resistant to stress. This is a serious problem:

on averaage $13^1/_2$ days a year are lost per head, of which 2 are due directly to mental ill health, and another 8 to physical ill health, which is in part also caused by stress.

Relaxation

Studies have been made of the effects of training workers in physiological relaxation techniques, which they are encouraged to practise for two 15-minute periods a day. This may include biofeedback, instruction in breathing, or special meditation techniques like TM, where the mind is emptied of thoughts and images by repeating a mantra for 20 minutes. All of these relaxation methods produce some physiological effects, especially lower blood pressure, heart rate, and generally improved health. Type A personalities benefit, with reduced scores on the Type A inventory. Mental health is improved, with reduced scores for anxiety, depression, hostility and so on, and employees become more satisfied and productive (Murphy, 1984). Leisure activities can also reduce the effects of stress: leisure satisfaction has been found to buffer the effects of stress at work.

Holidays are good for people, too. Table 10.12 shows the difference in rate of minor symptoms reported by a large sample of Americans, while on holiday and during the rest of the year.

Table 10.12   Percentages reporting symptoms while on vacation, and during the past year

		Vacation	During past year
Tired	34	12	
Irritable		8	30
Constipation, worry, anxiety		7	27
Loss of interest in sex		6	12
Digestive prooblems		6	16
Insomnia		4	11
Headaches		3	21

Source: Rubenstein, 1980

Stress-management training

We have seen that coping style affects vulnerability to stress. Some employees have succeeded in improving the mental health of their workers by teaching them better ways of coping. A form of cognitive therapy has been used, in which employees are shown that a lot of stress is due to the way in which they perceive and interpret situations, and taught that stressful situations can be seen in less threatening ways. For example, instead of reacting to overload by feeling incompetent, workers could blame the supervisor for mismanaging the work allocation. Individuals can also be trained in positive imagery, time-management and goal-setting.

This approach could be extended, making use of what has been learnt about coping styles. What people should do when experiencing stress is:

1 try to tackle the problem directly,
2 seek help from family, friends or work-mates,
3 take some physical exercise (see below).

What they should *not* do is:

1 sit and brood about it,
2 wait for it to go away,
3 eat, drink, smoke, take drugs.

Many popular books are now available on how to relax and how to cope with stress, and it seems likely that this information will soon be widely known, and perhaps widely acted upon.

Exercise

We saw in the last chapter that exercise is very beneficial for physical health. Other studies have found that aerobic exercise relieves depression. Hayes and Ross (1986) studied a sample of 401 people, and found that exercise predicted psychological health, especially for people in the low- and middle-income groups.

Firms which have introduced exercise programmes for their workers have found that not only is their bodily health much improved, but in addition they become less anxious, tense and depressed, especially on exercise days, and have improved work performance (Falkenburg, 1987). We shall show in the next chapter that exercise is one of the commonest sources of positive emotions, and this may be how it affects mental health. Exercise is often done in the company of other people, and the combination of physical and social activities, as in dancing, tennis and other sports, is a particularly potent source of joy.

Stress-reduction in organisations

A number of employers have taken steps to reduce the stresses to which their employees are exposed – and thus to reduce the costs of stress in terms of illness, absence and loss of efficiency. Very often it is possible to alter the working arrangements in various ways:

1 *Improving the job* – for example, by job enlargement or enrichment; reducing repetition, physical overload or time pressures; reducing travel and hours of work for managers; improving equipment or automating parts of the job which are boring or dangerous; reducing noise levels and making other environmental improvements.

2 *Organisational changes*, such as fewer levels in the hierarchy, decentralisation, reduced role conflict and ambiguity, and better-designed socio-technical systems. Wall and Clegg (1981) studied a sweet factory where work identity, work-group autonomy and job complexity were increased, a lot of control being transferred from supervisors to the work-group. This led to increased mental health and job satisfaction, and reduced labour turnover.

3 *Increased social support*, by the creation of small work-teams, and encouraging and training supervisors and managers to be more supportive.

4 *More participation in decisions* by structures of industrial democracy, consultation by supervisors and managers, surveys of job satisfaction, suggestion schemes.

However, some jobs are intrinsically stressful and such changes are not always possible – for example, for police, firemen or deep-sea divers. What can be done here is to improve selection methods, so that those selected can cope with stress, or even enjoy it; training can be given in stress management as described above; job rotation can give periods away from the most stressful work; part-time work, with short periods of work, has been used for divers and radar plotters.

Provision of social support

We saw the importance of social support for mental as well as physical health. It is possible to make some provision to help those who live alone or are socially isolated. Self-help groups are available for them in a number of specific areas, such as Alcoholics Anonymous. Many lonely people do join evening classes, churches, and other clubs and leisure groups which are open to all. The most likely place to find a friend is at a club in the neighbourhood, because there will be people who share an interest there, and who live nearby. In fact this is a very widespread activity, and some of the main kinds of club activity are shown in Table 5.4 (p. 115).

The members, and especially the leaders, of clubs and classes are often very good at welcoming new members and trying to integrate them. There have even been experiments in training hairdressers and barman as counsellors, since many people discuss problems with them (Argyle and Henderson, 1985). There have also been experiments on the provision of social support by creating networks for long-term psychiatric patients living alone, organised by social workers and linking the patients to local networks (Sorensen, 1985).

It is possible to improve the mental health of a community by the provision of community centres, places where clubs can meet and groups can form. The design of buildings is important. Some big apartment blocks have had so much vandalism and crime that they had to be demolished. It is now thought that one of the main factors was the absence of areas where residents could meet, get to know one another, and cooperate over keeping order (Newman, 1972).

Social treatment of mental illness

We saw earlier that poor social skills make people more vulnerable to stress, and less able to benefit from social support. Many neurotics are deficient in everyday social skills, and the same is true of mental patients of all kinds.

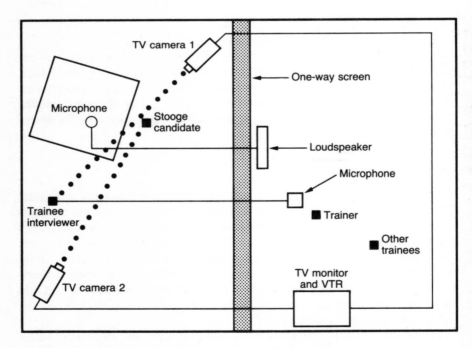

Figure 10.3 Laboratory arrangements for interviewer training
Source: Argyle, 1983

The most widely used form of social skills training (SST) is role-playing, often done in groups of about 6. The trainer coaches trainees in a social skill, modelling is done live or provided on videotape, a trainee role-plays a situation in which the skill can be used, either with other trainees or with assistants from outside, the performance is video-recorded and played back, together with tactful and constructive comments from the trainer. There may be 6–10 sessions, including some individual ones, for special problems faced by individuals. This is ideally done in a training lab, as is shown in Figure 10.3, complete with video-recorder and one-way screen.

There have been many controlled follow-up studies of the effectiveness of SST with patients. The conclusion has been that it is quite successful, though no more so than cognitive therapy, for example. A major problem is that of 'generalisation', enabling patients to transfer their newly acquired skills to their real-life settings. The usual solution has been 'homework' – persuading them to try their skills out between therapy sessions and report back (Hollin and Trower, 1986).

In the case of some patients treated by the author and colleagues, the recovery was very rapid (Trower, Bryant and Argyle, 1978). In these cases there was a specific deficit in social performance, which could be treated directly. Since then a lot of new research has been done, suggesting a number of forms of SST, as alternatives to traditional role-playing, which can be used to help people with particular difficulties. Here are some examples:

1 *Non-verbal communication*. Many patients, as we saw, smile, look and gesture less, and have a less expressive tone of voice than those without difficulties. All this can be improved quite easily with the help of a mirror, tape-recorder, video tape-recorder, and some simple modelling (Argyle, 1988).

2 *Verbal communication*. Many patients are very unsatisfactory conversationalists; for example, being unable to sustain a conversation at all. This can be corrected by spotting what they are doing wrong, such as replying to questions but not handing the conversation over. They can then be taught to get this right by coaching and role-playing.

3 *Self-presentation*. Some people present themselves inappropriately, via their clothes, hair, voice or general demeanour. The author has known people lose their jobs, or be socially rejected for this alone. The 'treatment' consists of showing them how to dress or speak differently, and this is quite easily done.

4 *Relationship skills*. One of the commonest spheres of social difficulty is in relationships with other people – making friends, for example. People can be helped by educational methods, giving better understanding of different relationships and the rules which should be folllowed to sustain this. This was discussed in Chapter 3.

CONCLUSIONS

Mental disturbance of different degrees is widespread in the community. It is more common among working-class people, and women. Mental patients are socially incompetent in several ways. Stressful life events like bereavement, unemployment and some kinds of work are partly responsible, as are more minor daily hassles. Social support can reduce the effects of stress; intimate relationships provide practical and emotional support and have a buffering effect; friendship networks have a main effect, mainly via companionship; work-mates provide support over work problems.

Individual differences in mental disorder are partly genetic, partly the result of socialisation. Hardiness is due to low neuroticism, high self-esteem, coping style and social competence; such competence leads to the mobilisation of social support.

Social factors can contribute to the prevention of mental illness, by training in relaxation, stress management techniques and the encouragement of exercise. Organisations can reduce stress levels by the modification of jobs. Social support in the community can be increased by the provision of community centres. Social skills training can contribute to the treatment of mental disorders, by correcting the social deficits of patients.

REFERENCES

Argyle, M. (1983) *The Psychology of Interpersonal Behaviour*. 4th edition. Harmondsworth: Penguin.
——(1987) *The Psychology of Happiness*. London: Methuen.
——(1988) *Bodily Communication*. 2nd edition. London: Methuen.
——(1989) *The Social Psychology of Work*. 2nd edition. Harmondsworth: Penguin.
——(1991) *Cooperation: The Basis of Sociability*. London: Routledge.
Argyle, M. and Furnham, A. (1982) The ecology of relationships: choice of situation as a function of relationship. *British Journal of Social Psychology*, *21*, 259–62.
Argyle, M. and Henderson, M. (1985) *The Anatomy of Relationships*. London: Heinemann; Harmondsworth: Penguin.
Baumrind, D. (1980) New directions in socialisation research. *Psychological Bulletin*, *35*, 639–52.
Bolger, N. and Eckenrode, J. (1990) Social relationships, personality and mental health during a major stressful event. Paper to ISSPR Conference, Oxford.
Bradburn, M. (1969) *The Structure of Psychological Well-being*. Chicago: Aldine.
Brown, G.W. and Harris, T. (1978) *Social Origins of Depression*. London: Tavistock.
Bruning, N.S. and Frew, D.R. (1987) Effects of exercise, relaxation, and management skills training on physiological stress indicators: a field experiment. *Journal of Applied Psychology*, *72*, 515–21.
Caplan, R.D., Cobb, S., French, J.R.P., Harrison, R.V. and Pinneau, S.R. (1975) *Job Demands and Worker Health*. Washington, DC: US Department of Health, Education and Welfare.
Cochrane, R. (1988) Marriage, separation and divorce. *In* S. Fisher and J. Reason (eds) *Handbook of Life Stress, Cognition and Health*. Chichester: Wiley.
Cohen, S. and Wills, T.A. (1985) Stress, social support, and the buffering hypothesis. *Psychological Bulletin*, *98*, 310–57.

Cohen, S., Mermelstein, R., Kamarck, T. and Hoberman, H.N. (1985) Measuring the functional components of social support. *In* I.G. Sarason and B.R. Sarason (eds) *Social Support: Theory, Research and Applications*. Dordrecht: Nijhoff.

Cooper, C.L. (1985) Your place in the stress league. *Sunday Times*, 24 Feb.

Costa, P.T., Zonderman, A.B. and McCrae, R.R. (1985) Longitudinal course of social support among men in the Baltimore longitudinal study of aging. *In* I.G. Sarason and B.R. Sarason (eds) *Social Support: Theory, Research and Applications*. Dordrecht: Nijhoff.

Crandall, J.E. (1984) Social interest as a moderator of life stress. *Journal of Personality and Social Psychology*, 47, 164–74.

Cronkite, R.C. and Moos, R.H. (1984) The role of predisposing and moderating features in the stress–illness relationship. *Journal of Health and Social Behavior*, 25, 372–93.

Depue, R.A. and Monroe, S.M. (1985) Life stress and human disorder: conceptualization and measurement of the disordered group. *In* I.G. Sarason and B.R. Sarason (eds) *Social Support: Theory, Research and Applications*. Dordrecht: Nijhoff.

Dohrenwend, B.P. (1975) Sociocultural and socio-psychological factors in the genesis of mental disorders. *Journal of Health and Social Behavior*, 16, 365–92.

Eysenck, H.L. (1976) *The Measurement of Personality*. Lancaster: MTP Press.

Falkenburg, L.E. (1987) Employee fitness programs: their impact on the employee and the organization. *Academy of Management Review*, 12, 511–22.

General Household Survey (1980, 1983) Nos 11 and 12. London: HMSO.

Goldberg, D. (1978) *Manual of the General Health Questionnaire*. Windsor: NFER.

Gurin, G., Veroff, J. and Feld, S. (1960) *Americans View their Mental Health*. New York: Basic Books.

Hannay, D.R. (1979) *The Symptoms Iceberg*. London and Boston: Routledge and Kegan Paul.

Hayes, D. and Ross, C.E. (1986) Body and mind: the effect of exercise, overweight, and physical health on psychological well-being. *Journal of Health and Social Behavior*, 27, 387–400.

Heller, K. and Lakey, B. (1985) Perceived support and social interaction among friends and confidants. *In* I.G. Sarason and B.R. Sarason (eds) *Social Support: Theory, Research and Applications*. Dordrecht: Nijhoff.

Hobfoll, S.E. (1988) *The Ecology of Stress*. New York: Hemisphere.

Hollin, C.R. and Trower, P. (1986) *Handbook of Social Skills Training*. Oxford: Pergamon.

Holmes, T.H. and Rahe, R.H. (1967) The social readjustment rating scale. *Journal of Psychosomatic Research*, 11, 213–18.

House, J.S. (1981) *Work Stress and Social Support*. Reading, MA: Addison-Wesley.

Ingram, R.E. (1990) Self-focused attention in clinical disorders: review and a conceptual model. *Psychological Bulletin*, 107, 156–76.

Jahoda, M. (1958) *Current Concepts of Positive Mental Health*. New York: Basic Books.

Jones, W.H. (1985) The psychology of loneliness: some personality issues in the study of social support. *In* I.G. Sarason and B.R. Sarason (eds) *Social Support: Theory, Research and Applications*. Dordrecht: Nijhoff.

Kanner, A.D., Coyne, J.C., Schaefer, C. and Lazarus, R.S. (1981) Comparison of two methods of stress measurement: daily hassles and uplifts versus major life events. *Journal of Behavioral Medicine*, 4, 1–30.

Kessler, R.C., Brown, R.L. and Broman, C.L. (1984) Sex differences in psychiatric help-seeking: evidence from four large-scale surveys. *Journal of Health and Social Behavior*, 22, 49–64.

Kessler, R.C. and McLeod, J.D. (1984) Sex differences in vulnerability to undesirable life events. *American Sociological Review*, 49, 620–31.

Kobasa, S.C. (1982) The hardy personality: towards a social psychology of stress and health. *In* G.S. Sanders and J. Suls (eds) *Social Psychology of Health and Illness*. Hillsdale, NJ: Erlbaum.

Lazarus, R.S. and Folkman, S. (1984) *Stress, Appraisal and Coping*. New York: Springer.

Libet, J.M. and Lewinsohn, P.M. (1973) Concept of social skills with special reference to the behavior of depressed patients. *Journal of Consulting and Clinical Psychology*, 40, 304–12.

Lin, N., Simeone, R.S., Ensel, W.M. and Kuo, W. (1979) Social support, stressful life events, and illness: a model and an empirical test. *Journal of Health and Social Behavior*, 20, 108–19.

Lynch, J.J. (1977) *The Broken Heart*. New York: Basic Books.

Lynn, R. (1981) Cross-cultural differences in neuroticism, extraversion and psychoticism. *In* R. Lynn (ed.) *Dimensions of Personality*. Oxford: Pergamon.

McLeod, J.D. and Kessler, R.C. (1990) Socioeconomic status differences in vulnerability to undersirable life events. *Journal of Health and Social Behavior*, 31, 162–72.

Marsella, A.J. (1980) Depressive experience and disorder across cultures. *In* H. Triandis and J. Draguns (eds) *Handbook of Cross-Cultural Psychology*, Vol.6. Boston, MA: Allyn & Bacon.

Maslach, C. and Jackson, S.E. (1982) Burnout in health professions: a social psychological analysis. *In* G.S. Sanders and J. Suls (eds) *Social Psychology of Health and Illness*. Hillsdale, NJ: Erlbaum.

Murphy, L.R. (1984) Occupational stress management: a review and appraisal. *Journal of Occupational Psychology*, 57, 1–15.

Newman, P. (1972) *Defensible Space*. New York: Macmillan.

Nolen-Hoeksema, S. (1987) Sex differences in unipolar depression: evidence and theory. *Psychological Bulletin*, 101, 259–82.

Parkes, K.R. (1984) Locus of control, cognitive appraisal, and coping in stressful episodes. *Journal of Personality and Social Psychology*, 46, 655–68.

——(1986) Coping in stressful episodes: the role of individual differences, environmental factors and situational characteristics. *Journal of Personality and Social Psychology*, 51, 1277–92.

——(1990) Coping, negative affecty, and the work environment: addition and interactive predictors of mental health. *Journal of Applied Psychology*, 75, 399–409.

Paykel, E.S. (1985) Life events, social support and clinical psychiatric disorder. *In* I.G. Sarason and B.R. Sarason (eds) *Social Support: Theory, Research and Applications*. Dordrecht: Nijhoff.

Phillips, E.P. (1978) *The Social Skills Basis of Psychopathology*. New York: Grune & Stratton.

Rabkin, J.G. and Struening, E.L. (1976) Life events, stress and illness. *Science*, 194, 1013–20.

Ross, C.E. and Mirowsky, J. (1989) Explaining the social patterns of depression: control and problem-solving – or support and talking? *Journal of Health and Social Behavior*, 30, 206–19.

Rubenstein, C. (1980) Vacations. *Psychology Today*, 13, May, 62–76.

Santer, S.L., Murphy, L.R. and Hurrell, J.J. (1990) Prevention of work-related psychological disorders. *American Psychologist*, *45*, 1146–58.

Sarason, B.R. Sarason, I.G., Hacker, T.A. and Basham, R.B. (1985) Concomitants of social support: social skills, physical attractiveness and gender. *Journal of Personality and Social Psychology*, *49*, 469–80.

Sarason, I.G. and Sarason, B.R. (eds) (1985) *Social Support: Theory, Research and Applications*. Dordrecht: Nijhoff.

Sorensen, T. (1985) Social network stimulation as preventive method among psychiatric long-term patients in a neighbourhood in Oslo. *International Journal of Family Psychiatry*, *6*, 189–208.

Steptoe, A. and Appels, A. (eds) (1990) *Stress, Personal Control and Health*. Chichester: Wiley.

Stroebe, W. and Stroebe, M.S. (1987) *Bereavement and Health*. Cambridge: Cambridge University Press.

Trower, P., Bryant, B. and Argyle, M. (1978) *Social Skills and Mental Health*. London: Methuen.

Vanfossen, B.E. (1981) Sex differences in the mental health effects of spouse support and equity. *Journal of Health and Social Behavior*, *22*, 130–43.

Veroff, J., Douvan, E. and Kulka, R.A. (1981) *The Inner American*. New York: Basic Books.

Wall, T.D. and Clegg, C.W. (1981) A longitudinal study of group work redesign. *Journal of Occupational Behaviour*, *2*, 31–44.

Warr, P. and Payne, R. (1982) Experience of strain and pleasure among British adults. *Social Science and Medicine*, *16*, 1691–7.

Wellman, B. (1985) From social support to social networks. *In* I.G. Sarason and B.R. Sarason (eds) *Social Support: Theory, Research and Applications*. Dordrecht: Nijhoff.

Williams, A.W., Ware, J.E. and Donald, C.A. (1981) A model of mental health, life events, and social supports applicable to general populations. *Journal of Health and Social Behavior*, *22*, 324–36.

Wing, J.K. (1976) A technique for studying psychiatric morbidity in inpatient and outpatient series and in general population samples. *Psychological Medicine*, *6*, 665–72.

Chapter 11

Happiness

Research on happiness is relatively new in psychology, but has taken off very quickly and produced a flood of research papers, several conferences and some books. The main issues have been mapped and largely solved in record time.

What is happiness? If people are asked what they mean by this word they give two kinds of answer. Some describe it in terms of positive emotions – joy, fun, euphoria – others in terms of satisfaction and contentment, with life as a whole, job, spouse, home and so on, a reflective state of mind. 'Happiness' includes both components. In a British survey 38 per cent said they were 'very happy', 58 per cent 'quite happy', and 4 per cent 'not very happy' (Harding, 1985).

Satisfaction can be measured by asking questions like 'How satisfied are you with your life as a whole these days?' The replies from a large American sample were as follows:

Completely dissatisfied			Neutral			Completely satisfied
1	2	3	4	5	6	7
0.9%	2.1%	3.7%	11.3%	20.7%	39.6%	21.7%

Source: Campbell, Converse and Rodgers, 1976

There are many ways of putting this question, but they all produce very similar answers, giving us some faith in their validity. It is also possible to ask about satisfaction with different areas of life. Table 11.1 shows how people rated the importance of several domains, and how well each predicted their overall satisfaction. It can be seen that family life and marriage scored high on both criteria.

Do people give a truthful and accurate account of their levels of satisfaction? One problem is that their reported satisfaction is found to vary a lot with the immediate situation – whether the sun is shining, whether their favourite football team has won or lost, whether they are tested in a nice room (Table

Table 11.1   The relative importance of some domains of satisfaction

	Mean importance rating	Regression coefficient
Family life	1.46	.41
Marriage	1.44	.36
Financial situation	2.94	.33
Housing	2.10	.30
Job	2.19	.27
Friendship	2.08	.26
Health	1.37	.22
Leisure activities	2.79	.21

Source: Campbell et al., 1976

11.2). It looks as if satisfaction is affected quite a lot by mood, as well as by enduring objective features of an individual's life.

Another doubt is over how far people are deceiving the interviewer, or themselves, when reporting their satisfaction. Most people report very high levels of marital satisfaction, but then 35 per cent or more later get divorced, which is a bit worrying for the investigator.

So much for satisfaction. Positive moods can be assessed by similar kinds of question. Figure 11.1 shows a non-verbal kind of question, and the percentages of a large American sample who checked different alternatives.

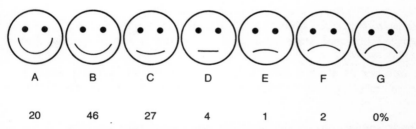

A	B	C	D	E	F	G
20	46	27	4	1	2	0%

Figure 11.1   Here are some faces expressing various feelings. Which face comes closest to expressing how you feel about your life as a whole?
Source: Andrews and Withey, 1986

Emotional states also vary in intensity. We found an intensity dimension, describing the emotions produced, for example, by listening to a beautiful piece of music, being overwhelmed by the beauty of nature, or getting on well with loved ones (Argyle and Crossland, 1987).

But is happiness the opposite of unhappiness, is joy the opposite of depression? This is a very important issue: if they are the opposite of each other, happiness research is not necessary – simply turn to the literature on depression. And to make normal people happier, give them the same treatment that is used for depressives – electric shocks, anti-depressive drugs and so on. But if happiness is *not* the opposite of depression, then 'happiness therapy' for normal people might have to take a different direction. This issue has been tackled in a number of ways. The main finding is that measures of happiness and unhappiness *are* negatively correlated, but at about −.50, so that they are also partly independent of one another (Watson, 1988).

Table 11.2   Life satisfaction and weather, football and rooms

Pleasant room	9.4
Unpleasant room	8.1
German team won	+ 2.5
German team lost	− 2.8
Sun shining	7.4
Rainy day	5.0

Source: Schwarz *et al.*, 1984

It follows that, in order to measure a person's happiness we also need to take account of the absence of depression and other negative emotional states. This can be done by measures such as the Beck Depression Inventory, or questionnaires for general neuroticism or mental ill health, which were described above (p. 255ff). And as we have seen, those in a negative emotional state also tend to report a lot of bodily illness (p. 225).

A number of studies have led to the conclusion that happiness has *three* main components, loosely correlated with one another. These are:

1 The frequency of experience of joy, and its intensity.
2 Level of satisfaction, with life as a whole.
3 The absence of depression, anxiety or other negative states.

There are several happiness scales. We have devised a new one, the Oxford Happiness Inventory, with 29 items in the 4-choice format shown in Table 11.3. This scale was derived from the Beck Depression Inventory, by reversing the items, revising them and adding more, followed by item analysis. It correlates .43 with ratings by friends, it is very stable over time, and correlates as expected with other measures of the three components listed above, for example −.52 with the BDI. Our research, which is described later, used the OHI.

Table 11.3   Oxford Happiness Index

On this questionnaire are groups of statements. Please read each group of statements carefully. Then pick out the one statement in each group which best describes the way you have been feeling the PAST WEEK, INCLUDING TODAY! Circle the number beside the statement you picked. If several statements in the group seem to apply equally well, circle each one.. Be sure to read all the statements in each group before making your choice.

1. 0 I do not feel happy.
    1 I feel fairly happy.
    2 I am very happy.

    3 I am incredibly happy.
2. 0 I am not particularly optimistic about the future.
    1 I feel optimistic about the future.
    2 I feel I have so much to look forward to.
    3 I feel that the future is overflowing with hope and promise

A recent study has suggested that, while such measures of happiness do form a general factor, they leave out another aspect of well-being. Ryff (1989) found that other aspects of well-being were less closely related, including measures of trusting, positive relations with others, purpose in life, personal growth and autonomy. We made a similar point earlier, in discussing depth of joy.

THE EFFECTS OF GENDER, AGE, CLASS AND CULTURE

Gender

The most striking difference between the sexes we have examined already – women are twice as likely to become depressed as men. On the other hand, the overall happiness of women is on average slightly greater than that of men, though this only holds for married women (Wood et al., 1989). Women also feel emotions, both positive and negative, with greater intensity. While women are happier than men when they are young, up to age 40, they are less happy later, partly because of their declining attractiveness, possibly because of less satisfaction from work.

Age

It may seen surprising that older people are considerably more satisfied than younger ones. The findings from a British survey are shown in Table 11.4. The explanation is simple, however: as we get older our ambitions and expectations decline and our achievements rise, until the two meet; the 'goal–achievement gap' disappears (Campbell *et al.*, 1976). On the other hand, the level of joy, or positive affect, definitely falls with age; this is because the number of pleasant events is smaller, and because older people have less intense emotional experiences; the same is true for negative experiences – older people simply have less intense emotions, and do less. As people get older their health deteriorates, and they have less sex but they usually become richer.

Table 11.4(a)   'Feeling very pleased with things yesterday'
(in relation to age)

	age			
	16–24 (%)	25–44 (%)	45–64 (%)	65+ (%)
All of the time	19	22	28	35
Most of the time	38	39	30	25

Table 11.4(b)   'Feeling very pleased with things yesterday'
(in relation to class differences)

	Classes		
	ABC1	*C2*	*DE*
All of the time	60	62	55
Most of the time	12	15	23

Source: Warr and Payne, 1982

Mental health on the whole improves with age, often after a bad period in the thirties, because of young children and early career problems. This is partly due to accommodation to situations, partly because older people have more resources for coping with problems – more money, social skills and contacts.

Class

This leads us to a very interesting and controversial question – does money make people happy? In American studies a surprisingly small relationship has been found, corresponding to a correlation of about .15. And whereas American incomes have greatly increased over the last 25 years, happiness has not; in fact, it has slightly declined (Campbell, 1981). However, in British studies, as in earlier American ones, a rather stronger relationship has been found (Table 11.5).

It can be seen that there is a clear effect of income on several measures of happiness, especially between the lowest income or social class group and the others. Similar differences are found between occupations, as we show later. In this study, people in classes D and E (unskilled manual, unemployed etc) were rather less pleased with things. In this and some other studies there is some effect of wealth or class on happiness, at the lower end of the financial scale – presumably because being very poor is very distressing.

Table 11.5   Happiness and income

	Income groups		
	High	Middle	Low
Very happy	44	42	30
Not happy	1	3	9
Satisfaction (1–10)	7.8	7.7	7.4
Positive affeect	3.2	2.7	2.3

Source: Harding, 1985

Does being very rich increase happiness? Yes, but not much. Diener and colleagues (1985) tested 49 people earning over $10 million a year and compared them with a control group from the same areas, with the results shown in Table 11.6. The millionaires were a little happier, but the difference is less than might be produced by, for example, getting married.

Table 11.6   Happiness of the very rich

	Very rich	Controls
% of the time happy	77	62
Life satisfaction	4.77	3.70
Positive affect	15.35	13.97
Negative affect	4.92	7.65
Self-esteem	.66	.46
Self-actualisation	.71	.55

Source: Diener et al., 1985

Cultural differences

There are great differences between countries in standard of living and the material conditions of life. Some earlier studies suggested that levels of satisfaction are not very different. However, according to a Gallup Poll there are actually quite big differences (Table 11.7). And a recent re-analysis by Veenhoven has found that there is a clear relationship between happiness and average income.

Table 11.7   Percentages 'very happy' in different parts of the world

	Very happy	Highly satisfied with		
		Standard of living	Housing	Family life
N. America	40	46	55	73
Australia	37	–	–	–
Europe	20	35	49	64
Latin America	32	36	37	60
Africa	18	5	14	18
Far East	7	8	14	18

Source: Gallup, 1976

THE CAUSES OF JOY

Joy can easily be induced in the lab by a variety of 'mood-induction' procedures. Here are some of the main methods:
1 Subjects read aloud a list of statements such as 'I feel really good', and try to put themselves in the mood suggested (The 'Velten' method).
2 Listening to cheerful music, again trying to get into the mood. The Delibes 'Coppélia' suite has been used for this.
3 Watching funny films (for example, of Peter Sellars) or cheerful films (such as of puppies at play).
4 Subjects are allowed to 'succeed' at a task, or told how well they have done.
5 Sitting and thinking for 10 minutes about the happiest recent events.
6 Talking about such events with another person.
7 Being with another person who is in a good mood; laughter in particular is contagious.

We compared methods 5 and 6, thinking and talking about recent happy events, and found that they had identical positive effects. However, some kinds of people are affected more by talking, others by thinking about happy events. Extraverts greatly enjoy meeting other extraverts, and get into a fairly euphoric state. Introverts on the other hand benefit more from sitting in a room by themselves, listening to music, and reading art magazines.

All of these methods work; they are effective in putting most people in a good mood, but the effect is usually short-lived, and often lasts only 10–15 minutes. This is fine for research purposes, but of limited use for real life. One direction of research is to find ways of generating longer-lasting effects.

How about joy experienced in everyday life? A study was carried out, with students in 5 European countries, asking them to think of a recent occasion of joy, saying what caused it. Friends were the main source (see p. 291).

MacPhillamy and Lewinsohn (1976) drew up a Pleasant Events Schedule, containing 320 such events. Research found that 49 per cent of these produced a good mood for the whole day for many people – mainly American young people. However, they did not spill over to the next day.

From these and other studies it appears that there are 8 main sources of joy:

1 Eating and drinking,
2 Sex,
3 Social relationships, especially being in love,
4 Success,
5 Using skills, doing interesting work or similar leisure occupation,
6 Sport and exercise,
7 Music, nature and reading a good book,
8 Alcohol (in modest doses).

This is a very interesting list. Some of the items make sense psychologically, others we don't really understand yet, e.g. item 7. As we have seen, different events work for different kinds of person; in fact there is quite a lot of variation in what works best. Presumably there is some kind of final common path, probably leading to stimulation of the pleasure centres. It is clear why there need to be negative emotions, such as anger and fear, too motivate fight or flight, but why are there positive ones? Joy may be the opposite of pain, an amplifiied signal to reward biologically desirable activities. Or it may arise from rapid proggress towards goals – both immediate goals, and towards more important long-term goals related to the ideal self and producing self-esteem (Carver and Scheier, 1990).

THE CAUSES OF SATISFACTION

The most obvious cause of satisfaction is the real satisfaction of needs by the objective conditions of life. And in fact a number of factors are found to be predictive of happiness – income, health, interesting and high-status work, marriage and other social relationships, and satisfying leisure (see Argyle, 1987).

How about people whose conditions suddenly improve, from winning football pools or lotteries? This is quite an interesting story: some of them are a little happier than before, but their lives are often seriously disrupted – as a result of giving up jobs, and moving house to more prosperous neighbourhoods where they are not accepted. So their objective conditions of life have not really improved much. Meanwhile it is interesting that wealth has so little effect on happiness, because it is widely believed that it is one of the main causes of happiness (Kammann and Campbell, 1982).

We saw earlier that self-reported satisfaction is affected by the weather, the fate of football teams and other sources of joy (Table 11.2). This has led to a theory about the satisfaction component of happiness – that it is a judgement based on assessment samples of current and recent life experiences, so that satisfaction can be altered by attention to different samples (Schwarz and Strack, 1991).

Table 11.2 showed that subjects report greater satisfaction if they are tested in a nice room. But they also reported *lower* satisfaction with their homes, because their homes compared unfavourably with the testing room. Comparisons with the past can have this effect: Strack *et al.* (1985) found that subjects reported satisfaction levels of 7.27 after thinking of 3 particularly unpleasant events in the past, but 6.85 after thinking of very happy events. Comparisons with other people do it too. A Cambridge study found that British manual workers in the top third of British incomes were more satisfied than non-manual workers with the same salaries – because the manual workers compared themselves with other manual workers, most of whom were paid less, while the non-manual workers were paid less than many other non-manual workers (Runciman, 1966). In fact this is one of the main areas where comparisons are important: industrial workers are very concerned about fair payment, and what other workers are being paid. Such comparisons are a major source of pay satisfaction (Berkowitz *et al.*, 1987), and there are several cases of workers choosing to lose their jobs entirely rather than be paid less than another group.

The gap between aspirations and achievement predicts satisfaction quite well – typically .50 in a series of studies (Michalos, 1986). The 'Michigan model' states that the goal – achievement gap is partly based on comparisons with past life, partly on comparisons with 'average folks'. We showed above that this model gives a good explanation of why satisfaction increases with age. It can also explain why satisfaction sometimes falls while objective conditions are improving. The falling satisfaction of Americans during the last 25 years may be because aspirations are rising faster than economic achievement can realise. The same process could explain the decline in the satisfaction of educated blacks over this period.

It is normal for us to have hopes and aspirations, and to revise them upwards if they are attained – like a high jumper raising the bar. However, over-high aspirations can be a threat to happiness, and happiness therapy sometimes includes persuading people to lower them.

People can get used to almost anything, and one theory of satisfaction is that they do, and only respond to recent changes in conditions. This was given some support from the reported finding that accident victims who become para- and quadri-plegic become nearly as happy as other people. However, as Veenhoven (1990) has pointed out, these patients were in fact less satisfied than controls, and they were interviewed face-to-face, while controls were telephoned: it is found that higher satisfaction is reported in face-to-face interviews. Furthermore, other kinds of victim report quite low levels of satisfaction: for example, mothers of handicapped children, and widows.

One group of people who obviously have not adapted to their situation are those suffering from depression. There is one very striking example of adaptation, however, and that is to the weather. Although people are happier and more satisfied on sunny days, there is no general effect of climate on satisfaction, presumably because people get used to their weather.

Do the different domains of satisfaction produce general satisfaction, or does a more basic personality trait of satisfaction lead to satisfaction with particular domains? There is evidence that both directions of causation work, especially for broad and important domains like work. It has been found that there is a top-down effect for satisfaction with social activities perhaps due to extraversion (see p. 297), and a bottom-up effect for marital satisfaction (Lance *et al.*, 1989).

THE EFFECT OF SOCIAL RELATIONSHIPS

The recent study of happiness arose partly from research on social relationships – which found that relationships make people happy. In the *Quality of American Life* study satisfaction with various relationships was the strongest predictor of overall satisfaction (Table 11.1). We shall now look at the effects of different relationships on joy and on satisfaction, and try to explain these effects.

Joy

Being with friends is the most common source of joy. In one study the main causes of joy were said to be relationships with friends (36 per cent), especially by middle-class, female and psychology students; basic pleasures (food, drink and sex) (9 per cent); and success experiences (16 per cent). The accounts of joy episodes with friends generally describe either reunions with long-lost friends or gatherings at which friends talk, laugh, relax and feel close (Schwartz and O'Connor, 1984). There is a weekly mood cycle, for students and probably for others, Friday and Saturday being high, Monday and Tuesday low, probably because of the social and leisure activities taking place at weekends (Larsen and Kasimatis, 1990).

If different relationships are compared, the most powerful source of joy is of course being in love, partly as a result of sexual excitement, partly from the sheer closeness of the relationship, with a lot of self-disclosure and mutual concern. Being with friends is an important source of joy, more so than being with the family; doing things with friends somehow produces an immediate elevation of mood. There may be some reverse causation here as well – we have seen that people seek out their friends when in a good mood. And we shall see shortly that extraverts are more likely than introverts to seek out friends. Husbands and wives cause each other joy, but the main effect is satisfaction rather than joy. Children, especially young children, are another source of joy, though they are also a source of conflict and stress. We shall see later that relationships at work can also produce a lot of fun.

Why do friends in particular produce joy? One explanation is in terms of the things that friends do together. We found that friends typically engaged in a range of very enjoyable activities – eating, drinking, playing tennis, going to parties (Table 3.2, p. 46). These are all very enjoyable activities, and they need the cooperation of others to do them at all.

Another explanation is in terms of the positive non-verbal signals that friends send to one another – they smile, look, come close, sometimes touch. Table 11.8 shows that people at a bowling alley smiled a lot at one another, but rarely at the skittles. It is nice to be smiled at, and smiles are reciprocated.

Table 11.8   Smiling (a) At the bowling alley (%)

	Hit	Missed
At people	42	28
At skittles	4	3

(b) In the street (%)		
	Good weather	Bad weather
With others	61	57
Alone	12	5

Source: Kraut and Johnstone, 1979

Friends have a great deal of fun and laughter together – from jokes, games, dancing and fooling about. The same is true of work-mates, who spend quite a lot of time, in work-breaks, and not only in work-breaks, doing the same (see Chapter 4).

A third possible explanation is that closely synchronised and coordinated interaction gives rewards as well as strengthening interpersonal attraction. Mothers and babies do it, friends do it – when talking, dancing, playing games. Experiments have been done in which a stooge increases the level of bodily synchrony with subjects, and this produces increased positive mood and attraction (Dabbs, 1969). People enjoy encounters more if others are initially in a similar mood. Subjects who were either normal or mildly depressed enjoyed a 30-minute meeting more if paired with someone similar (Locke and Horowitz, 1990).

Satisfaction

We carried out a study of satisfaction in a number of relationships. We found 3 dimensions of satisfaction: material, tangible help; emotional support; and shared interests. It can be seen that the spouse is by far the greatest source of satisfaction, close relatives and friends next, and work-mates and neighbours last (Figure 3.2, p. 43).

Many studies have confirmed the effects of marriage on happiness; see Table 11.9. The relationship is still found when other variables, such as age, occupation and income, are held constant, and it has not changed over the last 15 years. Satisfaction with home life is quite a strong predictor of happiness, but women with children experience negative emotions like boredom, aggression and loneliness (Harding, 1985). Living with a partner is nearly as good as marriage. And the effect is much stronger for young people. It is possible, however, that happiness causes marriage, as well as vice versa. It is true that happy people are found more attractive (and possibly more marriageable); otherwise there is little evidence for reversed causation here.

Table 11.9   Happiness of the married, single and divorced

| | Percentage 'very happy' | |
	Men	Women
Married	35.0	41.5
Single	18.5	25.5
Divorced	18.5	15.5

Source: Veroff et al., 1981

The effect of ending marriage, by death, separation or divorce, is very strong – here something has been lost. It looks as if people who live alone are missing something important. This is partly described by the 3 factors in Figure 3.1 – material help, emotional support and shared interests – found by Argyle and Furnham (1983). There may be a more fundamental point here. Human beings are basically sociable and cooperative; many things cannot be done alone – sex and family life, most work, most leisure. Since various forms of cooperation are so important for human life, cooperation has acquired rewards to motivate it, as in the case of sex and friendship. Living alone denies those rewards, and so life is felt as incomplete and less meaningful (Argyle, 1991).

Other relationships also contribute to satisfaction, as Figure 3.1 showed. Friends certainly do, particularly to satisfaction from shared interests and activities, for which they are rated almost the same as spouses. Kin, especially parents and siblings, are important, especially as sources of material help. Other studies have found that work-mates can be greater sources of satisfaction than Figure 3.1 suggests. They can be major sources of help and cooperation (see Chapter 4).

Relationships can also be a source of conflict. Young lovers have to work through a lot of early disagreements; marriage is the greatest source of conflict as well as of satisfaction; parents often have a lot of trouble with their children, especially when they are adolescents. Nevertheless, relationships continue to provide the greatest single source of happiness (Argyle, 1987).

WORK

Since most people in the modern world spend 7–9 hours a day, 5–6 days a week at work for 40 years or so, it would be expected that the nature and conditions of work might affect happiness. As we shall see, they do. A great deal is known about job satisfaction, and this was discussed in Chapter 4. One of its main components is intrinsic job satisfaction, satisfaction from the work itself, which depends on how varied and interesting it is, how far skills can be used, the amount of autonomy possible, and so on. Another is social satisfaction, especially with immediate work-mates.

The correlation between job satisfaction and overall satisfaction was .27 in the *Quality of American Life* study, about the same as satisfaction with friends. But does job satisfaction cause happiness, or is it the other way round? Unfortunately researchers have arrived at different answers from longitudinal studies. One American study found that job satisfaction influences happiness, another found both affect each other, while an Australian study found that happiness affects job satisfaction (Headey and Veenhoven, 1989), but most find a two-way pattern of causation. Another possibility is that areas of work and non-work have a lot in common, such as friendship, status and similar styles of behaviour, and that they jointly affect satisfaction with life as a whole.

The unemployed are definitely unhappier than those at work, but there is more effect on unhappiness than on happiness (Table 11.10). For men, the unemployed were significantly less pleased with things than those in jobs; the retired were a lot more satisfied. Women at work reported less emotional strain than those at home; other studies have found that women at work are happier overall. But women were most pleased if they were retired or in part-time work. Similar results have been found in other countries. In American surveys, 10–12 per cent of the unemployed describe themselves as 'very happy' compared with 30 per cent of the general population.

The apparent happiness of retired people is surprising. We said earlier that they differ from the unemployed in feeling that they are experiencing a well-deserved rest, rather than rejection and failure. They can, however, be bored and lonely; that is, they may miss the two most important sources of job satisfaction – the work itself and work-mates. It also depends on what sort of work they were doing and how much they enjoyed it. Many people over the retiring age manage to carry on working, while others do part-time jobs, or engage in serious leisure, which has some of the properties of work. A study of 1,800 men and their wives, who had retired under favourable financial conditions and in good health, found that they engaged in 9 main kinds of activity:

1 Resting and relaxing – television, walking, gardening and so on;
2 Time spent with wife and family, and on domestic jobs;
3 Hobbies – music, DIY, golf, bird-watching, fishing, philately;

Table 11.10 The emotional state of the employed, unemployed and retired

	Full-time employment (%)	Part-time employment (%)	Unemployed – looking for work (%)	Unemployed – not looking for work (%)	Retired (%)
'Felt very pleased with things yesterday (all of the time)'					
Men	23	24	21	20	36
Women	17	28	19	24	35
'Unpleasant emotional strain yesterday (all or most of the time)'					
Men	6	16	16	17	12
Women	9	11	21	13	14

Source: Warr and Payne, 1982

4 Social life and travel;
5 Committees and clubs;
6 Voluntary work;
7 Further education;
8 Part-time jobs;
9 New jobs – slower and at a lower level (McGoldrick, 1982).

LEISURE

The distinction between work and leisure is quite subtle, since they may involve exactly the same activities: digging the garden, driving a car, decorating rooms, looking after other people, for example, may be either work or leisure. Some of the main differences are that leisure is more autonomous, although less when done in a group, there is little or no supervision, the product, if any, is one's own property, and there is little or no material reward. People have a lot of leisure time, on average 4.0 hours a day for men with jobs, on weekdays, 11.4 hours a day at weekends (see Chapter 5).

American surveys have compared the amount of satisfaction derived from work and from leisure. For those with jobs, 47 per cent derived more satisfaction from work, 19 per cent more from leisure, and 34 per cent found they were equally satisfying (Veroff et al., 1981). For housewives and for single men, the level of satisfaction derived from leisure is higher.

How far does leisure affect happiness? A narrow definition of leisure emphasising 'hobbies' gave a rather poor prediction in the *Quality of American Life* study, but leisure defined as 'life outside work' was one of the best predictors of overall satisfaction. As we showed in Chapter 5, different kinds of leisure have major effects on mood and on happiness, but especially committed leisure, sport and social leisure.

In most simpler societies there is no clear distinction between work and leisure, there are no defined periods of leisure, and there is a lot of singing and story-telling at work (Thomas, 1964). Leisure, as opposed to work, has often been said to have started or become more salient in Britain from the time of the Industrial Revolution, when people started to work in factories, for set hours, often under unpleasant conditions. It was Engels who first proposed that leisure is a kind of compensation for work.

THE EFFECT OF PERSONALITY ON HAPPINESS

Are there happy people? We have seen that circumstances and activities affect happiness, but are there individuals who are consistently above or below average, as there are people who are depressed? Research shows very clearly that there are happy people, and we now know quite a lot about who they are, and why they are happy.

Part of the evidence for there being a consistent happiness trait is that measures of happiness are stable over a number of years. In one study happiness was successfully predicted from associated traits like extraversion over a 10–17-year interval (Costa, McCrae and Norris, 1981). Twin studies have shown that happiness is about 30 per cent inherited (Arvey *et al.*, 1989), and this is confirmed by the finding that children are similar in happiness to their biological parents, but not to adoptive parents (Sandvik *et al.*, unpublished).

The strongest correlate of happiness is extraversion: we find a correlation of .48. If extraversion is divided into sociability and impulsiveness components, it is sociability that predicts happiness. And extraversion particularly predicts positive moods during social interaction.

Headey and Wearing (1991) carried out a 4-stage panel study, at 2-year intervals, of 649 Australians. They found that extraversion was a cause of later positive affect, and did so by generating favourable life-events, especially in the spheres of friendship and work. So while friendship and work were causes of happiness, they were themselves, in part, due to extraverts seeking out and generating positive activities. However, favourable or unfavourable life-events also acted independently of personality, and were able to enhance or depress well-being. Other studies have found that extraverts choose certain kinds of situation: Furnham (1981) found that they choose social and physical activities.

We recently studied participation in 39 different social and other activities. Factor analysis produced a number of factors (Table 5.9, p. 124). Statistical analysis found that extraverts engaged more in the activities in Factor 4 (clubs and teams) and 6 (parties and dancing), and that this partly explained the happiness of extraverts (Argyle and Lu, 1990a).

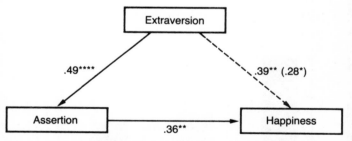

Figure 11.2 Assertion as a mediator of the extraversion–happiness relation
Note: The figure in parentheses is the reduced coefficient when the mediator was present
Source: Argyle and Lu, 1990b

The happiness of extraverts is partly explained by their choice of enjoyable social activities. In addition, extraverts possess certain skills. We found that extraverts score high in assertiveness, and in a longitudinal study this predicted later happiness and partly explained the happiness of extraverts (Figure 11.2). This shows how extraversion causes happiness via the route: extraversion – assertiveness – happiness (Argyle and Lu, 1990b). In a similar study we found that certain aspects of cooperativeness also predicted happiness, in particular enjoying engaging in joint leisure with friends.

When discussing mood induction methods earlier, we said that extraverts are made most cheerful by social situations, introverts by solitary ones. In one of our recent experiments subjects were asked to discuss recent happy events, and we analysed the events which they talked about; the results are shown in Figure 11.3. It can be seen that extraverts chose to talk about social and physical events, introverts about solitary and 'para-social' ones; that is, social behaviour at second hand, such as watching TV.

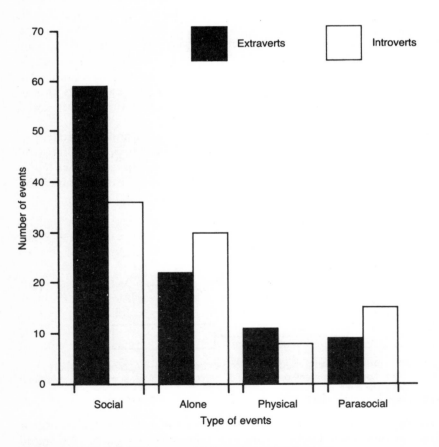

Figure 11.3 Recall of happy events by extraverts/introverts
Source: Argyle and Lu, 1990a

Why do extraverts enjoy social events so much? From a wide range of studies it has become clear that they have a special social style – positive non-verbal communication (smile, gaze and so on), positive verbal communication (more of it, especially questions, compliments and agreement), greater social skill, and an expectation that they are going to get on well and enjoy one another's company.

Several other aspects of personality are related to happiness, though less intensive research has been done on them so far. These are:

1 *Attributional style*. Depressed people blame themselves for bad things that happen. However, this is not so much a cause of depression as an effect of it. Happy people attribute good events to themselves, not bad ones, but we don't know the direction of causation yet (Argyle *et al.* 1989).

2 *Positive thinking*. Depressed people ruminate about unhappy things; if happy things come to mind they wonder how they might go wrong. Happy people ruminate about good things; if bad things come to mind they wonder how to put them right (Argyle *et al.*, 1989). Happy people have an optimistic, rosy view of life; they recall good things in the past, expect good things to happen in the future, think well of themselves, and of others. This may be a cause of happiness, or simply part of it.

3 *Internal control*. We saw that this is important for health and mental health. It is also important for happiness. Individuals with good resources of various kinds are a little happier: there are small effects of intelligence, physical attractiveness, education and so on.

4 *Neuroticism* is a strong predictor of unhappiness. It has little effect on positive affect, but influences negative affect, and it also reduces satisfaction. And it does so by leading to adverse events, especially over work and money, just as extraversion leads to favourable events (Headey and Wearing, 1991).

5 *Religion and politics*. Modest correlations are found between happiness and church attendance. Rather more important is a sense of inner meaning of life. Freedman (1978) described cases of successful and prosperous people who did not have this, and asked themselves, 'Why am I doing all this?', 'What is it all for?'. People with radical, revolutionary political attitudes are a good deal less happy than others (Harding, 1985).

THE EFFECTS OF HAPPINESS AND POSITIVE MOODS

Is happiness good for us in other ways? Perhaps it makes us idle or selfish. A recent conference at the University of Rotterdam was devoted to examining the positive and possible negative effects of happiness (Veenhoven, 1989a).

1 Length of life

A Dutch longitudinal study of 3,149 people has followed them up since 1955–57. Several satisfaction variables were found to be predictors of longevity – satisfaction with health, ageing, evaluation of income, and perceived value of life in old age. The effect of health satisfaction was still present, though much reduced if actual health was taken into account. The effect of satisfaction was greatest for married men, and was worth another 20 months of life for men one standard deviation above the mean for happiness (Deeg and Zonneveld, 1990).

2 Health and mental health

The average correlation between happiness and health, from many studies, is .32 (Okun *et al.*, 1984). We have seen that there is a stronger relationship with subjective health. We have also seen that health is rated as one of the most important domains of satisfaction. However, we do not yet know whether happiness causes health more than vice versa, or whether they are better regarded as components of the same condition.

3 Helping behaviour and sociability

If subjects are put in a good mood, they are more likely to help another person. When the sun is shining, people leave waitresses larger tips. And individuals who are rated by others as happy are much less likely to be rated as selfish (Table 11.11).

Table 11.11   Perceptions of relationship between happiness and selfishness

		Happy	
		Yes (%)	No (%)
Selfish	Yes	3.9	37.0
	No	41.6	17.5

Source: Rimland, 1982

If people are put in a depressed mood they are also more likely to help, but the reason is different. Subjects in a depressed mood only help if the task is interesting, or if they believe helping will improve their mood. Subjects in a good mood, however, help whether the task is interesting or not, and even if told that they have taken a drug so that they cannot influence their own mood (Manucia *et al.*, 1984). The explanation is less clear. The phenomenon has been described as 'an overflow of good will'; perhaps happy people want everyone else to be happy too, in order to avoid too much inequity; or perhaps good moods shift attention away from personal concerns in some way to broader ones (Cunningham *et al.*, 1990).

If subjects are put in a good mood they become more sociable, they talk more and disclose more (Cunningham, 1988), they like other people more and evaluate them more highly; they say they want to be with friends or go to a party. And as was mentioned earlier, positive moods are contagious, so that others catch them too.

4 Work

Do happy workers work harder? The average correlation between job satisfaction and rate of work, from 217 studies, is .17, but for supervisors and above the correlation is .31, which means that in half of these studies it was higher than this. However, it is not yet known whether job satisfaction results in higher rate of work, or whether there is some different causal chain.

Satisfied workers are also absent less (−.09, −.22 in two meta-analyses) especially for voluntary absences, but there is no evidence that satisfaction predicts absenteeism. Satisfied workers are less likely to leave: labour turnover correlates −.22 with satisfaction on average; the relationship is much stronger when there is high unemployment; later it has been confirmed that (low) job satisfaction is the final step in the chain (Argyle, 1990). Happiness does not lead to idleness: in a large Dutch sample it was found that happiness predicted the likelihood of finding a job, and also of keeping it (Verkley and Stolk, 1990).

5 Mental activity

People in good moods tackle problems in a different way from those in neutral or sad moods. They move more quickly, adopt the simplest strategy, and accept the first solution they find. In one experiment the problem was attaching a candle to a wall with a box of drawing pins and a book of matches. The solution is to use the drawing-pin box as a base, pinned to the wall; 75 per cent of those who had seen a comedy film found the solution, compared with 13 per cent who had seen no film and 20 per cent who had seen a non-humorous film (Clark and Isen, 1982).

There is evidence that positive mood leads to more unusual and diverse word associations, showing that a broader range of associations can be tapped; more fringe items are accepted as members of categories, such as furniture, vegetables and vehicles. This would make for enhanced creativity and problem-solving.

ENHANCING HAPPINESS

Could people be made happy? Or could they make themselves happier? Some of the methods which have been suggested entail professional help from a psychologist, but others could be a matter of do-it-yourself. Early methods of happiness enhancement have not been very successful. In a meta-analysis of 31 follow-up studies of courses for old people, it was found that experience of increased social activity, increased control over the environment and increasing knowledge or skills, all had substantial short-term effects, but little effect after 30 days (Okun *et al.*, 1990). Perhaps more specialised methods can do better.

1 Regular mood induction

We described earlier the success of twice-daily relaxation methods. Twice-a-day positive mood induction is equally feasible. The trouble with the methods described in Chapter 10 is that the effects don't last very long – the Velten technique, happy music, and so on. Some forms of exercise – running, swimming, cycling – may have stronger effects. And it is possible to combine several components. A friend of mine in Nevada starts the day by a run across the desert, which is spectacularly beautiful, sometimes with 'Walkman' music, or with his wife.

2 Pleasant activities

Different activities cheer up different individuals. Lewinsohn devised the following way to find out: clients keep a record of performing any of the 320 pleasant activities on his list, and their overall mood for each day, for 30 days. A little statistical analysis shows which are the activities that are most successful for each person. They are then encouraged to engage in these more often – provided that these are not too expensive, antisocial or interfere with family life. This has been found to be effective both with depressed patients and with normals (Lewinsohn *et al.*, 1982).

This all sounds a bit like unrestrained hedonism, the selfish pursuit of pleasure. In fact many of these pleasant activities are quite harmless, and if they make people happier they can be engaged in without causing problems: seeing friends, engaging in sport or exercise, going to church, listening to music, spending more time with the children, getting enough sleep, are some examples.

It is perhaps surprising that many people don't know already what cheers them up, and also surprising that they need some persuasion to do it. It may be necessary to use behaviour therapy methods such as goal-setting, and approximation in small steps.

3 Cognitive therapy

We saw that cognitive therapy can be used to prevent the effects of stress at work; depressed patients can be helped in similar ways. Happiness training courses for normals have included some cognitive therapy, ascribing the causes of good events, but not bad ones to self, identifying and removing irrational beliefs, such as 'To be happy I must be liked by everyone', lowering over-high aspirations, and giving insight and understanding of the causes of positive and negative feelings. A happiness training course based on these principles lasted for 4 weeks, with 2-hour sessions twice a week. The results were quite successful, as shown in Figure 11.4.

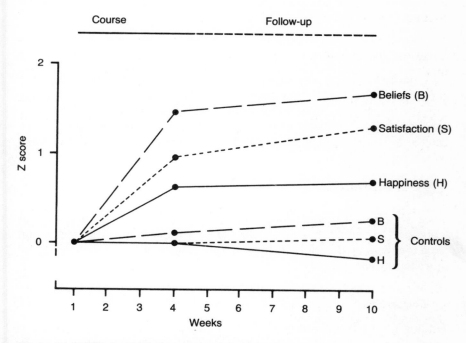

Figure 11.4: Effects of a happiness training course
Source: Lichter, Haye and Kammann, 1980

4 Social skills training (SST)

This was discussed more fully in Chapter 10. Which kinds of SST are relevant to happiness? We have seen that close relationships are probably the greatest source of happiness; in order to establish and keep relationships, certain relationship skills, such as rewardingness, are most important. Extraverts are happy, and it seems likely that their styles of social behaviour might make others happy too. We found that assertiveness was partly responsible – and assertiveness training has been successfully used as part of happiness training courses (Blaney, 1981).

There are other aspects of extraverted behaviour which it may also be valuable to teach. Positive non-verbal communication (in face, voice, gaze) is one, together with positive verbal communication (question, agree, compliment, and so on), and a generally cooperative approach to social encounters.

5 Life style

Therapy may not be necessary for happiness, if the right way of life can be found.

(a) Social relationships

To enhance happiness, one should get married, stay married, have children, keep up with relatives, have plenty of friends, and keep on good terms with the neighbours. In order to do these things some social skills training may be needed. Experiments have been carried out in which subjects have been asked to strengthen their relationships for some weeks – with positive effects for happiness.

(b) Work

Since work is such an important source of satisfaction, it is desirable to be at work, and to find a job which is satisfying – with both intrinsic satisfaction from the work, and social satisfaction from congenial co-workers. Both are more important than pay or status.

(c) Leisure

Finding the right job can be difficult. Finding the right form of leisure is relatively easy. Serious leisure, which has some of the properties of work, is more satisfying than watching TV. Sport and exercise produce positive moods, so does the company of other people, while some relaxation is necessary too.

CONCLUSIONS

Happiness consists of a combination of positive moods and satisfaction, and the absence of negative states like depression. Older people are more satisfied, and there is a small positive correlation between happiness and social class.

Joy can be produced experimentally by various mood-induction methods. Satisfaction is affected by real sources of satisfaction like income, health, work and relationships, and by reducing the gap between aspirations and achievements. Relations with friends and spouses are one of the main sources of joy, and of satisfaction. Work and leisure are also important.

There are personality differences: extraverts tend to be happy, partly because of their enjoyable social life; neuroticism correlates with unhappiness. Happiness has positive effects on health, also on helpfulness and sociability.

Happiness can be enhanced, by regular positive mood induction, engaging in more frequent pleasant activities, cognitive therapy or social skills training. Alternatively, social relations can be strengthened, and more satisfying work and leisure found.

REFERENCES

Andrews, F.M. and Withey, S.B. (1986) *Social Indicators of Well-Being*. New York: Plenum.

Argyle, M. (1987) *The Psychology of Happiness*. London: Methuen.

——(1990) Do happy workers work harder? *In* R. Veenhoven (ed.) *How Harmful is Happiness?* Rotterdam: Universitaire Pers.

——(1991) *Cooperation: the Basis of Sociability*. London: Routledge.

Argyle, M. and Crossland, J. (1987) The dimensions of positive emotions. *British Journal of Social Psychology*, *26*, 127–37.

Argyle, M. and Furnham, A. (1982) The ecology of relationships: choice of situation as a function of relationships. *British Journal of Social Psychology*, *21*, 259–62.

——(1983) Sources of satisfaction and conflict in long-term relationships. *Journal of Marriage and the Family*, *45*, 481–93.

Argyle, M. and Lu, L. (1990a) The happiness of extraverts. *Personality and Individual Differences*, *11*, 1011–17.

——(1990b) Happiness and social skills. *Personality and Individual Differences*, *11*, 1255–61.

Argyle, M., Martin, M. and Crossland, J. (1989) Happiness as a function of personality and social encounters. *In* J.P. Forgas and J.M. Innes (eds) *Recent Developments in Social Psychology*. Amsterdam: Elsevier.

Arvey, R.D, Bouchard, T.J., Segal, N.L. and Abraham, L.M. (1989) Job satisfaction: environmental and genetic components. *Journal of Applied Psychology*, *74*, 187–92.

Berkowitz, L., Fraser, C., Treasure, F.P. and Cochran, S. (1987) Pay equity, job qualifications, and comparisons in pay satisfaction. *Journal of Applied Psychology*, *72*, 544–51.

Blaney, P.H. (1981) The effectiveness of cognitive and behavioral therapies. *In* L.P. Rehm (ed.) *Behavior Therapy for Depression*. New York: Academic Press.

Campbell, A. (1981) *The Sense of Well-being in America*. New York: McGraw Hill.

Campbell, A., Converse, P.E. and Rodgers, W.L. (1976) *The Quality of American Life*. New York: Sage.

Carver, C.S. and Scheier, M.F. (1990) Origins and functions of positive and negative affect: a control-process view. *Psychological Review*, 97, 19–35.

Clark, M.S. and Isen, A.M. (1982) Toward understanding the relationship between feeling states and social behaviour. *In* A. Hastorf and A.M. Isen (eds) *Cognitive Social Psychology*. New York: Elsevier.

Costa, P.T., McRae, R.R. and Norris, A.H. (1981) Personal adjustment to aging: longitudinal prediction from neuroticism and extraversion. *Journal of Gerontology*, 36, 78–85.

Csikszentmihalyi, M. and Kubey, R. (1981) Television and the rest of life: a systematic comparison of subjective experiences. *Public Opinion Quarterly*, 45, 317–28.

Cunningham, M.R. (1988) What do you do when you're happy or blue? Mood expectancies, and behavioral interest. *Motivation and Emotion*, 12, 309–31.

Cunningham, M.R., Shaffen, D.R., Barber, A.P., Wolff, P.L. and Kelley, D.J. (1990) Separate processes in the relation of elation and depression to helping: social versus personal concerns. *Journal of Experimental Social Psychology*, 26, 13–33.

Dabbs, J.M. (1969) Similarity of gestures and interpersonal influence. *Proceedings of the Annual Convention of the APA*, 4, 337–8.

Deeg, D. and Zonneveld, R. van. (1990) Does happiness lengthen life? *In* R. Veenhoven (ed.) *How Harmful is Happiness*? Rotterdam: Universitaire Pers.

Diener, E., Horowitz, J. and Emmons, R.A. (1985) Happiness of the very wealthy. *Social Indicators Research*, 16, 263–74.

Diener, E., Larsen, S., Levine, S. and Emmons, R.A. (1985) Intensity and frequency: dimensions underlying positive and negative affect. *Journal of Personality and Social Psychology*, 48, 1253–65.

Freedman, J.L. (1978) *Happy People*. New York: Harcourt Brace Jovanovich.

Furnham, A. (1981) Personality and activity preference. *British Journal of Social Psychology*, 20, 57–68.

Gallup, G.H. (1976) Human needs and satisfaction: a global survey. *Public Opinion Quarterly*, 40, 459–67.

Harding, S. (1985) Values and the nature of psychological well-being. *In* M. Abrams, D. Gerard and N. Timms (eds) *Values and Social Change in Britain*. Basingstoke: Macmillan.

Headey, B. and Veenhoven, R. (1989) Does happiness induce a rosy outlook? *In* R. Veenhoven (ed.) *How Harmful is Happiness*? Rotterdam: Universitaire Pers.

Headey, B. and Wearing A. (1991) Subjective well-being: a stocks and flows framework. *In* F. Strack, M. Argyle and N. Schwarz (eds) *Subjective Well-Being*. Oxford: Pergamon.

Kammann, R. and Campbell, K. (1982) Illusory correlation in popular beliefs about the causes of happiness. *New Zealand Psychologist*, 11, 52–62.

Kraut, R.E. and Johnston, R.E. (1979) Social and emotional messages of smiling: an ethological approach. *Journal of Personality and Social Psychology*, 37, 1539–53.

Lance, C.E., Lautenschlager, G.J., Sloan, C.E. and Vance, P.E. (1989) A comparison between bottom-up, top-down, and bidirectional models of relationships between global and life facet satisfaction. *Journal of Personality*, 57, 601–24.

Larsen, R.J. and Kasimatis, M. (1990) Individual differences in entrainment of mood to the weekly calendar. *Journal of Personality and Social Psychology*, 58, 164–71.

Lewinsohn, P.M., Sullivan, J.M. and Grosscup, S.J. (1982) Behavioral therapy:

clinical applications. *In* A.J. Rush (ed.) *Short-term Therapies for Depression*. New York: Guilford.

Lichter, S., Haye, K. and Kammann, R. (1980) Increasing happiness through cognitive training. *New Zealand Psychologist*, 9, 57–64.

Locke, K.D. and Horowitz, L.M. (1990) Satisfaction in interpersonal interactions as a function of similarity in level of dysphoria. *Journal of Personality and Social Psychology*, 58, 823–31.

McGoldrick, A. (1982) Early retirement: a new leisure opportunity. *In* Leisure Studies Association Series. *Work and Leisure*, 15, 73–89.

MacPhillamy, D.J. and Lewinsohn, P.M. (1976) Manual for the *Pleasant Events Schedule*. University of Oregon.

Manucia, C.K., Baumann, D.J. and Cialdini, R.B. (1984) Mood influences on helping: direct effects or side effects? *Journal of Personality and Social Psychology*, 46, 357–64.

Michalos, A.C. (1986) Job satisfaction, marital satisfaction, and the quality of life: a review and a preview. *In* F.M. Andrews (ed.) *Research on the Quality of Life*. Ann Arbor: University of Michigan Survey Research Center.

Okun, M.A., Olding, R.W. and Cohn, C.M.G. (1990) A meta-analysis of subjective well-being interventions among elders. *Psychological Bulletin*, 108, 257–66.

Okun, M.A., Stock, W.A., Haring, M.J. and Witten, R.A. (1984) Health and subjective well-being: a meta-analysis. *International Journal of Aging and Human Development*, 19, 111–32.

Rimland, B. (1982) The altruism paradox. *Psychological Reports*, 51, 521–2.

Runciman, W.G. (1966) *Relative Deprivation and Social Justice*. London: Routledge and Kegan Paul.

Ryff, C.D. (1989) Happiness is everything, or is it? Explorations on the meaning of psychological well-being. *Journal of Personality and Social Psychology*, 57, 1069–81.

Sandik, E., Diener, E. and Larsen, R.J. (unpublished) Affective similarity among children and their parents in biologically related and adoptive families.

Scherer, K.R., Walbott, H.G. and Summerfield, A.B. (1986) *Experiencing Emotion*. Cambridge: Cambridge University Press.

Schwartz, J.C. and O'Connor, C.J. (1984) The social ecology of memorable emotional experiences. Paper at the Second International Conference on Personal Relationships, Madison, Wisconsin.

Schwarz, N. and Clore, G.L. (1983) Mood, misattribution and judgments of well-being: information and directive functions of affective states. *Journal of Personality and Social Psychology*, 45, 513–23.

Schwarz, N. and Strack, F. (1991) Evaluating one's life: a judgment model of subjective well-being. *In* F. Strack, M. Argyle and N. Schwarz (eds) *Subjective Well-Being*. Oxford: Pergamon.

Schwarz, N., Strack, F., Kommer, D. and Wagner, D. (1984) Success, rooms and the quality of your life: further evidence on the informative function of affective states. Conference of the European Association of Experimental Social Psychology, Tilburg.

Strack, F., Schwarz, N. and Gschneidinger, E. (1985) Happiness and reminiscing: the role of time perspective, affect, and mode of thinking. *Journal of Personality and Social Psychology*, 49.

Thomas, K. (1964) Work and leisure in pre-industrial society. *Past and Present*, 29, 50–62.

Veenhoven, R. (ed.) (1989) *How Harmful is Happiness*? Rotterdam: Universitaire Pers.

——(1991) Is happiness relative? *In* F. Strack, M. Argyle and N. Schwarz (eds) *Subjective Well-Being*. Oxford: Pergamon.

Verkley, H. and Stolk, J. (1990) Does happiness lead to idleness? *In* R. Veenhoven (ed.) *How Harmful is Happiness?* Rotterdam: Universitaire Pers.

Veroff, J., Douvan, E. and Kulka, R. (1981) *The Inner American*. New York: Basic Books.

Warr, P. and Payne, R. (1982) Experience of strain and pleasure among British adults. *Social Science and Medicine*, *16*, 1691–7.

Watson, D. (1988) The vicissitudes of mood measurement: effects of varying descriptors, time frames, and response formats on measures of positive and negative effect. *Journal of Personality and Social Psychology*, *55*, 128–41.

Wood, W., Rhodes, N. and Whelan, M. (1989) Sex differences in positive well-being: a consideration of emotional style and marital status. *Psychological Bulletin, 106*, 249–64.

Name index

Abrams, M. 177
Abrams, P. 149
Adams, J. 62
Adler, P.A. *and* Adler, P. 91
Ajzen, I. 244
Allan, G. 64, 205, 207
Allport, G.W. 133
Alvaro, J.L. 93
Andrews, D.W. 57
Andrews, F.M. 105
Appels, A. 234, 270
Argyle, M., on child-rearing 205;
  on conversation 9, 12, 19, 29, 31;
  on cooperation 268; on dress 209,
  216; on emotions 140, 283, 289,
  293, 296–8; on family relationships
  239; on job satisfaction 89, 300;
  on leaders 199; on leisure 112,
  114, 124–5; on mental health 262,
  264, 271, 275, 276; on neighbours
  208; on physical appearance 220;
  on relationships 40, 44, 47, 50,
  53, 55, 56, 58, 66, 67, 116, 207;
  on religious behaviour 133, 136,
  145, 147, 150, 151, 152, 155, 156,
  210; on sex differences in health
  259–60; on work and health 235,
  239, 269; on work relationships 78,
  80, 81, 84, 86, 202
Aronson, E. 185
Arvey, R.D. 90, 296
Ash, R.A. 86
Atkinson, M. 25
Au, P. 152
Austin, J. 8
Avedon, E.M. 112

Bakan, P. 141

Baker, M. 150
Bales, R.F. 31
Bandura, A. 166
Banks, M.H. 93
Barling, J. 87
Baron, R.A. 171, 188
Batson, C.D. 134–5, 150, 155, 157, 162
Baumrind, D. 269
Beard, J.G. 106
Beattie, G.W. 15, 16, 21, 29
Beehr, T.A. 94
Beit-Hallahmi, B. 133, 136, 145, 147,
  150, 152, 156, 210
Benewick, R. 179
Bentler, P.M. 244
Berger, P.L. 144
Bergin, A.E. 155
Berkman, L.F. 236, 237
Berkowitz, L. 90, 168, 290
Berne, E. 34
Bernstein, B. 27
Bilous, F.R. 21
Birch, F. 115
Black, D. 230
Blakar, R.M. 9
Blaney, P.H. 304
Blaney, R. 225
Blauner, R. 90
Bluen, S.D. 87
Bolger, N. 268
Bowlby, J. 41
Boyatzis, R.E. 87
Bradburn, M. 257
Braiker, B. 56
Brannon, L. 248, 250
Brenner, M. 14
Brewer, M.B. 176
Brislin, R.W. 187

Subject index

To Sujata